Y0-BRV-546

Expanding Media

Expanding Media

Edited by Deirdre Boyle

A Neal-Schuman Professional Book

 ORYX PRESS

Operation Oryx, started more than 10 years ago at the Phoenix Zoo to save the rare white antelope—believed to have inspired the unicorn of mythology—has apparently succeeded.

An original herd of nine, put together through Operation Oryx by five world organizations, now numbers 34 in Phoenix with another 22 farmed out to the San Diego Wild Game Farm.

The operation was launched in 1962 when it became evident that the animals were facing extinction in their native habitat of the Arabian peninsula.

Copyright © 1977 by Deirdre Boyle
Published by The Oryx Press
3930 E. Camelback Road
Phoenix, AZ 85018

Printed and Bound in the United States of America

Library of Congress Cataloging in Publication Data
Main entry under title:

Expanding media.

(A Neal-Schuman professional book)
Includes bibliographical references and index.
1. Libraries—Special collections—Non-book materials—Addresses, essays, lectures. 2. Audio-visual library service—Addresses, essays, lectures. I. Boyle, Deirdre.
Z688.N6E95   025.17'7   77-23335
ISBN 0-912700-03-3

Contents

Preface   ix

Introduction   xi

Contributors   xv

PART I Why Media?   1

In the Beginning was the Word . . . Libraries and Media
  Deirdre Boyle   **3**
This Matter of Media *Evelyn Geller*   **12**
Audiovisual Aids: Fallout from the McLuhan Galaxy
  William R. Eshelman   **22**
In Advance of Controversy: Visual Literacy.
  An Editorial in "School Library Journal"
  Lillian N. Gerhardt   **25**
  Response *John L. Debes*   **25**
The Media Religion *Harry Foster*   **28**
  Response to "The Media Religion" *Estelle Jussim*   **30**
Confronting Our Media Biases: The Social Dimensions of Media
  Theory *Estelle Jussim*   **33**
Introduction to "Differentiating the Media" *Lester Asheim*   **41**
The Human Element: Why Nonprint Managers Turn Gray
  James W. Ramey   **52**

PART II Selection and Evaluation   67

Collecting Nonprint Media in Academic Libraries
  Angie LeClercq   **69**
Fundamentals of Evaluation *Masha R. Porte*   **76**
Distributors vs. Buyers *Carol A. Emmens*   **80**
The Evaluation Gap: The State of the Art in AV Reviewing, with
  Special Emphasis on Filmstrips *Janet French*   **86**
The Slide as a Communication Tool: A State-of-the-Art Survey
  Juan R. Freudenthal   **99**

PART III Programming   109

Establishing a Cassette Program for a Public Library
  Carol M. Egan   **111**
The Library as Guardian of Oral History Materials: An Example
  from Berkeley *Willa Baum*   **119**

Photography! *Dennis Maness*   **127**
An Eye for an I *Susan Rice*   **130**
Building a Coherent Features Program *Ted Perry*   **134**
Programming Independent Film *Peter Feinstein*   **139**
Eight Millimeter Circulation Policies and Ranganathan's First
    Law *Joseph W. Palmer*   **149**
CATV: Visual Library Service
    Brigitte L. Kenney and Frank W. Norwood   **154**
Programming Video *Seth Feldman*   **161**
Guerrilla Television in the Public Library *Jay R. Peyser*   **175**

PART IV Production   181

Filmstrips—How to Make Your Own *William Cloke*   **183**
Production of Slide-Tape Programs *Carl F. Orgren*   **186**
Do-It-Yourself Videotape for Library Orientation Based on a
    Term Paper Project *Barbara Foster*   **195**

PART V Audiovisual Equipment   201

The Selection of Audiovisual Equipment: A Few Basics
    Kenyon C. Rosenberg   **203**
Look before You Leap. Tape Recorders: Open Reel vs.
    Cassettes *Kenyon C. Rosenberg*   **220**
One-On-One AV: The User's Point of View
    H. Michael Eisler   **231**
Where to Kick: A Troubleshooter's Guide for Teachers Who
    Don't Need Trouble *Phyllis Ward*   **236**
Whatever Happened to Videodisc? *Deirdre Boyle*   **241**

PART VI Standards and Cataloging   247

Thoughts on Media Programs: District and School
    William E. Hug   **249**
A New Version of Chapter 12 of the "Anglo-American Cataloging
    Rules" *B. R. Tucker*   **256**
Rules for Cataloging Audiovisual Materials at Hennepin County
    Library *Sanford Berman*   **265**
The Mystery of Ips and Mono, or, Do Students Understand AV
    Card Catalog Terms?
    Jane Schlueter and Robert D. Little   **273**

PART VII Education   277

Library Education and Nonprint Media: Where It's At
    Herman L. Totten   **279**
Scope and Content of Nonprint Media Courses Taught in
    Graduate Library Schools
    Herman L. Totten and Martin L. Mitchell   **285**

A Systematic Examination and Analysis of Nonprint Media
Courses in Library Schools
Karen S. Munday and John W. Ellison   **293**

PART VIII   Media Politics   299

Ivory Tower Ghettos   *Bill Hinchliff*   **301**
Cable Television: Should Librarians Get into the Act?
George C. Stoney   **307**
A Study in Censorship: The Los Angeles "19"
Ronald F. Sigler   **312**
Radical Mediacy   *Don Roberts*   **323**
"Printism" and Nonprint Censorship   *Don Roberts*   **330**

INDEX   333

Preface

The stormy history of libraries and media has raged alternately from enthusiastic endorsement to apathetic neglect. The continuing love-hate relationship with media arises from the lack of any profession-wide understanding of media as vital to the library's future. In the absence of a professional stance there is a disparity of media acceptance; like Babel each branch of librarianship speaks to itself, addressing media separately from all others. One glance at the standards and guidelines for school, public, academic, and community college libraries will quickly verify this. A look at the numerous sub-groups within ALA, each devoted to media, should resolve any lingering doubts.

Isolated from one another, librarians often have not shared media knowledge and expertise with those outside their specialization. How many public librarians have profited from the experiences of school media specialists or community college librarians? How many students have not received any introduction to "nonprint" media because they were not training to be school librarians?

Despite resistance to media in libraries, formats such as film, audio, and video are vital to the library's functioning in the modern world. Librarians, regardless of their specialization, need to know how to select and evaluate audio and visual media as well as print, how to program and administer media, how to handle equipment dilemmas and, through cataloging, make media information available to all users.

There have been readers on media and the academic library, and media and the school library but there is no recent collection which examines the broad applications of "newer" media to all libraries and librarians, regardless of type. This collection is directed to the library student *and* public librarian *and* school media specialist *and* academic librarian *and* library educator *and* the librarian who has yet to decide what s/he thinks of "media." It is designed to answer some of the philosophical and practical questions raised by media.

In researching I went back ten years in library literature, combing approximately 35 periodicals in the process, to see what librarians have said about media. I found a 1967 issue of *Library Trends* devoted to the subject: not surprisingly the authors discussed many issues which are still unresolved ten years later. In the interest of providing more current information, the scope of this collection was limited to articles published since 1969.

Films, slides, audio, video, and photography are some of the media forms discussed. The emphasis here is not on technology but on humanistic concerns. Paradigms for efficiency replete with flow charts and computer modules have a definite place in the literature, but plain talk on basic issues seems more pertinent to the general reader.

Those who think compiling a collection of articles is easy are crazy. One begins by trading literary talents for sleuthing skills in tracking down elusive articles. What one comes up with are "gaps" more often than articles—about as frustrating as finding a boot on the end of your fishing hook. For example, little material is available on media and special groups, such as the physically handicapped, prisoners, and ethnic groups; there are few commentaries on standards and media guidelines for various library programs; significant coverage of such maligned formats as realia and kits is yet to be written. When the problem is not a "lacuna," the articles found are often dated. The final selection of articles here is an effort to indicate what progress has been made to integrate media into library thinking. A few older articles have been included because they are either classic or unique studies of a subject.

Acknowledgements

I am grateful to those authors and publications who gave permission to reprint their articles. I wish to acknowledge my thanks to the following people: Patricia Glass Schuman saw a need for this book and suggested that I do it; she gave me the time and intellectual freedom to develop it; as always she is the supportive editor and friend every writer needs. Stephen Calvert advised me at various stages of the book and gave inestimable assistance in refining the index. In the Library Science Library at Pratt Institute's Graduate School of Library and Information Science, Margot Karp graciously offered me the resources of her fine collection and her own expert assistance. I am also grateful to Jana Varlejs who expressed enthusiasm for this project and gave needed criticism and to Lillian Shapiro who read the draft manuscript and offered valuable advice and support.

Deirdre Boyle

Introduction

*One of the facts that invariably emerges from any study
of human communications is that anxiety, suspicion,
and pessimism accompany communication changes.*
Neil Postman and Charles Weingartner

Some may think that film was the first upstart to demand disgruntled attention from the wise. Socrates judged the written word inferior to the spoken word and expressed his hostility in this passage from Plato's *Phaedrus:*

A terrible thing about writing, Phaedrus, is this, and here, in truth, it is like painting. I mean, the creations of the painter stand like living creatures, but if you ask them anything, they maintain a solemn silence. And so it is with writings; you might think they spoke as if they had intelligence, but if you put a question with a wish for information on a point in what is said, there is one, one only, invariable reply. Further, once a word is written, it goes rolling all about, comes indifferently among those who understand it and all those whom it no wise concerns, and is unaware to whom it should address itself and to whom it should not do so.

Of course, had we abided by Socrates' strong prejudice, recorded words would have faded away and along with them science, law, Christianity, stable governments and other aspects of civilization indebted to this once controversial communications medium.

Time is needed to recognize the value of a new medium and even more time is required to appreciate its full impact. In our haste, we look for quick explanations and find them in terms of what is already known. This makes for misleading distinctions like "print" and "nonprint." We do not see the unique advantages and disadvantages of new media, but rather only a negative expectation of how they do not conform to the familiar: films are awkward—they require projectionists and darkened rooms whereas print does not; videotapes are costly—they call for expensive equipment while books, newspapers, and magazines require no machinery at all. It is easy to dismiss the new by judging it only in terms of the familiar.

Librarians need a realistic understanding of media, and a total concept which embraces print equally with the audio and visual forms of film, photography, records, tapes, video—all those modes by which modern men and women explore the information which shape their lives and futures.

This collection is aimed at expanding an understanding of media in libraries. The book begins with "Why Media?", eight articles which argue the value and necessity of including media in libraries. Evelyn Geller and I explore the philosophy and issues underlying media in the library. William R. Eshelman expresses some of the reservations many have felt towards new media. His article is followed by two lively exchanges in *School Library Journal* and *American Libraries* exposing some of the controversies media provoke for librarians: Lillian N. Gerhardt questions the validity of "visual literacy" and John L. Debes, who coined the term, responds; Harry Foster criticizes the media invasion of libraries and is answered by Estelle Jussim. Next, in a full-length article, Jussim investigates some of our print biases. In an introduction to "Differentiating the Media," Lester Asheim advocates increased attention to how each medium communicates. Concluding this section is a view of the problems and solutions to media management by James W. Ramey.

Selection and evaluation of newer media present problems for most librarians, problems prompted by the lack of a central mediagraphic tool for locating current media materials and the relative inadequacy of existing reviewing sources. The National Commission on Libraries and Information Science has recently formed a Task Force on Nonbook Media to investigate the characteristics a national bibliographic database on nonprint materials should have. Even if the goal of a national nonprint database is realized, we are still far from a mediagraphic tool to provide information by *content* rather than form.

In "Selection and Evaluation" Angie LeClercq offers a useful guide to collecting media which has applications for all librarians. Next, Masha R. Porte thumbnails the essentials of film evaluation. Carol A. Emmens follows by reviewing the problems encountered in ordering films, from preview and rental hitches to copying issues to the quandary of locating independently distributed films. Janet French's article is one of the few in the literature to examine filmstrips—in it she offers valuable criticism of media reviewing practices. In the final article of this section, Juan R. Freudenthal gives an overview on slides, zeroing in on sources and acquisition problems which arise in various library situations.

Programming media means getting information out to the public. Two articles on audio in the library open up the section on "Programming." Carol M. Egan recounts the steps taken to establish a pilot cassette program in a suburban public library. The introduction of audio can lead to interest in oral history and Willa Baum offers useful information on setting up such a program. Twenty-five common-sense ideas on how to program photographs is given by Dennis Maness. Film is one of the oldest audiovisual media to have a place in libraries. Children and film are naturals, but just what responses one can realistically expect from children is outlined in Susan Rice's humorously pointed article. Ted Perry encourages more adventurous film selection by librarians. In discussing independent films, Peter Feinstein makes practical suggestions applicable to planning any film program. One of the finest articles on libraries and cable TV, written by Brigitte L. Kenney and Frank W. Norwood, begins a group of three articles on video. Seth Feldman reviews video ideas and resources and Jay R. Peyser explores video's potential as a community information tool.

Librarians, transformed into "audiovisual specialists," clamor for help with technical problems. "Production" and "Audiovisual Equipment" may help. Clearly three articles on media production will not substitute for complex training, but they do indicate that producing a simple media program is possible if suitable technical help, equipment, and above all, interest can be found. William Cloke covers filmstrips, Carl F. Orgren offers hints on slide-tape programs and Barbara Foster explains how a successful videotape for library instruction was made.

Two articles by Kenyon C. Rosenberg answer a host of questions on selecting audiovisual equipment. H. Michael Eisler points out specific needs when planning for individual media access. For those who shudder at the thought of machines, Phyllis Ward reveals some useful hints at solving common yet nerve-frazzling equipment foul-ups. For those who hang back, waiting for the videodisc to revolutionize library media collections, I include my report on the status and future of the disc.

Three significant documents have recently appeared: *Media Programs: District and School, Standards for Cataloging Nonprint Materials,* and chapter 12 of the *Anglo-American Cataloging Rules.* But, commentaries on media guidelines and standards are not plentiful. William E. Hug offers here his thoughts on *Media Programs: District and School.* B. R. Tucker reports on the new version of chapter 12. Sanford Berman, editor of *HCL Cataloging Bulletin,* explores how Hennepin County Library resolves some media cataloging questions. Finally Jane Schlueter and Robert D. Little discuss whether abbreviations of media terminology confuse users.

Consulting some of the standards for media collections one finds that the Public Library Association has revised their audiovisual guidelines for small and medium-sized, as well as large public libraries. They recognize that "all formalized communication formats are of interest to librarians," that "audiovisual resources and services should have equal weight, concern, familiarity, and support of library administrations and staff as those of printed materials," and further that "all library staff should be familiar with audiovisual resources, as well as program planning."

Audiovisual guidelines for four-year academic libraries, not revised since 1968, weakly call for an audiovisual librarian without outlining the expertise or training necessary for such a person. Recently published "Standards for College Libraries" do not recognize the need for integrated collections, offer no guidelines for "nonprint collections," and merely state that "every college library should have nonprint resources appropriate to institutional needs" without any elaboration of the range, extent, or configuration of nonprint services. As for staffing, no mention is made of an audiovisual librarian, and figures for computing the number of librarians are based on the number of volumes and students without any mention of nonprint resources. It is apparent that academic libraries have a distance to go in catching up with media-minded community college and school libraries.

The "Guidelines for Two-Year College Learning Resources Programs," issued in 1972, reflect the philosophy behind the standards for school media programs, emphasizing "programs" rather than geographically limited libraries and urging unified media programs. The guidelines require that learning resource centers encompass all learning and teaching media, regardless of form. They also note that a degree in library science is not the only road to acceptance of professional training.

This brings us to media in library education. The training of media professionals is vital if standards for libraries are to be met and user needs served. Library schools might heed the warning sounded in the guidelines above if they do not want to be passed by when future students are searching for suitable training. In order for a total concept of media in libraries to take root, the seeds must be planted in library school. Herman L. Totten reviews how media education fares and, with Martin L. Mitchell, surveys the scope and content of library media courses in a 1972 study. Karen C. Munday and John W. Ellison update and validate the earlier study in their later findings.

The mere inclusion of "nonprint" materials in a library may be the cause for heated arguments, yet media raise the subtler, more volatile issues of freedom of access, censorship, and other political controversies. Bill Hinchliff's late-sixties article recommends library reforms which include a total media concept. George C. Stoney emphasizes the time and commitment which cable involvement requires, warning librarians that controversy and activism are part of the medium. Censorship of nonprint media has rarely been documented. A case history of film censorship in a public library is detailed by Ronald F. Sigler. A subtle yet pervasive form of media censorship exists in the exclusion of alternative media. Don Roberts urges that the same attention that is given to alternative print be given alternate media sources. Finally, Roberts, reporting on the results of a study sponsored by the Council for Library Resources on media censorship in United States libraries, warns of the dangers of "printism."

Expanding Media is a title which borrows from the legacy of the sixties, the decade of expanded consciousness, expanded cinema, and expanded interpersonal relationships. It is an appropriate title for this book because the status of media in libraries is barely emerging into an "expanded" awareness long overdue. Many along the way have hoped that these new "fads" would fade away just as Socrates must have hoped that written words would disappear. History has proven their hopes groundless. Media have always been with us—from hieroglyphs to videograms—and they will always be with us, in whatever forms we devise to convey information and express our art. These articles on media reveal what the library profession has thought about and fought over in the last decade. Reading between the lines, they also point to what further expansion is needed in our media consciousness. I hope this collection may be instrumental in realizing this goal.

Contributors

Lester Asheim is the William Rand Kenan Jr. Professor of Library Science at the University of North Carolina in Chapel Hill. "Introduction to 'Differentiating the Media' " is reprinted with permission from *Library Quarterly,* (January 1975, p. 1–12). Copyright © 1975 by the University of Chicago Press.

Willa Baum is Department Head of the Regional Oral History Office at the Bancroft Library, University of California at Berkeley. "The Library as Guardian of Oral History Materials: An Example from Berkeley" is reprinted with permission from *Catholic Library World,* (October 1975, p. 112–117). Copyright © 1975 by the Catholic Library Association.

Sanford Berman is Head Cataloger of the Hennepin County Library and editor of *HCL Cataloging Bulletin.* "Rules for Cataloging Audio-Visual Materials at Hennepin County Library" is reprinted with permission from *The U*N*A*B*A*S*H*E*D℗ Librarian, the "How I Run My Library Good" Letter,* (Spring 1973, p. 6–8). Copyright © 1973 by the U*N*-A*B*A*S*H*E*D℗ Librarian.

Deirdre Boyle writes the monthly column "Media Minded" in *American Libraries* and is the editor of *Children's Media Market Place* (Neal-Schuman Publishers/Gaylord). "In the beginning was the Word . . . Libraries and Media" is reprinted with permission from *Library Journal,* (January 1, 1976, p. 125–129). Published by R. R. Bowker Co. (a Xerox company). Copyright © 1976 by Xerox Corporation. "Whatever Happened to Videodisc?" is reprinted with permission from *American Libraries,* (February 1977, p. 97–98). Copyright © 1977 by the American Library Association.

William Cloke teaches fourth grade in the Santa Monica Unified School District in California and is an independent filmmaker and freelance writer. "Filmstrips—How to Make Your Own" is reprinted with permission from *California School Librarian,* (Winter 1976, p. 15–18). Copyright © 1976 by the California School Librarian.

John L. Debes is Coordinator, Visual Learning for Eastman Kodak Company in Rochester, NY. He is advisor to the National Center for Visual Literacy. "Reply to a *School Library Journal* editorial" is reprinted with permission from *School Library Journal,* (December 1975, p. 4). Published by R. R. Bowker Co. (a Xerox company). Copyright © 1975 by Xerox Corporation.

Carol M. Egan is a public information and media consultant for libraries. She is secretary of the American Library Association's Public Relations Section and director-at-large of the Executive Board of the Illinois Library Association's Public Library Section. "Establishing a Cassette Program for a Public Library" is reprinted with permission from *Illinois Libraries,* (March 1974, p. 239–243). Copyright © 1974 by Illinois Library Association.

H. Michael Eisler is Managing Editor of Media Development for J. B. Lippincott Co. in Philadelphia. "One-On-One AV: The User's Point of View" is reprinted with permission from *LJ/SLJ Previews* (December 1973, p. 12–13). Published by R. R. Bowker Co. (a Xerox company). Copyright © 1973 by Xerox Corporation.

John W. Ellison is an Associate Professor at the School of Information and Library Studies, SUNY at Buffalo. "A Systematic Examination and Analysis of Nonprint Media Courses in Library Schools" is reprinted with permission from the *Journal of Education for Librarianship,* (vol. 16, Winter 1976, p. 189–194), a publication of the Association of American Library Schools. Copyright © 1976 by the Association of American Library Schools.

Carol A. Emmens is reference librarian for the Educational Film Library Association and a freelance writer specializing in film. "Distributors vs. Buyers" is reprinted with permission from *Sightlines* (Winter 1975/ 76, p. 5–8), the journal of the Educational Film Library Association. Copyright © 1975 by the Educational Film Library Association.

William R. Eshelman is the editor of *Wilson Library Bulletin.* "Audio-Visual Aids: Fallout From the McLuhan Galaxy" is reprinted with permission from *The New York Times Book Review,* (May 6, 1973, p. 32–33). Copyright © 1973 by The New York Times Company.

Peter Feinstein is presently a consultant specializing in film and television. He was formerly the Director of the University Film Study Center in Cambridge, MA, and was the founder of the Film Forum in New York City. "Programming Independent Film" is reprinted with permission from *Film Library Quarterly* (vol. 7 no. 3–4, 1974, p. 8–16). Copyright © 1974 by the Film Library Information Council. Acknowledgement is gratefully extended to FLIC.

Seth Feldman is a member of the English Department at the University of Western Ontario. "Programming Video" is reprinted with permission from *Film Library Quarterly* (vol. 7 no. 3–4, 1974, p. 91–102). Copyright © 1974 by the Film Library Information Council. Acknowledgement is gratefully extended to FLIC.

Barbara Foster is an Assistant Professor at Hunter College Library. "Do-It-Yourself Videotape for Library Orientation Based on a Term Paper Project" is reprinted with permission from *Wilson Library Bulletin*

(February 1974, p. 476–477, 480–481). Copyright © 1974 by the H. W. Wilson Co.

Harry Foster is the librarian at Anne Arundel Community College in Arnold, MD. "The Media Religion" is reprinted with permission from *American Libraries* (March 1975, p. 132–134). Copyright © 1975 by the American Library Association.

Janet French is library coordinator for Centennial School District in Warminster, PA. "The Evaluation Gap—the State of the Art in AV Reviewing with Special Emphasis on Filmstrips" is reprinted with permission from *School Library Journal* (March 1970, p. 104–108, 118). Published by R. R. Bowker Co. (a Xerox company). Copyright © 1970 by Xerox Corporation.

Juan R. Freudenthal is Assistant Professor in the Graduate School of Library Science, Simmons College in Boston. "The Slide as a Communication Tool: A State-of-the-Art Survey" is reprinted with permission from *School Media Quarterly* (Winter 1974, p. 109–115). Copyright © 1974 by the American Library Association.

Evelyn Geller, former editor of *School Library Journal,* is completing a doctorate in library science and sociology at Columbia University. "This Matter of Media" is reprinted with permission from *Library Journal* (June 15, 1971, p. 2048–2053). Published by R. R. Bowker Co. (a Xerox company). Copyright © 1971 by Xerox Corporation.

Lillian N. Gerhardt is editor-in-chief of *School Library Journal.* "In Advance of Controversy: Visual Literacy" is reprinted with permission from *School Library Journal* (December 1974, p. 3). Published by R. R. Bowker Co. (a Xerox company). Copyright © 1974 by Xerox Corporation.

Bill Hinchliff is a freelance community bibliographer and author of the bibliography *America's Counter-Productive Criminal Justice System and the Search for Alternatives.* "Ivory Tower Ghettos" is reprinted with permission from *Library Journal* (November 1969, pages 3971–3974). Published by R. R. Bowker Co. (a Xerox company). Copyright © 1969 by Xerox Corporation.

William E. Hug is Associate Professor, Department of Curriculum and Teaching, Teachers College, Columbia University. "Thoughts on Media Programs: District and School" is reprinted with permission from *School Media Quarterly* (Winter 1975, p. 109–114). Copyright © 1975 by the American Library Association.

Estelle Jussim is Associate Professor, Graduate School of Library Science, Simmons College in Boston. She is author of *Visual Communication and the Graphic Arts* (Bowker) and is a frequent contributor to symposia and journals on the national and international level. "Reply to 'The Media Religion' " is reprinted with permission from *American Li-*

braries (March 1975, p. 132–134). Copyright © 1975 by the American Library Association. "Confronting Our Media Biases: the Social Dimensions of Media Theory" is reprinted with permission from *School Libraries* (Summer 1972, p. 12–17). Copyright © 1972 by the American Library Association.

Brigitte L. Kenney is Associate Professor, Graduate School of Library Science, Drexel University in Philadelphia. "CATV: Visual Library Service" is reprinted with permission from *American Libraries* (July–August 1971, p. 723–726). Copyright © 1971 by the American Library Association.

Angie LeClercq is Head of the Nonprint Department in the library of the University of Tennessee in Knoxville. "Collecting Nonprint Media in Academic Libraries" is reprinted with permission from *Tennessee Librarian* (Summer 1975, p. 84–87). Copyright © 1975 by the Tennessee Library Association.

Robert D. Little is Associate Professor and Chairperson, Department of Library Science, Indiana State University in Terre Haute. "The Mystery of Ips and Mono, or, Do Students Understand AV Card Catalog Terms?" is reprinted with permission from *Wisconsin Library Bulletin* (November–December 1973, p. 381–383). Copyright © 1973 by the Division of Library Services, Department of Public Instruction, State of Wisconsin.

Dennis Maness is Senior Librarian, Literature Department, San Francisco Public Library and is a freelance photographer. "Photography!" is reprinted with permission from *Synergy* (no. 38, September 1972, p. 20–22). Copyright © 1972 by San Francisco Public Library.

Martin L. Mitchell is supervisor of secondary school libraries for the Columbus Public School System in Columbus, OH. He is the author of numerous articles on school libraries. "Scope and Content of Nonprint Media Courses Taught in Graduate Library Schools" is reprinted with permission from the *Journal of Education for Librarianship* (vol. 14, Summer 1973, p. 58–66), a publication of the Association of American Library Schools. Copyright © 1973 by the Association of American Library Schools.

Karen S. Munday is Head of the Audiovisual Department of Charles B. Sears Law Library, SUNY at Buffalo. "A Systematic Examination and Analysis of Nonprint Media Courses in Library Schools" is reprinted with permission from the *Journal of Education for Librarianship* (vol. 17, Winter 1976, p. 189–194), a publication of the Association of American Library Schools. Copyright © 1976 by the Association of American Library Schools.

Frank W. Norwood is Executive Director of the Joint Council on Educational Telecommunications, a national consortium of those concerned with communications technology and public policy. "CATV: Visual Library Service" is reprinted with permission from *American Libraries* (July–August 1971, p. 723–726). Copyright © 1971 by the American Library Association.

Carl F. Orgren is Associate Professor in the School of Library Science at the University of Iowa. "Production of Slide-Tape Programs" is reprinted with permission from *The U*N*A*B*A*S*H*E*D*™ *Librarian, the "How I Run My Library Good" Letter*, (Summer 1975, p. 25–28). Copyright © 1975 by The U*N*A*B*A*S*H*E*D™ Librarian.

Joseph W. Palmer is Associate Professor of Library Science at California State University at Fullerton. "Eight Millimeter Circulation Policies and Ranganathan's First Law" is reprinted by permission from *California Librarian* (October 1974, p. 43–46). Copyright © 1974 by the California Library Association.

Ted Perry is the Director of the Department of Film at the Museum of Modern Art in New York City. "Building a Coherent Features Program" is reprinted with permission from *Film Library Quarterly* (vol. 8 no. 2, 1975, p. 7–10). Copyright © 1975 by the Film Library Information Council. Acknowledgement is gratefully extended to FLIC.

Jay R. Peyser is a librarian at Harborfield Public Library in Greenlawn, NY. "Guerrilla Television in the Public Library" is reprinted with permission from *School Library Journal* (April 15, 1973, p. 22–25). Published by R. R. Bowker Co. (a Xerox company). Copyright © 1973 by Xerox Corporation.

Masha R. Porte is Head of the film library of Dallas Public Library. She was film review editor of *FLQ* and now evaluates films for *Film News* and EFLA. "Fundamentals of Evaluation" is reprinted with permission from *Film Library Quarterly* (vol. 5 no. 4, Fall 1972, p. 37–39). Copyright © 1972 by the Film Library Information Council. Acknowledgement is gratefully extended to FLIC.

James W. Ramey is Senior Research Associate at the Center for Policy Research, New York University and a consultant for the University of Southern California School of Medicine in Los Angeles. "The Human Element: Why Nonprint Managers Turn Gray" is reprinted with permission from *Drexel Library Quarterly* (April 1971, p. 91–106). Copyright © 1971 by Graduate School of Library Science, Drexel University.

Susan Rice is a film critic, screenwriter, and author of the book *Films Kids Like*, volume 1 (American Library Association). "An Eye for an I" is reprinted with permission from *Sightlines* (Fall 1974, p. 3–4), the journal of the Educational Film Library Association. Copyright © 1974 by the Educational Film Library Association.

Don Roberts, former AV librarian at Hennepin County Library, is a consultant for Pyramid Films and the WAVE Project. "Radical Mediacy" is reprinted with permission from *Booklegger Magazine* (no. 11, September/October 1975, p. 8–13). Copyright © 1975 by Booklegger. " 'Printism' and Nonprint Censorship" is reprinted with permission from *Catholic Library World* (December 1976, p. 223–224). Copyright © 1976 by the Catholic Library Association.

Kenyon C. Rosenberg is Assistant Director of Public Services for Kent State University Libraries in Ohio. "Look Before You Leap. Tape Recorders: Open Reel vs. Cassettes" is reprinted with permission from *LJ/SLJ Previews* (October 1972, p. 5–11). Published by R. R. Bowker Co. (a Xerox company). Copyright © 1972 by Xerox Corporation. "The Selection of Audiovisual Equipment—A Few Basics" is reprinted with permission from *LJ/SLJ Previews* (January 1975, p. 7–15). Published by R. R. Bowker Co. (a Xerox company). Copyright © 1975 by Xerox Corporation.

Jane Schlueter is now working as a volunteer in Robles Elementary School Library in Tampa, FL, while raising her family. "The Mystery of Ips and Mono, or, Do Students Understand AV Card Catalog Terms?" is reprinted with permission from *Wisconsin Library Bulletin* (November–December 1973, p. 381–383). Copyright © 1973 by Division of Library Services, Department of Public Instruction, State of Wisconsin.

Ronald F. Sigler is Associate Professor, School of Library Science, University of Wisconsin in Milwaukee. "A Study in Censorship: the Los Angeles '19' " is reprinted with permission from *Film Library Quarterly* (vol. 4 no. 2, Spring 1971, p. 35–46). Copyright © 1971 by the Film Library Information Council. Acknowledgement is gratefully extended FLIC.

George C. Stoney is a Professor in the Department of Film/TV at New York University and Co-Director of the Alternate Media Center. "Cable Television: Should Librarians Get Into the Act?" is reprinted with permission from *Film Library Quarterly* (vol. 7 no. 3–4, 1974, p. 85–90). Copyright © 1974 by the Film Library Information Council. Acknowledgement is gratefully extended FLIC.

Herman L. Totten is Dean of the School of Librarianship, University of Oregon in Eugene. "Library Education and Nonprint Media: Where It's At" is reprinted with permission from the *Journal of Education for Librarianship* (vol. 13, Winter 1973, p. 182–187), a publication of the Association of American Library Schools. Copyright © 1973 by the Association of American Library Schools. "Scope and Content of Nonprint Media Courses Taught in Graduate Library Schools" is reprinted with permission from the *Journal of Education for Librarianship* (vol. 14, Summer 1973, p. 58–66), a publication of the Association of American Library Schools. Copyright © 1973 by the Association of American Library Schools.

B. R. Tucker is Principal Descriptive Cataloger for the Library of Congress. "A New Version of Chapter 12 of the *Anglo-American Cataloging Rules*" is reprinted with permission from *Library Resources & Technical Services* (Summer 1975, p. 260–267).

Phyllis Ward is a Media Specialist for the Falls Church Virginia Schools. "Where to Kick: a troubleshooter's guide for teachers who don't need trouble" is reprinted with permission from *Learning Resources* (*Audiovisual Instruction* supplement), (March 1974, p. 2–4). Copyright © 1974 by the Association of Educational Communications and Technology.

Expanding Media

PART

WHY MEDIA?

In the Beginning Was the Word . . . Libraries and Media

by Deirdre Boyle

If you are surfeited with apocalyptic visions, so am I. I find it very difficult to predict the future, partly because the rate of change today makes such predictions instantly obsolete and partly because I tend to reject both visions of doom and utopia. So I find myself about to draw conclusions, make recommendations, and predict the future of media in libraries trying to resist dire prophesies, with doubts and a hope that resolution of the problems ahead lies within our reach.

I have long had ambiguous attitudes towards media. For a time I interpreted "understanding media" to mean a wholesale endorsement of media technologies, some sort of mindless enthusiasm for kinetic images and groovy sounds. My only brush with media theory in college was a cursory reading of Marshall McLuhan's *Understanding Media* which, like many before and after me, I violently rejected, thinking he was attacking print. Years later my perceptions of what McLuhan was expressing have been radically altered, but not without the struggle to understand a startling and revolutionary concept.

My attitudes towards media were first tested when I found myself an AV Coordinator in a private high school, knowing little about libraries and even less about media. From sheer survival instincts I set out to learn something about what these "audiovisual services" were that I was supposed to provide. Like many media librarians, I was "lugging and plugging" equipment, building a media collection from the rather mediocre educational offerings available, teaching about mass media to senior English students and thinking about what treatment media deserved in libraries and how our media environment affects us. Media study, once you've become aware of it, has a way of hounding you into everlasting consciousness.

Over the course of the last few years I've found that attitudes toward media among my librarian friends ran the gamut from mystical devotion to atheistic scepticism. Media enthusiasts seem to fall into two categories:

on the one hand, the intuitive, nonverbal people who do not articulate in the traditional media of print and the spoken word. They sometimes hamper their effectiveness at conveying the impact media have for libraries. On the other hand, there are the media theorists with a profound sense of the social, psychological, and political impact of media but who are so scholarly in their expression that those most in need of instruction are turned off by erudite tone and language. Both proponents attempt to counteract a lack of knowledge and negativism felt about media: one reveals the media to be worthy of serious reflection and scholarly study, the other demonstrates how other modes of expression and awareness are available through auditory and visual means. Neither one has yet succeeded in convincing the doubting Thomases among us that media are vital to the library's future.

Obviously the basic issue here is that media, that ambiguous, even elusive, term hasn't yet been defined in such a way that it brings that shiver of professional commitment which "the Word" invokes.

THE "WORD" IS A MEDIUM

From time immemorial the Word—capable of symbolically representing the reality of God—has held a sacred meaning. How do you go about convincing people whose dedication to knowledge and information can be equated with a holy reverence for words (books, newspapers, magazines, the printed medium) that media are worthy of such a commitment? Continued resistance to a concept of media, which of course encompasses the word not as primary code but as one of several communications' languages, indicates the enormity of this task. The problem is not so much a matter of informing librarians, as it is of converting them to a new religion in which one god is now revealed as having several persons.

The library profession has no one ideological stance on media. Attitudes toward media vary from one branch of librarianship to another as from one librarian to another. At the risk of losing all anti-McLuhanites, what seems needed is for the profession to arrive at an understanding of media as McLuhan saw them, as *codes of communication*. When media as a concept is limited to *audiovisual aids* or *nonprint*, when media mean filmstrips, transparencies, and simulation games, few are likely to deem such codes equal partners of the powerful and sophisticated language of words. But, when media are viewed as those sources of information which dominate us, print, television, film, radio, telephone, among others, a total concept of a new information environment created only in the last hundred years becomes apparent. The definition of the goals of librarianship, "to provide user-oriented service and information to all" expressed by ALA President Allie Beth Martin, requires a new understanding of media as the information environment in which users live. Understanding media becomes then a basic task for librarians who will provide for Mediaman's information needs.

THE INDUSTRIALIZED MIND

Hans Magnus Enzensberger, writing in *Partisan Review*, identified this fearsome reality imposed by media: "Hardly anyone seems to be aware of the phenomenon as a whole: the industrialization of the human mind . . . The mind industry's main business and concern is not to sell its product: it is to 'sell' the existing order, to perpetuate the prevailing pattern of man's domination by man, no matter who runs the society and by what means. Its main task is to expand and train our consciousness—in order to exploit it."

Man has become *mass man* as a direct result of the mass technologies altering life styles, work patterns, information structures. There is always that fear that all this "progress" may lead to a mass mind programmed to think certain thoughts and act in specified ways. Libraries like to envision themselves as trustees of information, guarantors of intellectual freedom. But today, the information upon which freedom depends is not just preservable in books. Denied access to media information and the techniques necessary to decipher their full meaning, we fall prey to what Jacques Ellul calls the most dangerous form of determinism, the technological phenomenon, or as Enzensberger puts it, the industrialization of the mind. One need only look at television, a most familiar technological phenomena, to realize that for most people in this country, television provides their principal source of education, entertainment, information, and opinion. The solution to the problem technology poses is not to abolish them (which is impossible) nor to ignore them (worse yet) but to become aware of how any medium—print as well as electronic communications media—affects us, informs us. It is only by becoming aware of the dangers of these technologies that we can hope to transcend them.

But, in an endeavor to recognize the potential harms of media, we must not overlook the fact that the symbolic and value communication of our culture is now being carried out largely within these media. While media technologies may serve as agents of mind control, they also extend our ways of knowing, increase our knowledge, and expand our consciousness.

To provide user-oriented service and information in our mass media environment, librarians will need to think about how people learn, why people turn to the mass media and why people read, how electronic media communicate differently from print. Help in answering questions like these comes not only from thoughtful librarians researching these areas, but also from the social sciences of psychology and sociology, from philosophy and communications theory.

A STATE OF RESONANCE

Tony Schwartz in *The Responsive Chord* explores how electronic communication differs from the traditional concept of information transportation. The transportation theory involves a sender, a message, and a receiver. The sender, or author/publisher, transmits the message, or book, to the receiver, librarian/patron. In this equation, all communications' information is contained in the message. A transportation theory of communication is useful only when the *movement* of information is a central problem. But, when someone is overloaded with information, as we are of late, the transportation theory ceases to be meaningful. What we are really dealing with is information flow, a much more complex process than the mere transportation of messages.

With electronically mediated human communication, the communicator's function is to achieve a "state of resonance" with the person receiving visual and auditory stimuli from media. Listeners or viewers bring far more information to the communication event than any communicator can put into a program, commercial, or message. The problem becomes one of understanding the kinds of information and experiences stored in the audience, the patterning of this information, and the "interactive resonance" process by which stimuli evoke this stored information. "In communicating at electronic speed," Schwartz tells us, "we no longer direct information into an audience, but try to evoke stored information out of them, in a patterned way."

Schwartz' analysis not only throws light on how the electronic media of television and radio can manipulate our minds to "sell" their message, but it also has implications for how librarians must approach information seekers in our media environment.

In assessing the information needs of a user, the librarian as communicator must take into account the information and experience already stored in the user's brain to provide the right stimuli—be it book, film, or leading questions, which will evoke the meaning sought. A more involving process is called for. The library user, no matter how "culturally deprived," comes with a vast array of information and experiences already stored in his brain. Meeting information needs may no longer just mean locating books or films, "directing information into an audience." It will probably mean a more active service, discovering what the user knows, what he or she needs to know, and how this information can best be revealed. Lengthy interviews, placing telephone calls, exploring several media resources will be part of this process.

FEAR OF TECHNOLOGY

Once media are recognized for their penetrating, far-reaching effect upon the information environment of the library user, once the profession understands the importance of a total concept of media as vital to user-oriented library collections and services, then related issues raised by media technologies can be dealt with one by one. Among the most pressing is the gut-level issue—fear of technology. There are several reasons for such fear. One is the myth that women (and librarianship remains largely a woman's profession) are not mechanically inclined or capable of handling heavy, complicated equipment. This is a "myth" because the female sex is not so biologically limited. Intimidation by machinery comes from a lack of confidence governed by cultural conditioning. While the women's movement has helped in shooting down such myths, there are still many who believe that they simply can not handle equipment, who remain traumatized by technology.

Fear of media technology is often accompanied by the fear of exposing oneself as lacking in knowledge. Toffler cautioned us in *Future Shock* that "new knowledge compels those for whom it is relevant . . . to reorganize their store of images. It forces them to relearn today what they thought they knew yesterday." Confronting a lack of knowledge and expertise, especially in an alien world of machinery, is particularly difficult for people with a high stake in their self-image as "competent professionals."

I have great sympathy for people plagued by such fears. Faced with five different brands of 16mm projectors and indecipherable instruction manuals, caught in classrooms and auditoriums when bulbs blew and the natives grew restless, I know the anger and frustration media technologies prompt. My first video experience was so devastating to my self-confidence—after having misthreaded the tape and ruining a 20-minute documentary—that I was ready to give up on media then and there. Fortunately I did not. Challenge and conflict are the stuff upon which self-confidence is built. Overcoming such fears will not only offer librarians cause for self-congratulation but, in the grander scale of things, insure increased access to all information codes.

The time has come for all librarians to face the realities technology presents to them. "The functions and services of all professions are determined by the technologies at their disposal. Librarianship is no exception. If the profession fails to understand and appropriately utilize the communications technologies which are available it has failed in its social function," comments library educator Estelle Jussim.

Communications technology is not going to disappear nor slow down long enough for people still operating in a linear mode to grab hold of its tail. "A lot of people are waiting for the technological cycle to stop. You have to stick your finger in that spinning wheel sometime," is good advice from Bruce Fairley of the Metro Toronto Central Library. The point is that technology goes on reinventing itself. Many are now waiting for the advent of the videodisc to resolve their video format dilemmas. Some are' holding off on any video activity until a standardized format is proclaimed. I can't help but imagine that, based on the rate of change and number of discoveries we've seen appear in recent years, some new invention will appear on the horizon—perhaps holographic video—which will postpone decision for the cautious once again.

The videodisc, foreseen in the next two years, will make acquisition of preprogrammed video as easy as collecting phonodiscs, but it will not replace portapak or studio video which fulfills another function, helping users create their own information. What may happen is that the videodisc will *displace* portapak video by discouraging its growth, a sorry fate for the community-centered, user-oriented library. An awareness of the different capabilities media technologies offer us is needed so that we don't, in our ignorance, trade-off information we make locally for mere ease of retrieval we can buy.

LAST HIRED . . .

Another issue, crucial now because of its potential to seriously set back media programs and media consciousness is the crisis of funding. So long as there are librarians who still view media as aids peripheral to the main functions of the library, the first items to be cut will be media services and staff. Shout it from the highest library rooftops, this is a major mistake.

No one likes to finger the guy who's got to go, but why does it always seem to be the media person? Huge investments are squandered as media systems are relegated to closets because the only person who knew how to operate them is crossed off the budget. Enormous potential for community and school participation is being denied or frustrated by such cuts. This stems from another version of that hierarchical notion that words are more valuable than images and sounds, books si, media no.

And when it comes to dollar value, who is to say that books are cheaper than audiovisual media? The library profession doesn't subscribe to any theory of supplying only "bargain-basement information." Quality and comprehension are at stake here. A single half-hour film may fulfill a need that 50 books on the subject are inadequate to fill. For example, to provide a youngster born in the last ten years with information about John Kennedy's assassination, newspaper, magazine and book accounts, useful in themselves, do not equal the invaluable information that the actual Super-8mm footage of the tragedy offers or the complex feelings expressed through the collage of television and radio coverage in Bruce Conner's film, *Report*.

MEDIA CONSCIOUSNESS IS FREE

While cut backs are inevitable, cut outs are more than foolish, they're dangerous. Different media formats can not be viewed as unrelated, dispensable entities. A library wiping out its video program is about as sensible as their cancelling all magazine subscriptions or ceasing to collect fiction. Ignoring important information sources merely because they are inconvenient to store endangers our basic freedom of access to information.

Strategies are at our disposal for dealing with the harsh realities limited funding implies for media services. Increased cooperation of public and school libraries, of local libraries with their regional groupings, consortia of libraries, universities, museums, and community information centers, will help hold down costs through the sharing of expenses, resources, and staff. Time and effort will be needed to work out such cooperative efforts but, if deemed a priority, the initial expenditures of time in planning will be rewarded by continued and increased access to media information. And interlibrary loan systems will figure as a major factor in the containment of materials expenses.

Remedies such as those outlined here are no doubt being expanded upon by writers exploring other issues because cooperation is going to be the key to all strategies defending libraries against the onslaught of rising costs versus shrinking finances.

In the meantime, libraries faced with severe financial limitations need not abandon media commitment because of no cash. While sophisticated video systems bear high price tags, media consciousness is free for the asking. James Brown in his soon-to-be-published study *New Media in Public Libraries* comments on many innovative media activities he examined. "I don't think that it was money that did it always, it was the determination on the parts of people with ideas about what a library could be and ought to be—the vision of involved librarians."

Libraries must not overlook the fact that they have access to numerous media technologies capable of extending their abilities to locate and deliver information to their users. George Stoney, Director of New York University's Alternate Media Center, reminds us that books are media too and that collecting books on media is a beginning for media service. Film, audio, and video are media "superstars," but low-profile media such as the telephone, photocopier, and typewriter offer libraries an untapped potential for revolutionizing information services. For example, the telephone, as Ted Carpenter tells us, turns men into "angels," capable of being in more than one place at the same time. Creative use of the telephone turns static information into kinetic information. Calling up the Department of Social Services or the local NOW chapter, the librarian gets up-to-the-minute information, which as we know only too well changes radically from day to day. Book information is dated before it even comes out. Newspapers and magazines, though more current, do not give one the opportunity to dialogue, to ask an authority a question followed by a further question in seeking out answers to a dilemma. People-to-people information service via the telephone is a positive, readily available media service which all libraries could implement.

Reorienting libraries to the belief that media service begins with an attitude of mind, that inexpensive media technologies are available in every library, that media are not just for the richly endowed, may be a significant step towards actualizing a new concept of library information service.

What is needed now is the profession's understanding of our media environment and commitment to a total media concept for libraries; a freedom from the fear media technologies evoke; and cooperative efforts on the parts of all branches of librarianship in coordinating activities to provide for the needs of future library users.

FREEDOM INCLUDES ALL MEDIA

Filling user needs through media technologies will present numerous difficulties which librarians will have to resolve. Some librarians are worried that media technologies place them in more controversial positions than books ever did. But book service is a public act too, which puts the library and librarian on the line each time users are provided with materials. People hesitating to engage in media activity for such reasons had best examine their attitudes about books and freedom of access.

Free access to media information is often not the policy of libraries which, while they would hesitate about violating the library bill of rights with regard to print, do not give a second thought to the propriety of limiting media access to individuals, groups, or minors. Don Robert's current study on media censorship, sponsored in part by the Council on Library Resources will lay the groundwork for further investigation and action in this area.

Standards for cataloging "non-print" media are being revised by library and media education groups. The revised Anglo-American Cataloging Rules, scheduled to appear in 1977, may help resolve some questions. But, before then, guidelines need to be followed and unified media collections need to be established so that users will not be frustrated in their attempts at locating information. Somehow, someone will finally meet the crying need for a mediagraphic tool which will assemble all data on media so that acquisitions librarians and library users can see what materials are available and where to find them.

MEDIA CREDIBILITY

There are many other problems raised by media which are too numerous to mention here. While a philosophical, psychological, and financial disposition to a total concept of media for libraries may help librarians in resolving their media dilemmas, we wait for this great moment. Sound judgments and implementation of media programs are called for now.

Will libraries survive without a total media concept? Probably, but libraries will not be able to meet the information needs of users without taking seriously the implications of our media environment, without recognizing the awesome influence of mass media. The library can not expect to remain vital if it maintains that the portable book is the only carrier of information and communication which it is mandated to provide. And so long as controversies over the validity of auditory and visual literacy persist, chauvinistically discriminating against other codes and other learning styles, the library will lose its credibility as an institution preserving and making accessible all human knowledge.

I am not sure how ready librarians are for that "religious conversion" that adoption of a total media concept seems to imply. It is within the power of the profession, as within each individual, to reinvent the future.

If we recognize the importance of a total media concept for libraries we are at least on our way to finding out what the future may bring. If not, we may look forward to this vision, portrayed by Jorge Luis Borges in "The Library of Babel":

> The human species—the unique species—is about to be extinguished, but the library will endure: illuminated, solitary, infinite, perfectly motionless, equipped with precious volumes, useless, incorruptible, secret.

This Matter of Media

by Evelyn Geller

It has been a disappointment, over the last several years, to observe how discussions of "integrating media" inevitably boil down to two dreary cliches: One is that the library is no longer the storehouse of printed information, that librarians have to swing with the media revolution if they want to hold on to their patrons. Or, the other side, that the book is not really dead—which is probably a more popular suggestion.

The trouble is that both statements are true, yet both are irrelevant. And it is disturbing that people can rally about these slogans as if they were opposing causes. This really shows how far we are from integrating media. And the reason, at least among those of us who are well-meaning, is that we simply cannot evaluate the current communications revolution in terms of both its good and unfortunate impact upon us. Marshall McLuhan has said, in one of his less popularized, yet brilliant, statements, "If we understood our older media, such as roads, and the written word, and if we valued their human effects sufficiently, we could reduce or even eliminate the electronic factor from our lives."

How great is this "electronic factor"? It is often repeated that a student will have spent 5400 hours in school before he gets his high school diploma. By that time, he will also have spent 7500 hours watching movies on television. Yet in education, or in the nontheatrical or noncommercial film field, an opposite situation prevails. Not only are media less prominent than books, they have not been well used, or used enough, to make a difference in teaching. In its report *To Improve Learning* the Commission on Instructional Technology shows only the inconclusiveness of experiments and research in that field.

A QUESTION OF TEXTURE

The trouble is, in part, that we are not talking about the same thing when we use that word—media, or even film. The educational film is only a textbook put on a screen, a safe venture for a producer who needs a solid market, who can not afford the investment entailed by the entertainment film, and who cannot expect to make a profit on a single film until its third year of production. At the other end of the film spectrum is the independent poetic film producer, more likely to have the public library or various film clubs as his target audience. He has had trouble finding a distributor or may even have only two prints of his small masterpiece. His work is analogous to that of an unpublished manuscript circulated almost privately. When we talk about even one medium, film, we must thus make distinctions that would be analogous to various kinds of books with differing appeals to librarians. The distinction is one of content, or aesthetics, a distinction of texture.

In the school situation, the past history of the "a/v market" combined with an all-too-slowly moving trend toward freedom from curriculum, and the split between librarians and a/v specialists has not produced a very happy situation in film selection. Librarians are really in a bad way when— as one Long Island public library did—they can't find a film to work into a children's literature program in handsomely funded and expensive local BOCES (regional school system) film collection and are forced to write to the New York State Library for help.

On the other hand, I wonder if the public libraries have been much better in conceptualizing and programming media, even if one grants that they are way ahead of the schools in the quality of film selection. Public libraries still fail to integrate print and nonprint into one total program. Most public libraries have a separate audiovisual specialist. Budgets are not combined so that print and nonprint materials might be selected together, to complement each other, for a given purpose. There is still an emphasis on 16mm film, with neglect of other media—notably recordings—which would be easier to handle and loan. There is little concern with media circulation at the local branch level. Even the recent program of films on EVR seems to have been compiled hurriedly, out of expediency, relying heavily on noncopyrighted works simply because they would not run into trouble, rather than with any specific intent in mind. Conducted fragmentally and in isolation, the use of media in public libraries does little to relate people to other media, or to the communications media in their lives.

THE REAL DICHOTOMIES

So we return to the old print vs. non-print argument which rests on a bastardized McLuhanism. "The medium is the message." Aha! Content is irrelevant. And thus we lose the gist of some of the most perceptive statements on the nature of media in the contemporary world. It is a pity that librarians, of all people, should share in the simplistic journalistic interpretations of this very perceptive thinker. McLuhan has been misunderstood most because he discusses media in terms of impact rather than content. It is not that he doesn't care about content, but because for McLuhan content does not completely explain the impact of communications media as forms of technology. The McLuhan analysis is, much the same as Lewis Mumford's, a linking of social patterns to stages of technological development, or similar even to the way that Karl Marx related social forms and moral values to the underlying modes of production in society. Thus for McLuhan the clock is a medium. It quantified our description of time, divorcing it from the emotion and the conditions of our experience; it made speed measurable. The electric light bulb is a medium, transforming our notions of what could be done by day or by night, and, hence our lifestyles. ("Will night baseball replace sex?")

As the alphabet and papyrus, and later, the manuscript, created a breed of scribes, the book—the first case of mass production—freed literacy from control by a small cult, and made possible the homogeneity of large communities. Today the paperback is a different medium from the hardback, because of the different conditions of accessibility it enjoys —even though the content is the same. Photo-reproduction is a different medium from the published book, because of its impact on the economics of publishing. The fact that every man can become his own "publisher" radically changes our notion of accessible information—and hopefully, will change our conception of "valuable" information to something more broad than what is commercially marketable.

The distinction between print and nonprint as related to oral and written cultures must be seen in proper perspective. All of us, from literary critics pondering the origins of the *Iliad* to children's librarians telling stories, know that our literary culture stems originally from an oral tradition that present technology is recreating. One major literary medium, drama, in print form is necessary only as a kind of bookkeeping device for what was a visual performance. If that original performance can be preserved on the screen, the importance of the written play is diminished, except as the direction or manual for performers. Similarly, the book and the press, both print, are different media. To go back to McLuhan:

> The book is a private confessional form that provides a "point of view." The press is a group confessional form that provides communal participation. It can "color" events by using them or by not using them at all. But it is the daily communal exposure of multiple items in juxtaposition that gives the press its complex dimension of human interest.
>
> The book form is not a communal mosaic or corporate image but a private voice. One of the unexpected effects of TV on the press has been a great increase in the popularity of *Time* and *Newsweek*. Quite inexplicably to themselves and without any new effort at subscription, their circulations have more than doubled since TV. These news magazines are preeminently mosaic in form, offering not windows on the world like the old picture magazines, but presenting corporate images of society in action.

What does all this mean for the children in our schools? And for adults? That they are barraged by the constant play of information about contemporary events—about which they are learning, for good or for ill —outside of school, rather than in the classroom. Abraham Cohen observed this a few years back in the *School Library Journal* when he noted that TV sets are in 90 percent of our homes. By January 1969 they were in

95 percent. (There were telephones in only 80 per cent of our homes.) Similarly, there were some 17,000 movie theaters, including drive-ins, in our country. In 1969-70 there were only 10,252 bookstores. Students and adults are learning from newspapers, magazines, and comic books, to a degree that our schools and libraries seldom acknowledge.

TOWARD CONCEPTUAL INTEGRATION

Conceptually, we have to end the tired discussion of "print vs. non-print" when we talk about media, and about integrating them. We should be talking about perspective, about relating our clients to the words and images around them, and to the past, in ways most of our schools and libraries do not. With so many centrifugal forces in society, it is crucial that we all try to supply a connecting link. But so far neither our training nor our job structure has prepared us for this kind of work. We are trained in a discipline without content, dealing rather with the organization of knowledge, and that not in any sophisticated form. If we cannot really link books to each other conceptually or thematically, how can we expect to relate them to other media—chosen through a separate and inadequate budget, by a separate person, with different aesthetic and practical criteria, hindered by the present use of media in the system, by the lack of facilities, by administrative restrictions.

It is ironic that the school librarians, who have gone furthest in trying to alleviate both problems—that of print vs. nonprint, and that of curricular vs. societal relevance—have been getting it in the neck from both audiovisual specialists and public librarians. The *Standards for School Media Programs*, which emphasized conceptual and thematic connections across the media, have been fought by experts in "communications media" on the grounds that a projector constitutes a separate discipline.

A second solution, offered in the New York State report of the Commissioner's Committee on Library Development, ran into equally vehement opposition. Yet its controversial tenet—that schools take over most of the responsibility for library service to children at the preschool and elementary levels—was only an extension of a position that Frank Stevens expressed years ago, when he was coordinator of school libraries in New York State. Refusing to set up required lists for the schools, he said: "Give me any book, and I'll fit it into the curriculum." I don't see how any professional school librarian could take a different stand, could rule out this conception of responsibility. What the public library can do is support the concept of enrichment of services, of greater variety and freedom of service that will, nevertheless, always be changing if we are lucky enough to have the schools improve. If this is not a viable philosophy, I would like to see public librarians develop a proposal for school reform, including school library reform, that would not include a concept of total responsibility, or that school administrators could not possibly, philosophically accept.

There are, to be sure, *pragmatic* problems that we know are not so easy
—questions of aesthetics and liberality of support, the concept of library
service that does not always come so easily to a school administrator, and
above all the problems of censorship, which stem from the American
watchdog attitude toward schools. But I'm not certain that these are issues
of philosophy. Philosophically, the school library movement is an attempt
to see the library as a total environment, to move from instruction to
culture, to the broad concept of education that the public library also
represents, with the sole distinction that it also serves the child during his
formative years at a time, in a place where the love of intellectual exploration can be cultivated for all children as they learn, regardless of the
preference, or indifference, of their parents.

One may argue that the school library, as a "special library" serving
the professional staff as well as students in curricular areas, is carrying out
a rather narrow function in relation to this ambitious conception. This
notion, however, embodies—quite to the contrary—a concept of service
that public libraries are, for the most part, failing to perform for their
clientele. The result is that few people—literate people who used the
public library assiduously while they were children—have retained their
interest in library service. I include myself among them. My own branch
library ranks among the better ones in New York City. Yet its hours are
inconvenient for the working person. The new books are never in stock;
fiction cannot be reserved; if the book is out, I wait a month. It's easier, as
the middle class has learned, to buy a paperback.

THE PUBLIC AS SPECIAL LIBRARY

Of course the public library has for decades been pussyfooting on its
function regarding the public. Even if it has extended its service beyond
pushing mysteries, sports, home care, bestsellers, and other books that
"move," it has not really advanced far beyond the little rental library writ
large. Some years back, when the Public Library Inquiry was made, it was
suggested that the library address itself to the small segment of in-
tellectuals who actually use it. This philosophy, plus the increasing size of
cities and the move to the suburbs, deflected the library from its original
goal of trying to serve, or elevate, its entire community, including the
working class. This is one reason, of course, why the libraries are not
getting even reasonable support these days.

Even granted that the sources of recreation through books once used
by workers have now been preempted by television, the library still has a
useful function to perform for all people, founded upon the principles of
Jeffersonian democracy, which, for all their outdatedness, underlie our
concept of the functioning of the state: a belief in the common citizen's
ability to rule himself, to keep any one power from taking over society, if
only he has access to information. If this is not the purpose that justifies
libraries as a *public* service, then a valid rationalization will be difficult to

find. The 1966 public library standards talk about self improvement in only the vaguest terms, leaving the active work of cultivating awareness to individual initiative. They are so all-encompassing that they offer the libraries few priorities within a limited budget.

The concept of the public library as a "special library" is only now beginning to take root among urban communities on an experimental basis and generally with federal funds. In these communities, populations are deprived of access to information on the public agencies that can help them, and "special" information services to fill this and other needs are being tried.

But there are other critical issues in the integration of information in which libraries must be involved at this juncture in time—especially when economic power is increasingly concentrated among a few TV networks, film producers, publishing enterprises (the small ones, including the small children's departments, having been drastically affected by the Depression). The dimensions of their power and audience are overwhelming compared to those of the book.

According to the latest (1969) figures for the publishing industry, sales for adult and juvenile trade books, hardback and paperback, came to $380 million. If you want to add to it sales of wholesale paperbacks and sales through book clubs, you come out with $773 million. If you add university press books, you can reach a total of $810 million.

How does this compare with the figures for a few other media? Commercial movie sales in 1969 came to $1.1 billion; TV advertising expenditures totaled $3.585 billion; radio broadcast revenues—another $1.27 billion; newspaper advertising expenditures reached $5.85 billion (on a national and local level); magazines of all kinds got $1.375 billion in advertising that year.

And these media do not include many channels, such as the vast government publishing industry.

So, if we limit our function to serving as institutional outlets for the commercial trade book publisher, we have ignored media of overwhelming importance, in the face of which the publishing industry really shrivels. It is not a question of deferring to these media, but of recognizing, and perhaps countervailing, their impact.

It is interesting to note in this connection the recent Roper survey of people's attitudes to television. It is now considered by 49 percent of Americans asked to be the most credible and least dispensible of the news media; three-fourths of the parents surveyed would allow commercials on children's programs, to keep those programs going; and the subjects of the survey believe, eight to one, that the ads are well worth the benefit of a free show. Roy Danish, director of the Television Information Office, concluded that the criticism of TV by persons who claim to speak for the public runs counter to the findings of the Roper study. This may merely be a good selling job, and while the average man may not be a great expert on the forces manipulating him, at least he is not aping Agnew.

A PHILOSOPHY OF REFERENCE SERVICE

Yet, however favorably inclined we may be toward television, we know that it doesn't tell all the story, that like other media, it gives us a fractured and fragmented view of reality. In fact, in the current paranoid atmosphere of charges and countercharges, there is hardly anyone to serve as a mediator, or referee; to check up on charges and references, to restore balance and accurate context to the dialectic of debate. Somehow librarians seem to feel that just choosing a "balanced" collection will create that order. In a way, the cataloging is supposed to do that for you. Or, if you're really with it, some well-selected, annotated booklist will do the job.

If we are really trying to carry out a valuable function, however, what we should be doing is, in a way, both more primitive and far more sophisticated.

For example, I had the occasion last fall to read Edward Banfield's *The Unheavenly City* with a view to exploring its implications for library service to the deprived. In addition to writing the book specifically to contradict Kenneth Clark's *Dark Ghetto,* Banfield had constructed a kind of philosophy of class culture based on the research of others. This claim led me to a backward tracking of his sources. What I discovered was a gross and rather arbitrary distortion of other people's ideas—including those of Oscar Lewis and Herbert Gans—though he was using these authorities for his own argument. Checking the *Library Journal* review for the book, I found that it had been called a case of "skillful" reasoning, a "provocative" book that all libraries should buy.

While I agree with the conclusion, it seems pretty apparent that such cheery and noncommittal acceptance of a book like Banfield's, especially if translated into library purchase or student reliance on its findings, is cavalier and even dangerous. The use of a book like this—which describes the philosophy of the Nixon administration and its kiss of death on the War on Poverty—warrants more than the kind of casual reader's guidance we generally accord a book. If the job of cataloging or classification is truly intellectual, placing a piece of knowledge in a conceptual framework, this should be extended toward understanding the content of this book. In this case, a responsible librarian would have to display and cite the book, along with its sources, comparing them and pointing out distinctions for the readers. That is, if we were really interested in integrating information by engaging in a little added research.

The trouble again lies in the fact that we are not encouraged to be specialists in content. If authorities conflict, you let them slug it out. The result: the most sophisticated kind of reference work, in the grand public, research, or academic library, becomes simply a matter of chasing down citations for some scholar. This banal exercise glorified as "reference service," basing our so-called professionalism on the accidental flaws of the bibliographic network—which is really nothing more than a massive bookkeeping system—has done as much as anything in librarianship to keep reference work sterile and irrelevant. There is only one segment of the profession that has gone beyond this conception of service—again, school librarianship.

If you read the *Standards for School Media Programs*, you will see why. Although the term "media specialist" prevails, it soon becomes clear that, in terms of education and function, the librarian is not a "media" specialist at all, but a specialist of another kind—based either on subject matter or grade level. He is a cross between the teacher and the librarian as we normally conceive of both. He does not leave content to the subject specialist, yet he is not quite a teacher. He is not confined to the mere transmission of "knowledge," nor is he a researcher engaged in his own narrow enterprise. If the idea were extended to the public library or the college library, the librarian could indeed become a kind of bibliographic umpire, creating balance out of the partisan published feuding in the disciplines.

A different but related reference function would provide background documentation on issues of obvious currency. I read a little squib in the *New York Times* recently about how AT&T had been denied the right to experiment with the picture telephone because it first had to clean up the mess it had made with the traditional phone service. That was nice. On second thought, however, why couldn't that experimental money be turned back into the company to keep my telephone bill down?

Out of curiosity I checked the *World Almanac*, where AT&T is listed as the third largest company in the United States (outranked only by GM and Standard Oil), but number one in profit. Out of sales of $14.1 billion, it had had a net profit of over $2 billion—the highest in the country. Now these figures are two years old, which is a reference problem in itself. If AT&T enjoys this profit largely because it has a virtual monopoly supported by you and me, why don't the costs of its inefficiencies come out of its profits, rather than its client's pockets? Is it naive to expect that the library might prepare, or anticipate, information on such a subject—or on various subjects of community interest—based on documents and non-trade sources—in advance, and publicize them? Or is this kind of service to be provided, say, in Minneapolis, by Ervin Gaines only for business interests?

BEYOND "ADVOCACY"

This may seem close to that much publicized idea of advocacy which has been so badly misinterpreted in the profession, but it is something very different. To me, the public library's main function today is to extend the concept of journalism to its services: find out what the important issues are, issues to highlight, to display, upon which to spend valuable research time, upon which to run film programs, and to build collections about. This requires a decision like that of the newspaper or television station on what the library is to cover in depth. The decision is not about the point of view: it is about what the important questions are. Libraries must avoid, for example, what one large inner-city system did last spring: running a gardening display in branch after branch, in the middle of an urban slum. As for magazines, tear some of them up, put them on bulletin boards. Don't bury the clippings in the vertical file. Keep track of a story as it breaks in the press, get letters to the editor and arguments. Do libraries have to wait for CBS Television to do "The Selling of the Pentagon" when the H. W. Wilson Company published a "Reference Shelf" book on a similar topic, based on magazine articles, for high school libraries earlier this spring? This issue could have been exposed in the libraries when it was still in the newspaper and magazines and before CBS made it big news. Buttressed with government documents (put to much better use than usual), public libraries could have done an important and better-documented job on the Pentagon. Why should we force library school students to learn the bibliography of government publication if we do not wish to free libraries from captivity to, and relevance as decided by, the commercial media? How can we claim to be "information specialists" if we don't want to go beyond what private industry sees as saleable and popular information—if we don't want to go beyond the middle ground of accepted opinion?

Of course, then, libraries must use all media—recordings which run the gamut from children's fairy tales to the sound of current events as they happen, the passion of contemporary debate, and the social commentary of rock music.

Libraries must use experimental film, which, like poetry, will surely die without support, and which, at another extreme, is producing an archive of social documentary more immediate and vivid than any book. Libraries must do this to a degree greater than ever conceived, breaking down the administrative and financial barriers to acquisition across media boundaries, to acquisition for purpose.

But purpose does come first, and I would suggest that libraries and librarians exist, above all, to create a better pattern out of the mosaic of contemporary experience than that provided by newspapers or television in their datelines of simultaneous happenings. The job can be done through print and other media, but most important, we must understand the content of both, and the impact of all media upon human life in our society.

Remember that even in *Fahrenheit 451*, where an entire culture based on book-burning was narcotized by wall-tall television entertainment while the ruling powers engaged in secret war, the great preserver of the book, Faber, did not blame other media—he blamed the truth. "Do you see why books are hated and feared? They show the pores in the face of life. The comfortable people want only wax moon faces, poreless, hairless, expressionless."

But Faber also said:

> It's not books you need, it's some of the things that once were in books. The same things could be in the [television] "parlor families" today. The same infinite detail and awareness could be projected through the radios and

televisors, but are not. No, no, it's not books at all you're looking for! Take it where you can find it, in old phonograph records, old motion pictures, and in old friends; look for it in nature and look for it in yourself. Books were only one type of receptacle where we stored a lot of things we were afraid we might forget. There is nothing magical in them, at all. The magic is only in what books say, how they stitched the patches of the universe together into one garment for us.

"Stitching the patches of the universe together." I hope that's what we're all about.

REFERENCES

Edward Banfield. *The Unheavenly City.* Little, 1970.

Ray Bradbury. *Fahrenheit 451.* S. & S.. 1967. Ballantine (pap.), 1969.

Commission on Instructional Technology. *To Improve Learning.* Bowker. 1971.

Marshall McLuhan. *Understanding Media.* McGraw, 1964. pap., 1965.

Audio-Visual Aids: Fallout From the McLuhan Galaxy

by William R. Eshelman

The orbiting of Sputnik in the fifties was viewed in the United States as a kind of handwriting on the sky: our educational system must be thoroughly reformed. Among those who hastened to make the most of the crisis were the advocates of audio-visual aids. Claiming successes with military training films and language labs during World War II, they intensified their campaign to revolutionize teaching methods. It was old hat to require students to use their imaginations while reading, they argued. Such devices as slides and filmstrips, films and television would motivate students to read and increase their appreciation of literature.

The A-V proponents based their claims on research, usually summarized like this: Learners retain about 10 per cent of what they read, 20 per cent of what they hear, 30 per cent of what they see. Of what they see and hear the retention is 50 percent, of what they see as they speak 70 per cent, of what they say as they participate in activities fully 90 per cent.

In the sixties the McLuhan galaxy swam into our ken, creating a new cultural shock. We were informed that the long dominance of print had forced us into being linear creatures. Print is made up of words strung together in sentences and paragraphs, separate elements that can be arranged only in linear chains. Thus we think step by step, a clumsy, time-consuming method when contrasted with what is possible through the means of the new electronic media. Now, according to Marshall McLuhan, because of TV, computers and other such gear it behoved everyone to become an involved, simultaneous thinker.

The argument raised questions and problems that Mr. McLuhan and his followers never got around to answering. Who can think in TV's split images? How many can speak in film or slides? Are computer programs the language of love? The development of TV's instant replay technique is a concession to the linear process. Like print, it allows the viewer to "re-read" and so to comprehend.

The individual uses language internally to encode ideas and to communicate them. Thus he is both a sender and a receiver of verbal messages. The vast majority of people never encode ideas in filmic terms, nor do they interact with others who do. We may receive nonprint messages, but seldom if ever are they our tools of thought. Where are the enduring classics of the filmstrip? Who quotes them? Who remembers them?

The chief characteristic of the multi-media techniques used in teaching (the simultaneous presentation, for example, of slides, films and filmstrips) is over-stimulus without time for response. Without interactions, there can be little learning. One rises from such a presentation battered and bemused, having tried to drink, as it were, from a fire hydrant. Where is the grammar of this new A-V language? What is its syntax? Is there an electronic Fowler to rail against the blurring of useful distinctions?

The McLuhan rage produced a dramatic change of heart among American schools and libraries in 1969. In that year, the National Educational Association (which had absorbed the national visual aid group back in 1923) and the American Library Association (which had urged its members to collect films as early as 1925) jointly published a "set of standards," the effect of which was to upgrade the educational importance of A-V software and hardware and to substitute the phrase "school media center" for the word "library."

Typical of the new media packages now currently being urged upon school librarians by their two national associations is one made up of eight filmstrips plus cassettes which claims to put "the civil rights movement into meaningful perspective." The two-hour show consists of more than 900 color frames, with the narration highlighted by the voices of Martin Luther King, Medgar Evers, Orval Faubus, John F. Kennedy, George Wallace, among others. The school library possessing plenty of copies of books by Claude Brown, Malcolm X, Angela Davis, Eldridge Cleaver, plus a collection of the views of Spiro Agnew, Barry Goldwater, William F. Buckley and the John Birch Society will find the set a useful aid in achieving the aim of every worthy school and public library—an increase in the number of thoughtful, independent citizens. If it can afford the $142 the package costs.

Anyone who thoughtfully examines the two associations' school media standards inevitably finds himself weighing the relative priorities of books and A-V materials. If one filmstrip title costs $142, the cost of reaching the minimum standard set for A-V materials in a 2000-student high school library would be $71,000. This to complement a book collection of 40,000 volumes, in itself a completely unrealistic goal!

In less than 20 years the mystique of A-V has grown from a helpful aid to reading and learning into a titan that threatens to supplant reading entirely. Equipment sales in 1971, the latest year for which figures are available, reached $544-million, while sales of films, filmstrips, recordings and the like totaled $887-million. For the same year, sales of textbooks to all elementary and secondary schools came to $448-million.

The growing drain of A-V purchases on library budgets may well have a secondary but equally disquieting effect: Book publishers, dis-

couraged by the sagging market, will publish fewer books. They will take
fewer risks in making selections for publication. The chances for manuscripts espousing dissident views will grow dimmer. The present reading
generation loses, the oncoming generation never learns to read.

A recently published research study contradicts the earlier findings
that A-V aids are effective with the general run of students. It shows that
filmstrips are not effective even for learning by rote and that films improved the learning of a skill only by students whose verbal reasoning
ability was underdeveloped. For those who scored high on verbal reasoning tests, the films were a hinderance; the "spoonfeeding" interfered with
their performance.

Libraries—the ideal tool for self-paced instruction and life-time
learning—are the chief targets of the Nixon Administration's fusillade
against social programs. In cutting off federal funds, the President suggested that the worth of libraries was so self-evident that he was confident
the states and local governmental units would deal them a portion of their
revenue-sharing dollars. Librarians, who recall that the federal programs
were initiated in 1956 precisely because these governmental units had
failed to support library service, are understandably less sanguine.

Most libraries in this country have always been undersupported; they
have never been financed well enough to show what they could really do
to help the mass of the people. If you doubt this, make a little experiment.
Compile your own list of books that have changed the world, that should
be in every library, and then go look for them in your local library. Do not
be satisfied that the titles appear in the card catalogue; are the books
actually on the shelf? That is the test of a library collection—are the books
available when you need them?

Librarians who participate in children's story hour programs are
frustrated and saddened by a situation that occurs all too frequently. At
the end of a typical hour, they find a dozen children clamoring to take "the
book" home. But no. The librarian is forced to favor only one or two of the
children. There just aren't enough copies of any book to go around.

Libraries have not been tried and found wanting; they have not been
tried. It is in this context that the demands for libraries to give priority to
films and filmstrips, games and realia, must be examined. Some nonprint
media are needed, of course—to attract non-readers, to stimulate latent
readers, to supplement and enrich. But A-V must not become the end, it is
an aid; indispensable but auxiliary.

In Advance of Controversy: Visual Literacy

An Editorial in *School Library Journal*

by Lillian N. Gerhardt

The latest fad among librarians and educators in hot pursuit of higher status and budgets for AV materials is something idiotically called "visual literacy," a contradiction in terms if ever there was one. It is a matter of fact and good practice for every book-loving librarian today to recognize that building library collections demands more than the acquisition of printed materials. However, there is still only one meaning for "literacy"—the ability to read and write. It does not mean the ability to look at single or sequential pictures and grasp what's going on. Looking at pictures and listening to sound tracks is pleasant, engaging, informative. It is not a *literate* activity. Never was. Never will be. It's bad enough that school librarians supinely accept "media center" as the designation of their points of service, and "media specialist" as a part of their titles without ever rising to protect and preserve the time-honored, encompassing terms "library" and "librarian." It would be far worse to accept that there is any other form of literacy than the ability to decode letters and assemble them in easily decodable combinations. The audio and the visual are aids, not ends, in achieving or testing the chief goal of publicly supported education in a democracy. That educational goal is a population able to read the laws and write to their legislators. Analysis of the graphic seems to be the intention of courses and conferences currently called "visual literacy." Let them be called "graphic analysis" and keep "literacy" as a clear goal in education and "literate" an undebased distinction for those who learn and can handle letters in receiving or producing communications.

Response

by John L. Debes

What prerequisites must exist in order to have a literate society? In the history of literate civilizations, Hsu says that the first requirement for a literate society is a body of "literature," that is, "written" materials: history, description, exposition, art forms, etc. There are three other requirements: the "written" material must permit wide distribution and access; it must be possible for "readers" to perceive and agree on an author's meanings; and it must be possible for any citizen to add to the "written" treasure in such a way that his contribution can become available to all.

Taking these four prerequisites in order, first, that we are now blessed with a considerable body of film and other visual literature few would deny; second, that the technology of visual reproduction and/or dissemination permits wide access is ostensible; third, that citizens understand visual communication is something that we assume; and fourth, that a citizen may create material of merit and have it become available to all has certainly been demonstrated. Accordingly, we are clearly on our way to satisfying these prerequisites, and, therefore, we have already established the basis for a visually literate civilization.

Literacy requires a language. What about the nature of language? A language is a set of conventional signs that can be offered in culturally established patterns by one human in his endeavor to communicate with others, and that can be perceived and understood by those others. The signs can be noises, but they need not be. Deaf people in the United States use a language called American Sign Language (Ameslan); it is not English, it is one of the visual languages.

All languages do not have "spoken" forms; some, such as the computer languages, have only "written" forms. Some "spoken" languages have two or more "written" forms. These need not represent the sounds of a spoken language, but may represent the ideas. An example of the latter is the visual language of the Japanese called Kanji. Kanji signs contain no clue to the sounds of Japanese words.

The kind of literacy developed, then, depends in part on the nature of the language. Literacy, then, becomes much more complex than is premised in your remarks. A learned Japanese person, being literate, must be so in a *visual* language that has only a "written" form; and a deaf person to be literate must be so in a visual language that up till recently had only a "spoken" form. So, your statement "it would be far worse to accept that there is any other form of literacy than the ability to decode letters and assemble them in easily decodable combinations" is not understandable.

You said that "Looking at pictures . . . is not a literate activity." If one literate activity is "reading," then we must ask ourselves what "reading" is. One definition describes "reading" as perceiving and interpreting the meaning from a set of visible signs ordered sequentially by someone to express an idea. By that definition, perceiving and interpreting a filmed exposition of the flow of electrons in a circuit is "reading."

You said that the goal of education is "a population able to read the laws and write to their legislators." The students of a certain upstate city in New York might have written a verbal letter, or a group letter to their community leaders about how rundown the town appeared. But those letters could have been ignored or perhaps had the fate that letters to the White House have sometimes earned: to be piled on a scale and weighed. So, instead of letters, the students shot and composed a slide "program" (a group statement) and got permission to show it at a community meeting. The visual statements (pictures) had been carefully made and carefully edited and sequenced, so the cumulative message was unmistakable and powerful. Steps to clean up and fix up began almost at once. We may well ask which citizen is the most effectively educated, the man whose letter is thrown on the scale or the student whose slide essay wins action? One goal of education may indeed be effective communication between government and citizen. If so, few citizens *ever* read laws *verbally*, but they often "read" common signs for laws, such as traffic signals, and locks on doors.

The questions you have raised may be basic, in some ways, but the answers, right now, seem to be growing less clear; our knowledge about human languaging is becoming steadily more sophisticated and complex. Perhaps when we are more sure of what languaging is and of the new and unusual forms in which it can be developed, we will be more sure of what we mean by literacy. In that light, we may see that among the goals of education ought to be *many* literacies of which traditional verbal literacy will be only one.

The Media Religion

by Harry Foster

Phony dichotomies have been set up to divert libraries from their purpose. Old libraries were "book-centered"; the new are "people-centered." The library was dark, musty, silent, forbidding, traditional; the media center is attractive, exciting, relevant, bustling, innovative. These comparisons, as invalid as they are, betray preoccupation with image, indifference to values. Moreover they constitute a presumptuous and cynical devaluation of the abilities and needs of the library's legitimate clientele, whether the library be school, academic, or public. On my mind is the need for the library profession to take a more discriminating look at what many of its practitioners today call "media," "learning resources," or "educational technology." I believe the reassessment would result in a fresh recognition of the paramount value to education of the printed page, and in a renewed dedication to our proper concerns.

Educational technologists, with the industry they support, have nearly completed their invasion of library territory, undertaken 15 or 20 years ago. The success of the operation can be seen in the epidemic conversion of school and college libraries into media or learning resources centers; it is also apparent in state and national library standards, and in the curricula of library schools. Through the recognition of such dubious concepts as "learning resources," "information science," and "learning styles," the printed page has been demoted in favor of other "commodities."

The surrender has not escaped criticism. Jean Stafford, for example, does not admire the new library in her *New York Times Book Review* (May 5, 1974) article entitled "Contagious Imbecility." William R. Eshelman objects to "Audio-visual Aids: Fallout from the McLuhan Galaxy" in the same publication (May 6, 1973). Pauline Kael warns readers of *The New Yorker* (Oct. 3, 1970) in a review entitled "Numbing the Audience" that "the media men, with the teachers at their heels, [are] indoctrinating school kids to be the film generation." The Council for Basic Education, which objectively maintains that the hardware boys should be given a fair chance, publishes in its *C.B.E. Bulletin* for May 1974 your present contributor's "The Debasement of School Libraries." And in the daily press, columnists Sydney Harris, James Kilpatrick, and Ernest Furgerson, among others, frequently notify their readers that it is time for the restoration of books and reading to their former esteem. Librarians who are guided by trends should perhaps be on the alert.

The subjugation of librarianship to educational technology is apparent in standards endorsed by the American Library Association. Two of them are *Standards for School Media Programs* (1969), and *Guidelines for Two-Year College Learning Resources Programs* (1972). The absence of the word "library" in both titles should anger all librarians. Their indifference is a dismaying symptom of the contagion Jean Stafford has diagnosed. Both documents are written in the kind of educational jargon that funding authorities and taxpayers are at last beginning to suspect. The two-year college standards also employ the vocabulary of systems analysis. There is, for example "instructional delivery system," fortified by "instructional development functions" and "configuration of resources," engineered to fill up passive minds like boxes and bottles. Is it any wonder that a group of Canadian librarians was seen to walk out in despair over the mentality they found prevailing at a section meeting last year, where a slide-sound presentation of these standards was being discussed?

Neither the two-year college nor the school standards are subject to precise interpretation, but they clearly mean big business to those who use them. The 1969 cost of implementing the school media programs is calculated to be $38 billion, with a continuing annual maintenance cost of $11 billion. These figures appear in Vol. 2 of *To Improve Learning; An Evaluation of Instructional Technology*, edited by Sidney G. Tickton with the staff of the Academy for Educational Development, Inc., (Bowker [A Xerox Company], 1971). In supporting tables the only "items of equipment and materials" which appear to relate to books and reading are "reading devices" and "reading programs." These account for only a small fraction of the costs. Will the forthcoming revision of the media standards call for larger outlays?

The 1975 revision of a third set of ALA standards may possibly include a statement to the effect that "a library's holdings comprise all institutional collections of instructional and learning materials, including multi-dimensional, pictorial, aural, and print materials" (from a working paper, June 20, 1974). The revision committee seeks the views of all who have an interest in college libraries. Let those who oppose the subordination of the library to learning resources or media centers convey their opinions to the ACRL Ad Hoc Committee to Revise *Standards for College Libraries*. Let those who have tried it, didn't like it, and have been fortunate enough to return to former administrative "configurations," render a great service by speaking out.

Standards, professional schools and associations, certification requirements, and accreditation procedures as interlocking instruments demand more cautious scrutiny than they now receive. Many readers of *American Libraries* will not agree that they serve to degrade our libraries. I ask them to consider, however, that there are educators and socio-political scientists who seriously propose that reading is nonessential, and that reading and writing are the weapons of a cruel and greedy elite. A few librarians consciously support these theories. Others believe that novelty equals validity, change denotes progress, technology rules the future, "a picture is worth a thousand words," and that the retrieval of data constitutes education. Are these beliefs in harmony with the historic and valid ideals of librarianship?

Response to "The Media Religion"

by Estelle Jussim

It is undoubtedly calming to observe that the pendulum is beginning to make a necessary and self-correcting swing back from the excesses of the 1960's media hysteria. It is undoubtedly satisfying that the costly, gaudy Utopian baubles which audiovisual specialists used to dangle before us as the ultimate panaceas to all educational problems are observed gathering the dust they may richly deserve. It is undoubtedly heartening that librarians are smiting the Philistines. But it is not at all calming, satisfying, or heartening to discover that many librarians—for example, Harry Foster, in his article "The Media Religion" in *On My Mind* for October, 1974—still have not the faintest idea of what the media revolution was all about, why it was historically and technologically inevitable, and why its benefits and its opportunities can be denied only at the risk of vitiating our basic professional responsibilities.

In the simplest possible terms, the media revolution occurred because there were technological developments which made it possible to encode reality in new forms with a greater approximation to reality than had ever been possible before. These technological developments, like film and television, totally unrelated to library functions at first, were discovered to perform certain communications tasks extremely well. Those tasks of transmitting information, knowledge, or wisdom, which had been previously dependent on print, drawings, and paintings, now could find media appropriate to specific communications necessities, including the visual recording of events happening in "real time," longitudinal studies of changing visual phenomena like cell mitosis or urban decay, not to mention the sound and shape of famous persons. Why any librarian would want to stop the world and get off when so much opportunity is now afforded us is a perplexity deserving of close scrutiny.

First, it is imperative that we agree with Mr. Foster's loathing for the educational jargon which masks the old passive-student view of communication under the pomposities of "instructional delivery systems." It is even necessary to go well beyond Mr. Foster's position to remark that the single most observable fact of the learning resource centers erected in the technological fever of the mid-1960's is this: the costly equipment stands idle for lack of creative imagination and appropriately educated staffs to use it. Part of the problem is the measurement hang-up. There are several sub-species of instructional technologists who have no sense of humor about their trade because they have had no adequate education in philosophy. They believe that all interactions can, indeed must, be structured and measured, rather than recognize that much of life is beautifully, humanely random and creative, and far more complex than the simplistic behavioral objectifying would have us believe. If learners do not fit the Procrustean bed, head and shoulders are removed to make the behavioral objectives narrow enough to be measured.

The gestalt of human existence, with its encrustations of values, prejudices, loves, ambitions, hates, and fantasies, seems utterly and futilely remote from these humorless pseudo-scientists. Motivation through interest in content and competence often seems beyond their range as well, surprisingly because many well-meaning instructional specialists have fallen into the trap of believing that only gadgets will motivate.

But agreeing with some of Mr. Foster's revulsions against the extremes of the instructional technologists is not for one moment to agree with some of his preposterous overstatements. To claim Jean Stafford's infamously elitist *New York Times* article (May 5, 1974) as support for his opinions is to admit that he did not really perceive Mrs. Stafford's profound confusions about condescending public library signs involving poor grammar and the presence of media other than print. I cannot agree more heartily that we are losing the mastery of our most concise and flexible symbol system: language. The word is still supreme—for all the things it can do, including bring you this message from me, a message which in no way could be brought to you in pure iconic terms. If anyone is unconvinced that language has peculiar and unique virtues, let him/her draw, in succession: "a daisy," "the quality of stoniness," and, lastly, "liberty." Not the Statue of Liberty, but the generalization about a human condition for which many million humans have given their lives.

No more than Marshall McLuhan can expound his fascinating and irritating theories through any medium other than print—and anyone who has seen/heard the dreadfully turgid video tape and film on and about him can verify this paradox—than I believe we can do without the written word, and the book. The book is the most ingenious random access, portable information/experience machine ever invented. But what Mr. Foster will not admit is that the book is simply a technology like all others with which librarians must now concern themselves. Once he gets over the typical humanist confusion of mistaking the content of a medium (books are "good" for you because they presumably talk about human values: shall we read *Mein Kampf* or *The 120 Days of Sodom* by de Sade?) with its format, he must try to recognize what any intelligent media specialist will tell you: that each medium, print included, has a specific and unique set of characteristics which enable it to perform certain specific communications tasks. The word excels at generalizations, the still photograph and the slide in isolating visual moments of history, both natural and human; the motion picture cannot be surpassed for its ability to transmit an illusion of ongoing events; the hologram is unique in its three-dimensionality; the computer uniquely manipulates large masses of data and rearranges them on command. And so on. What begins to stick in the craw are the ponderously expensive dial-access systems, the inappropriate televised lecture, the mounds of a/v junk littering the selection tables, and the whole and suspect idea that *every* librarian needs to be able to *produce* complex audiovisual messages while all they really might need to do is to know how, and know how very well, to evaluate what is being produced.

I would rather contend that any human member of any profession who does not know how to use a camera, and how to think visually (see Sir Herbert Read on *Art and Education*) is missing out on a vitally important aspect of communication, one which involves the right-hand kinetic and visual hemisphere of the brain rather than only the left-hand, speech-making, logical hemisphere. If you want to have a whole brain and to learn how to use your faculties, learn how to *see*, and how to listen. Not many people know how to do that—which is of course why the library profession has been so excruciatingly laggard in its development of storage and retrieval systems for visual and auditory information. Indeed, many librarians still do not understand that you really need a picture of a daisy if you have never seen one, and that even one of our oldest forms of books, namely dictionaries, have graphic illustrations of weird entomological freaks difficult to find on an urban street.

But it is time for the pendulum to swing back toward the word, so economical, so graceful, so enigmatic, and so able to generate ferocious quarrels. It is time to reestablish reading as the primary technological skill of our age. It is time to stop pretending that expensive equipment, by itself, can solve any problems. Yet, instead of reading Jean Stafford or James Kilpatrick—as Mr. Foster so amazingly exhorts us to do—let us read the ethnopsychiatrist J. C. Carothers or David Riesman on the social implications of print. And let librarians/media specialists concentrate on learning how to evaluate a/v materials and why and when to use them before they plunge into producing more of the same themselves. We except from this last suggestion, of course, the school librarians who are fighting for survival against the influx of the a/v specialist.

The problem with pendulums swinging is that they have to keep going to extremes before they come to rest at the center of gravity. Our center will always be those long-lived arts and skills of selection, acquisition, organization, and dissemination of recorded experience. Let's not allow the seeming newness of a form of recording confabulate our responsibilities concerning *all forms* of transmitting human knowledge.

Confronting Our Media Biases: The Social Dimensions of Media Theory

by Estelle Jussim

There are probably few professional educators who explicitly question that their function, goal, and purpose is to equip young people for "adult life." Until the social explosions of the past years shattered the general American complacency, there seemed to be no urgent reason to examine assumptions about the specifics of adult life: children were expected to "grow up" so that they could be "successful" economically, socially, and psychologically. Training in self-discipline, flexibility, standards of self-performance, was all important, as

> The central and perhaps most crucial commitment of American civilization is to the inevitability and, in most cases, the desirability of change. The activities and events of everyday life are interpreted through such terms as "progress," "advancement," and "development" within the context of the never-constant environment in which we live. . . . Even those not motivated by promises of success know that stagnation is penalized. . . . The successful meeting of the new demands requires, first of all, readiness to abandon the present, whether it be locality, associations, or activity.[1]

Print-literate individuals were obviously best equipped to uproot themselves from family and friends, hometown, and home job, as they had already—by the act of learning to read—sufficiently individuated and divorced themselves from any absolute need for tribal continuity or face-to-face, oral/aural transmission of information. In all good faith, educators have stressed *reading* as the single skill which can ensure a safe journey upward from youthful ambition to full adult accomplishment. How poor black Americans, denied access to decent schools which could teach them the quintessential skill needed for success within the value system of the white society, have been crucified by this stringent requirement of print-literacy, is an important part of our present history and, very probably, our future problem for a long time to come.

The paradox, which seems intolerable to educators who have been confronted by black rage, is that one of the ways in which certain black militant groups have come to grips with their need to survive is by denying any value to the white culture. "Whitey's" emphasis on print-literacy is viewed as only one of many cooptations into a society which denies any value to the identity of negritude, simultaneously stressing inter-changeable parts/dehumanization/superficiality/consumerism/individual greed/oppression of creativity, and all the other evils characteristically ascribed to modern capitalist white America. For an educator who has been offering READING as the panacea, as *the* key to the door of golden opportunity, to be rejected as an oppressive part of the Establishment must seem the most inexplicable irony. When black groups in England recently urged the BBC to reject *Sesame Street* on the grounds that this delightful television instruction emphasized white middle-class virtues, there was confusion in the ranks of American educators, who could not imagine what they had been doing wrong.

It is difficult enough to recognize our cultural biases, our life-style ethnocentricities; it is probably even more difficult, if we are to credit Lewis Mumford and Marshall McLuhan, to recognize our media-cen-tricity, to discover and to relinquish, *if necessary*, what might be called our *bias of communication:* an unconscious reliance upon a single medium of communication whose social and psychological influence is so profound that—no more than we recognized the air we breathe as having substance before Lavoisier demonstrated it to us—we simply cannot examine it without examining all that we are.[2] What seems difficult to grasp is that "the environments set up by different media are not just containers for people: they are processes which shape people."[3]

To any student of media theory, it hardly seems possible that we can understand socialization, the educational process, acculturation, or any other social dynamic without understanding not how *we* process media, but how media process *us*.

PRINT AS A MEDIUM

The basic hypothesis of contemporary media theory has been stated in this form:

> ... every medium of communication possesses a logic or grammar that constitutes a set of devices for organizing experience. The logic or grammar of each medium that dominates an age impresses itself on the users of the medium, thus dictating what is defined as truth and knowledge. Commu-nications media, then, determine not only what one thinks about but literally how one thinks.[4]

The basic "set of devices" we encounter is the phonetic alphabet, which codes the sounds of speech into a visual channel (print or writing), decoded in turn by "reading." The phonetic alphabet, with its twenty-six unvarying elements, which must be memorized not only as individual sound symbols but in a mnemonic sequence of ABCD, etc., has a logic or code which is epitomized in the medium of *print*. While typographic fonts may differ in mood, they are identical in essence: each represents the idea of interchangeability of parts, of sequence, of uniformity of symbol, of repeatability of total statement. Set in rows of unvarying width, read sequentially from left to right, with a jump of the eyes back to the left again, uniformly down a page and up to the top of the next, print conditions us to certain visual expectations. More importantly, it teaches us, by the process of transmitting metacommunication "cues," that *thought* should be as orderly as the printed page, that communication must be linearly sequential, that it consists largely of the proper labeling of items, and that deduction is preferable to induction. All of this has been well documented in McLuhan's *Gutenberg Galaxy*.

The coding logic of the phonetic alphabet extends far beyond the end product which appears on the printed page to the process of the manufacture of print. It seems fairly certain that printers perforce organized the first assembly lines. Each step of the process was completely rationalized.

> . . . the printed sheet, even before the military uniform, was the first complet-ely standardized product, manufactured in series, and the movable types themselves were the first example of completely standardized and inter-changeable parts. Truly a revolutionary invention in every department.[5]

Printing, then, represented a "logic" of manufacture, a suggestion as to how to proceed with other manufactures, a "logic" of technocratization. Printing, more than mining or any other heavy industry, altered the means of production and its homogeneous repeatability became the stan-dard for every other product. The assembly line and the psychology of man-as-machine are still with us.[6] Not everyone would agree that this "logic" has been humane or joy-enducing.

As importantly, print created a new psychological experience. In Lewis Mumford's view,

> More than any other device, the printed book released people from the domination of the immediate and the local. Doing so, it contributed further to the disassociation of the medieval society; *print made a greater impression than actual events* (emphasis added), and by centering attention on the printed word, people lost that balance between the sensuous and the intellectual, between image and sound, between the concrete and the abstract, which was to be achieved momentarily by the best minds of the fifteenth century— Michelangelo, Leonardo, Alberti—before it passed out, and was replaced by printed letters alone. To *exist was to exist in print* (emphasis added): the rest of the world tended gradually to become more shadowy.[7]

The social impact of print was more than matched by psychological effects. We recognize many deleterious effects, for example, the mad fantasies of Don Quixote, brought on by reading too many romances, or the sexual gaming of Emma Bovary, similarly the result of reading un-balanced romantic balderdash. But there are less obvious effects which the sociologists have discovered. Again, for example:

> . . . tradition-directed persons not only had a traditional standard of living but a traditional standard of how hard and long (they) should work; and print served, along with other agencies of socialization, to destroy both of these

standards. The inner-directed man, open to "reason" via print, often develops a character structure which drives him to work longer hours and to live on lower budgets of leisure and laxity than would have been deemed possible before. He can be driven because he is ready to drive himself.[8]

It is perfectly conceivable—and the counter-culture reveals it as fact —that an American subculture could reject this model of print-driven man as without human value. The substitution of an isolated life style, masquerading as "independence," profoundly disturbed David Reisman. The absence of adult mediation in the act of youthful reading deprived children of corrective feedback, taking

> ... the process of socialization out of the communal chimney corner ... the child is allowed to gird himself for the battle of life in the small circle of light cast by his reading lamp. ... [9]

Surely this is equivalent criticism of a medium to that voiced recently by educators in despair that children were being "tended" by television sets instead of people.

In the face of all well-intentioned educators and media specialists who exhort children to READ stands one of the most extreme condemnations of verbal symbol structures by a writer consumed with the desire to unmask Western biases, Aldous Huxley:

> Children should be taught that words are indispensable but also can be fatal— the only begetters of all civilization, all science, all consistency of high purpose, all angelic goodness, and the only begetter at the same time of all superstition, all collective madness and stupidity, all worse-than-bestial diabolism, all the dismal historical succession of crimes in the name of God, King, Nation, Party, Dogma. ... [10]

Yet another writer views the logic of print in very favorable terms. In his *Fahrenheit 451*, Ray Bradbury presents colorful, individualistic, prideful, brave, independent, lively *book readers and word addicts* as saviors of human values in a world where politically controlled television feeds infantile pap to submissive, unthinking, hyperemotional, drug-dependent, low-energy, marginally literate television viewers, who live only for present pleasures. The mistake Bradbury makes, of course, is to equate *print and reading* with *thinking and acting*. We have only to remind ourselves of the tons of cheap detective stories, dull historical romances, or obscene magazines which are published in print form and which are devoured by "readers," to see how mistaken he is. Television primacy does not, fortunately, equal totalitarianism, although, in another essay, we could analyze the logic of television and discover that it has a propensity—thanks to the cost of its production facilities—to nurture centralized political control. But then we have only to look back to the history of censorship of the press and the royal printing privileges of England and France to remember that it may be the ideological posture that precedes thought control.

To continue with another interweaving of individual development and social style: the ethnopsychiatrist, J. C. Carothers, noted that there seemed to be marked differences in behavioral patterns between literate Western Europeans and nonliterate rural Africans. He found that various delusional systems, widely prevalent among literate people, e.g., paranoia, depressional states, obsessional neuroses, or schizophrenia, were almost absent among the nonliterates, although a state of mental confusion—short-lived but violent, bordering on acute panic, which tended to resolve itself quickly—was regularly observed. Seeking the etiology of these differences, Carothers observed that these rural nonliterate Africans did not progress beyond what Piaget defined as the second stage of development. Unlike their European counterparts, who had learned to read by the time they were seven or eight, the nonliterate Africans were unable to search for "generality of principle, to recognize the need for continuity and contact in causation. . . ."[11] They remained in that stage (viewed as "normal" in literate children between the ages of three and eight) where

> . . . superficial similarities between objects are regarded as indicative of causal bonds, even though there is no continuity in space or time; all manner of objects are imbued with a life or force of their own; all things are possible. . . .[12]

Carothers postulated that the interiorization of the phonetic alphabet and the exteriorization of ideas through the written word assisted in the separation of thought from deed, so closely associated in oral/aural cultures. The so-called "childish" behavior of the nonliterate Africans was therefore no reflection whatever on their intelligence, whatever racist governments propounded. As they had not been conditioned by the concentrated utilization of a single medium, writing or print, they had not intensely structured their thought processes along the lines of those symbolic verbal structures, nor had they acquired the delusional systems which literate children and adults receive from reading.

It might be possible to extrapolate from Carothers' observations of nonliterate black Africans to the problems of nonliterate black Americans.

ISSUES ENGENDERED BY THE PRIMACY OF PRINT

If nonliterate black Americans constitute a distinct subculture whose characteristics may seem unfamiliar and difficult for both literate blacks and literate whites, we can well understand why they fail to be integrated into the print-literate (relatively) majority culture. Without even addressing ourselves to the crucial questions of economic exploitation, we can perceive differences in life styles which belong to each culture. Literate and print-structured personalities and groups may say, "You are proving once again that the most crucial task is to teach black children to read." Yet another question ought to be staring us in the face. Pushing the logic of the situation to its extreme, we should perhaps ask ourselves: "What right do we have to force a member of a different subculture, the black minor-

ity, to acquire the characteristics of the majority?,", and "Are we so sure
that the characteristics of the majority will guarantee joy or happiness or
anything but some degree of skill in competing in the technological
world?," or "Does the nonliterate have any characteristics that we should
admire?"

Whether we decide that reading and print culture are intrinsically
valuable or not, we can certainly agree that tremendously important
moral and philosophical issues are raised by merely examining the assumptions we have been conditioned to accept. Certainly, if we agree that
the very logic of print, regardless of content, socializes black children into
behavior patterns regarded as identical with those of a group viewed as
the hated oppressor, we can begin to understand why some black leaders,
trying to preserve what is good in their own culture, in their own individual behavior patterns, should reject any undue emphasis upon reading.

And they are not alone in condemning total stress on print-literacy:
educators, artists, cultural anthropologists, social psychologists, view the
development of all *learning* modes as vital to the maximization of human
potential. Excessive emphasis on print-literacy, to the almost total exclusion of training and enlargement of other modes of apprehension,
may result in deep frustration and a serious sense of alienation from the
"real world."

> Reality, as modern man understands it, eludes language in two directions.
> Language has become too clumsy an instrument for men of science; yet for
> the man in the street it is too abstract, too unrelated to practical skills and the
> handling of all those appliances in daily use which have completely taken the
> place of nature as the frame of human lives.[13]

We can hardly wonder any longer why restless children turn from the
irrelevant nonsense of reading *Silas Marner* to the sweaty satisfactions of
the machine shop. We should perhaps begin to explore the possibility that
children deserve not only THE RIGHT TO READ, but much, much
more. Perhaps they deserve the right to encounter realities outside their
own limited ones, the right to smell and taste interesting foods, the right to
selectively view television without being overwhelmed by consumer advertising and subliminal manipulations, the right to understand how to
learn from a film, the right to dance, to paint, to be warm in winter, the
right to respect from adults.

THE NEED FOR NEW PERSPECTIVES

Concern for heightening the child's personal awareness and our
recognition of all the senses as perceptual systems should encourage us to
master the grammars of media and to understand and to modify their
effects upon cognitive and psychosocial behaviors.[14]

> All our mental processes depend upon perception. Inadequate perceiving
> results in poor thinking, inadequate feeling, diminished interest in and
> enjoyment of life. Systematic training of perception should be an essential
> element in all education.[15]

The first step toward the mastery of media theory is to acknowledge that there seems to be evidence that we are "processed" by media, and that, given the stress placed upon print-literacy in our society, we are products of a print-dominated culture, despite the proliferation of other media. The second step should be to accept that there are other kinds of literacies which we neglect at our own peril.

What is really being asked, of course, is: can books' monopoly of knowledge survive the challenge of the new languages? The answer is: no. What should be asked is: what can print do better than any other medium and is that worth doing?[16]

Thus, the third step is to admit our ignorance of the grammars of the new media, and simply to go back to "school" and start learning them. In time, instead of remaining passive recipients of what the communications industries decide to manufacture, we could ourselves contribute.

At the very least, we can begin to offer a true range of services to young people, not only recognizing that they learn at different speeds and in differing modes, but that they also respond out of different cultural matrices: they require their educators to be as trained in perception as their educators require them to be. Starting from where *they* are, instead of where *we* are, we can help them use recorded knowledge, not as a substitute for real-life experience, but as an avenue into becoming what they want to be in ways which are acceptable to their own cultures.

REFERENCES

1. George D. Spindler, *Education and Culture: Anthropological Approaches* (1963), p. 275.

2. Harold A. Innis titled a major work, *The Bias of Communication* (1951). Note that he did not use this phrase to describe the bias of persons toward media, but rather the internal bias of each medium toward influencing social structures in specified ways. The phrase is useful.

3. John S. Culkin, "A Schoolman's Guide to Marshall McLuhan," in Harry Crosby and George Bond, *The McLuhan Explosion* (1969), p. 180.

4. James W. Carey, "Harold Adams Innis and Marshall McLuhan," in Raymond Rosenthal, *McLuhan: Pro and Con* (1968), p. 289.

5. Lewis Mumford, *Technics and Civilization* (1962), p. 135.

6. For an extensive examination of the interactions between technology and culture, see Siegfried Giedion's *Mechanization Takes Command*.

7. Mumford, *Technics*, p. 136.

8. David Reisman, "The Socializing Functions of Print," in Charles Steinberg, *Mass Media and Communication* (1966), p. 416.

9. Ibid., p. 417.

10. Aldous Huxley, "Education on the Nonverbal Level," in Alfred de Grazia and David A. Sohn, *Revolution in Teaching* (1964), p. 72.

11. J. C. Carothers, "Culture, Psychiatry, and the Written Word," *Psychiatry* 22:316 (Nov. 1959).

12. Ibid.

13. J. L. Aranguren, *Human Communication* (1967), p. 216.

14. See James J. Gibson, *The Senses Considered as Perceptual Systems* (1966).

15. Huxley, *Education*, p. 73.

16. Edmund Carpenter, "The New Languages," in Carpenter and McLuhan, *Explorations in Communication* (1966), p. 179.

Note: For the interactions of capacities for information transfer with artistic expression, see Abraham Moles' Information Theory and Esthetic Perception *(1958), and the present writer's* Visual Communication and the Graphic Arts *(1974).*

Introduction to "Differentiating the Media"

by Lester Asheim

In the introductory pages of the Conference program—which also served as an advertisement in advance of these formal meetings—it is suggested that "the most important questions concerning the several media may no longer be those that still seem to dominate the literature of librarianship." We were referring, of course, to the either/or, book/non-book kind of debates and their holier-than-thou rhetoric. This Conference, instead, assumes that it may be taken for granted that libraries, as centers of communication, will be multimedia agencies in this indisputably multimedia age, and the question should not be which one medium is the best, but rather for what purposes is each medium best? If that be so, we suggest that what does need exploration is the nature of each of the several media, each in its own terms. And from that it follows that the analysis of the proper use of each medium must be based upon standards relevant to *it*, not to some generalized single standard derived from another medium.

The focus of the Conference, then, is upon identifying those characteristics—technical, aesthetic, social, and psychological—that determine the effectiveness of each medium for different kinds of content, for different kinds of users and for different kinds of purposes. "Out of this objective and unpolemical emphasis," as the program presents it, "we hope to make a useful first step towards realistically and fairly differentiating the effectiveness of each medium in providing the information, education, entertainment and intellectual stimulation that are wanted and needed by the several publics that libraries serve."

Thus, in broad and—we thought—clear-cut terms, we defined our aims and, in effect, our most likely audience. The aims we saw as quite specific. The audience we saw as very broad indeed.

Now it is notorious that people who are formally and officially concerned with the art and process of communication are the ones who have the most difficulty in communicating. I like to think that this is not because we are even less adept than others in performing the communication act, but rather that we may be more sensitive to communication failures when they occur. Like the city which keeps the most complete police records and therefore seems to have more crime than any other, I want to believe that the popular image of the inarticulate communicator derives not from more communication failures, but from his more complete awareness of them. Whatever the cause, I think the response to our Conference publicity illustrates something of the problem.

Our major difficulty lies in the term "media," which carries a variety of connotations depending upon the special outlook or practice of the group perceiving the term. We tried to indicate the usage to which we are committed by specifying those media with which we are concerned: the broadcast media in their several forms (i.e., radio and television); the film, both as an art form and as a communication carrier; and the media of print in both traditional and new contexts. More specifically, we tried to suggest that our focus would be on content, and the influence of the particular medium upon the content it can most effectively carry, and not on gadgetry or technical operations as such.

Yet—predictably—the immediate response of many who were exposed to our press releases was to think of "media" in a variety of other contexts. There were those media specialists whose emphasis is on the apparatus rather than on the content, who clearly thought our Conference would provide them with a chance to see new devices and learn how to run them. This is a perfectly legitimate objective, but it is not—this time —ours.

There were those to whom the "new technology" means reprographic and miniaturizing devices, and who thought we would most certainly include discussions of the use of microfilm, microfiche, and the like. To our way of thinking, this kind of format is not so much a new form of communication as it is a way to solve certain problems of book acquisition, storage, and cost. A book page is still a book page, however much it is reduced for storage purposes. Our concern is with those media which create new content—and under this heading we would include those uses of one medium which record the content of another, but in the very act of so recording it transform it into something else. Filmed plays are of this nature; the medium interposes itself between audience and content and transforms the product. This will indeed be one of the areas of our exploration, for it is central to our concern about whether the one is truly a substitute for the other. Where it is not, we have a phenomenon amenable to the kind of analysis that we are proposing.

There were those whose interest in "media" focuses strictly on *non-book* devices, ignoring completely our warning that the book is one of the media to which we would pay particular attention, stressing by our very attention to all the media that which is unique and indispensable in each of them, the book included.

There were the proponents of the learning-resources approach, who include in their concept of media study carrels, language laboratories, and a world of "realia," from live hamsters to dead leaves, which never for a moment had, I must confess, occurred to us, although we accept without question the communication and educational role that they can play.

And there were those to whom media means, quite specifically, *not* the major commercial channels of mass communication, whereas—in our own private understanding of the term—it was those very media which presently constitute the major commercial channels with which we hope to be much concerned.

I have carefully tried to word that last sentence—"those media which presently constitute the major commercial channels"—to suggest an important distinction, between the medium itself (film or television, for example) and the commercial-channel application of it. Film and television need not be, as you are all well aware, simply mass commercial media; they are forms of communication capable of quite small-scale, non-commercial, private or artistic or educational uses as well. What we do suggest, however, is that whether on a mass scale or in intimate face-to-face use, the effectiveness of the message carried on such a medium does indeed depend upon adaptation of the content to that medium. Thus, in the production of a film, let us say—whether by Hollywood or the kid next door with his hand-held camera—the way the medium is used will affect the impact of the communication experience. We were pleased to see in the special section on "New Media Publishing" in *Publishers Weekly* last June[1] a report that makers of educational films had, as a result of the decline in the use of their traditional products, come to a new insight. What they had decided is that artistic use of the medium is more effective and desirable than "instructing" in a heavy-handed manner; their new look will be to create good *films*, which will make their point more effectively precisely because they are *good films*.

This conviction, apparently somewhat reluctantly arrived at by the information industry, is the basic theme of this Conference. And the library relevance of this tenet harks back to the mission of the librarian as identified by Ortega y Gasset some forty years ago.[2] In his statement, the librarian was described as a filter interposed between man and the torrent of books. We would today, of course, broaden the concept to read: "a filter interposed between the users of communications and the torrent of sources of communication content," but the idea remains the same: the librarian has a role to play in identifying the most effective means for the dissemination of different kinds of messages to serve different purposes for different audiences. The stress is not so much on the format or the document in itself, but on its effectiveness in meeting the needs of its users, and this imposes a responsibility for selection.

We realize that not all librarians today accept the centrality of selection in the librarian's obligation. In their concern for intellectual freedom, which we share, there are those who see the ideal library as that which has everything, imposing no exclusions for any reason—either quality, accuracy, sound factual authority, or social importance, since all of these elements are subject to personal interpretation.

This approach seems to us unrealistic on two counts. The first is obvious: no library can have every item in every medium, so selection of some kind, by the very nature of budgetary and space realities, must take place. The second reflects what seems to us to be a hidden assumption: that where librarians accept the responsibility for selection they will inevitably become self-serving, imposing their own preferences, ignoring the needs of their patrons, and building an elitist collection that is oriented to administrative convenience rather than service to users. We reject this as an operating premise—which is not to say that it cannot ever happen or that it never has. But any system can be abused by those who would misuse it; it is our hope that we can identify selection criteria which will help to promote user rather than supplier satisfaction, by placing emphasis upon use, not simply collection. And if there is a danger of selector bias in the building of collections, we see it as more likely to be manifested where decisions are based on format rather than where they are based on content related to users.

That is why we have suggested in our program announcement that the continuing confrontation between the hard-sell advocates of the "New Media" and the die-hard defenders of The Book is really no longer fruitful—they are both, in their separate ways, format-oriented. The librarian who would not consider anything unless it is a book (or, more liberally, print) is really no more misguided than the media specialist who will accept anything as long as it is not a book. The criterion in any medium, therefore, is not format *in and of itself*; the criterion should be the value of the content. And we are suggesting that the value of the content is considerably affected by the extent to which the format is properly used in relation to the content and to the needs of the audience to whom it is addressed. Thus we are suggesting that the selection of materials is still one of the librarian's most important functions, and we are hypothesizing that despite their growing hospitality to a variety of materials and not just the materials of print, librarians do not impose criteria of selection with the same rigor when choosing the so-called newer media as they have traditionally employed—or at least used to pride themselves that they employed—in the selection of books.

We are not saying that choice and selection do not take place in the acquisition of the newer media, but we are suggesting that there are two possible directions in which librarians err when they make their selections. One is in the willingness to impose much lower standards on newer media, simply because they *are* the newer media. Many librarians feel that we need more films or tapes or cassettes in our libraries to show that we are in the new multimedia mainstream, and so they accept inept filmmaking, for example, where they would never accept comparably inept writing. Bad writing is a definite mark against book purchase, but poor filmmaking seems seldom to enter as a criterion in the purchase of a film.

Closely related to this error is that of applying to all of the other media criteria derived from the evaluation of literary productions. This may seem to be a contradiction rather than a parallel of the fault of debased standards, but the failure in both cases lies in the application of criteria inadequate to assess the particular medium under review. Librarians of course are, historically, book-oriented, and *book* selection was, for a long time, a staple of library school instruction. Today the title of the course has been changed to "Selection of Materials," but we are guessing that the content and the criteria have been altered very little. A film adaptation of a novel, for example, is judged on its fidelity to the novel, not on its quality as a film. As an illustrative aside, there is a very interesting review of the film *The Great Gatsby* in the *Chronicle of Higher Education* which casts a critical eye on the many angry and bitter reviews of the film by critics whose touchstone is the book. Landon Jones suggests that "there is no way for a movie to carry the full weight of Fitzgerald's symbolism."[3] I would question this unequivocal assertion, although I would accept his corollary: "The real question is whether *Gatsby* succeeds as a movie." His conclusion is that one should not judge the film by standards of literary art, but rather by the standards of romantic film entertainment, of which *The Great Gatsby* is a quite respectable example. "In other words," according to Jones, "*The Great Gatsby* is not a bad *good* movie; it is a good *bad* movie."

Virginia Wexman will explore in more detail the kinds of problems that are involved in adapting from one medium to another, and will point up more specifically the kinds of conflicts, adaptations, and cross-media equivalents that occur in the transition from one form to another. Suffice it to say here simply that the librarians' book orientation has led us to see all other media as supplementary or subordinate to the book, as our own standard terminology so clearly reveals. "Nonbook," "nonprint," "audio-visual *aids*," we say condescendingly, leaving no question as to which format we place at the heart of the learning process or the aesthetic experience. With that kind of bias, often unrecognized in ourselves, we tend to expect of the other media that which we like best about the book, and to ignore the peculiar strengths and weaknesses of each of the media, including the book, that could help us select more wisely among them.

Selection of materials is less easy than it would appear to be, for a variety of reasons. When we select, we do so on the basis of a considerable mix of criteria: we are interested in subject matter, in form, in treatment, in public demand, in cost, and in a number of these combined. Thus it must be recognized that the selection of each and every film or recording or book may not necessarily be concerned with the art of the particular medium. There are reasons to preserve certain content for purposes other than the art of the carrier. There is a film of Pavlova dancing the Dying Swan, for example, which is an indispensable document of a specific dancer's performance. Its value might be enhanced if it were really a good film, but the fact that it is not does not deny it its place in a dance collection. This kind of record is extremely important for libraries —but having said this, we have said all that needs to be said in the context of this Conference. We are not, in this kind of situation, concerned with the effectiveness of the medium in its own right, but simply with its value as a preserver of something else. This puts it, as an art form, into the class of a Xerox copy or a microfilm, which is not to underestimate its importance or even its social implications.

We are all used to this kind of selection—for the record rather than for the art—but in either case, the peculiar strengths of the medium for carrying particular kinds of content are involved. This visual presentation

of the *movement* of the dance is better conveyed by moving picture film
than by a film strip or a verbal description, even when the art—not just the
attributes of the film—is not involved. A documents collection, a collection of archives, is not limited to those which are well written, but even
here the medium may make a difference. No one in 1974 needs to be
reminded that an edited transcript is not as good as an unexpurgated tape
if what we want is a record of everything that was said *and* the intonations
that help interpret meaning and intent. On the other hand, if our purpose
is to get a quick overview of the general topics discussed, an edited and
interpreted document that cuts out all the repetitions and irrelevancies
and interprets the high spots might well be more useful. The nature of the
medium employed does make a difference in the use to which the content
can be put.

Thus a major concern of this Conference will be this very point: what
does the nature of the medium itself do to the content? Ron Powers'
paper, concerned with identical content carried in three different formats, explores some of the differences imposed by the medium. Out of
this interesting case history should come some useful generalizations as to
the impact of each medium for particular purposes, and the reservations
one must make about the substitution of one medium as an equivalent for
another.

This use of substitute media has been a popular basis for speculation
in education these days. Why not get a filmed lecture of an outstanding
teacher, the argument goes, and then simply project that in classrooms
across the country, so that all classes would have the same educational
experience that is now limited to the students in the original classroom?
My guess is that Mr. Powers' answer would be that it is *not* the same
educational experience. This is not to say that the filmed lecture might not
be a useful educational experience in its own right, but it is to say that one
is not the equivalent of the other, and that identification of the "best" one
depends upon the purpose to be served.

Precisely because we now have a variety of media from which to
choose, we can today select content to serve a variety of purposes and
users. When the book was, to all intents and purposes, the only format
that carried intellectual content amenable to wide dissemination, the book
was, indeed, *the* medium of communication, and the librarian was concerned quite literally with finding the right book for the right person at
the right time. If the book was not the right medium for some persons,
then they could not be served by us. But today they can be, for we are able
now to see libraries, not as book agencies only, but as agencies of communication; the standards need not be less strict, but the performance of our
task can be broader and more varied. Depending on the nature of the
content, the needs of the user, and the ways in which the user wants to
employ the content, we can provide it in the book form for one purpose,
on film for another, on taped recording for a third.

The value of this new freedom is clear enough where the content
differs in each medium. We all recognize that one may wish to listen to a

piece of music, look at a painting, but read about the lives of the artists who created them. But already librarians know that they may need all three formats even when the content is ostensibly the same, because each serves at least one purpose or one audience better than either of the other two.

There is no possibility, within this short Conference, to deal with the kinds of technical and psychological problems that we are beginning to approach if we follow this line of thought to its logical conclusion. Experts in the media know a great deal about the ways in which effects are gained through informed use of each medium—but this is knowledge gained over a lifetime of experience, experiment, theory, and trial and error. Filmmakers know, for example, that a wipe from left to right has an emotional effect different from a wipe from right to left; a painter can direct the sequence of a viewer's attention by establishing a kinship between three points of visual relatedness—shape or color—within a composition; the composers of movie music have a bagful of sure-fire tricks to manipulate our moods and emotions in response to musical cues of which we are often not even aware. This is fascinating stuff, and pertinent to our discussion, but we cannot cover everything. We will have to limit ourselves, for the most part, to more general conclusions about the attributes of the several media, and what these suggest as to affects and effects to be expected from them. But this does suggest that selectors will have to be more sensitive to the subtleties and nuances in each format that go beyond the simple description of the dominant subject matter. Donald Gordon, for example, will explore some of the ways, besides the use of language as such, in which print is used to attract attention, arouse emotion, impose a pattern of thinking, and create an atmosphere of receptivity for the verbal message. We may one day have to be as expert in evaluating the work of the compositor as of the author, as we select the materials of print for library uses.

While an in-depth exploration of these specific subtleties is beyond the scope of this Conference, we do not mean to suggest they are not an important part of the approach to media differentiation with which we are concerned. Certainly we are eager to go beyond the fairly simple-minded distinction which points out merely that moving pictures are better for depicting movement than still pictures are. On the other hand, a look at some of the uses to which film is put suggests that even so obvious an insight as that is not always mastered by those who make films or who use the product.

Still we should be careful about jumping to conclusions about the attributes or limitations of a medium. Michael J. Arlen has said: "I used to think automatically that television was primarily a visual medium . . . but I no longer am quite so sure about how visual television really is. . . . It occurred to me . . . that if one had to choose, during most of the hours in which television stations broadcast, and certainly during most of the daylight hours, between having the sounds on one's set turned off and having the picture turned off, it would somehow make more sense, be more useful, more intelligible, to have the picture off, because what you have so much of the time on television is static (almost still) pictures of people sitting down and talking."[4] This use of the television medium may actually fulfill a need felt by many of its so-called viewers, but it certainly does not capitalize upon that which the medium is supposed to do best. The study of television as a medium is not yet sufficiently advanced to determine what it does do best; the experiments are still being carried on by the trial-and-error method of the marketplace. The point to be made here is simply that it is dangerous to come too readily to one-dimensional judgments about the characteristic attributes of a medium; they could lead us to overlook the inventive and creative uses of the medium which move beyond these snap judgments about media limitations.

As an example: One of the great silent films—at least to my mind—is Carl Dreyer's *The Passion of Joan of Arc*, which utilizes a subject which, it would appear on the surface, is a highly unlikely one for film treatment. One setting, very little action, and lots of talk—surely not the stuff of effective silent filmmaking, as some critics were quick to point out at the time. Yet Dreyer knows what the camera can do besides follow breakneck chases; he moves in close on faces, he utilizes camera angles and lighting to probe the nuances of changing facial expression in a way that no other medium could, and he creates—by his use of the qualities that the moving camera alone can achieve—a film of almost unbearable emotional impact. My point is that there are much more subtle uses of each of the media than the usual inventory of attributes provides us, and alertness to these uses is certainly a faculty to be employed in selection.

Study of the media, pretty much in this very context, has come a long way in the field of education. Much of what is now known through educational research is pertinent to our concerns in this Conference—but there are also subtle differences between an evaluation of group use of a medium and individual use; of children's use of a medium and that of adults; and—despite the growing emphasis in the classroom upon learning rather than on teaching—between the in-school and out-of-school experience. Teaching devices and methods, highly successful in the classroom under the kind of controlled conditions that prevail there (even permissiveness is built into a classroom situation) may have the opposite effect when imposed upon an adult, self-motivated learner—and even more, upon a seeker of entertainment, relaxation, specific factual information, or a personal, aesthetic experience. Approaches which really motivate kids in the third grade are not necessarily equally effective with adults on their own. I am not suggesting that we should ignore the findings of educational research, but I am suggesting that we may have to select carefully from these findings those that are truly applicable to a different set of surrounding circumstances.

For example, a great number of the studies which compare the effectiveness of one medium against another—the book against the film or the taped lecture against the live one—have found no significant difference between one medium and another in facilitating the attainment of a wide range of teaching objectives. While this may seem to invalidate the major premise of this Conference, I am inclined to doubt it. In many of these cases, the studies have shown merely that a not very inventive use of one medium is no worse than a not very inventive use of another. The emphasis has been almost solely on the feedback on examinations of certain factual or other readily measurable data—an incomplete assessment of the varied richness of communication experiences. By and large, the purpose has been merely to show that the hardware can be used in teaching, and I guess that there was a time when that needed to be demonstrated. But now let us accept the fact that hardware can indeed be employed in such situations; our concern is with the software to which, until very recently, little attention was paid at all. In other words, instructional uses of the media tend to be more concerned with response rather than with stimulus; with "what the learner does rather than what is done to the learner."[5] But when one is concerned with emotional appeals to adults on matters of social outlook, for example, our concern is less with such behavioral analysis and more with the various types of stimuli.

We are well aware that the points we are stressing in this Conference are not particularly new to librarians. Librarians have been in the multimedia business for a long time—long before it was the popular rallying cry it is today. Frances Henne's paper will remind us of some of the kinds of activities to which librarians have long been accustomed which are not necessarily tied to the formats of print, and which have for a long time applied other criteria than literary ones. But, by and large, these nonbook (there's that giveaway word again) activities have been seen as secondary and supplemental; their purpose has been seen as motivational, and their value has been gauged by the extent to which they can be used to lead people to books. This attitude is changing, and one contemporary library school dean has stated our purpose very well indeed: "We must have, and as educators we must transmit, a far better knowledge than we presently have of the relationship of print, of sound, and of image. We must develop integrated systems that can fruitfully amalgamate all media, understanding the place and power of each within the context of all."[6] We could not have said it better, but it is disturbing to realize that the dean in question, in pursuit of the ideal he has so well expressed, believes that it cannot be attained in a school hampered by the weight of the tradition implied in the term "library"; he has changed the name of his school from "School of Library Science" to "School of Information Studies" in order to be free to take the broader, wider, deeper approach that his statement implies.

We like to think that this new approach is *not* in conflict with the library ideal but a contemporary expression of it, utilizing the new tools at hand to accomplish what is implicit in the traditional objectives. It is true, of course, that many of the older generation of librarians came to the newer media after we had been firmly attached to the book tradition, and that for many of us the newer media simply do not speak as rich a language. But some of us can understand intellectually, if not emotionally and in practice, that this may be a reflection of our own limitations and not necessarily those of the media themselves. We see a new generation of library users coming up who are not so deeply wedded to the literary tradition, and understandably we wonder if we can communicate with them. But do not forget that today's and tomorrow's librarians are part of this new generation too, sharing with them their highly developed skills in the many new languages that are represented by recordings, tapes, films, and multimedia events. We have only to be hospitable to desirable change in library outlook and practice to have it come about; the agents of change are waiting in the wings for their cues.

We are thus speaking about the impact of the multimedia orientation upon libraries and librarians. This means that libraries and librarians are elements in the equation, and therefore they introduce constraints and considerations in the processes of selection and use that may not be recognized if we hold ourselves exclusively to the analysis of media based on the qualities of the media alone. Wesley Doak will deal with some of these librarian-imposed constraints as they affect, both positively and negatively, the library's full use of all media. The identification of difficulties, however, is not an argument for abandoning a good course of action. The challenge lies in surmounting difficulties in order to attain desirable ends. To surmount the difficulties we must know what they are, so that we can balance them against values and potentialities to determine whether it is worthwhile to face the difficulties. It is our hope that the papers in this Conference will make more clear the justification for taking on the task we propose.

Our approach in this Conference is concerned with stimulating a truly multimedia approach; with an attempt, insofar as that is possible, to start all of the media off on the same foot, and to measure the value of each one in terms of its effectiveness for users, and not in terms of historically acculturated preconceptions about format. Whenever a librarian speaks to librarians in this tone, the suspicion immediately arises that he or she is really antibook, and that this is some kind of covert way of attacking the values of print, not only in our own time, but even in their historical context. When—in 1955—the Graduate Library School held a Conference entitled *The Future of the Book*, which suggested that the book format should be seen as a means and not as an end in itself, it became necessary to add an "Afterword"[7] to the proceedings volume, to refute a widely disseminated report that the Graduate Library School had assumed the imminent and inevitable demise of the book, which would soon be replaced by movies, television, and mechanical devices, and that, indeed, we welcomed this overthrow of the tyranny of print. Actually the Conference had determined almost exactly the opposite: that the book has had more to say, has said it more clearly, and has preserved it for future consultation better than any other communication device, new or old. But for a librarian even to hit upon a title like "the future of the book" was threat enough to the traditionally book-oriented to trigger a violent reaction.

It is our hope that the intervening twenty years have done away with that kind of automatic defensiveness, and that we are now ready—indeed, more than ready—to weigh the worth of all media by the kind of standard which will in each individual instance give us the most accurate measure of its qualities. As we have suggested, this may require different standards for each one, if we are to get a true assessment and not a distorted one. It is our belief that the things that the book does best will continue to be apparent in such a comparative study, and that the book is not really threatened because there are many things that our media do better. To find the appropriate uses to which each of the media can be put, and thus not to misuse any of them to accomplish ends to which they are not truly suited, is to enhance the value of each one of them—including the book. And in the context of this Conference, that is the once and future role of the librarian: to act as a filter, as a mediator, as a selector. This is the area of the librarian's traditional expertise, enhanced and broadened but not —in its essentials—altered by acceptance of the multimedia approach to the collection and dissemination of the materials of knowledge, information, and ideas.

REFERENCES

1. Doebler, Paul. "New Films Aim for Leading Role in Schools and Adult Education." *Publishers Weekly*, June 18, 1973, pp. 57–60.

2. Ortega y Gasset, José. "The Mission of the Librarian." *Antioch Review* 21 (Summer 1961): 133–154.

3. Jones, Landon Y. "Review of *The Great Gatsby*." *Chronicle of Higher Education*, May 6, 1974, p. 8.

4. Arlen, Michael J. *The Living-Room War*. New York: Viking Press, 1969, pp. 23–24.

5. Levie, W. H., and Dickie, K. E. "The Analysis and Application of Media." In *Second Handbook of Research on Teaching*, edited by R. M. W. Travers. Chicago: Rand McNally & Co., 1973.

6. Taylor, Robert S. *Curriculum Design for Library and Information Science.*. Education and Curriculum Series, no. 1. Syracuse, N.Y.: Syracuse University, School of Library Science, 1973, p. 64.

7. Asheim, Lester, ed. *The Future of the Book: Implications of the Newer Developments in Communication*. Papers presented before the 12th Annual Conference of the Graduate Library School of the University of Chicago, June 20–24, 1955. Chicago: University of Chicago Press, 1955, pp. 104–105.

The Human Element:
Why Nonprint Managers
Turn Gray

by James W. Ramey

All the world is divided into three camps—the nonprint fanatics, the nonprint haters, and the silent majority that just doesn't give a damn! Why is there massive indifference (read passive resistance) to all forms of nonprint media in libraries? Why are so few collections cataloged? Why doesn't the equipment work? Why isn't software available? Why, after all these years, haven't nonprint media made the grade as a technological innovation in schools, colleges, and libraries, considering its over-whelming impact in the great big world outside these institutions? Why is the AV department such a whipping boy that we are now willing to call it almost anything except "the AV department" in order to avoid (we hope) the onus of being "low man on the totem pole?" This paper will attempt to raise and discuss some of these issues and many other "human factors" that enter into the poor showing of the nonprint media department. Some of these issues are seldom voiced, although they come through loud and clear at the non-verbal level.

It should be clear at the outset that we are speaking about the AV department, in all its many guises. It may be called the nonprint media center, the instructional materials center, the audiovisual instruction center, the learning laboratory, the communications center, the mixed media center, the visual education department, the self-study center, etc. In some places it may not even have a name. Nevertheless, we are talking about that unit that provides one or more types of nonprint media, usually those accessed with an electromechanical device—media such as films, filmstrips, audio tapes, videotapes, slides, magnetic tape data bases, records, microfilm, fiche, cartridge film, cassette tape, cartridge tape, wet carrels, radio, television, CATV, EVR, CCTV, opaque projection, over-head projectors, and associated production and service facilities. Teaching and research operations may be included as well as the service function.

The traditional villain, in discussions of nonprint media problems, is lack of funds. This lovely rationalization takes the blame for just about everything that is not done or that is done poorly. Like so many myths, this one is not based on fact. The key to successful operation of the nonprint media department is not related to the size of its budget or to the amount of capital investment in equipment, but to who is running the department now, and whose idea it was in the first place.[1] Acceptance of the department director as a peer of the professional staff is the most critical factor, but it is almost as important to have the operation initiated by someone at a level high enough in the organization to give it unquestioned administrative and professional sanction from the beginning. Lacking these factors, the operation is typically perceived as a low-level, low-priority service function that really has little to do with the mission of the organization. We have witnessed dramatic confirmation of this in the past decade. The Federal government poured millions of dollars into audiovisual departments in public schools and higher education. Many institutions with little or no commitment to nonprint media accepted these funds because they were available. Today, with the funds dried up, many audiovisual departments languish or have died because the local institutions are unwilling to allocate sufficient resources to maintain them.

What are the elements which help or hinder the use of nonprint materials in the school or academic setting? First, a look at some of the plus factors. The young instructor may well regard nonprint media as a bonanza. He is interested in making a name for himself. What better way than to become identified with the latest advances in instructional technology so as to be regarded as a progressive, "with it" fellow? Besides, it is much easier to publish articles about new methods and techniques than about work in the older, more mature areas. The computer technology area is very expensive and any innovation in this area must involve massive organizational commitment and often involves bringing in specialists. It is, therefore, much easier for the young instructor to turn to the audiovisual area where he will not have to compete with specialists or become quite so involved in learning special skills. Further, computers are generally associated with certain disciplines within the academic community, whereas the audiovisual media area has universal application. Assuming our young instructor is not in a computer field, or not associated with an organization that has a computer, he may then decide to become an AV evangelist. He has the time, the energy, and the enthusiasm to forge ahead and to put up with the problems, unless he happens to be part of a faculty that does not accept the nonprint media. Without official sanction, the young instructor would be out of his mind to champion nonprint media.

The high-ranking, high-status professor is a very different case. He has already made his reputation and is secure in the knowledge that whatever he is doing in the classroom, it must be right. To expect him to innovate, by adding nonprint media to his already successful operation is to expect a great deal. By doing so he will greatly increase his workload. It isn't easy to integrate audiovisual aids into a presentation. It takes much time, planning, coordination, and headache—it can even double preparation time for a presentation. The professor is well aware that research has tended to prove the null hypothesis about audiovisual presentations, i.e., they teach as well as the same presentation without audiovisual aids. The professor is already pressed for time. Unlike the new instructor, his time is oversubscribed, his energy is limited because he doesn't really get enough rest, and his enthusiasm is tempered with wisdom—he weighs innovations in terms of trade-offs and payoffs before commiting himself.

How much more effective will the presentation be? Enough so that it is worth both the additional investment of time and energy and the negative potential in loss of control? If the professor makes a "boo-boo," he has only himself to blame, but if the AV department makes a mistake, it is the professor who has egg on his face, not the AV department. It is the professor whose reputation is in jeopardy when he risks dependence on the AV department for part of his presentation instead of retaining complete control. If the equipment is not set up, or the tape is improperly threaded, or an adjustment cannot be made because of union rules, then the reflection is on him. Only a very secure professor will take the risk and put up with the potential aggravation.

The University of Kansas Medical Center was the first Medical School to use television, back in 1947. So many high status professors in the Surgical Department, which initiated this program, objected to directors, script girls, rehearsals of operations, and the perpetual foul-ups that reflected on them and their capabilities as surgeons and instructors that they finally kicked out the chairman of the department (who had initiated the program) *and* the television.

What about the rest of us—the in-betweens? Part of the reason we haven't "caught fire" with AV enthusiasm is that we are afraid of the nonprint media. We blundered into this era of gadgets and we aren't really comfortable with them. Alvin Toffler calls it "future shock."[2] We watch with wonder and just a touch of envy the deft ability of six year olds to handle complicated electromechanical equipment that have us baffled. They grew up with the stuff. They accept it as easily as we accepted keeping the fire going in the coal stove. This seems especially to be true among females. We've been brainwashed to the notion that females are not mechanically inclined. We are unaware that this "old wives tale" has long been exposed as another myth and that, as a matter of fact, companies that do delicate electronic assembly work employ women almost exclusively because they do the job so much better than men. It simply is not true that a woman cannot deal with audiovisual equipment. All of us, male and female, can learn to handle such equipment if we are sufficiently motivated.

Another reason we "in-betweens" have avoided nonprint media is laziness. We aren't likely to admit it, but we really do not coordinate our time very well, and by the time we think about the presentation we must make on Wednesday and remember the visual aids to be made for that program, it is already Tuesday afternoon. It is then easy to rationalize the unresponsiveness of the AV department as incompetence on their part, and add one more little bit of non-objective "evidence" to our unspecific feeling that "AV doesn't serve any good purpose" anyway.

Thus far we've concentrated on the teaching staff and their resistance to nonprint media. What about the librarian? Why should there be resistance to nonprint material by "insiders?" One reason is that librarians share with teachers the feeling that AV people are "outsiders." In many situations the head of the nonprint media department is not a professional. He may be an engineer, a "show biz" type from the entertainment media, a technician, or a jack-of-all-trades. In any case, he is neither an educator nor a librarian—if he is one of these other "types,"—he is an outsider. Furthermore, he is almost invariably male. And to add insult to injury, he is often better paid than the librarian who may be his nominal superior. Not only is he not a peer, he doesn't even speak the same language. Instead of pedagese, he speaks a wild mixture of technicalese and "show biz" that reduces many people to quivering impotence. Not only is he scary, if he is an engineer or a theatrical type, but he is likely also to have "delusions of grandeur," seeing himself as the "impresario" doing *his* thing, and the librarians and teachers are expected to fall in line, playing Trilby to his Svengali. Even if these characterizations are not true, they make lovely rationalizations for avoiding nonprint media.

In addition, there is the problem of cataloging. Not only does the librarian feel out of her depth vis-a-vis the nonprint media equipment and production, but also she is made to feel inadequate in her *own* area of cataloging, because we've had nonprint media around for four generations and still haven't arrived at any standard way of cataloging the darn stuff! While this is certainly ludicrous, it is no laughing matter for the librarian who desperately needs to find some way of asserting her professional superiority over an AV technician with a high school education and a bigger paycheck.

An even more horrible situation, for many librarians, is to be saddled with the responsibility for nonprint media *without* a technician around. How many times have you nosed around in a library, poking into cabinets and drawers, and discovered all kinds of audiovisual equipment that the librarian "doesn't know anything about?" "It was here when I came," is the favorite rationalization for the "junk" in the closet. Somehow this disclaimer is supposed to explain why the librarian relegates to the closet (out of sight, out of mind) equipment that may well represent 50 percent of the capital investment in the library. Another dodge is to let the equipment break down and then feel relieved of responsibility because "it doesn't work." This technique may have been borrowed from the language department, which developed a whole series of "reasonable reasons" for not using the "language lab" installed at great expense, after Sputnik. What is the reason for such tactics?

Lack of commitment is the basic problem. All the "reasonable reasons"—unfamiliarity with the equipment; ignorance of nonprint media; lack of time to deal with AV materials; no budget to keep nonprint media up-to-date; lack of help to catalog, to maintain equipment, to acquire software, to train teachers or users, etc.,—are really meaningless. These excuses could just as well be applied to print media. The plain truth of the matter is that most librarians are book-oriented and plan to stay book-oriented if they possibly can. Books are comfortable, easy to deal with, uncomplicated, and familiar. "Conversions" are relatively rare, among either teachers or librarians.

Placing a book-oriented librarian in a media center doesn't change the librarian. Unfortunately, all too often it does change the media center. One favorite way in which this is accomplished is through use of the "security" gambit. In order to keep all that expensive equipment safe, the librarian has it moved to an inside room, preferably on the third floor, where nobody can break in and steal it. After all, the argument goes, the library is not very secure, what with all those windows and doors, and the coming and going of patrons. Once the nonprint material and equipment is physically removed from the library it is much easier to ease it out of the operation, particularly if it is not cataloged. The user must get the librarian to trudge up to the third floor to secure materials. This is a huge deterrent, especially in the light of the ploys the librarian can use to stymie the patron who persists. Either she can't leave the desk uncovered, or she issues audiovisual equipment only between 8:53 PM and 9:07 PM on the first Wednesday after the full moon, except in months with names containing the letter "a," during which the schedule is 7:28 AM to 7:39 AM on the second Tuesday after the board meeting. The unfortunate thing about this is that it isn't funny. It happens. So why aren't more librarians committed?

Maybe so few librarians are committed because so few library school instructors are committed. In the typical library school course, nonprint media gets a fast verbal nod once in a while and the local "AV Nut" teaches a course or two. But an actual survey of the use of audiovisual equipment by instructors in a major library school, conducted in 1970, revealed that over a period of eighteen weeks elapsed time, requests for the set up of AV equipment was as follows: (Note, these were requests—a subsequent check with students revealed that in some classes equipment was often present, seldom used.)

16 mm projector and screen—28 times
overhead projector—41 times
slide projector—7 times
opaque projector—3 times
record player—1 time

During this period approximately forty classes were scheduled per week, but three weeks should be subtracted for exams and holidays or breaks between semesters. The resulting use ratio figures are a bit staggering because approximately 600 class sessions occurred within this period, and believe it or not, the survey was undertaken because a staff member felt that there was a great need for additional audiovisual equipment!

In the light of figures like these, is it any wonder that the library student gets the message loud and clear, "Don't bother with nonprint media, it isn't really very important"! Until we convince our library school instructors that nonprint media are important enough for them to use in their classes, we can hardly expect great changes in the attitudes of practicing librarians toward such media.

What makes this situation even more absurd is that the library school curriculum lends itself especially well to the use of audiovisual techniques, since much of it is "how to" type teaching (like medicine, which has already discovered the value of AV techniques) rather than abstract learning. The armed forces have demonstrated beyond any shadow of a doubt that familiarization and skill teaching is best handled through a combination of audiovisual techniques and "mock-up" training aids, and that, furthermore, much of the basic theory can be handled best through self-instruction. This frees instructors to deal with questions and advanced work through seminar and discussion sessions. Knowing this and doing something about it are two different things, however. Armed forces instructors are "captive" instructors. They can be told what to do and how to do it. Library school instructors are not so open to persuasion unless one happens to be in the fortunate position of being able to choose only instructors who are willing to work with a curriculum that leans heavily on utilizing such techniques.

Suppose you have been hired to establish an AV department in an existing college or school setting. What can you do to establish a beachhead in a situation like this? Begin by understanding how tenuous your position really is. Knowing this ahead of time can save your job, especially if you take proper precautions. A major part of your difficulty may be the administrator who "blows hot and cold." He may have hired you during a "hot" phase—don't be surprised if he forgets you during his "cold" phases. Especially in those city school systems where the AV budget is handled as "discretionary funds" by the principal, the "cold" phase is most likely to occur while AV funds are still available. In such a situation "discretionary funds" become "slush funds" and, in some cases, they just never seem to filter through. Some librarians have had the equally disheartening experience of an administrator who "blows hot" when he sees an interesting AV gadget (salesmen love these guys), buys it, (on *your* budget), plays with it for a week or two, and suddenly hands it off to you. The first time you may have heard about his purchase could be when he asks you to send someone around to cart it out of his office! If you were lucky, it was a $75 item. A recent graduate student of mine discovered that 92.8 percent of her annual equipment budget had been spent this way when the principal spent $6,500 on a videotape production outfit!

The Big Donor whim is much like the executive whim, except that it is likely to produce much larger white elephants. A well known eastern school of dentistry lost several of its most promising young professors when a Big Donor was so impressed with their use of television in the classroom that he wanted to build a $60,000 studio for them. The dean informed them of their good fortune and they almost cried, for the last thing in the world they needed or wanted was a studio. They explained to the dean that the essence of their use of the medium was the immediacy of moving from lecture to demonstration to discussion all in the same room, with the television serving to give every student a live view of the patient's mouth while they were working on and discussing it. They did not want a studio because they had no use for one. But their protests were to no avail. The dean felt that he could not afford to offend a Big Donor, so in due time the studio was built and all the TV equipment was moved to the studio from the classrooms where it was being used. Of course it was not possible to teach classes in a studio, so it was no longer possible to utilize TV in teaching. Soon the professors who had pioneered in this activity moved to schools that appreciated what they were doing, and to this day, the $60,000 television studio gathers dust, because it is of no use to a school of dentistry.

Fortunately, there is something you can do about many of the white elephants you collect, whether you inherited them, had them dumped on you, or simply find them no longer suitable for your program. Check with your local big game hunters in nearby schools and universities. They too, will have white elephants on their hands, and you can do what the zoos do —trade elephants. Barter is not out of fashion. You may develop a reputation of being a wonder worker by indulging in a little judicious trading—for what is a white elephant for one may be a bonanza for another.

Before leaving the subject of administrators, before you take that job, make sure the man in charge of the organization knows where the costs are in a nonprint media department and is willing to support them. Most executives seem to be under the impression that the hardware is the big ticket item in the nonprint media department. A few careful questions during the job interview may disclose that the hardware in the new AV center is being provided by a grant, by Federal funds, or by that Big Donor. If this is the case, be very wary. The executive may not know that he is committing himself to an *annual* expenditure approximately three times the size of the hardware cost.

First of all, the most generous average life of AV equipment is five years, and for many nonprint media centers it is as little as three years. This means that you will have to replace 20–33 percent of the hardware each year. This replacement figure does not include additions to hardware, and you will note, we have indicated percentage replacement, *not* percentage cost. The dollar figure will be even greater because of constant inflation.

Next, consider the software. A "heads-up" operation spends at least as much on software each year as it does on hardware initially, i.e., if your initial investment in hardware is $20,000, you should be spending $20,000 *per year* on software. If you aren't, your cost/effectiveness ratio is zilch and you deserve the hard time they give you about all that expensive equipment just sitting there.

Finally, your operating costs will probably run about twice the initial equipment investment, annually. This figure includes all personnel and production costs. In a larger operation the costs will be greater, so that over time, the hardware accounts for a very small proportion of the costs.

As you can see, the problem of commitment is an administrative problem, not just a teacher/librarian problem. Cost/effectiveness assumes much greater importance in the nonprint media center than in the library that is book-oriented, because the expensive hardware sticks out like a sore thumb. If it is important to have the library open from 7 AM to 2 AM seven days a week, it is *doubly* important to have the nonprint media center open at least that long, if not on a 24 hour basis. If you are one of the vast number of librarians who just don't think in such terms, it is high time you started. The investment in the nonprint media department is greater by an order of magnitude than in other parts of the library, and anything that can be done to up the utilization factor should be done. Some costs can be shared, for example by accepting outside production assignments, using a time-shared computer, operating a film exchange, using the carrier signal of your FM station for commercial muzak, selling access to your mag tape data base to business users (either on a direct charge basis or by setting up "business associates" at an annual fee, as many universities do). In addition, the nonprint media department can participate in the more usual cost-sharing techniques familiar to most libraries (pools, union catalogs, co-ops, etc.)

An example of how the budget might look, annually, if the organization gets a grant that provides $20,000 worth of initial hardware:

Annual Budget

Hardware replacement	$ 5,000
Software	20,000
Personnel & Operations	40,000
sub-total	$65,000

Add to this amount additional hardware, and consider raising the personnel budget, because this one is *very* tight. It only provides one professional ($10,000), one clerical ($5,000), one technician ($8,500), and student help ($7,000). This amount of student help at $1.85/hr amounts to only 473 man/days. We now have only $10,000 left for all other costs, hardly an adequate budget, yet a surprising number of organizations try to make do on less.

Unfortunately, this budget, inadequate as it is, only covers one of the three areas in which the nonprint media department should be involved —the service area. It does not take care of either teaching or research. The mature nonprint media center is involved in all three areas.

Existence may be tenuous indeed for the AV center that is not heavily engaged in teaching, preferably at three levels: teaching staff members/ instructors, teaching technicians/helpers, and teaching users/students. When I say teaching, I do not have in mind a two hour orientation or an occasional "production" workshop. I mean a regularly scheduled credit course in the institution's curriculum. I mean released-time assignment to the nonprint media center of staff or instructors, either full released time for one semester, or part released time for a longer period. I mean a state-certified and approved program of training for technicians that includes a planned curriculum and a certificate of completion. Nothing changes the image of the nonprint media center quite so drastically as to raise it to full teaching department status. Furthermore, this step is within the range and capability of most AV centers, whereas doing research, which is also strongly recommended, may not be as easy for some librarians.

Like teaching, research responsibility enhances the image of the AV center. It need not be funded research dependent on outside grants. A well thought-out program of record keeping should be the first task. One needs to know what is being accomplished. The nonprint media department is the most vulnerable department in the library, school, or college. During a budget crisis the first thing the trustees want to cut is the "fat," the "fads and frills," i.e., the big price tag items that seem least vital to the mission of the institution. That's *you* they're talking about, Baby! Unless you can document, chapter and verse, how indispensable your department is to the program, you may find yourself pounding the pavement. It is absolutely amazing how few AV departments keep records. It isn't amazing that so many of them have disappeared. Your annual report should read like a corporate annual report. You should be able to document strengths and weaknesses and use this analysis to back up your budget requests, just as you use it to defend the department if need be. Self-evaluation is important as part of this annual effort. Few people are willing to "ask for trouble" but this is one of the most effective means known to further growth and development. It works for nonprint media as well as it does elsewhere. Don't be afraid to weigh your program in the balance. It may prevent worse mistakes in the future. If you are in a college or university, call on your colleagues in the business, engineering and education schools. Ask them to assign graduate students to projects in your department. They can help you with design, with carrying through projects, even with scut work, and in the end you will not only have the research done, but you will also have cemented relations with faculty members in a few more places. If you are in a public school, involve a curriculum specialist in this activity, or contact the local school of education and invite them to use your department as a laboratory setting for research by their students. Some people have been known to double their manpower by such means.

When setting up those records, be sure to include accurate figures on equipment downtime. This is *all* the time a piece of equipment is unavailable for use, for whatever reason. When you want to purchase replacement equipment downtime records are very helpful. When you are calculating total equipment needs you will need to know how much downtime you have in order to arrive at accurate figures. Finally, downtime figures are essential to an accurate assessment of the cost/effectiveness of your operation.

Returning to the ways and means of establishing a nonprint media department, there are a few rules of thumb that will help keep you out of trouble. The basic one is START LITTLE! Don't start big. The temptation to begin in a fancy set of studios is especially hard to resist when television is involved. Organizations that have had no previous experience with an organized AV department, or that have the opportunity to design facilities into a new building are especially vulnerable in this respect. I discussed this problem with Professor Preben Kirkegaard, Rektor of the Danmarks Bibliotekskole in Copenhagen last September while he was showing me through their beautiful new building. He had cautiously resisted any involvement in television after being told by the architect that a minimal layout would add about 2.5 million dollars to the cost of the building. Incidentally, his solution to integrating nonprint media into the curriculum is a lovely one. The front of the classroom is paneled with cabinets containing various types of AV equipment, including stereo audio equipment. A motorized screen and automated 16 mm and carousel slide projector equipment can be operated by the instructor from his lectern in the front of the room. He can also control lights on a dimmer circuit and draw motorized blinds from this lectern.

The high priced response is not an unusual one from architects. Unfortunately some consultants are as unreasonable as the architects in this regard. The problem is that they are hardware-oriented instead of program-oriented. I was visiting an eastern medical center that was already in the bricks and mortar stage of building and was shown the plans for the new television and nonprint media center. One studio was two stories high, 30' × 60', and the other somewhat smaller. I knew they did not have an AV director and asked about their existing program. They explained that they currently had a graphics department (one girl) and a secretary who handled AV equipment as an ancillary activity because it was stored in the hall closet near her office. My suggestion to them was that they immediately relabel all the blueprints, calling the TV studios "electrical equipment rooms" and that the doors be locked, no keys issued, and signs put on them reading "Danger—High Voltage." I suggested that they secure an AV director and start a small program, combined with the graphics department, and strongly suggested that the AV director be a member of the existing faculty, interested in nonprint media, who could begin missionary work among his colleagues. As awareness of, familiarity with, and interest in AV aids increased, he could up the complexity of available aids until at some time in the future, when some of his colleagues felt a desperate and justifiable need for a studio, the *small* studio could be "carved out of existing space" for them, and so on until the faculty was actually ready for and comfortable with the complete facilities being built.

This is not as silly as it may sound. The sudden acquisition of big-time studios with their overwhelming equipment and, perhaps, a producer, a director, a script girl, and who knows what else, spells just one thing to most faculty members—Broadcast Entertainment Television—almost guaranteed to turn most faculty members into "goats" and a few into "hams." Either situation is unfortunate because both involve a role reversal: AV suddenly becomes the tail that wags the dog. The nonprint media department should exist to facilitate the mission of the institution, *not* the other way around. All over the country there are underutilized TV production facilities in schools and colleges because the facilities were built before a program need required them. Few things can kill an AV department more quickly or more permanently than starting BIG.

How do you start little? Begin by concentrating your efforts on ONE item. Do not try to be all things to all people. Find out what your users want most. Bend your efforts to providing that aid, whatever it is, in spades. Insist on involving them in the task—selecting hardware—selecting software. Foolproof the operation so they can all become as involved in producing software as they wish, with assistance from your department only if they want help. Don't do it for them if you can help it. By selecting a type of nonprint media many people want and involving them in the task, you should soon have a number of "old hands" at using that item. Don't buy the fancy version of the hardware. Keep it as simple as possible so everybody will soon have it mastered. When the faculty/users have exploited all the capabilities of the hardware and are actually able to demonstrate their need for more complex equipment in terms of projects they are undertaking, *then* get a fancier version of the equipment. This process may be slower than you would like, but it is solid. By building capability as the need and desire and *ability* of the group to handle more complexity increases, you are actually participating in the development of *real* nonprint capability and orientation in the mission of the organization. Once the initial type of hardware has become as familiar as chalk and blackboard, you can move on to another type, *if* the faculty is ready to add another type.

What steps are involved in developing the use of a particular type of nonprint medium? The following guidelines will provide a standardized pattern that can be adapted to fit your particular situation.

1. Begin with a one paragraph policy statement of the rationale for using the media you are choosing in your library or organization.
2. In several sentences, describe the users for whom these media are intended.
3. Use standard reference sources plus the Yellow Pages to find hardware. Devise a hardware evaluation form and use it when you are discussing hardware with dealers or checking out hardware they lend you. Use such guides as the *Library Technology Reports* at this step. When you finalize your choice, write down why you chose this particular hardware.
4. Duplicate step three for software. Be sure to involve faculty.
5. Prepare inventory cards for hardware, including insurance and maintenance and downtime information. Don't forget security arrangements.
6. Prepare catalog cards for your software.
7. Plan and conduct training programs that include both equipment and production "hands-on" opportunity.
8. Make arrangements to observe users using the equipment and devise user evaluation forms for feedback from them to add to your own notes.

Your job is not complete until you have completed this last step. The proof of the pudding is in the eating. As you can see, with little modification you will have completed a section of your annual report when you have gone through these steps. You will only need to write a summary statement of the project as a whole and the response of users to form a basis for your own reaction as to whether this was a wise media choice for your institution.

One last word about this procedure. Don't choose a single piece of equipment. Choose two, borrow them from the vendors for evaluation and, keeping software constant, try them on your users before making a final choice of equipment. This procedure often turns up objections you never would have thought about without such a test.

This procedure also provides a start on another aid that should be put into operation early in the life of your nonprint media department—a combination handbook and policy manual. The reason for the handbook is to give comfort to the user by not only telling him what, when, how, why, and where; but also provide simple comparison charts to indicate what equipment best fills a particular need; recommend room arrangements, etc. provide checklists for preparing a presentation; and furnish additional, useful material. The policy portion of the manual serves two purposes: the more obvious, public purpose of informing others and the private purpose of forcing you to think through the mission of your department fully and completely. This process will take time. It will involve many discussions with both faculty and adminstration before you will have hammered out the real purpose of your operation to be expressed in the policy manual. This is the first and most important task you can undertake in a nonprint media center.

In our guidelines for developing a capability in a particular type of nonprint medium, we moved rather rapidly over the software step. What about the gripe that comes up in almost every discussion of nonprint media: "There just isn't any software available!"? How many times have you heard such a statement? As a matter of fact, for many areas of instruction the amount of AV software available is simply staggering. There are available, for example, over 800 psychiatric 16 mm movies. Departments of psychiatry will tell you this isn't so, but one researcher actually compiled a listing, including information on how to obtain the films, etc. What we really mean when we say no software is available is one of three things. Either we mean that we haven't bothered to look; or we mean that in our cursory appraisal of the situation, we previewed a couple of items that didn't really quite fit what we wanted to get across to our group; or we mean it is too hard to get stuff when we want it.

If you must order three months in advance, specifying date and time of use, can't preview the material until it arrives the night before, and can't be sure you will be ready to use it at that specific time and date three months hence, you are trusting providence more than most of us are willing to trust people. This is emphasized especially when you have the horrible experience of receiving the film only a few minutes before it is scheduled to be shown, so that you cannot preview it, and discover, upon taking a chance and running it anyway, that you were sent the film on opium dens instead of one on fox dens. I just went through such an experience. I was the visiting speaker on a strange campus. Four hundred undergraduates had *paid* to see a 90 minute film at the opening session of a workshop. The film distributor goofed and sent the 20 minute preview instead of the 90 minute feature! We were lucky not to have had a riot on our hands.

There are several answers to this software availability problem. The first and most obvious is the responsibility of the nonprint media department to secure and make available to users listings of available software. It is very easy to assemble a thousand catalogs of available materials, and such a collection of resource references would hardly scrape the surface of reference material that could be stocked, the great bulk of it free.

The second answer to this problem is one I have already mentioned. Involve users in the production of their own software. This is more rewarding and results in material tailored to the need. Whether the faculty member does it or assigns production as a classroom project, can be determined by the instructor and the need of the class. The AV department can do many things, given sufficient notice, that the instructor or the class cannot do. But nothing is quite so satisfying to a class as to be turned loose with 8 mm camera or slide camera or portable ½ inch TV to produce their own classroom materials. Such projects need not be expensive and they are both doubly instructive and very apt means of focusing the attention of students who may not be challenged by other types of presentation.

At the higher education level, television and videotape can be used in many situations to bridge the gap between classroom and real life with a minimum of investment. You can start with $1,400 worth of portable equipment. This would allow you to try videotape simulation of problem situations,[3] to provide students with a means of self evaluation,[4] and to tape actual situations outside the classroom for playback and discussion by the class.[5]

Finally, I can hardly end a series of remarks on the human element in managing nonprint media without repeating Emerson's apothegm: "Do you not see that a man is a bundle of relations, that his entire strength consists not in his properties, but in his innumerable relations?"[6]

REFERENCES

1. James W. Ramey, *Television in Medical Teaching and Research* (Washington, Government Printing Office, 1965).

2. Alvin Toffler, *Future Shock* (New York, Random House, 1970).

3. James W. Ramey, "Simulation in Library Administration," *Journal of Education for Librarianship* 8 (Fall 1967).

4. James W. Ramey, "Self-Instructional Uses of Television in Health Science Education," *Proceedings of the Fourth Rochester Conference on*

Self-Instruction in Medical Education, edited by J. P. Lysaught (Rochester, University of Rochester Press, 1971).

5. James W. Ramey, "The Underlying Challenge of Medical Television," *Health Sciences TV Bulletin,* new series 1 (July 1964).

6. Ralph Waldo Emerson, *Journals of Ralph Waldo Emerson,* edited by Edward Waldo Emerson and Waldo Emerson Forbes (New York, Houghton Mifflin, 1909), Journal IV, p. 167.

PART

SELECTION AND EVALUATION

Collecting Non-Print Media in Academic Libraries

by Angie LeClercq

WHY NON-PRINT MEDIA?

A librarian might legitimately ask what qualities non-print materials have which enhance learning and communication in ways that are different from print materials. For those who need convincing, it is possible to identify four salient characteristics of non-print media which are unique.

Non-print materials have a quality of immediacy. Their sounds and images provide a witness to the entire range of man's activity. The performing artist can study his art in the light of many varied interpretations. The student of human affairs can find all the fluctuating dilemmas of man in war and peace more fully comprehended when the sounds and images that characterize them are recorded and preserved.

Non-print materials have the ability to capture mood and style. The inflections and gestures of a speaker—John F. Kennedy's use of his hand, Richard Nixon's use of his finger—are more acutely perceived. The nuances of a dramatic or tense situation are more evident when heard and viewed. The drama of the McCarthy investigations, the humor of a Falstaff, the ethos of an FDR fireside chat can only be fully captured in a plastic medium.

Non-print materials have the capability of individualizing instruction. While they have most often been used for their mass communication, qualities, they can be easily adapted for one to one communication. Advances in technology—the audio cassette, the video cassette, and the sound/slide package—provide an individualized playback mode.

Finally, complexity of subject matter, and the realistic recording of visual data are possible when all the senses are involved. It is possible through non-print media to experience an eclipse of the sun, examine the interior of a beehive, watch a glacier moving, or participate in an old-time circus parade. Thus, the added dimensions of immediacy, mood and style, individualization, and realism which non-print materials can bring to the teaching/learning process make their acquisition by libraries significant, and perhaps crucial.

BIBLIOGRAPHIC ORGANIZATION IN
THE NON-PRINT AREA

The guides, current review journals, indexes, retrospective selection aids, and subject listings we use depend on our intentions. A recreation leader, a church program planner, an instructor, a librarian, or a student will each potentially have differing needs when approaching bibliographic tools.

Instructors, librarians, and instructional technologists will need reviewing media which help in evaluating materials for selection and acquisition. Program planners will need selective indexes to help them find materials on specific subjects. Students often want selective indexes which will help them locate reviews on a specific title or compile a subject listing. The following list of non-print selection aids should help the user match his needs with the right type of reference tool.

NON-PRINT SELECTION AIDS

I. **GUIDES**
   Guides to Educational Media (Rusfvold & Guss); *Guides to Educational Technology* (Frankle); *Media Indexes and Review Sources* (Chisholm); *Programmed Learning and Individually Paced Instruction* (Hendershot).

II. **CURRENT REVIEW JOURNALS**
   American Record Guide; Audiovisual Instruction; Booklist, Cassette Information Services; EFLA Review Cards; Film News; Learning Resources; Media and Methods; Previews; Sightlines.

III. **INDEXES TO REVIEWS**
   Media Review Digest (1970—formerly *Multi Media Review Index); Film Review Index,* 1974.

IV. **RETROSPECTIVE SELECTION GUIDES**
   The Elementary School Library Collection (Gaver); *Feature Films on 8mm and 16mm* (EFLA); *Learning Directory,* 1970+; *NICEM* (National Information Center for Educational Media, 13 indexes to various media); *Schwann Record and Tape Guide; Spoken Records* (Roach).

V. **SUBJECT LISTINGS**
   AUDIO:
   Directory of Cassette Producers (Cassette House, 1973); "A Discography of Commercially Recorded Speeches," (Thomas and Potter in *The Speech Teacher); "*Radio and the Grand Illusion" *(Media & Methods,* January, 1973); *Index of Literary Recordings* (U.S. Military Academy, 1971); *The White House Record Library* (Recording Industry Association, 1973).

   SLIDES & FILMSTRIPS:
   "Slides" *(Booklist,* September 15, 1971; February 1, 1973; April 15, 1972; October 15, 1973); "Slides Acquisitions" (in *Previews,* November 1972); *Slide Buyers Guide* (DeLaurier, 1974); *Some Sources of 2 × 2 Inch Color Slides* (Kodak, 1974); "Sound Filmstrip Programs" (in *Media & Methods,* February 1974).

VIDEOTAPES AND FILM:
"The Campaign Trail" (in *Media & Methods,* September 1972); "A Checklist of Medieval and Renaissance Plays on Film, Tape and Recording" (in *Research Opportunities in Renaissance Drama,* 1974 #17); "Featuring Films" (in *SLJ,* 1972); "Information Sources: Programmers' Tools" (in *Film Library Quarterly,* Winter, 1975); *The Video-play Program Guide* (C. S. Tepfer Co., 1974); "Programming Video" (in *FLQ,* Winter, 1975); "Video and Cable: A Source List" (EFLA, 1973); "Video-cassettes, The Dream Medium" (in *Media & Methods,* March, 1974).

CHARACTERISTICS OF CURRENT REVIEW JOURNALS

While the specific needs of the user will vary, there are definite characteristics of the current review journals which are essential to their reliability. The user should evaluate a review journal to see if it is *comprehensive,* if it contains reviews which are based on *wide participation* by reviewers with a variety of motivations, biases, viewpoints and concerns, and finally whether the posture of the reviews is *critical* and discriminating.

No journal will embody these qualities of comprehensiveness, wide participation, and critical posture to the same extent. While *Previews* is fairly comprehensive for most media formats (excluding slides and video-tapes) and has a broadly based band of reviewers from around the country, their reviews are generally unreliable because their critical standard varies so markedly. *Booklist,* on the other hand, contains media reviews of an impeccable critical standard, but is comprehensive only in the areas of 16mm films and filmstrips. Many of the non-print reviewing journals *(Film News, Sightlines)* provide notification services in their brief descriptive lists of newly released materials.

The crucial nature of comprehensiveness in enhancing the reliability of current review journals can best be demonstrated by *Booklist's* recent attempt to review video productions. I have coordinated this effort with the assistance of volunteer reviewers from a variety of educational institutions and geographical locations. There is an enormous volume of video productions listed in distributors' catalogs. Our reviews to date have been highly selective, and truly represent only the tip of the iceberg. There is an enormous amount remaining which has not been critically analyzed or compared with other material on the same subject for possible merit or lack thereof. How then to judge the reliability of these reviews? I am extremely sympathetic with the media center director who, having just purchased a video-cassette based on one of our reviews, angrily called to say that the production did not meet any of the expectations which had been generated by the review.

A further problem in getting a reviewing service off the ground is the stance of distributors. They are more than willing to provide the reviewer with a single preselected program from a series for evaluation. However, they are unwilling to provide the other thirty programs in the series for critical evaluation.

Despite the obvious deficiencies of non-print bibliographic aids, the oft-repeated statement that there is chaos in the bibliographic control of non-print materials is increasingly untrue. The current journals are becoming more comprehensive, critical in their stance, and broader in their scope of coverage. The newly reorganized *Media Review Digest* is truly an excellent tool for finding reviews of specific titles, for keeping up with discographies and filmographies, and for keeping abreast of awards and citations. It can be used for selecting, programming, and as a cataloging aid.

In the retrospective area, the NICEM indexes are developing coverage, and with their supplements are providing more up-to-date coverage. They deserve the reputation of a *Books in Print*. In the selective retrospective area such a tool as Mary Gaver's *Elementary School Collection* provides a buying guide similar to the long famed *Reader's Advisor*. From the vantage point of a user, the tools for developing an on-going collection of non-print materials are becoming more reliable and useful. Perhaps the greatest current need is for the development of a workable collection development model.

A MODEL FOR COLLECTION DEVELOPMENT

The idea that print and non-print materials should be combined as instructional resources for use in the teaching/learning process is increasingly accepted by academic libraries. However, procedures for developing well-rounded, diverse collections of media in all formats are still in their incipient stages.

The procedures which librarians have used to select and acquire print collections should have some applicability to non-print collection building. In developing print collections librarians have relied heavily on four sources: 1) evaluative reviews in library and subject literature; 2) book subscription plans; 3) subject bibliographies; and 4) faculty requests. In developing non-print collections a-v specialists in universities have relied to a great extent on two sources—their own expertise or faculty requests. The reasons for this are multifarious: 1) review sources have in the past tended not to be evaluative, comprehensive or reliable; 2) subscription plans such as Baker and Taylor's *Media Quick Lists* provide adequate coverage for elementary and secondary schools, but only about 20% of their listings are in the adult or higher education range.

As a result of the limited range of sources and individuals involved in building non-print collections, these collections tend to be overweighted with expensive 16mm films designed to support classroom instruction. A factor which further reinforces the sterility of non-print collections is that a-v specialists tend to be only slightly involved in planning for curricula changes and teaching/learning innovation.

During the summer of 1974, the Council on Library Resources funded my proposal to survey non-print departments within college and university libraries to study their present state of organization and to propose an organizational and collection development model for the future. A few examples from my survey can both highlight the problems, and perhaps point the way toward organized procedures for collection building.

One institution visited was a senior college (3rd and 4th year and graduate studies) in the midwest. Its stated goal for the teaching/learning process is the total individualization of instruction with high emphasis on mediated learning packages or modules. Administratively both the library and the a-v center fall under the Dean of Instructional Services. The charge to build a media collection was delegated to the Media Librarian. In the course of ten months, the Media Librarian developed the 16mm film collection from 150 titles to 650 titles. Several comments can be made about this collection. First, 16mm films are a notoriously poor format for individualization of instruction. The learning center was totally unequipped to make this large, expensive collection accessible to students. Second, the collection had been selected on the basis of the personal predilections of the Media Librarian. There was no organized procedure for relating collection to curricula or faculty interests. It is no wonder then that the collection resembled a public library film collection, heavy in film as art titles, general social documentaries, and series on the environment. Needless to say, the media formats most suitable for individualized learning—filmstrips, audio cassettes, slide/sound sets—had been underdeveloped as a result of the emphasis on 16mm films. However, some attempt had been made at developing an audio collection: a blanket purchase of the *Big Sur Audio Tape Catalog*. While this misexpenditure of funds seems especially egregious, it is not atypical. The procedures and tools for developing an opening day media collection have not been finely honed.

Media collection development can be seen as a double-faced coin, with producers, distributors and bibliographic tools on one face, and faculty, students and the instructional system on the other face. The collection building specialist is the mediator between these two forces. An obvious imbalance is created where one side is given more weighted consideration than the other. The producer-distributor side is a finely organized lobbying force that has been extremely skillful in persuading media specialists of the value of their wares. The faculty, student, user side of the coin is unusually inept, often unconcerned or unaware that they have a responsibility and a right to participate in the media selection process. How can the a-v center organize its collection building procedures to bring these two forces into equilibrium?

Bergen Community College in Paramus, New Jersey, is one institution which has refined its collection building procedures for both print and non-print into a truly workable model. The Library and Learning Resources Center provide print and non-print resources for approximately 250 faculty and 2,500 students. Peter Heulf, Head of Educational

Media, is responsible for the total range of audio-visual services including production, distribution of software and equipment, and collection development.

Collection building and utilization at Bergen are the responsibility of seven reference librarians who have the title of Media Utilization Advisors. Each of these individuals has a masters in librarianship and in instruction media. Each Media Utilization Advisor is assigned to two academic departments, and is expected to spend at least 15 hours a week in contact with their designated faculty. Mr. Heulf stresses face-to-face contact, feeling that a reliance on telephone or mail reinforces the faculty member's image of the faceless librarian. The librarian is charged with the responsibility of bringing about a relationship between faculty and potential resources. The Media Utilization Advisor is the chief negotiator or liaison between library selection tools such as *Choice, Booklist, Library Journal, Previews, Media and Methods,* and faculty. Advisors send reviews of books and media to faculty, faculty initiate a request, and in this fashion the library assures itself of maximum faculty involvement in the selection process.

The intimate relationship between collection building and utilization which exists at Bergen is enhanced by the Library's information dissemination techniques. All print and non-print material is cataloged by the LC system. The computer-based catalog makes material accessible in several different ways. Media are retrieved by LC classification in print-outs, and by media format print-outs. Media Utilization Advisors regularly provide faculty with LC print-outs in their area of subject interest. A computer based faculty profile enhances dissemination of acquisition information. The Library collects non-print materials suitable for use in large group instruction (16mm films, transparencies, slides) and individualized instruction (8mm loops, filmstrips, videocassettes, and audio-cassettes). Thus print-outs by media format allow faculty who wish to pursue a particular instructional mode to select materials suitable to that mode.

The Bergen Library does not rely solely on its Media Utilization Advisors and its bibliographic system for communication with faculty. The Library also offers an a-v course and a bibliographic course for faculty. Broad faculty participation in these courses has apparently stimulated a fuller utilization of library resources.

The only aspect of the Bergen collection development model which is unique to that institution is its enthusiastic staff. Basic features, such as assigning staff collection building responsibilities in coordination with academic department liaison work, are adaptable in any college library.

Given a workable collection building model, comprehensive, evaluating review literature, and a willingness to include non-print in one's library collection, there will continue to be a number of academic libraries where print-only collections prevail. While such reasons for non-inclusion as budget priorities, and problems of cataloging and circulating non-print materials are all too real in the short run, they seem unjustified in the long range view.

The need for non-print materials to support the teaching/learning process is acute. If libraries do not collect information regardless of format, other campus agencies will assume this mission. Such agencies as a-v centers, and instructional materials centers tend to be equipment oriented, lack a means of generating funds for purchasing materials, and do not have the training or skills to organize and service non-print collections. Access to these resources for both faculty and students will suffer if libraries fail to assume a mandate to collect information regardless of format.

Fundamentals of Evaluation

by Masha R. Porte

Film selection is perhaps the most important function of the film librarian. Certainly, it is in this activity that one is functioning at the highest professional level. One is called upon to utilize talent, knowledge, and imagination. Selection/evaluation, two sides of the same coin, require that the librarian be responsible and responsive on the one hand to the film medium itself and on the other to the community that is served.

Film evaluation all boils down to the interrelation of the nature of film and the individual's personal predilections.

A film may meet the highest artistic and technical standards, but the subject may not appeal to the viewer, or it may be presented with emphases which repel the viewer. Or, conversely, it may be a rough production technically and artistically, but deal with a subject considered vital to the needs of the community by the evaluator, and therefore merit praise and recommendation.

Although the viewing of films is still mostly a group process, response to the moving image is personal, individual, and often unique. The viewer brings to the screening his own background, experience, viewpoint, and in fact, his mood at the time of the screening. These, plus the circumstances surrounding the showing (physical environment and screening companions), color the viewer's assessment of a film. It has often been noted that one's attitude toward a film may be different with a change in physical environment, the group viewing the film, or personal state of an individual viewer.

In the case of the non-theatrical film which is being considered for public library circulating collections or for library programs, another important element enters the evaluation: utilization. When previewing films for possible purchase, the librarian is very much aware of their potential audiences. The evaluation is based in part on the amount of usefulness the films will have.

If abstract evaluation results in a wide spectrum of opinion, the added factor of a film's usefulness may cause even further varieties of viewpoint. For each library has its own constituency, its own unique types of audiences. Even though audiences may be classified in general as, for example, women's clubs, minority groups, consumer groups, men's business or civic clubs, etc.—in each community the character of these organizations differs with the tenor of the community as a whole. Some areas are more sophisticated, more socially aware than others. In some cities there is more interest in one subject than in others. Patrons in some libraries may be more amenable to the avant-garde than borrowers in other institutions. All these differences, of degree and of emphasis, tend to influence the selection of films for a given collection, and therefore constitute one general criterion for evaluation.

A CLUTCH OF CRITERIA

Among the more abstract criteria, also general, are such components as those listed in the following outline, compiled by a committee of the American Library Association as a guide for selection of films. Technical aspects (presentation): how a filmmaker conveys his ideas.
- Visual aspects of camera work: expressiveness, mobility, visual viewpoint, clarity befitting the intended style, aptness of color, contrasts and image.
- Sound elements: appropriateness to approach, subject and style of film concept; use of music, sound effects, balance; synchronization; tone, pitch, inflection, enunciation, and pacing of speakers; level and balance of sound.
- Editing: pacing and rhythm; length of sequence; method of cutting (transitions); choice of cuts and clips.
- Suitability to intended purpose, audience, and subject matter.
- Adequacy of development for the concept.
- Elements of vocabulary in sight and sound (freedom from wordiness, condescension, faddishness, jargon; levels of sophistication).
- Honesty, accuracy, authenticity, objectivity, slant or bias.
- Comprehensiveness or superficiality of coverage. Creativity.
- Cinematic validity (appropriate use of the medium; effectiveness of means or techniques; literacy of film language).
- Originality of style, freshness of viewpoint, inventiveness of approach.
- Insight.

These are all valid elements of which the experienced evaluator is aware (consciously or subliminally) while screening films. The problem is to define some of the terms, particularly in relation to what are "good" and "bad" qualities of each film component. Here the key words are "aptness" and "appropriateness." What may be "good" filmmaking for one purpose, may be "bad" use of the medium for another. It is not always true, for example, that a film without narration or dialogue is preferable to one which uses these factors. In such films as *The Red Balloon, The Golden Fish, The String Bean*, the absence of words intensifies the focus on the action and the story. The very minimal dialogue in *Occurrence at Owl Creek Bridge* heightens the sense of suspense and fantasy. Suspense, the mood of a town, and the character of some of the people, are revealed in the dialogue of *The Lottery*. The storybook quality, the slightly condescending tone of the narration, make of *The Lady or the Tiger?* not only a provocative story, but a kind of parable.

And consider nature films: *White Throat* without any but natural sounds, conveys the sense of peace, spiritual refreshment, and the dignity of living things. *Morning on the Lievre* could have done the same thing without narration, but the reading of the poem which describes the river as the morning unfolds adds a lyrical dimension. The English countryside in *Journey into Spring* could also be enjoyed without words, but the reading of the minister's descriptions, written two centuries ago, lends a feeling of continuity and stability to the natural beauty.

It almost goes without saying that in most cases films of fact require that verbal information be provided on the soundtrack, although there are some notable exceptions in which the visuals give ample explanations. Cinematic treatment of social issues nearly always use either off-screen narration or a cinema-verite style in which the actual participants speak. These methods are necessary to state facts, present a viewpoint, stimulate action or discussion.

It is the viewer's individual sense of what is apt or appropriate which affects his ultimate evaluation of a film. This sense can never be made uniform; and so long as there is personal, individual judgment, there will be differences of opinion with regard to a film's value (except in the cases of some of those few outstandingly excellent productions on which there is universal agreement).

AWARENESS OF MULTI-PURPOSE USE

In a democracy, differences are supposed to be looked on favorably as enriching the fabric of life. In the case of film evaluations, particularly those which are made public as in reviews, such differences can have at least two major disadvantages. In the first place, a favorable evaluation of a patently inadequate film fails to deter the filmmaker from continued production of inferior work. And secondly, varying reviews of a film can be frustrating and confusing to the librarian looking for recommendations for purchase or programming.

A partial, long-range answer to the matter of the filmmaker's work lies in the practice of letting him or the distributor know the librarian's assessment of the film. There will be a variety of responses, but they may weigh more heavily on one or another side of acceptance, and in that way may be a guide for the filmmaker's future efforts.

As for the confused librarian, he must eventually determine which source of evaluations may be considered the most authoritative, which seems to fit most often his own estimations of quality and usefulness. In this respect, differences of opinion have the advantage of allowing for a broad latitude of choices.

Film as a medium lends itself to much versatility in the way it is ultimately used. A film may have been made with a specific purpose in mind (to consider a given subject, to solve a challenging technical problem, etc.). That film could be shown as a discussion-starter on the topic, or on related subjects. It could be presented as an example of a given aspect of the art of filmmaking (animation, e.g., or time manipulation, etc.). Or it might be used solely for entertainment, even though it might have more profound aims.

An evaluator should be aware of this multi-faceted use of film and should know something of the technicalities of filmmaking, should base his assessments on this knowledge and on the ability to judge from having seen many, many other films. In the end it is the evaluator's knowledge, experience and innate taste and broad cultural background which will give him the keenest perception of the film.

Distributors vs. Buyers

by Carol A. Emmens

When Sputnik went up in 1958, the sale of audio-visual materials soon went up, too. In the panic that ensued, the U.S. government became convinced that spending more for education would get us to the moon first. Money poured into schools through Title I and Title II and both hardware and software sales rocketed. Producers, publishers, television stations, and others thought the pot of gold was just over the horizon. The number of companies producing AV materials naturally multiplied and today the U.S. has the largest distribution network for non-theatrical films in the world. *Hope Reports* indicate approximately 4,500 films are produced annually. At least half actually enter the educational market.

The sudden growth and success quickly ended when the government cut the funds for schools. Significantly, all three major networks stopped distributing their own programs during the '70s when the AV market was hit with a double whammy—increased costs and decreased funds.

INCREASED COSTS, DECREASED BUDGETS

An EFLA questionnaire sent out in May of 1975 revealed that buyers and distributors alike are affected. The latter must pass on increased lab and postage costs as well as increases in overhead expenditures, such as salaries. One consequence is that fewer films are bought, and as Gene Feldman (Wombat Productions) stated, "When public libraries [institutions] have less money to spend for new films, it is immediately apparent that uncommon films (and frequently very meaningful, important films) will suffer." According to a former sales representative, schools are interested in buying "package deals." The quality is less important than the quantity when end-of-the-year numbers reports are due. Small distributors are hit hard because they can't compete with the "deals" that salesmen from large companies make in the field.

Public libraries and universities are also faced with increased costs and reduced budgets. Many institutions are coping with the problem by joining together in circuits or consortiums. The latter are groups of schools or colleges/universities which band together to buy films cooperatively. Frank Moynihan (Billy Budd Films) views the trend favorably as do most distributors, who allow discounts or give bonus prints. Even disgruntled distributors agree that the floodgates are open; they must swim with the consortium tide.

One factor which contributes to increased prices is slow payment by many institutions. Institutions need to streamline and speed up the processing and payment of invoices. The majority of distributors are small businesses, which can not afford to carry deficits.

RENTAL COLLECTIONS

Budget dollars are stretched by renting prints from large rental libraries, such as the University of Michigan or Indiana University, whose fees are less expensive than most distributors' charges. However, restrictions placed by filmmakers and distributors on the use of films sold to universities undermine this service. According to Karen Sayer Higgins, AV consultant at the University of Michigan, there are four types of restrictions:

1. Minimum rentals set by the distributors.
2. Circulation only within the state in which the institution is located.
3. Circulation only within the institution; sometimes further restricted by a prohibition on announcements. (It is the producers of feature films who generally forbid advertising.)
4. Circulation only within classrooms.

Because many universities will not buy films that carry restrictions, distributors suffer as well as the users who can't afford higher rental fees. Ms. Higgins contends that wide rental distribution stimulates rentals and purchases by other organizations, as evidenced by the numerous requests she receives for film sources. Based on their own experience, many distributors concur with this view. In addition, when rental libraries receive more requests for a title than they can fill with one print, duplicate prints are bought.

PREVIEW PROBLEMS

Some distributors are attempting to combat shrinking profits by eliminating free previews and charging a rental fee, which may be applied to the purchase price. This growing trend is prevalent primarily among small companies and the chief executive of one such company confided that after less than a year the results are "poor." In fact, free previews are permitted for "legitimate" buyers, i.e., those known to the company. The AV budgets of many organizations do not contain funds for rentals or preview fees. Since approximately 90,000 films are listed in the latest

NICEM guide, librarians and teachers know (or hope) that substitutes are available for films they can't preview free. Therefore, many buyers will not even consider a film for which there is a preview charge.

The majority of companies still allow free previews, actually a misnomer since previewing is time-consuming, and therefore, costly. Henk Newenhouse (Perennial Education) wrote, "We would not dream of charging preview fees because we sell our films through previews . . ." Unfortunately, the industry does not have standard procedures for previewing. A general feeling exists among distributors questioned that preview privileges are abused. Some distributors encourage classroom "testing" of their products, but often the same school or teacher will request free "preview" prints of the same film several years running, or will request to preview films "for possible purchase" when the institution does not have funds for buying films. Similarly, two or more representatives within a district will request preview prints, perhaps inadvertently.

Late returns or loss of preview prints play havoc with the distributors' shipping departments (and marketing and finances). Many libraries, especially film circuits, and school systems screen new films once a month. Prints which arrive late may be "held over," sometimes without notifying the distributor, by the same persons who charge a fine if a borrower returns *their* prints late. Purchasers then express surprise and annoyance when reminders are sent to them automatically by a mailing house or computer.

"Missing" prints tie up inventory records and previews for other customers; insurance reimbursement covers only a part of the total loss. The post office is the acknowledged culprit. (No, Virginia, the mail doesn't always get through in rain or sleet or snow.) Postal service has become less dependable, but sometimes previewers say (and believe) they returned prints which are still sitting on their shelves due to in-house carelessness or oversight.

A footnote to this major problem is described by Henk Newenhouse, "A minor annoyance is the stealing of shipping cases. We use certain high quality cases which cost us an average of $6.00 [and] we have customers who consistently keep our new cases . . . "

Institutions can help resolve the complex problem of previewing in the following ways:

1. Adhere to the policies of each company.
2. Return prints on time or notify the distributor of your intent to keep the print longer. (Reviewers are particularly lax about this.)
3. Appoint a central clearing person to eliminate duplicate requests.
4. Give the distributors an alternate date for previewing.
5. Take care to handle films properly.

Following these guidelines can also help to alleviate some of the complaints of film previewers: long waiting periods for preview prints, receiving damaged prints which can't be projected, or receiving prints late.

COPYCOPYCOPYCOPYCOPYCOPYCOPY

Slow payment, declining budgets, and preview tie-ups cause headaches, but illegal duplication of films causes migraines. One distributor said he knew nothing about black market buying; others hope the problem will go away; still others admit that the black market is flourishing despite the recent F.B.I. crackdowns, which will simply force pirateers further underground. Professional pirates generally steal and dupe feature or commercial films, but non-professionals are hard at work, especially in schools. Video equipment makes child's play out of copying films and distributors are faced by a two-headed monster—ignorance and rationalization. Confused by the Supreme Court's ruling over "fair use" in copying materials, many individuals believe taping a film for classroom use is acceptable despite the warnings tacked on to the film can or leader.

Those who know that videotaping copyrighted films is illegal often convince themselves it isn't wrong if:

1. The school cannot afford the film.
2. The budget does not allow rentals.
3. It's shown on television. (Stealing from big corporations is not really stealing, is it? Time-Life salesmen regularly spot taped versions of such series as the "Ascent of Man," which was shown on NET.)
4. It will be erased after five hours, five days, five months (five years?)
5. The school owns one copy and just needs three more.
6. It's for the children!

Arthur Mokin, a producer and distributor, taught a film course at a New York college where a faculty member suggested taping all of their films so that they would be more "accessible."

Teachers torn between the dilemma of providing illegal tapes of films or no films at all must consider the impact on the industry. As Robert Churchill wrote (*Media and Methods,* February 1973), "If . . . producers' films are duplicated without compensation, soon there will be no films. The goose is dead." A filmmaker/producer must make money to finance his next film. Rick Schilling (Time-Life) estimates that in today's market only 300–400 prints are sold for a "good seller" and that's over a two to three-year period. Others place the figure at only 200 prints. Many companies rely on selling two, three, four, ten or even fifteen or twenty prints of a film to the same customer in order to make a profit. Yet re-sales are dwindling.

Unmoved by ethical arguments? Afraid of getting caught? In response to the problems its members face, the National Audio-Visual Association, with the approval of the U.S. Justice Department, is instituting an Information Exchange program. Customers who repeatedly "misbehave," i.e., return prints late, tape films, fail to pay, will be listed as violators and this list will be made available to NAVA members. Unlike McCarthy-type blacklisting, the violators will be notified that a signed complaint was issued against them and the accused will have an opportunity to respond to the charges. Complaints must be specific; for example, Paul Purchaser failed to return a preview print of "Why the AV Industry is Confusing." When the difficulty is corrected, the violator's name will be removed from the list.

In the past, distributors exchanged personal lists of customers who preview but never buy. NAVA also wrote letters to persons/institutions who/which violated the policies of distributors. In January 1975, one company alone asked NAVA to send out 12 letters of complaint.

Technology, creator of the problem, may be cast in the dual role of villain and hero. Systems to foil illegal copying of ¾" videotapes are on the market. Trans-American Video, Inc. introduced its Copy Guard Encoder last March. Copies of protected tapes come out blank yet the original is not affected. Critics of the system claim it is easily overcome and that only "casual thieves" are deterred. An industry spokesman has said that with a dry cell, two transistors and a little know-how, a student could bypass the system, but TAV maintains its system will eliminate as much as "95% of the videocassette piracy" in education and industry. The *Video Publisher* (June 27, 1975) also stated that all the duplication houses it contacted said Copy Guard is inadequate against "professional" pirates. However, Richard H. Irvine, Vice President of TAV, claims duplicates made by overcoming Copy Guard can be detected electronically. Many companies are using the system and other companies claim to be working on new methods.

The majority of illegal duplicates are made from 16mm films and no method for protecting them is available. Industry spokesmen claim that ubiquitous copying will continue until film or videocassettes become as inexpensive as phonograph records or books. Producer/distributor Arthur Mokin pointed out that the lab costs for prints is a small portion of the total price. What the customer is really paying for is the production costs. A scripted, edited *videotape* costs $5,000 or more to produce (*Hope Reports*, 1975); even a "talking head" tape runs $1,000 to $4,999; therefore $20,000 for producing a 16mm film is not a lot. One solution to the problem, which satisfies both buyers and distributors, is the *authorized* duplication of film onto video. Under a standard contract the duplicator pays 75% of the price of the film for the first copy and 50% for subsequent copies.

DISTRIBUTORS VS. FILMMAKERS

Some distributors produce the bulk of their materials, but other companies are literally the middlemen between purchasers and filmmakers, who are demanding a larger percentage of the take. The pie is usually divided 75%–25%, but the distributor pays for all lab fees and promotion, which averages $3,000–5,000 per film for adequate promotion. Several distributors say their profit is only 25% or less, so that the filmmakers are receiving a fair share.

The representatives of Colour Images Unlimited, Inc., a newly formed company, disagree, "We feel that many young producers are not receiving their fair share of the gross dollar generated by the distributor. Much of that is due to lack of marketing knowledge on the part of the producer at the outset. A better informed producer could negotiate for better royalty percentages in the beginning. We also feel that there are very few distributors doing a complete and efficient job of distribution."

Jerry Bruck, Jr., producer and distributor of I. F. STONE'S WEEKLY, concurs. At the 1975 Mid-West Film Conference he said, "Distributors do not distribute." He and others who have achieved a degree of success in distributing their own films are encouraging filmmakers to jump on the bandwagon. And many are. But they are entering a market which some believe is already saturated with too many films and too many sources. Moreover, many creative filmmakers lack the necessary business skills to distribute their films successfully. This can lead to conflicts and misunderstandings between the filmmaker/distributor and the potential buyer. Many institutions are cautious about buying films from individuals or new companies. By dealing with larger, established companies, institutions can get discounts or bonus prints on bulk purchases. They can also be assured of getting prompt service if new prints, replacement footage, or repairs of used prints are needed. As one school AV director pointed out to a filmmaker: "This is not to imply that we would compromise our selection policies to obtain all these advantages, but the 'big guys' have good films too. In the tight economy in which we now exist, and with money to buy less than half of the films our committees approve, I find myself, if faced with two equally fine films, in the position both of choosing the best buy and of protecting my long term investment."

All too often, buyers find that they are unable to locate a filmmaker when they want to buy additional prints or need replacement footage, or they discover that a promising new company went bankrupt. On the other hand, no one denies the vital role of independent producers/distributors as outlets for controversial, non-commercial, or avant-garde films. No wonder the AV purchaser is lost in a maze!

The audio-visual picture, painted here predominantly in shades of black and gray, also has patches of rose. Despite all the problems, 16mm sales were up 17% in 1974 according to a report published by the Educational Media Producers Council; and our continuing dialogue with buyers, producers, and distributors indicates that all are making efforts to resolve the difficulties plaguing the industry.

The Evaluation Gap:
The State of the Art in A/V Reviewing, With Special Emphasis on Filmstrips

by Janet French

The problems posed by the formidable production of information today are compounded by an equally remarkable multiplicity of information carriers. Anyone wishing to search for, make use of, or transmit information is faced with a dizzying number of possibilities. Certainly the educator is among those suffering from what appear to be an excess of choices. Charged with identifying "appropriate" information carriers, he must bear in mind his agency's curriculum, the competencies and idiosyncrasies of both staff and students, the physical limitations of his plant, the financial limitations of his budget. He must then relate all these variables to the range of available materials. Even without considering any exotic equipment, the educator is still faced with a host of possible carriers and possible combinations of features: print and nonprint, sound or silent, motion or still, simple or complex. And he must decide whether he wants the material for individual, small group, or large group use, or some combination of these elements, since materials are not all equally adaptable to all these uses.

These are by no means the only factors to be considered. The selector must know that not all formats are equally suited to any given educational task. Wide variations in quality also exist in the handling of any given topic in a *given* medium. Even when superior materials have been identified, the person charged with selection cannot assume that his job is done. Either his information or its treatment may be outdated tomorrow by new discoveries, new approaches in the original medium, or a superior presentation in an entirely different format.

Under the circumstances it seems reasonable to expect that a main goal of educational selection agents would be to establish national services for the bibliographic control and evaluation of all widely used instructional materials. Trade books long ago succumbed to such controls in response to the needs of librarians. To a substantial degree, 16mm films and educational records are also subject to control and evaluation procedures. As the matter now stands, however, no comparable systematic evaluation services have been established for the other media.

A "FRUSTRATING TASK"[1]

Is there a substantial need for a comprehensive evaluation of the neglected nonprint media? How useful are the currently available selection aids? What suggestions might be made for general and local evaluation procedures? This study attempts to answer such questions for that unpretentious but widely used medium, the filmstrip, for reasons noted below.

For those who believe that nonprint media represent a new order of things, it may be worth noting that filmstrips have been around for 50 years.[2] It would not be fair to insinuate, however, that most films produced during this long period of time have been especially good. In fact, the brevity and mediocrity of filmstrips as a class before the Sixties may well explain their past exclusion from critical consideration.

The situation today has changed substantially. Color has almost entirely replaced the old black-and-white format, and the average new film is almost twice as long as films produced in the Fifties. Sound has been introduced through the use of synchronized records and tapes, and while it has not been uniformly successful, it can at its best add a lively dimension of depth and excitement to the visual presentation. Most important, several producers new to the field have been using the medium with respect and sensibility and are making films of aesthetic as well as educational value. (Let anyone who doubts it see Guidance Associates' *Streets, Prairies, and Valleys: The Life of Carl Sandburg.*) Their superior films may be helping to stimulate a general upgrading of standards. Certainly substantial improvements in both technical and instructional quality have been evident and this fact, coupled with the filmstrip's original virtues of inexpensiveness and simplicity, probably account for its present position as the most widely used of the nonprint instructional resources.

It would be foolhardy to try to unravel the precise relationships between new educational practices, improved materials, and increased allocations (now, disastrously, waning). All have contributed to a vast expansion of materials holdings. In 1966, the educational establishment bought $442 million worth of a/v materials and equipment.[3] In that year the filmstrips absorbed over $500,000 of the $165 million in ESEA Title II funds spent on a/v materials.[4] That this substantial investment has not been generated solely by Title II pressures is shown by the fact that in the past eight years there has been an increase of 1000 percent in filmstrip sales to schools.[5] More surprising, perhaps, but fully compatible are the results of an NEA survey made in spring 1967, which showed that of some 1600 elementary and high school teachers polled, 81.2 percent were using silent filmstrips, a figure which surpassed the reported use of any other material including records.[6]

BIBLIOGRAPHIC CONTROL AND SELECTION

To what extent has the substantial investment in filmstrips and their evident popularity prompted the development of useful selection tools? It should be noted first that a basic catalog of recommended titles on the order of the Wilson or ALA (book) catalogs has never been produced; anyone contemplating the development of a filmstrip collection must be prepared to build it from scratch. Help appears to be coming, however, from at least two sources.

The dimensions of the selection problem for both backlisted and current titles take on sharper focus when viewed in relation to the more than 25,000 individual titles listed in NICEM's *Index to 35mm Filmstrips,* published by Bowker last fall. To be fair, it must be admitted that some of these are no longer in print and that others were designed for adult rather than classroom use. Yet, even if we tentatively eliminate several thousand filmstrips, the residue represents a formidable challenge to building a superior filmstrip collection.

The NICEM *Index* itself, despite the grandeur of its proportions, is a puzzling tool to use even as a simple finding guide. The only information on the bases for inclusion is that the entries represent titles recorded in the data bank of the University of California since 1958. The user has no way of knowing, therefore, whether the *Index* is intended to be a comprehensive list of all filmstrips produced in this country (or elsewhere) from any given date or whether an effort was made to trace all such productions or whether the list merely represents items submitted for entry by those producers who were moved to cooperate. If the *Index* is not a comprehensive guide, neither is it a simple key to current materials on the order of *Books in Print* since the alphabetic title list is peppered with "out of print" entries. Even such basic bits of information as the total number of entries listed and the number of o/p titles in the list have been omitted; the only way to approach either figure is through page sampling. The *Index* may not seem worth such extensive carping, but it was produced with substantial fanfare and represents a much-needed step towards the bibliographic control of the medium. Unfortunately, it also represents the cavalier attitude towards media control and evaluation evidenced by many of the agencies presently engaged in either enterprise.

A fervor for systematizing is undoubtably a distinguishing feature of librarianship. Responding to the accelerated growth of the nonprint media in school libraries, *School Library Journal,* a principal source of critical book reviews, launched a semiannual *Audio-visual Guide* in November 1967. In an editorial introducing it, Evelyn Geller accurately reflected both the needs of the field and a professional passion:

> We felt that the main obstacle to better incorporation of a/v materials has been the failure to impose on them the same genius for organization that librarians, dictating their need for bibliographic control and systematic evaluation, have been able to stamp on the book industry.[7]

She picked up the challenge by publishing this nonevaluative but highly useful subject index to the current output of media in the pre-K to 12 range. The list, systematically expanded since its inception, now includes films, filmstrips, 8mm loops, slides and transparencies, discs and tapes, study prints, maps and charts, and a few miscellaneous items. It offers some useful figures for comparision.

CURRENT VALUATION: SLIM PICKINGS

In November 1967, 204 filmstrips and filmstrip series were reported in the *Guide*. This figure increased to 250 in April 1968 and spurted again to 291 in November that year. Thus school-oriented filmstrip production from January 1968 to February 1969, as reported by the major producers, came to 541 series and individual titles. (The total for 1969, as reported in the April and November 1969 *A/V Guides*, come to 617, but we are using the 1968 figures for comparison.)

It is instructive to compare the 1968 filmstrip or filmstrip series reported—541—with the number of filmstrip reviews published during the same period. Though for many obvious reasons such a comparison is on wobbly statistical ground, it still provides an indication of evaluative activity in relation to production.

The "Index to Audiovisual Reviews," published at frequent intervals in *Audiovisual Instruction*, reveals a total of 230 filmstrip reviews identified in the index in 1968. While it is perfectly possible that many reviews were overlooked, it is also true that large numbers of the listings were repeaters —reviews in different journals reported for the same filmstrip series. Numerically, then, filmstrip reviewing activity is well behind production, though the output for school consumption is certainly amenable to complete coverage. The man on the firing line—the selection agent—not only lacks selection tools for backlisted titles, but faces an increasing disparity between total production and items critically reviewed.

Seven readily obtainable journals carry most of the reviews listed: *Educational Screen and AV Guide, Film News, The Grade Teacher, The Instructor, School Library Journal, Science Teacher, Senior Scholastic's* teacher edition, and *Social Education*. In addition, the ALA *Booklist* last fall launched its filmstrip reviews. Of these publications, *Educational Screen, School Library Journal*, and *Film News* offer the greatest number of reviews, the first two covering an average of six to seven filmstrips or filmstrip series per month, the latter publishing ten or 11 reviews per bimonthly issue. The rest publish their reviews on a rather irregular basis, averaging three or less a month. Considering both the quantity and quality of their evaluations, *School Library Journal* and *Film News* warrant consideration by the selection agent as prime sources of responsible reviews, but neither provides the volume of service necessary to keep pace with production.

Booklist, long established as a critical guide to current books, 16mm films, and reference materials, may provide a comprehensive source of critical evaluation. In answer to the question on the extensiveness of *Booklist's* planned coverage, Paul Brawley, editor of the nonprint reviews, wrote a year ago:

> The number of nonprint items to be reviewed will be directly proportional to the quality of the items received. Every known producer and distributor of nonprint materials [e.g., in the first year, filmstrips and 8mm loops] is being contacted in an effort to preview and evaluate as close to 100 percent of the educational market as possible.[8]

However, general access to ALA's evaluations is not as broad as this statement implies since reviews are being published only for material which "meets our criteria of selection and therefore is recommended for purchase."[9] Though there are doubtless many good reasons for limiting the reviews to recommended materials, space being an obvious factor, *Booklist* has seriously abridged the usefulness of its projected service through this decision. The reader will not know whether titles omitted are the victims of oversight or have been actively rejected. Though *Booklist* does seriously qualify its recommendations, as a concession to the generally poorer quality of production in the audiovisual field, its cautiously worded criticisms militate against their effectiveness.

Less obvious, but of greater consequence, a publication's ban on outright negative reviews damages the whole industry by withholding from public discussion the feedback producers need to improve their films. Perceptive and carefully considered reviews, both positive and negative, perform an essential service: at their best they represent a kind of ongoing, in-service education for the selection agent, calling attention to considerations that might otherwise have been overlooked, identifying the flaws and merits of a film, comparing it with others of superior or poorer quality.

Despite the manifold advantages of publishing reviews which reflect a full range of opinions, at present only *School Library Journal* does so as a matter of policy. Considering the modest number of filmstrip reviews published in *SLJ,* it is obvious that both producers and purchasers are receiving very little information about rejected materials. This is without question one of the most serious deficiencies of current a/v selection tools and a marked contrast to the publication policies of the major book reviews.

A number of agencies have award programs for filmstrips they judge to have special merit. Of these, Educational Film Library Association's Blue Ribbon awards, given annually at the American Film Festival competition, are the most important; they have been described as being "in the same tradition as ALA's Newbery-Caldecott Award."[10] Though one may doubt that they are as significant as the Newbery-Caldecott prizes, their choices are worthy of attention. EFLA makes a descriptive list of contenders available it its annual publication, *American Film Festival: The Best of 19–.*

HEARTS AND FLOWERS EVALUATION

While the end of any selection procedure is presumably the same—to identify the best material for a given purpose—the degrees of responsibility imposed on persons evaluating materials vary substantially. The person selecting materials for his own use obviously accounts to no one save himself, but as the circle of persons affected by an evaluative decision increases, so does his measure of responsibility. The judgment of the evaluator may affect only one group of students, if he is a teacher choosing material for his class, or it may affect a whole school or school district, if judgment is being brought to bear on purchases for the media collection. If the results of evaluation are made public, as in printed reviews, the number of persons and institutions potentially affected by the evaluation increases enormously and, to the same degree, so does the evaluator's responsibility to provide a carefully considered and informative review.

It is possible, of course, to become so overwhelmed with these responsibilities that a kind of mental paralysis sets in. In an article on materials evaluation, one author indicated both a total abnegation of her critical faculties and a denial of the existence of objective criteria:

> Ethics involve one's professional responsibilities to make an evaluation that is fair to both the producer and the consumer. It is anticipated that material receiving poor ratings may be used successfully by some teachers, or for some children and, conversely, that materials receiving good ratings could be unsuccessful in many cases. There is also a general concern about the effect of the variability of teacher-pupil-classroom transactions upon ratings; recognition is given to the possibility that the time of day or the weather may play some role in the success or failure of a material, and that success with materials varies according to the ability of the teacher to use them creatively. Even under hypothetically ideal conditions, the variabilities of a pupil, teacher, and environment are such that evaluation of a material is by nature intrinsically qualified.[11]

Not too far removed from the impotence of this point of view, and quite as useless to someone seeking guidance, are the evaluators who feel a greater obligation to be kind to the producer than to be honest with the user. In her excellent *Manual on Film Evaluation* Emily Jones admonished:

> In the past evaluators have tended to be overkind rather than overcritical. They have been trained in the theory "if you can't say something good don't say anything." This was based partly on the lack of materials which made it necessary to accept mediocre productions provided they dealt with the subject called for. This is no longer necessary, and mediocre films should be judged as severely as mediocre anything else. No one wants to hurt the

feelings of film producers . . . but the responsibility of the evaluator is to the user, and there is no point saying "The film may be useful with some . . . groups," when what you mean is "The subject is unimportant, the treatment is uninteresting, and it is impossible to imagine any group of normal intelligence sitting through it."[12]

Despite Miss Jones' reference to past practice, the hearts-and-flowers approach is still evident in many reviews. It seems likely, too, that the lack of adverse recommendations in journals that carry reviews is as symptomatic of the sentiments she describes as lack of space or the desire to push good materials.

The fact is that it is both possible and reasonable to establish useful guidelines to cover the important features of any given medium. There is no need to examine them here in depth since virtually every treatise on a/v materials includes a list of evaluative criteria. Suffice it to say that the technical aspects of a filmstrip, for instance and an accompanying record or tape admit readily to objective evaluation: they either are or are not clear and free from distortion, synchronized with the sense of the captions or script, or relevant to the apparent subject of the film. With regard to the content itself, the questions of whether the material is up to date and accurate also seem beyond the influence of the time of day, the weather, or the creativity of the teacher.

Perhaps when the evaluator considers the coherence or logic of the presentation, he has entered into the arena of subjective judgment, and certainly this is true with regard to whether or not he finds the film stimulating, imaginative, or effective. If the evaluator takes his charge seriously, however, there is no reason for him to apologize for his subjective responses. Quite the contrary, in direct proportion to his appreciation for the film medium and his understanding of children and teaching needs, these personal responses will comprise a valuable aspect of his evaluation.

Of substantial bearing, too, on the usefulness of an evaluation, is the evaluator's familiarity with the medium and, in particular, with comparable titles in the subject area. The old maxim to the contrary, comparisons are not odious, and a knowledge of similar materials will give the evaluator a concrete basis for his appraisal of the relative merits of two or more titles. Furthermore, where such comparisons are possible, the subsequent review, to be of maximum value, will indicate the order of preference and the reasons for ranking. While references to related titles are an expected feature of book evaluation, they are almost totally absent from media reviews. The need for this kind of guidance is pressing, however, in view of the vast outpouring of new materials, the duplication of coverage, and the lack of basic selection tools for recommended titles. Another factor which makes comparisons particularly important in film evaluation is the special vulnerability of the medium to obsolescence and the need to find satisfactory replacements for aging titles.

It does not suffice that all these considerations enter into an estimate of the material's value. If the evaluator expects others to use the results of his effort, and particularly if his review is to be published, it is essential that his written evaluation indicates clearly:

1. The material's physical features
2. Its content
3. Its possible uses
4. Its comparative merits
5. The strengths or weaknesses which led to the final evaluation

As Emily Jones warns, "The evaluator must keep in mind the fact that he is acting for someone else. . . . He is being the eyes and ears of a potential user."[13]

Perhaps it would be useful to cite—without comment—the total content of two typical reviews. Their usefulness, or lack of it, should be self-evident, though it may be worth noting that the first review purports to offer guidance to the purchase of an 18-filmstrip set priced at $108, while the second reviews a single film sold by the New York Times for $7.95.

Review A

Here are some answers to the endless and always recurring questions: Why do we need maps? What's inside us? What makes morning, noon, and night? The strips can be used by either class or individuals doing special study and research. Pupils are encouraged to think about the questions and answers and to understand the explanations offered. The material is adapted to the learning needs of young pupils.[14]

Review B

If the librarian, teacher, or group leader can bear exposure to yet another word on the "youth rebellion," this filmstrip should be provocative, for it poses the ultimate question: "So what happens when you're 31?" (Don't trust anyone over 30.) The introduction by Russell Baker, in the discussion manual, is worth the price alone and should be required reading for parents and young people on either side of 30.

The filmstrip captures the youth phenomenon, reinforced by expert shots of their native habitats, by charts that signify their staggering presence among us, and by the veracity of their own dulcet tones and sounds. The black and white prints are dramatic in their straightforward reportage; the sound track well-matched to them. Both sides of the record are audibly cued; Side Two, however, allows for discussion breaks after frames 25 and 54. The manual lists activities, discussion questions, and books and pamphlets especially for young adults.

Since it lends itself to discussion, *Generation* . . . may be used effectively by a library club, guidance department, church group, social studies class, or even a PTA "happening." It may give hope to disadvantaged parents.[15]

A question may fairly be raised about the length of the second review; a little judicious surgery would not bridge the value of its content. But if the main concern of either the evaluators or the journals carrying reviews hinges on their brevity, the whole undertaking becomes pointless. The substance of the reviews should be weighed, not against the price tag of the materials reviewed, but in consideration of the degree to which they accurately mirror their potential service to the users. Insofar as an evaluation fulfills this end, it is successful; insofar as it falls short, it represents a waste of time and money for the reviewer and the journal, as well as for the selection agent who stopped to read it.

IN-DISTRICT EVALUATION: AN AWFUL EXAMPLE

Despite the surface advantage of systematic in-district evaluation, the literature is full of cases of catch-as-catch-can practices euphemistically described as "evaluation." Were these projects pursued as a fringe activity, they would still be a waste of energy; when they are employed to identify materials which are to be a central factor in the educational program, they are inexcusable. A case in point was reported in *Audiovisual Instruction* describing preparations for an individualized instruction program. With pride and fantastic naiveté, the author reported:

> About this time the teachers were ready to evaluate instructional materials as they related to their objectives. The Audio-Visual Department called in the complete nonprint libraries of EBF and SVE, as well as the "quick-strip" library of Eye Gate for evaluation and possible purchase. For the next few weeks the teachers looked through catalogs of all the known producers of nonprint materials. [They] were free to . . . order for evaluation any nonprint materials which they felt might have merit for our program. . . . By April, after the evaluation of many hundreds of filmstrips, tapes, records, and programmed materials, the teachers were ready to start ordering instructional materials with particular instructional objectives in mind.[16]

Overlooking the fact that the main suppliers reported are more noteworthy for the size of their catalogs than for the consistent quality of their products, the description of this project's "evaluation" procedures reads like a catalog of unsupportable practices. Nowhere is there any ·suggestion that criteria were established or adopted for the media under consideration, or that the teachers were given training in their implementation. One of the principal hazards to sound evaluation is that the skills and understandings necessary to the enterprise are so often underestimated. In-district selection practices appear to be based, time and again, on the assumption that the teacher who uses the material is, by virtue of that fact, fully equipped to judge it. Unfortunately, for systems operating under such assumptions, the use of a material does not of itself promote or guarantee expertise in its choice. A cardinal tenet of *any* evaluation process is that it should be preceded by careful indoctrination of the participants so that they fully understand the selection criteria and the nature of the responses required of them.

If the designer of this undertaking failed to appreciate the need for criteria, he performed as poorly in providing guidance in identifying materials for preview. With a very large staff and a great deal of time it might be feasible (if not desirable) to call in "complete libraries" of the major producers; but the present tidal wave of production will soon make such innocent unselective approaches to evaluation an impossibility.

Given the size of the author's task force—12 teachers—and the time allotted for evaluation—three hours a week for about six weeks, their reported activities are nothing less than preposterous. In the time available to them they are described as having examined "the catalogs of all the known producers of nonprint material," previewed "the complete nonprint libraries of EBF, SVE and Eye Gate," and evaluated (apparently to their satisfaction) "many hundreds of filmstrips, tapes, records, and programmed materials." In view of the fact that the average filmstrip runs about 15 minutes and one side of an average LP a half hour, this reported evaluation activity can serve the profession solely in the capacity of an Awful Example. In the absence of any real commitment to guide the evaluation process and participate in it, in how many other districts have media specialists promoted—or at least accepted—similar debacles?

RESPONSIBILITIES OF THE MEDIA SPECIALIST

If these harried pseudoevaluation programs are not to become—or remain—general practice, media specialists must take on their full responsibilities for the selection of materials. They must develop or adopt valid criteria for evaluation and train other media specialists and selected classroom teachers to apply them to materials being considered. They must know both the physical aspects of the media and their content, and they should know which materials and producers are most likely to meet specific needs.

Responsible selection agents will try to bring order and purposefulness to evaluation, seeing it as an ongoing process, not a series of crash programs. To this end they will develop selective lists and systematically reevaluate their holdings to maintain a collection of genuine merit. Insofar as possible, they will structure each evaluation project so that evaluation can take place in the context of comparison—both of the viewpoints of the participants and of the materials themselves. On the other hand, they will *not* be cajoled into previewing massive portions of a producer's catalog, a practice which reduces the possibility of careful comparisons and tends to create a sense of obligation to the producer or his agent. Occasionally this arrangement gets an added fillip through the offer of a bonus if a certain number of items are purchased. Such inducements, when accepted, virtually paralyze any genuine evaluative effort.

The media specialist will make use of the selection tools available to him and encourage the development of better ones. I admit they are not now and probably never will be wholly satisfactory. Yet they provide a means of identifying promising materials, some of which might otherwise be overlooked, with far more hope of success than simple faith in the descriptive listings of a catalog or Herculean assaults on complete libraries of materials. The present lack of selective catalogs or adequate reviews suggests that persons responsible for buying media have never seen the need for such selection tools. If this is so, it follows that they have either failed to understand their responsibilities as selection agents, or they have failed to assume them.

That is really my main point here. The media specialist cannot properly take responsibility solely for the *form* of the materials he administers; he is equally responsible for its *content*. The teachers and others whom he draws into selection will have, at best, a fragmented acquaintance with the media collection. It is the specialist who must be familiar with it *all*—its strengths and weaknesses, the gaps that need filling, the material that needs replacing. He must be aware of what is available in the collection if he is to advise on its use. He must know what promising new materials are on the market and what superior materials appear on the backlists if his selection procedures are to be anything but exercises in serendipity. Of all the persons involved in selection, he alone is responsive to the total curriculum; he alone is knowledgeable about the complete collection and the needs of all its users. It is his responsibility, therefore, to initiate the selection process, guide its functioning, and see that it is brought to a satisfactory consummation.

At this juncture it may be worthwhile to consider the mystique of group evaluation. In 1957 Paul Reed wrote unequivocally:

> Selection of materials should be based upon the judgments of those who are to use them. Group judgments are superior to individual judgments. Teacher judgments are best when they are based upon actual experience in using the materials in classroom situations.[17]

In 1963 Edward Schofield, addressing a symposium, quoted this statement almost word for word.[18] In 1968 Carlton Erickson used it verbatim in his handbook *Administering Instructional Media Programs*. It may, of course, be perfectly true, though none of the exponents offers supporting evidence, and precisely how the "best" selections might be determined is difficult to conceive. What is apparent is that in 1957, when Mr. Reed enunciated this doctrine, the dimensions of both media budgets and production were modest enough to contemplate in-district selection programs which strictly adhered to it.

It may seem heretical to suggest this, but the fact remains that group evaluation is neither the only nor necessarily the best approach to media selection. It should seem reasonable to suggest that the results of group evaluation can only be as good as the training, motivation, and experience of the participants. It is therefore a practice qualified in value and one which can readily degenerate into a parody of genuine evaluation: witness the example quoted earlier. Furthermore, considering the logistics of enormously increased production and demand, evaluation procedures which involve large numbers of volunteers (not to mention those impressed into service) may prove to be a luxury better suited to the infancy than to present dimensions of media production.

Regardless of who participates in the preliminary events, the media specialist remains the central figure in the selection process, not merely its agent, and the final ordering of priorities is his to make. Responsibly conceived, his selections will be based on the merits of the material available, the nature of his collection, the needs of his users, and the size of his budget. A decision to buy or not to buy based fairly upon these considerations will represent the proper culmination of the evaluative process.

REFERENCES

1. Rufsvold, Margaret. "Guides to the Selection and Evaluation of the Newer Media," *Audiovisual Instruction,* January 1967, p. 11.

2. NICEM, *Index to 35mm Educational Filmstrips.* Bowker, 1969, p.v.

3. Geller, Evelyn. "Media Mix at Midpoint," *School Library Journal,* November 1968, p. 11.

4. ———. "The ESEA Title II Report for 1966: The Difference It Made," *School Library Journal,* April 1968, p. 70.

5. Lembo, Diana. "A Stepchild Comes of Age," *School Library Journal,* September 1967, p. 54.

6. "Instructional Resources in the Classroom," *Audiovisual Instruction,* March 1968, p. 284.

7. Geller, Evelyn. "Small Ways out of Chaos," *School Library Journal,* November 1967, p. 19.

8. Brawley, Paul L. Letter, February 27, 1969.

9. Ibid.

10. Lembo. *op. cit.,* p. 55.

11. Moss, Margaret H. "Evaluation as a Responsibility of the IMC Network," *Exceptional Children,* December 1968, p. 304.

12. Jones, Emily S. *Manual on Film Evaluation.* Educational Film Library Association, 1967, p. 5.

13. Ibid.

14. Cypher, Irene. "Filmstrips," *The Instructor,* October 1968, p. 162.

15. Lembo, Diana. "Screenings," *School Library Journal,* September 1968, p. 65.

16. Ogston, Thomas J. "Individualized Instruction: Changing the Role of the Teacher," *Audiovisual Instruction,* March 1968, pp. 244–5.

17. Reed, Paul, quoted in Carlton Erickson's *Administering Instructional Media Programs.* Macmillan, 1968, p. 70.

18. Schofield, Edward. "Competencies Needed by School Librarians for Selecting and Organizing Materials for Materials Centers," *The School Library as a Materials Center;* Mary Helen Mahar, ed. U.S. Office of Education, 1963, p. 21.

OTHER REFERENCES

Brown, James W. and Kenneth D. Norberg. *Administering Instructional Media Programs.* Macmillan, 1968.

ALA Bulletin, January 1969, p. 56.

Mahar, Mary Helen. "Equalizing Educational Opportunity," *ALA Bulletin,* February 1969, pp. 226–230.

Meierhenry, W. C. "National Media Standards of Learning and Teaching," *ALA Bulletin,* February 1969, pp. 238–241.

Educational Screen and AV Guide.

Film News.

Grade Teacher.

Science Teacher.

Senior Scholastic, Teacher Edition.

Social Education.

EFLA. *American Film Festival: the Best of 19–.* Educational Film Library Association.

The Slide as a Communication Tool: A State-of-the-Art Survey

by Juan R. Freudenthal

INTRODUCTION

Photography has been acknowledged as a vital contemporary medium of expression, forcing the visual image upon all levels of cultural experience, either as a vehicle for instruction, information, entertainment, or as a tool for research.[1] The visual message has given a new meaning to our perception of and relation to things. The photographic slide—a long established component of the nonprint media—is one manifestation of this visual revolution. Its lineage, however, antedates George Eastman's roll film system and can be traced to the magic lantern and lantern slides of the early seventeenth century. Despite its illustrious history, for the most part, only art historians, museum curators, and a handful of art librarians and teachers have consistently recognized the slide's unique properties and its importance as a medium of communication. Because of a greater emphasis on visual training in contemporary education, the most recent decade has seen the sudden multiplication of this inconspicuous and fragile photodocument on an unprecedented scale. In 1971 alone, commercially produced slide sales in the United States accounted for more than 2.2 million dollars.[2] This recent "slide explosion" (or "slide pollution" as some prefer to call it) has found many librarians and media specialists unprepared to deal with its implications and effects. We know little or nothing about communication through pictures, despite the fact that all kinds of visual representations have infiltrated every form of modern life.

How do we find out about the acquisition of slides, their physical arrangement, classification, cataloging, and the problems of intellectual access to visual information? In order to articulate objectives and user needs, to standardize cataloging procedures, terminology, and methods for storing slides, it seems necessary to find a comprehensive study describing the various operations practiced in slide collections in every type of library. Most encouraging is the announcement that one such study is to be published in 1974, Betty Jo Irvine's tentatively titled "Slide Libraries: A Guide for Academic Libraries and Museums." The academic emphasis of this survey is similar to the points of view of almost all previous library literature related to the development of slide collections in the United States.[3] And it could not be otherwise. It was in a few well-known American universities and museums during the 1880s that most lantern slide collections were first developed. Even with the advent of the more convenient $2'' \times 2''$ format, slide collections continued to be used, with very few exceptions, within the context of major art history libraries. Only very recently have the small academic and public libraries, and most important of all, school media centers, caught up with the slide. A 1964 study indicated a dramatic increase in the use of instructional media, with 96 percent of all elementary and secondary schools reporting the use of slide-filmstrip projectors, and with nearly 100 percent having at least one slide projector.[4]

The librarian or media specialist finds no immediate solutions to the baffling problems of selecting, purchasing, producing, arranging, and retrieving visual materials. It is my purpose in this state-of-the-art survey to comment on some of the most recent developments and activities related to the slide, as reflected primarily in library literature. This body of information produced largely during the 1960s, is scant indeed, and most articles are either too general or too much involved with single aspects of one slide collection to be broadly useful.

Organized interest in slides is very recent. During the late 1960s, art historians, art librarians, and slide and photograph curators began to exchange information and points of view at several professional meetings in the United States, Canada, and Great Britain. These resulted in publication of several newsletters which have since become a much needed forum and clearinghouse of information. Another important step forward was the publication, in 1970, of a general slide classification scheme (See Reference 12). These developments are encouraging, and point toward growing recognition of the slide as an important communication tool in our society. Notwithstanding that most existing professional literature discusses slides within an academic context, much of it is applicable to the special circumstances of school media centers.

ORGANIZATIONS AND PUBLICATIONS

Several library and nonlibrary organizations in the United States address themselves to the problems of visual communication in general and aspects of slide and photograph curatorship in particular. Some of these are well-known to most librarians: the ALA/ACRL Art Section; The Museums, Arts, and Humanities Division and the Picture Division of the Special Libraries Association; and the Slides and Photographs Division of the College Art Association.

Two relatively new associations, however, promise to voice very forcefully the concerns of teachers, art librarians, and media specialists interested in slides and other visual materials. The Art Libraries Society of North America (ARLIS/NA) was formed in 1972 based on an English model, the Art Libraries Society of the United Kingdom (ARLIS/UK). The latter organization was founded in 1969 by a group of British art librarians who felt that their particular interests and needs had not been met by the Library Association or ASLIB. The Art Libraries Society of North America, with membership in the United States and Canada, joined the Council of National Library Associations on May 4, 1973, and has become a separate, eloquent, and increasingly influential art library confederation. Its membership is a pragmatic conglomerate of publishers, booksellers, art librarians from all types of libraries, museums, galleries and art institutes, as well as others interested in visual librarianship. ARLIS/NA will soon have its own Slide and Photograph Special Interest Group. Projects are under way to publish handbooks on art librarianship, bibliographies, standards, directories, and other pertinent sources of information. Several state or local chapters of ARLIS/NA have already been formed. The most important link among members, however, is the ARLIS/NA *Newsletter*, 1972—, a well edited, informative, and readable bimonthly which vividly reflects the concerns, projects, and ongoing research of the membership.

The National Conference on Visual Literacy (NCVL), on the other hand, provides a multidisciplinary forum for the exploration of modes of visual communication, promoting research, and evaluation of practices growing out of these concepts. Founded in 1967 by individuals from many disciplines (art, psychology, linguistics, instructional technology, philosophy, etc.) NCVL has its headquarters at the Center for Visual Literacy, College of Education, University of Rochester. This center cooperates with conference organization, facilitates exchange of information, coordinates activities, and collects and organizes research data. *The Visual Literacy Newsletter*, 1972— is a practical, nonscholarly bimonthly for exchange of information and debate on aspects of visual literacy. The *Newsletter* features guest editorials, abstracts, brief reports, and articles on research projects in learning from pictures, and announcements about forthcoming conferences and workshops. There is no doubt that this publication is a timely spokesman for those educators, librarians, and scientists who are aware of the growing diversity of visual aspects in our culture.

SELECTION AND ACQUISITION

Selection and acquisition of slides varies from library to library according to the users and the characteristics of curricula. In this respect, the general principles of book selection apply to the selection of nonprint material as well. There is some variation in *who* selects the slides. This author was able to ascertain several approaches among libraries in the

Boston area. At the Museum of Fine Arts, for example, selection depends exclusively on the staff. At Harvard's Fogg Museum Art Library, where the collection is primarily for the use of faculty and graduate students, selection decisions are made to a great extent by the faculty. At the Massachusetts College of Arts, selections are made by faculty, students, and the slide staff.

Presently, the lack of sources of information for the acquisition of slides has been partially corrected by the publication of two invaluable lists: De Laurier's *A Slide Buyer's Guide* and Petrini and Bromberger's *A Handlist of Museum Sources for Slides and Photographs.*[5, 6] The former supplies preliminary information on slide sources, chiefly commercial, in the United States and abroad. In several cases it contains qualitative analyses of the sources described and also gives some brief but sound advice in the art of assessing the quality of slides. The latter compilation is a worldwide guide to the purchase of slides from museums and libraries, but its qualitative evaluations are limited only to the museum sources. De Laurier and Petrini complement each other. A third and still very useful sourcebook on slides is a booklet published by the Metropolitan Museum of Art entitled *Sources of Slides: The History of Art.* The 1973 edition can be obtained free of charge from the Met's Slide Library.

One of the best and most recent surveys on the acquisition of slides and photographs in selected colleges, museums, and libraries was undertaken by Peggy Ann Kusnerz of the University of Michigan.[7] The author reports on who selects the slides and photographs, selection policies, and how slides and photos are acquired. Kusnerz's survey revealed the following six sources for acquisitions, listed in order of frequency: professional photographer on staff, museum sales, commercial firms, professorial/curatorial photographs, clippings, and private exchange. Also of interest to slide librarians is Tom Lennox's evaluation of purchase sources for 35mm art history slides.[8] This study, which focused on the slide collections of five educational institutions in California, arrived at a consensus about purchase sources on art history slides and highlighted areas of necessary evaluation, such as the quality of the transparency itself, type of mounting, price, the chance to review and approve the slide before purchasing, and the offerings of the producer.

COPYRIGHT

There seems to be no happy solution to the problem of statutory copyright and the concept of "fair use" for librarians and educators.[9] Slides present new challenges to a prevailing national debate still deadlocked in Congress. A slide can be copyrighted by requesting an application from the Register of Copyright in the Library of Congress. This procedure can become prohibitively expensive for the claimant if more than a few slides are involved and, in general, has not been common practice. After talking to several librarians and photographers, and after a survey of the scant literature on the topic, this author can only conclude that almost all circulating photographs and slides are in the public domain. This has led to the consistent practice among photographers, museums, art galleries, art libraries, artists, librarians, and instructors to adhere to the "fair use" doctrine (or should it be called "fair abuse"?). By this doctrine, it is assumed that all slides and photographs *are* copyrighted. Most commercial sources and many photographers' personal names become registered trademarks. Some photographers purchase reproduction rights from museums or similar institutions and therefore have an obligation to protect these agreements.

A further problem is presented by those museums that do not permit photographs of their collections to be taken. As one author has observed:

> Most museums operate on the assumption that the owner of a work of art also owns the reproduction rights to it. . . . A legal interpretation might be welcome in regard to whether or not art works more than sixty years old . . . are in the public domain. In other words it may be that anyone has the right to photograph a Rembrandt for the same reason that Dover Press has the right to print copies of old books.[10]

At this juncture, librarians and media specialists interested in the copyright of visual materials will have to voice more forcefully their concerns regarding the newly proposed copyright law, which contains clauses delimiting the reproduction of print and nonprint materials. Presently, the copyright of slides, with very few exceptions, continues to fall within the purview of common law. The abuse of duplication or invasion of intellectual property, to which many photographers, museums, and publishers have been subjected by irresponsible citizens, is an issue that will continue to stand on the merits of the "fair use" doctrine until the copyright law becomes more specific and realistic.

ACCESS TO SLIDES

There are probably no issues in the development of slide collections that have received more attention during the late 1960s and thereafter than classification, cataloging, retrieval, and automated indexing. Presently, slide collections may be arranged by accession number, subject, geographical area, art form or medium, time period, or some combination of these. It has been traditional in American libraries with sizable slide holdings to adopt and/or adapt classification schemes of such well known art history research centers as the Metropolitan Museum of Art, the Fogg Art Museum, the Cleveland Museum of Art, and the Philadelphia Museum of Art.[11]

The problem of intellectual access to slides has been largely ignored by librarians and media specialists, even at a time when the multimedia approach to education is so prevalent, and visual materials in all formats are accepted as *bona fide* documents in core library collections. Providing subject access to nonprint material that carries no explicit self-description can present a baffling problem for the cataloger with little or no background in art history and no familiarity with the visual process. Search and retrieval logic has been applied with reasonable success to print materials but it is far from satisfactory when applied to a collection of 35mm slides. The many possible approaches to a subject and the prevailing interdisciplinary trend in learning experiences require the user to consider different points of access for the same visual message. A junior high school student, an art historian, a soldier, a specialist in literature, and a history teacher, all may be using a different set of categories in asking for a slide depicting a sixteenth century castle or a portrait of Henry VIII. School media centers in particular face an acute problem in regard to slide access. One slide tray or slide-tape may contain many photodocuments potentially useful in completely different contexts than originally intended. How can the individual slide within a set be made most accessible for a variety of purposes?

The index to a slide collection, whether in academic, public, special library, or school media center should permit the inquirer to locate easily those slides that will best meet his individual need. Furthermore, it should allow students and scholars from different subject fields to utilize the terminology of their own disciplines. One probable reason that so many teachers do not use visual materials, particularly slides, is the problem of accessibility; physical as well as intellectual.

Recent research on methods of classifying, cataloging, retrieving, and automated indexing of slides has provided some solutions and new insights. In 1968, the Council on Library Resources funded a project for the development of a classification system for slide and picture collections that could be adapted to automated indexing. This project, carried out at the University of California at Santa Cruz, resulted in the publication, in 1970, of a manual *A Slide Classification System for the Organization and Automatic Indexing of Interdisciplinary Collection of Slides and Pictures*.[12] Although this system does not provide all the answers to slide classification, its advantages are many. It is broad in concept, adaptable to slide collections of all sizes, interdisciplinary in its approach to teaching, and characterized by a filing system that encourages browsing. Finally, it enables the collection to be cataloged or indexed by automated as well as manual means.

Also of considerable interest, and an important complement to the Simons and Tansey slide classification system, is the work done by Robert M. Diamond and Associates, in developing a system designed for the search and retrieval of 35mm slides.[13] This project includes a prototype list of terms that can be used to describe a given slide for retrieval purposes.

A few articles in library literature dealing with access to slides are particularly relevant. At the Learning Resources Center of Prince George's Community College in Maryland, major slide sets are each classified according to the range of materials they contain. The circulating slide collection on general topics is arranged by category in a loose Library of Congress class order. Most of these slides are prepared by the media department from illustrations in books and magazines.[14] Elizabeth M. Lewis writes about the possibility of a key-punched graphic index to the 5,000 art slides in the collection of the U.S. Military Academy. Her article also reviews the earlier literature on slide classification and offers a summary of advantages of machine indexing of art slides.[15] Finally, coauthors Skoog and Evans discuss the pros and cons of using a modified and expanded DDC system for the classification and cataloging of 42,000 slides at the Hunt Library of the Carnegie-Mellon University.[16]

STANDARDS OF QUALITY

Mass production of slides has been characterized by carelessness, resulting in an inferior product and a great disrespect for the untrained eye. Poor quality notwithstanding, slides continue to be purchased on the basis of producers' biased and exaggerated blurbs or amateurish reviews. Too many librarians and media specialists do not seem to mind or are unable to assess critically faded or faked colors, out-of-focus or cropped subjects, or distortions resulting from poor camera angles. What at first seemed only a slide avalanche has now become a "slide pollution" in library collections.

Two major issues prevented, until a few years ago, the adoption of stringent quality control policies—namely, the limited availability of slides and their high cost. But as we enter a new era, when more and more libraries have their own media production specialists and staff photographers capable of producing less expensive, quality, in-house photodocuments, it is hoped that judgments of visual material can become more critical and the process of slide selection more discriminating.

One way to determine slide quality is to compare the projected piece of film with the object it represents. Since in most cases this is impossible, we must rely on our art history background, our memory, or simply on our intuition. Color fidelity is probably the most difficult quality to attain and to judge. Photodocuments reproduced from the original master slide are seldom accurate in color. Original slides, that is, photographs taken directly from the art work, give the best results for color quality and fidelity.[17] In order to assess an original slide critically, many factors have to be considered such as: (1) type of camera and film used; (2) the expert use of natural light, speed, and electronic flash; and (3) the care and methods by which film is developed. Patricia Sloane, in her "Color Slide for Teaching Art History," reports with adroitness and candor on the experience of working with inadequate color slides.[18] As an artist and teacher, she criticizes such institutions as the Metropolitan Museum of Art and Eastman Kodak, and goes so far as to call the Philadelphia Museum of Art the "rip-off magnate of the world of color slides."[19] The author complains, and rightly so, that most companies and museums use poor judgment concerning the particular works which ought to be photographed and comments on how slides of sculpture and architecture should be composed and taken, and how vendors may utilize existing technological possibilities.

It is evident, as we survey the available literature on slide production, that much of the criticism about poor quality of slides is well grounded and based on valid teaching experiences. To prevent our learning centers from becoming inundated with inferior products, librarians and media specialists will have to discipline their visual perceptions and develop pertinent criteria of visual excellence.

VISUAL LITERACY

A new generation is being brought up in an educational context where the visual dominates.

> Print is not dead yet, nor will it ever be ... nevertheless, our language-dominated culture has moved perceptibly toward the iconic.[20]

In order to achieve a major level of sophistication in the approach to visual materials, it is necessary to understand the nature of the visual process.

A considerable amount of research has been generated lately on nonverbal means of transmitting information and how people learn from pictures.[21] The psychology of perception and mental images is being scrutinized with care by behavioral scientists and psychologists. Probably no contemporary figure has discussed more lucidly the process of visual thinking than Rudolf Arnheim, Harvard professor of the psychology of art. Known throughout the world for his psychological studies of the forms and functions of art, Arnheim tries to reestablish the unity of perception and thought and suggests that intelligent understanding takes place within the realm of the image itself. The author's most important statements on this subject are summarized in *Visual Thinking.*[22]

Gyorgy Kepes, professor of visual design at M.I.T., is the editor of several anthologies concerned with the visual arts and the implications of visual training in modern society. In *Education of Vision,* Kepes affirms that

> Vision, our creative response to the world, is basic, regardless of the area of our involvement with the world. It is central in shaping our physical, spatial environment, in grasping the new aspects of nature revealed by modern science, and, above all, in the experience of artists .... [23]

The need for a broad overview and nontechnical discussion of visual literacy has been competently achieved by Donis A. Dondis' *A Primer of Visual Literacy.*[24] The author, currently at the Boston University School of Public Communication, has written a basic handbook which covers visual communication and expression and includes a survey of the major visual components.

Finally, a few sources should be mentioned in regard to the history and progress of photography: Helmut and Alison Gernsheim's *The History of Photography from the Camera Obscura to the Beginning of the Modern Era,* Beaumont Newhall's *The History of Photography from 1839 to the Present Day,* and the invaluable series *The LIFE Library of Photography.*[25-27]

In conclusion, it is this writer's belief that visual literacy and visual communications are areas hitherto unexplored by most librarians and media specialists. These aspects cannot be dismissed lightly if we expect to understand the nature of the ever increasing visual information infiltrating learning centers. There is a dire need for the systematic training of visual competencies. There may be more than a bit of truth in Laszlo Moholy-Nagy's dictum: "The illiterate of the future will be ignorant of pen and camera alike."[28]

REFERENCES

1. The implications of photography in modern society are masterfully discussed in Susan Sontag's "Photography," *The New York Review of Books* v. 20, no. 16 (18 Oct. 1973), p. 59-63; "Freak Show," *The New York Review of Books* v. 20, no. 18 (15 Nov. 1973), p. 13-19. A third essay by the same author is in preparation.

2. "Multimedia Moves Ahead Fast in Educational Publishing," *Publishers Weekly* 203:40 (21 May 1973).

3. One useful article, which gives a historical background of slide collections in the U.S., reports on a 1968 questionnaire directed to institutions having slide collections, and discusses needed areas of research, is Betty Jo Irvine's "Slide Classification: A Historical Survey," *College and Research Libraries* 32:23-30 (Jan. 1971).

4. Eleanor P. Godfrey, *Audiovisual Programs in the Public Schools* (Washington, D.C.: Bureau of Social Science Research, Inc., 1964), p. 12.

5. Nancy De Laurier, ed., *A Slide Buyer's Guide* (Univ. of Missouri: Kansas City Printing Office; Jan. 1972).

6. Sharon Petrini and Troy-Jjohn Bromberger, *A Handlist of Museum Sources for Slides and Photographs* (Santa Barbara: Univ. of California, 1972).

7. Peggy Ann Kusnerz, "Acquisition of Slides and Photographs: Results of a Survey of Colleges, Museums and Libraries," *Picturescope* 20:66-77 (Summer 1972).

8. Tom Lennox, "An Evaluation of Purchase Sources for 35mm Art History Slides," *Picturescope* 19:10-49 (Spring 1971).

9. Ivan Bender, "Copyright: Chaos or Compromise?" *LJ/SLJ Previews* 2:3-5 (Nov. 1973). The author discusses some of the major issues of the present copyright law revision and its implications for librarians, educators, publishers, and AV producers.

10. Patricia Sloane, "Color Slides for Teaching Art History," *Art Journal* 31:280 (Spring 1972).

11. Less well known is the fact that the School of Library Science at Case Western Reserve University acts as a clearinghouse for all types of classification schemes and subject heading lists in several fields.

12. Wendell W. Simons and Luraine C. Tansey, *A Slide Classification System for the Organization and Automatic Indexing of Interdisciplinary Collections of Slides and Pictures* (Santa Cruz, Calif.: Univ. of California; Aug. 1970).

13. Robert M. Diamond, "A Retrieval System for 35mm Slides Utilized in Art and Humanities Instruction," in *Bibliographic Control of Nonprint Media*, ed. by Pearce S. Grove and Evelyn G. Clement (Chicago: American Library Association, 1972), p. 346-59.

14. "Classification the Key to Slide Collection Vigor," *Library Journal* 97:965-66 (15 March 1972).

15. Elizabeth M. Lewis, "A Graphic Catalog Card Index," *American Documentation* 20:238-46 (July 1969).

16. Anne Skoog and Grace Evans, "A Slide Collection Classification," *Pennsylvania Library Association Bulletin* 24:15-22 (Jan. 1969).

17. Many art historians still prefer the black and white 3¼″ × 4″ or 2″ × 2″ slide which permits one to focus more readily on details of sculpture and architecture. This group contends that color reduces the impact of the total content and detracts from the main artistic elements.

18. Patricia Sloane, "Color Slides for Teaching."

19. Ibid., p. 276.

20. Donis A. Dondis, *A Primer of Visual Literacy* (Boston: M.I.T. Press, 1973), p. 7.

21. Of special interest is W. Howard Levie, ed., "Research on Learning from Pictures: A Review and Bibliography," *Viewpoints* 49 (March 1973). *Viewpoints* is the bulletin of the School of Education, Indiana University.

22. Rudolf Arnheim, *Visual Thinking* (Berkeley: Univ. of California Pr., 1969).

23. Gyorgy Kepes, ed., *Education of Vision* Vision and Value Series (New York: G. Braziller, 1965).

24. Donis A. Dondis, *A Primer of Visual Literacy*.

25. Helmut Gernsheim and Alison Gernsheim, *The History of Photography from the Camera Obscura to the Beginning of the Modern Era* (New York: McGraw-Hill, 1969).

26. Beaumont Newhall, *The History of Photography from 1839 to the Present Day* (New York: Museum of Modern Art, 1964).

27. *The LIFE Library of Photography* (New York: TIME-LIFE Books, 1970-1972). A fifteen-volume set, which includes such topics as photojournalism, caring for photographs, the studio, light and film, the print, color, scientific and industrial photography, travel photography, and so on.

28. As cited by Donis A. Dondis, *A Primer of Visual Literacy*, p. xi.

PART

PROGRAMMING

Establishing a Cassette Program for a Public Library

by Carol M. Egan

On October 15, 1972 the Suburban Library System in Hinsdale, Illinois began a cassette program that ranks in the category of a prototype. The collection of 6,279 cassettes includes spoken word and music and was placed in eight libraries in the system. What everyone wants to know is how we did it! How did we purchase the items? What selection tools and suppliers did we work with? How did we process the cassettes? What circulation policies did we establish? And most important—how is the public reacting to the service?

BACKGROUND

It seems like quite a large order to answer all those questions, but then the whole project was of a magnitude that boggles the mind. How did we get started on such an innovative and ambitious project? As in most cases it was a combination of an idea whose time had come coupled with money being available to test the idea. The Suburban Library System received an Enrichment Grant from the state of Illinois early in 1972. After polling the membership to determine priorities for system services, SLS decided to use the grant for innovative media. The grant contained stipulations which at times proved exasperating: (1) the money had to be spent by June 30, 1972 and (2) only adult materials and no duplicates could be purchased. Thus, within five months after I was hired, purchasing for all materials for two services—framed art prints and tape cassettes—had to be completed. The framed print program was established and on display in system libraries by June 1972 and the cassette program opened officially in October 1972.

ZONE SERVICES

The system membership decided to experiment with a new circulation concept, Zone Services. The suburban area comprising SLS is a very compact one; one suburb is contiguous to another. Because there is no great distance involved, many patrons use SLS cards frequently at neighboring suburban libraries. The reciprocal borrowing statistics show these common traffic patterns. Using these patterns the 58 libraries in the system were divided into eight zone clusters. Each zone includes seven or eight libraries with varying population counts. One library in each zone is the center for framed prints, another library in each zone houses the tape cassettes, and eventually a third library will house an experimental service that is unique to that zone. The ultimate plan being that each library in the zone will be able to offer some type of specialized collection. The rationale for this method of operation is based on several facts of modern life: (1) the library no longer has to be within easy walking distance for everyone in the community because the automobile makes the facilities of many libraries within easy reach of patrons and (2) with the high cost of new materials, the great proliferation of new media introduced every day, and local resources being tightened, local libraries can no longer realistically attempt to provide all services in depth for their patrons. Zone Services is a reasonable answer in this situation because many services are still available to the public but within a short driving distance. What has often happened in the past with new services is that each individual library will purchase titles or art prints or cassettes that comprise a "basic" collection. So as a patron travels from suburb to suburb he sees the same "basics" but no in depth collections. With Zone Services, the system is able to create a varied, in depth collection in one library in each zone by spending about the same amount of money as all the individual libraries in that zone would have spent to simply duplicate each other's collections.

The prospect of central housing and booking at SLS headquarters was also explored because some systems presently circulate framed art prints and cassettes in this manner. However, after exploring the cost of setting up such a central service, it was decided the zone concept was less costly and had the advantage of placing the materials directly before the patron which generally increases use of the material.

SELECTION AND ORDERING

On the basis of desire to house the collection and provide the staff, as well as hours open and space available—eight libraries were selected to house the cassettes.

Meetings were held with the member libraries in each of the eight zones to acquaint libraries in a particular zone with each other and to gather input as to procedures and collection content. The eight zone center libraries also met separately. Information from these discussions was evaluated in relation to two factors: the types of material available in the cassette format and what was available for purchase within the established time limit. The following categories were finally determined:

A. Music
   1. Popular
   2. Classical
   3. Show tunes, humor, and nostalgia
   4. Religious, international, and miscellaneous—sound effects, etc.
B. Spoken Word
   1. The Arts: Literature, Music, Theatre, Film, Dance, and Art
   2. Travel
   3. Languages
   4. Business
   5. Career Information
   6. Self-development
   7. Issues and Insights (current events)

In all, 39 suppliers provided the 6,279 tapes in the entire collection. Each zone center houses approximately 775 tapes. Although each collection includes the same categories, the contents of each collection are entirely different from the other seven collections. Only in the areas of languages and typing/shorthand were duplicates purchased. This was done on the recommendation of the membership so that each zone center would have a supply of these very popular items. SLS paid for all the duplicates from its own budget. Approximately two-thirds of the collection is spoken word and one-third is music.

We can relate many experiences with manufacturers and distributors, but let us suffice with just a few. There is a wide variety in the quality of *tape*, in the durability of the plastic cassette *case*, and in the level of *material* recorded on the tape (all of the SLS tapes were purchased prerecorded). My first suggestion is to order items with preview privileges—especially when the company name is an unfamiliar one. For example, RCA displays high levels of recording skill, but many small operations are jumping on the cassette bandwagon and oftentimes the tapes reflect this inexperience. Another suggestion—some music tapes are manufactured by means of a Dolbyized technique which means that the natural hiss noise of the tape is reduced and what results is a wonderfully clear recording. Classical recordings were the first to use the Dolby process. Better cassette players now have a built-in Dolby mechanism which makes even regular tapes sound clearer. A Dolbyized tape does not have to be played on a Dolbyized player, but as you can imagine, the combination of a Dolbyized tape and player is high class listening. The moral: look for the word Dolby on the cassette; when you have a choice of two recordings choose the Dolbyized one.

For selection tools and ordering information I would recommend the following as basics: *Schwann Record and Tape Guide,* published monthly, for sale at all record stores for $.85. Schwann concentrates on music, however it does offer some spoken word recordings. *Harrison Tape Catalogue* is published every two months, sells for $.75 at most record stores and is quite similar to Schwann in that it concentrates on music. Harrison only lists reel to reel tapes, cassettes, and 8 track tapes; Schwann lists records as well as tapes. For spoken word tapes consult *Directory of Spoken-Voice Audio Cassettes* which lists a good selection of distributors, a wide variety of subject matter and includes annotations. To obtain a copy, write: Cassette Information Services, Box 17727, Fay Station, Los Angeles, California 90057 ($5.00). *Listening Post* is a good source for *reviews* of current music and spoken word items. A yearly subscription (10 issues) is $9.00. Write Listening Post, 15255 East Don Julian Road, City of Industry, California 91749.

PROCESSING

In processing the cassettes, the main goal was simplicity. All processing was done at the system headquarters with the aid of summer help. As the tapes arrived they were checked against invoices, listened to for brief periods on each side to enable us to catch defects immediately, assigned accession numbers, given a code letter to designate the category of the content, for example C for classical (these letters were primarily for use later in compiling the catalog), and given one of eight arbitrary letters to correspond to the eight zone centers. The end product of the identification information looked like this: TC-S71-C15 L. TC stands for tape cassette. S71 means this is a system tape purchased in the 71-72 fiscal year. C refers to classical music and fifteen is simply the accession number. The letter L tells in which of the eight collections the tape belongs. We chose letters to identify the collections rather than the zone center's name because we wanted to be able to rotate the collections in the future and thus avoid labeling the collections as to a specific library. So, for example, all tapes in the collection at Hinsdale Library are labeled L. Those at Elmwood Park are P. After the rotation, LaGrange may house Collection L.

A shelflist card was then typed to include the following information: title, artist, arrival date, supplier's name, cost, and the above identification numbers and letters. The artist is the main entry for popular recordings; the title is the main entry for shows, films and musicals; and the composer is the main entry for classical recordings, followed by the title of the work and the performer. These cards were used as our controls during the hectic weeks of processing. We worked with the cards rather than the actual cassettes whenever we needed information. The cards were filed in accession number order, later they were put in order by zones and divided by content within the zone so that the information for the tape catalog could be typed directly from the cards.

The next concern was how to package the cassettes for ease of circulation and yet eliminate the problem of pilferage which so many of the libraries were concerned about. The method chosen has proven quite workable. Each cassette is placed in a heavy duty 6″ × 9″ manila envelope which has a tie on the back rather than a metal clip because the clip breaks too easily. A pocket is glued to the front of the envelope and a book card inserted. The pocket and book card display the following information: accession number, collection letter, title and artist. All this information is necessary on *both* the pocket and the book card because the book card is retained by the library as a circulation record. Thus, if the information is not on the pocket as well, and the patron checks out several tapes, he is unable to tell which package contains which tape. The book card also contains the list price of the cassette, so the librarian can immediately tell the patron the replacement fee if the item has been lost. The accession number and collection letter are also written on the front side of the manila envelope.

Another processing question arose: How to write the collection letter and accession number on both the plastic cassette case and on the paper covering on the outside case? After trial and error we finally discovered the Sharpie pen by Sanford ($.29). It's one of those miracles of our age that's designed to write clearly on anything and won't smudge.

MULTIPLE TAPE SETS

Another decision to be made was how to package sets with multiple tapes and single copies of booklets. In the case of a set with a large number of tapes and only one booklet we ordered extra copies of the booklet and included one with each package of two, three, or four tapes. We tried not to include more than four tapes to any one package to allow the individual parts on the set to circulate to as many people as possible at any one time. We stamped all booklets "Do not write on this material" with the hope that the booklets would be acceptable for numerous circulations before they would have to be replaced.

CATALOG

In each zone center, the cassettes in their manila envelopes are stored behind the circulation desk. The patron browses through a printed catalog that is color coded for each zone and organized by subject; for example, popular and classical music with items listed by accession number and title under the subject:

Popular Music   *Collection O*

Acc.#	Artist/Composer	Title
3787	The Mothers	Just Another Band from L.A.
3788	Pink Floyd	Obscured by Clouds

Large quantities of catalogs were printed so patrons may take a copy home. The front page of the catalog lists the procedures to be followed when borrowing cassettes. The patron selects the numbers he wants from the catalog and gives the list to a library staff member who retrieves the cassettes.

CIRCULATION PROCEDURES

The tapes are circulated for two weeks at a time and may be renewed for another two weeks. Reserves are available. Each zone center has its own overdue policy. Patrons are asked to limit themselves to a reasonable number of cassettes.

Each zone center also circulates ten cassette players and adapters with a canvas carrying bag. The players and adapters may be reserved.

DAMAGE

Because it is so difficult to prove who caused damage and because cassettes are a new format for many people and thus will probably be damaged often at the beginning of the service, it was decided that borrowers will not be held responsible for damaged cassettes, however they are responsible for lost cassettes. Our experience thus far reveals a minimal amount of both damage and loss considering the size of the collection (6,279). We estimate that in these first few months of the service 35 cassettes a month are returned to us damaged, while five are lost. Those of us dealing with the service are most amazed at the small amount of loss, but we feel this is attributable almost in full to the packaging and circulation procedures being used.

DUPLICATION

Considering the staff time and equipment it would take to repair damaged cassettes with the end result that the cassette is still weak in one spot and will probably break again soon, we decided it would be less expensive in the long run to buy a new cassette. Although SLS replaces damaged cassettes with new ones, many libraries and schools have chosen to make duplicates of their original tapes and circulate the duplicates. When damage does occur, they simply dispose of the damaged cassette and duplicate the original. However, there are several factors to consider in such an arrangement: (1) duplicators are expensive—$1500–2000 and up, (2) generally a clerk or skilled technician is needed to run the duplicator (depending on the complexity of the machinery) and someone has to type labels to affix to the new copies, (3) blank tape and labels need to be purchased, (4) occasionally the duplicator needs costly repair, and last but certainly not least, (5) the whole operation can be interpreted as a violation of the copyright laws unless specific permission for copying has been given (and few manufacturers will do this). In fact, the SLS Board decided that we could not duplicate any tape unless we acquired express permission from the manufacturer either in writing or from a printed statement on the cassette itself.

CIRCULATION STATISTICS

And now for the most important question of all—how is the public reacting to the tape cassette service? The response can be expressed in one word: fantastic! In the first full month of service 4,056 cassettes from a collection of 6,729 circulated. One library circulated 100 the first day. Every month since (the service has been in effect for 6½ months) the circulation has been hovering around 3,500–4,000. The public is surprised at finding cassettes in the library, astounded by the variety of the collection and amazed that cassette players and adapters can also be checked out free. Most people expect to find lots of music and little else, but when they discover cassettes on "How to be a Better Salesman" and "Tax Advantages" they are elated. One sales manager has his men check out cassettes and listen to them during their many hours on the road. Another lady gave her daughter some literature tapes read by Basil Rathbone to take to her elementary school literature class. One patron admits to giving up television viewing since the tape cassette service started—she finds the variety of tapes more interesting!

A side development in connection with the cassette and framed print services is the success of the Zone Services concept. Circulation for these two new services to people *other than the local* patrons of the zone center library has increased steadily since the service began. During the first month of the cassette service, 42 percent of the circulation was to patrons other than the local patrons of the zone center library. That figure has now increased to 62 percent of circulation. This zone circulation figure represents both those items requested at the local level then delivered to local libraries via the SLS van drivers and those circulations in which the patron physically travels to another library to pick up the materials. So it appears that not only is the cassette service being enthusiastically received by library patrons, but also the patrons are responding quite readily to the zone center concept of housing and circulating materials—an interesting development on which to base future library development plans.

PROMOTION

Promotion for the tape cassette service was approached from several angles. First a colorful poster announcing that cassettes were coming to the library was distributed to all the libraries in the system a few months prior to the actual availability of the cassettes. This created an interest and built up demand by the time the cassettes actually arrived on the scene. Next the tape cassette catalog for each zone was printed. It includes a cover sheet explaining the borrowing policies for the service and individual sheets with lists of tapes on various subject areas. The lists are arranged by accession number under the subject headings. Enough catalogs were printed so that patrons may take them home for browsing at their leisure. This allows the patron to become more familiar with the collection and to pass the booklet on to other friends with whom he discusses this new library service. A news release stressing the variety of the collection and the fact that both cassettes and cassette players are now available in libraries was sent to all libraries in the system to be distributed to local papers. Some papers sent reporters to take pictures of people checking cassettes out of the library. One patron became interested in the service, and wrote a feature article on the framed art print and cassette programs and the new concept of Zone Services for his newspaper. I have spoken to community groups using a traveling display of the new types of media available through their library. Our best publicity however is the surprised and pleased patron who tells his neighbors about what's new at the library!

ROTATION

The original plan of action called for all eight collections to be rotated from one zone center to another once a year. Thus each zone center will have an entirely new collection for its public to choose from each year and the present group of tapes will not reach exposure saturation for eight years. Hopefully, the rotation of tapes will keep interest alive in the cassette collection.

EVALUATION

There are still lots of decisions to make. Should the packaged tapes be put on open shelves rather than have the librarian do all the retrieving or will this lead to wholesale pilfering? What are the least and most popular titles? Should we buy duplicates of popular items or continue to buy single copies of new materials? Should the collections include materials for children? Do we want to purchase more cassette players or use this money for materials and expect patrons to begin buying their own players?

Even though we have had considerable experience in establishing a cassette collection there are still many questions about how to provide the most effective service, but we do feel we have taken a giant step in the right direction based on the public's response to the program thus far. Innovative media is an exciting and challenging area in which to work because it is new and developing and expanding in so many different directions.

The Library as Guardian of Oral History Materials: An Example from Berkeley

by Willa Baum

The tremendous growth of oral history in the last decade has meant that most libraries will be faced with the requirement to access, process, preserve, and service the materials of oral history. In addition, libraries may well be asked to direct the doing of an oral history project. Beyond the mention of a few how-to-do-it manuals in the bibliography, this article will deal only with the handling of oral history materials after they come to the library.

Oral history materials may be assigned to the library from a variety of sources. Perhaps they will be produced by the institution itself, either by a department of the library, or by an academic department of the school of which the library is a part. They may be produced by an independent group such as a historical society, a temporary research project, an ethnic or cultural group, a Bicentennial project, or an individual writer who is using interviewing as one means of acquiring data. Many excellent tape recorded interviews can come to the library as donated tapes from patrons who have recorded members of their family or someone else who has caught their interest.

The oral history materials will come in a motley variety of shapes, sizes, and conditions. There may be cassette or reel tapes; folders or binders of transcripts; photographs of assorted sizes, framed and unframed; supplementary materials ranging from diaries, scrapbooks, newspaper clippings, business ledgers, to wills and marriage certificates; and artifacts like political campaign buttons and academic gowns. All of these things may be clearly labeled and explained as to why and wherefore they were gotten together, or they may be almost without identifications. They may be donated for the open use of all patrons, or come in with all sorts of special conditions. Not having the simple format of an author, a title, and an assigned LC catalog number, they will pose problems in how to catalog them so that users can find them, even if the librarian has been successful in figuring out how to shelve them.

This article will present a few considerations for the librarian faced with handling oral history materials, and then describe how oral history materials are housed and serviced in The Bancroft Library. The system in The Bancroft Library is just evolving, all does not run routinely and smoothly yet, and what works for a large manuscript library like The Bancroft may not be suitable for another kind of library. But it is hoped these examples will be of some help to libraries in setting up their own system for handling oral history materials.

CONSIDERATIONS IN THE HANDLING OF MATERIALS

Provenance: The significance of any oral history collection will be substantially enhanced if the user knows something about the circumstances of its production and deposit in the library, as well as what it contains. Information the library should acquire at the time of accession includes: 1.) Name and identification of the person or group who conducted the interviews. 2.) Name and identification of the donor and how he got the collection (if he is not the interviewer). 3.) Why the interviews were done. (Were they done under the auspices of a centennial committee to research the town's history, a professor's history as a teaching exercise, a railroad buff recording old-time trainmen for his own interest, etc.). 4.) When were they recorded? 5.) Who were the interviewees?—names, dates of birth and death if available, description (occupation, participant in the Pullman Strike, longtime resident of Plumas County, etc.). 6.) A summary of the subject contents of the tapes/transcripts.

An easy way to get this information is to print up a form for donors of oral history materials to fill out. A copy of the filled-out form can be attached to the tapes, the transcript, and to any related materials. Another copy can go into the "oral history binder."

Permission to Use: The library should get a written statement of assignment from the donor of the oral history materials. This statement should indicate that the materials are open for scholarly or educational use. If the donor wishes to place restrictions on use, such as, for example, exclusive publication rights for a specified period of time, get that in writing with a definite date when the restrictions expire.

The library should ascertain from the donor whether the persons interviewed knew and agreed to have the interviews placed in a library for public use. If there is any question about this, it would be prudent for the library to itself, or through the good offices of the donor, request a signed release from the interviewee and the interviewer of each interview. A very simple printed release form will suffice. *(Figure 1: Donated Tapes Collection- Release Form)*

Shelving and Preservation: Tapes do well under the same conditions of housing as are recommended for papers and photographs; that is, a clean environment (no smoking, no eating) of stable humidity (40–60 percent) and stable temperature (60–70°F). Therefore, all oral history materials can be stored together in manuscript boxes. However, for reasons of maximum use of space, tapes are often stored separately from papers. If this is done, all the materials relating to one interview must be so catalogued that patrons know of the existence of all units and the librarian can reassemble them from their separate shelves.

Tapes should be stored upright in the box they came in, away from a magnetic field. Rewinding the tape once a year is recommended to reduce the chance of stretching portions that may have been wound too tightly and to reduce print-through. However, our office has twenty-year-old tapes that have only been listened to a few times and have not been rewound otherwise and they still produce excellent sound. But if possible, set up a system of routine rewinding, perhaps every five years.

Cataloging: Intelligently-done cataloging is the key to whether the library's oral history materials will prove an exciting new resource or will be lost on some dusty shelf, yet the irregular form of the materials may confuse the cataloguer. Oral history materials, tape or transcripts, should be listed in the main catalog, not relegated to a special catalog on audio-visual materials. The important thing about oral history is not that it is sound, although that can be important too, but that it is a first-person

FIGURE 1: DONATED TAPES COLLECTION—RELEASE FORM

Donated Tapes Collection
Regional Oral History Office
The Bancroft Library
University of California
Berkeley, California 94720

I hereby give to The Bancroft Library for such scholarly and educational use and purposes as the Director of The Bancroft Library shall determine the following tape(s) of Interviews recorded on ＿＿＿＿＿＿＿＿＿＿＿＿.
                                                                          date(s)

＿＿＿＿＿＿＿＿＿＿＿＿＿＿
Name of narrator

＿＿＿＿＿＿＿＿＿＿＿＿＿＿
Address of narrator

＿＿＿＿＿＿＿＿＿＿＿＿＿＿
Name of interviewer

＿＿＿＿＿＿＿＿＿＿＿＿＿＿
Address of interviewer

＿＿＿＿＿＿＿＿＿＿＿＿
Date of agreement
Subject of tape(s)

＿＿＿＿＿＿＿＿＿＿＿＿
＿＿＿＿＿＿＿＿＿＿＿＿
＿＿＿＿＿＿＿＿＿＿＿＿
＿＿＿＿＿＿＿＿＿＿＿＿
＿＿＿＿＿＿＿＿＿＿＿＿

account of past events or a way of life that is of historical interest. In order to establish catalog entries, the cataloguer will have to evaluate the probable uses for each collection of oral history materials. The narrator may be sufficiently well-known in his locality or field that his name is already a subject-identification (Earl Warren) or he may be unknown, his significance coming from the class of persons he belongs to (suffragists, pioneer women, the WPA accounts by former slaves) or the events he describes (a sailor in Pearl Harbor on December 7, 1941).

Most likely the main entry will be the narrator's name, but it could be the subject of a group of interviews, i.e., "San Francisco Earthquake and Fire, 1906—a collection of 30 interviews with survivors."

Added entries should be: 1.) One or several subjects the interview deals with, 2.) The group or individual under whose auspices the interview was conducted (Menlo Park Historical Society, Studs Terkel), 3.) The category "oral history"—because teachers, radio and TV producers, and writers are now searching for this type of personal material. The "oral history" card could simply refer patrons to a listing of all sound recordings, which could there be divided into oral history, speeches, radio broadcasts, performances, etc.

The main entry card should indicate interviewee, interviewer, date(s) of recording and/or completion of the interview, project series (if done as a series on a certain topic), major subjects discussed, medium (cassette or phonotape), speed, pages of transcript or time of a tape (don't indicate footage), additional materials (introduction, bibliography, photos, etc.), any restrictions, other materials available elsewhere as "Phonotape also available;" "transcript also available."

Servicing: As with any unique materials, precautions must be taken for the safety of the materials while in use by patrons. For transcripts and papers, this means the usual precautions relating to manuscripts, such as that they be noncirculating, used in the reading room only, no use of ink while using them, etc. For tapes, this means providing the patron with a play back machine that will play the tape or cassette and that has a lock affixed to the "record" button in such a way that the patron cannot erase the tape by error.

Of course, if the library can afford to make patron-use copies while retaining the archival copies, the patron-use copies can circulate just as any other replaceable item.

A second consideration is that any restrictions on use be strictly adhered to. This means the catalog card should be marked with the restrictions, and also each item should be clearly marked so that it cannot be brought to a patron in error without the librarian noticing the restriction. Items which are completely closed can be put away in a sealed-package, marked with the date of opening, and pose no problem, but those which, for example, can be used only with the written permission of the narrator, or by certain classes of persons (recognized scholars), etc., or under certain conditions have to be clearly marked on the tape/transcript so that anyone working at the service desk will be aware of the restrictions.

A routine way of handling any requirements on the use of oral history materials, as of any materials, needs to be worked out and made known to all service librarians.

Finding Aids: In addition to the in-library aids—catalog cards, maybe lists or guides for patrons on special materials in certain fields of research —full use of oral history materials requires that their existence be made known to the community of prospective users. This can be done in several ways: 1.) Announcement of the accession of the materials in the local newspaper, library newsletter, local or state historical newsletters, and journals in the field of the materials; 2.) Inclusion in a regional or state bibliography of oral history or local history resources; 3.) Inclusion in the National Union Catalog of Manuscript Collections. NUCMC will only accept notice of transcripts (not tapes; they are a directory of *manuscript* collections) which total at least a foot in shelf space so only substantial collections can be listed there; 4.) Oral History collection directories—the most recent finding aid for oral history is *Oral History Collections* (Bowker, 1975), which lists oral history projects, and interviews by narrator and subject. This first directory leaves much to be changed and improved, but if holders of significant oral history materials will submit information to the directory, subsequent editions can become a major finding aid.

HANDLING OF MATERIALS IN THE BANCROFT LIBRARY

The Bancroft Library is a major research center on the Berkeley campus of the University of California consisting of a non-circulating collection of books, manuscripts, pictures, maps, and other materials with an emphasis on the history of western North America. The Regional Oral History Office, a department of The Bancroft Library, tape-records the recollections of persons who have contributed significantly to the development of the West and the nation. Typed, indexed transcripts are prepared for scholarly use.

In addition, the Office collects tape recordings produced by individual researchers (the Donated Tapes Collection), and advises researchers in the use of oral history materials or methodology.

Transcripts and related papers are transferred to the Manuscripts Division, and tapes to the Microfilm/Audio-Visual Division for cataloging and preservation, and for patron use in the reading room in the following steps:

Transcripts and Papers: *(Figure 2: Transcript Catalog Card)* 1.)Completed transcript (with title, table of contents, photographs, index) is transferred to Manuscripts Division. Also transferred are any papers or photographs relevant to the transcript. 2.) Manuscripts Division accessions transcript and related papers and assigns a call number based on order of accession. 3.) The Manuscripts Division prepares catalog cards which include the following: name of interviewee, title of interview, dates of interview and completed transcript, name of interviewer, and

FIGURE 2: SAMPLE CATALOG CARDS FOR ORAL HISTORY MANUSCRIPT CATALOG CARDS

Partial phonotape also available
Please inquire at Desk

72/105 Rinder, Rose (Perlmutter)
    C   Music, Prayer and Religious Leadership, Temple Emanu-El, 1913–1969, Berkeley, Calif. 1971.

    [44], 1841. Ms. 28 cm.

    Photocopy of typed transcript of tape-recorded interviews conducted 1968–1969 by Malca Chall for Bancroft Library Regional Oral History Office. Introduction by Rabbi Louis I. Newman. Photographs inserted.

    SEALED UNTIL JANUARY 1973 EXCEPT WITH MRS. RINDER'S WRITTEN PERMISSION.

                        CONTINUED ON NEXT CARD

Notation: Phonotape available
Notation: Interview sealed until specified date

72/105 Rinder, Rose P. Music, Prayer . . . (card 2)
    C   Recollection of the years she and her husband Cantor Reuben Rinder were associated with Temple Emanu-El in San Francisco; their participation in musical life of the Bay Area; their friendship with many musicians including Ernest Bloch, Yehudi Menuhin, Isaac Stern and others.

    Copies of letters, programs, and other documentary material inserted.

                        (OVER)

1. Rinder, Reuben, 1887–1966 2. Jews in California 3. San Francisco, Temple Emanu-El x-3. Templ-El. San Francisco 4. Music—San Francisco 5. Musicians —Correspondence, reminiscences, etc. 6. Bloch, Ernest, 1880–1959 7. Menuhin, Yehudi, 1916– 8. Stern, Isaac, 1920–
I. Bancroft Library. Regional Oral History Office II. Newman, Louis Israel, 1893–

Tracings–Rinder, Rose. Cards crossfiled under these entries.

subject summary of contents. Any restrictions to use of the transcript are noted on the card. Availability of a phonotape is also noted. 4.) Catalog cards are filed in the manuscripts catalog under the name of the interviewee, with added entry cards for The Bancroft Library/Regional Oral History Office, and cards also for the major subjects covered. 5.) Patron requests transcript by call number. Text must be read in reading room. A limited number of pages can be copied by photocopy.

Tapes: *(Figure 3: Sound Recordings Catalog Card)* 1.) Tapes are transferred to Microfilm/Audio-Visual Division with notes about the recording such as names and addresses of narrator and interviewer, occasion for interview, order of subjects discussed, spelling of names, etc. 2.) Tapes are assigned call numbers by order of accession. 3.) A catalog card is

FIGURE 3: SOUND RECORDING CATALOG CARD

Rinder, Rose (Perlmutter)   (Mrs. Reuben)
Inquire at Desk for listing(s) for Phonotape 303

More information on phonotape listed in a notebook at desk.

FIGURE 4: SAMPLE PHONOTAPE LISTING

Leaf from the notebook reserved at the Bancroft Library Service Desk. Note that the phonotape listing also refers the user to the transcript. Users request phonotape by call number. The tape is brought to them with a compatible tape recorder and earphones for listening. (A = 5" reel; B = 7" reel; C = cassette.)

PHONOTAPE

302:1 Richardson, Leon Josiah, 1868–1964.
  B   cInterview on the history of the University of California Extension
          Division and President Benjamin Ide Wheeler, 1959.
          1 reel (7") 3¾ ips
          plastic; full track (1–575 ft.)
          Excerpt. ROHO interview by Amelia R. Fry.
          Transcript available as C-D 4048.
          ROHO transfer, May 1974.

303   Rinder, Rose (Perlmutter)   (Mrs. Reuben)
  A   cInterview on music and musicians in San Francisco in the 1930's,
          Oct. 3, 1968.
          1 reel (5") 3¾ ips
          plastic; ½ track
          track 1—1082 ft. track 2—508 ft.
          Includes comments on early training of Yehudi Menuhin.
          Jews in Calif. Interview No. 2. Complete tape. ROHO interview by
          Malca Chall.
          Transcript available as 72/105 c. *(reference to transcript)* ROHO trans-
          fer, May 1974.

prepared; main entry is by interviewee's name; added entries are major subject(s) discussed in the recording. The catalog cards are very brief and serve chiefly to guide the patron to a slightly more detailed list of recordings at the service desk. This listing indicates interviewee, subject of interview, interviewer, length of tape, possibly the availability of a transcript, interview notes, correspondence, clippings, etc. 4.) Catalog cards are entered in Motion Pictures and Sound Recordings catalog. 5.) Patron requests tape by call number. It is delivered to reading room with a suitable tape recorder and earphones for listening. Tapes may not be copied for patrons except by special permission from the interviewee and the Director of The Bancroft Library.

Other Retrieval Aids: *(Figure 4: Sample Phonotape Listings)* 1.) ROHO prepares lists of interviews by topic (agriculture, forestry, wine industry, labor, etc.) which are available in a binder at the service desk. 2.) ROHO maintains a cumulative index to all transcripts, which consists of a compilation of all the index cards made in the preparation of the indexes for each transcript. 3.) Transcript listings are submitted to the National Union Catalog of Manuscript Collections, Library of Congress, when a sufficient number have been done in one subject field to qualify as an entry. (ROHO—Regional Oral History Office)

BIBLIOGRAPHY

Baum, Willa K. *Oral History for the Local Historical Society*. American Association for State and Local History, 1315 Eighth Avenue South, Nashville, Tennessee 37203. 63p. 1974. $2.25 (order directly).

Custer, Arline. "Bibliographic Identification and Description of Oral History Records," in *Selections from the Fifth and Sixth National Colloquium on Oral History*. Oral History Association, 1970–71, pp. 99–102.

Forms Manual. Society of American Archivists, 1627 Fidelity Building, 123 South Broad St., Philadelphia Pa. 19106. 1973. $8.00. Good examples of library forms for control and servicing of oral history materials in large and small libraries. (Order directly.)

A Guide for Oral History Programs. Oral History Program, California State University, Fullerton, California 92634. 347 p. 1973 $8.00. A how-to-do-it manual that gives examples of catalog cards and a bibliographic listing of an interview series. (Order directly.)

The Handling and Storage of Magnetic Recording Tape. Product Communications Division. 3M Company, St. Paul, Minnesota 55101. Free. An excellent basic booklet on how to store tapes. (Order directly.)

McCracken, Jane (ed.). *Oral History-Basic Techniques*. Manitoba Museum, 190 Rupert Avenue, Winnipeg, Manitoba R38 ON 2, Canada. 20 p. 1974. $1.00. Good examples of an interview question outline and an index to an interview. (Order directly.)

Tyrrell, William G. *Tape Recording Local History*. American Association for State and Local History, 1315 Eighth Avenue South, Nashville, Tennessee 37203. 12p. 1966. 50 cents. (Order directly.)

Zachert, Martha Jane. "The Implications of Oral History for Librarians," *College and Research Libraries*, March, 1968. Pp. 101–103.

Note: The author wishes to thank Estelle Rebec, department head, Manuscript Division, and Vivian Fisher, department head, Microfilm/Audio-Visual Division, for their help in describing The Bancroft Library's procedures.

Photography!

by Dennis Maness

Instead of just collecting photographs, why not use them for functional and aesthetic purposes? Here are ways to brighten your library, improve your public relations, and have fun with your junior patrons.

1. Use photos in place of (or in addition to) posters, paintings, etc., as decoration. How about a great ski photo when it's 98° outside, or a stunningly backlit blossom in the middle of January, or a beautiful seascape anytime?

2. If a natural disaster strikes, e.g., oil-spills in California or the recent flooding, put together an exhibit showing before and after scenes, how the people reacted, etc. Both newspapers and amateur photographers are good sources for the photos.

3. Buy a lot of cheap (50¢ to $1) old box cameras and circulate these to kids when you have a program involving photography. A good source for old cameras is a thrift/second-hand store. Maybe your Friends organization will buy you a nice collection of the Instamatic-type of camera ($4 to $10); film may be easier to get for these.

4. Organizations such as Kodak, UNESCO, and the New York Museum of Modern Art send traveling exhibits around the country for just the price of postage. Apply for one of these.

5. If you can't get one of the above exhibits, make your own using your local photographers, both amateur and professional.

6. Perk up your building with a different kind of directional sign! Use photos of an outhouse or Mens' room sign; a copy machine; the circulation desk—all of these with a hand pointing in the right direction.

7. If your collection is departmentalized, or if you separate science fiction westerns, biography, etc., from the rest of the collection, use a photograph as a sign. It doesn't need to be a literal picture; an abstract photo suggesting a well-known person or a fantasy subject is sometimes more effective and eye-catching.

8. Use frames in which you can change the photos for #7 above and use prints either submitted by patrons or have a monthly contest to "fill the frame."

9. Photos can show how to use the library, e.g., a photo-essay on how to check out a book or how to use the audio-visual equipment.

10. Use a Polaroid to take portraits of kids who win contests or complete reading programs.
11. Use a Polaroid to take portraits of kids who don't win contests or complete reading programs. (In fact, I like this idea better.)
12. Photograph behind-the-scenes activities of the library such as book processing, ("My goodness, I didn't know you had to do all that!") and display them.
13. In conjunction with #12 above, invite your local camera club to do a photo-essay on what a librarian does besides read and check out books. Then display their prints.
14. If your city doesn't have a photo-center, invite teachers and lecturers to the library to give demonstrations. (Developing and printing photos doesn't really have to be messy, but you do need a light-tight room).
15. Have kids make their own cameras and award a prize for the biggest, smallest, prettiest, funniest, etc., *working* one. All they need is a light-tight box and some film. Kodak puts out an excellent pamphlet (free!) on the making and use of a pinhole camera.
16. For display, invite your local camera club to submit photos based on one theme. This could be different each month.
17. If your newspaper or city government doesn't sponsor a city-wide photo contest, you do it and display the results. If another organization does have a contest, invite them to use the library to display the entries.
18. If you have a bookmobile or a media-machine, photograph its activities. Use the photos for public relations and for your historical archives.
19. Have a businessman (policeman, teacher, worker, any type of person in your local community)-of-the-month. Photograph him, his business, at work, in the library (!) and display the prints in a prominent place. This is a good way to involve people in the library who wouldn't think of it otherwise.
20. If your library has a collection of photographs (the older the better) don't let it gather dust; use it as a traveling exhibit to hospitals, banks, booths at fairs and carnivals.
21. Photograph special activities or programs and use them either for displays, publicity, or a scrapbook.
22. Make a jigsaw puzzle from a picture of each child participating in a reading program. As each book is read, let him add another part to the prominently displayed puzzle.
23. If you use puppets or stuffed animals for your programs (or if your younger patrons make them) print real people's faces onto the face of the puppet. (Liquid photographic emulsion can be purchased so that a photo can be printed on practically anything.)
24. Have the kids make puppets or dolls by pasting photos of themselves onto cardboard and then tying the various parts of the body together with string.

25. Using Printing-Out-Paper (this is the red or sepia-toned paper that photographers' proofs come on) let the kids make photograms of anything small (hands or pocket/purse items). You don't need a darkroom or chemicals, just sunlight. The prints will fade after a while unless they are fixed, but they're fun while they last.

Two final bits of advice: use original prints—not photos cut out of magazines and newspapers or photocopied from some other source; when children are making the photographs, don't worry about the quality —it's fun no matter how it turns out.

An Eye for An I

by Susan Rice

Adult: "Would you like to see one long movie or a lot of short ones?"
Children: "A lot of long ones!"

Three years ago the Center for Understanding Media embarked on a program involving children and movies. We valued both and thought they could help each other. We didn't conceive of the Children's Film Theatre project as a particularly revolutionary or complex experiment; it wasn't regulated by the varia of scientific calibration. We did not seek to prove that children's reading levels would increase proportionally to their exposure to film through the administration of reading readiness tests, nor did we wire their brains to electrodes to establish a link between heightened psycho-motor responses and flickering wall stimuli. What we did do was simply to undertake a *documented* program involving regularly scheduled screenings and evaluation of children's films. We did this because no extensive or reasonably current listing of children's films—not to mention one based on the observed responses and feelings of *children* themselves—was available. Anyone interested in using films with children was forced to rely on the catalogue descriptions of the distribution companies (hardly a reliable resource) or on the repeated use of well-known children's film 'classics' (like *The Red Balloon* and *The Golden Fish*) with which many of the children were already familiar. Those impartial listings that did exist generally sprang from the fevered imaginations of adults whose experience with the films was restricted to the sanctity of preview screening rooms, whose evaluations were for the most part arrived at on the basis of what children *should* like rather than what they *do* like.

When we initiated the Children's Film Theatre, we took as 'given' the principle that children can develop good taste by tasting good things, that entertaining movies were always—directly or indirectly—'educational' (while the inverse did not always hold true), and that short films were a more appropriate medium for small people than features.

The project itself extended for two years and involved over 4000 children—from public, private and parochial schools, day-care centers, after-school programs, community groups and nurseries. The film programs were generally 40-60 minutes long. The size of the audience varied from 8-200, though we came to prefer much smaller groups (30-40) for the kinds of activities we liked to do after the films. The groups were economically and racially mixed and, in some cases, polylingual; some of the children spoke no English at all. Ages ranged from 3½-10. We did not often combine age groups at single screenings, although we did use most of the films with all age groups.

It has been over one year since the American Library Association published *Films Kids Like*, an annotated catalog of 225 short films for children that resulted from the Children's Film Theatre project. My purpose here is certainly not to reiterate or capsulize the information that can be found there. I am not, of course, above plugging the book and I do feel it is an invaluable aid to anyone interested in children, children's films and how to show films to kids. The philosophy and the nuts and bolts information are set forth in the Introduction to *FKL* as economically as I know how. Obviously, I commend the book to you.

Upon compiling *Films Kids Like*, I found myself one of a common contemporary phenomenon: the instant expert. I was invited to give speeches and lead seminars. I found myself lecturing people who had given more of themselves to children and children's media than I could ever hope to do. Some of them asked for more specific information, PROOF! (like electrodes) . . . others wanted to know what could possibly be educational about a film that didn't use words to convey its meaning . . . still others wondered why films should be any more effective than chalk as a medium of expression or inspiration . . . I paint a grim picture. Generally the response to our project was interested and enthusiastic. And I learned a great deal from the audiences I spoke to, much of which I wished we had thought to include in *Films Kids Like*. We didn't do it then, so I am going to do it now.

Because I am a strong believer in active participation rather than passive responses, I am going to ask you to play along with me as I administer this little True or False Quiz. (No looking at your neighbor's *Sightlines!*)

LITTLE TRUE OR FALSE QUIZ.

1. *American films for children fall far below the level of foreign films for children.*   T☐   F☐

False. Sort of. American animation generally falls below the level of animation done in countries like Czechoslovakia, Bulgaria, and Hungary (did I leave out Canada? Again?), but people like Eli Noyes, Jr. and Bruce Cayard are fast closing the gap. Americans tend to restrict themselves to line animation, clay animation and pixilation, while middle European animators seem to move just about anything they can work their hands on — glass, wool, wood, photographs, things you can't even identify. This may be explained by the generosity of the governments who put their money behind the ideology that childhood is the most vital and influential time of our lives, etc. etc., whereas children's filmmaking in the good old

U.S. of A. falls plumply into the arena of free enterprise. And we are just beginning to realize what a firm investment (literally) children are, even as consumers of animation. This has meant a boon for cartoons—mostly the television variety which involve little more than the animation of mouths and occasional hands or eyelids. But it also means that film distributors are beginning to recognize a real market for children's films. And some of those distributors would as soon spend their money on imaginative animation and imagination as they would on the predictable talking sticks. In the area of live-action filmmaking for children, this country is faring far better than even the largest producers of children's films—India and Japan. This subject is an apt one for much closer examination, so suffice it to say that (unlike almost anything else) things are looking better for American short films for children.

2. *Silence is Golden.*   T□ F□
False. Kids talk for a number of reasons . . . because they're bored (although they tend to move more than talk when that is the case), because they're interested, because they're frightened, because they're involved. When you use films with kids you become fairly sensitive to what the talk means. We found out as much about the children's feelings and reactions from what they said *during* the films as anything else. This is the TV generation—they have been reared to concentrate on small moving images and vague sounds while all kinds of hell is breaking loose around them. Think what a pleasure it is to have a *big* image and high fidelity sound to lose yourself in with all kinds of hell breaking loose around you. Kids do not seem to be terribly distracted by the talking of other kids; sometimes they are comforted by it.

3. *If a group gets too raucous, stop the projector.*   T□ F□
True. Let the punishment fit the crime.

4. *Movies for children should always be properly introduced.*   T□ F□
False. Movies for children should always be judiciously screened prior to showing to see if any introduction is required. Ushers in movie houses don't tell us anything about what we are going to see, why breed the expectation in children? Dwight MacDonald, one of the most revered American film critics, when he attempted to introduce classics of the screen for his course in film at Santa Cruz, was implored by his students often to "shut up and show the movie!" Children who can't read like to know the name of a movie. It's only fair that they should know. Unless you think you can do a better rendering of the subject matter than the filmmaker, that information should suffice, along with the number of films on the program. Kids like to know how much they're in for and they like to count down. I guess it makes them feel a part of things.

5. *Quality films work in every situation for audiences large and small.* T□ F□
False. Some films that work wonderfully in small groups (up to 40) fail miserably in large (100 or more) screening situations. Some that work well in large situations are flat in more intimate settings. Age, of course, of both the film and the audience is a major variable, as well. To find out

which films work in what situations, you can either toy with disaster or acquire a copy of *Films Kids Like*. We are currently looking more deeply into the matter of small and large audiences for children's films and will include a special section on this subject in the Supplement to *FKL* which should be out within a year.

6. *Kids like animated cartoons best.*   T☐ F☐

False. Kids are most familiar with animated cartoons and the recognition factor is a source of delight for them, a feeling of power. Kids also like live-action movies with kids in them that they can identify with. They like story films of books they have read (recognition again). And they also like straightforward, slow-moving, narrated, linear portraits that don't bear the slightest resemblance to TV commercials. Kids like movies that respect them and that allow them to respond (even if unconsciously) to a sensuous surface. Of course kids like some animated cartoons—but not a whole program of them. A whole program of any one genre is suicide. Mix it up . . . live action, animation, narrated, non-narrated, fairy tales, music films, story books, sports. You know.

7. *Movies make children violent.*   T☐ F☐

True. Not all movies by any means. But some. First, the bad news: I have actually seen children begin to hit one another upon viewing one of those sportsthrillclimax films. Now, the good news: There was no hitting or violence when the same film was shown with a warning prior to screening. Occasionally one must invoke Rice's Rule of Order: Use Threats Before Some Films. (e.g. "No more movies if I see anybody so much as move.") You'll recognize the films that require the invocation of this Rule the moment you pre-screen them. You have one other option in desperate situations: make the primary offenders light captains or projector watchers. If this seems like rewarding vice, it is. But it is far from punishing virtue which is what happens to the rest of the audience when a couple of chronically loud or aggressively angry kids begin to cut up.

8. *Movies work miracles.*   T☐ F☐

False. Movies cannot make the lame walk or the blind see. They are a medium; they are affected by those who generate them and those who receive them. In this respect, perhaps, movies are no more than a book, a painting or a piece of chalk. But they are also magic. I know of no other medium that so thoroughly widens the eyes, engages the senses and plunges us so intensely into a waking dream conjoining conscious and unconscious states. And movies do even more for children. At their best they provide feelings of identity, affiliation and power in most dramatic form. And these experiences can resonate for a lifetime.

Building a Coherent Features Program

by Ted Perry

The issue I am speaking to is the building of a collection of feature films in the public library. The principles also apply just as well to programming within libraries.

To begin with, let me relate two experiences of my own which will inform whatever I have to say about feature films for libraries.

First, as a member of the New York State Council on the Arts Film—TV and Media Panel for the past three years I have often reviewed requests for funds to place feature films in libraries. With very few exceptions, the list of proposed films was mundane, predictable, and consisted almost entirely of entertainment films, many of which are often available on television.

The second experience has to do with what happened when, several years ago, our department at New York University sent several students out into community centers, libraries, and museums to present film lectures. Often, the libraries and other sites insisted that we do programs on very popular topics, such as film comedy, the western, and gangster films.

With a few exceptions, then, my impression of what libraries want is feature films which are entertainment-oriented and safe, that is, presenting no controversial views about politics, sex, or even the experience of watching film as film. In many respects, then, the libraries are asking for the most typical mass consumer product, that is, films which are almost totally entertainment industry oriented. I'm sure that the reasons for this are extremely complex and much of it has to do with the fact that librarians have not been helped in the selection of films. Today's conference is certainly a step in that direction. Also, I doubt that librarians have been exposed to all the films that I personally would wish that they had seen. Only a few places, such as the Film Library Information Council, The Educational Film Library Association, and others, have been willing to render any service to the librarian when it came to selection. But, for whatever reasons and however justified, the library selections I have seen most often have been somewhat less than adventurous, to put it gracefully. A good librarian would never think of buying only Rod McKuen books for the poetry shelf, but that sometimes seems to be the attitude when contemplating feature film purchase or programming.

So, if I have anything at all to say to you, it is that I would hope that librarians would think more often in a broader and more adventurous spectrum in selecting films, seeking and expecting advice from film people and from whatever other sources are available.

How does one make a more adventurous selection of films? I can't give you a list of films today, because each library must have its own special needs. Some have special needs in relationship to their community. Others wish to buy only a few films, and some acquire titles in large numbers. In some respects, it would be quite easy for me to say to you that you should subscribe to the leading film periodicals that deal with narrative cinema. But that is the easy way out. What I would rather do is suggest, by giving certain guidelines, a means for selection in building a feature film library. I would like to supply some of the criteria which I think are important. These criteria revolve around several areas: history, genre, other media, countries, directors, and form.

In the first area, that of history, some attempt should be made to select films which represent important moments in the history of film, such as the birth of the cinema. In this category, up until 1911 or so, the term feature is not meaningful since most of the films were considerably shorter than the ninety minutes we usually associate with the term "feature film." Nevertheless, this early period is highly important, especially if one is interested in the development of film narrative during that period and the influence of various other media; cartoons, still photography, melodrama, popular literature, and so on. I've been quite amazed at the extraordinary response that the Museum of Modern Art has received for its D. W. Griffith retrospective. The audiences have responded overwhelmingly to the very earliest Griffith Biograph films. This is some indication, I think, that what seems like terribly adventurous programing in many cases turns out to be quite acceptable to large audiences. Another important historical period is the transition to sound, also the dissolution of the big studios in the fifties and the coming of the independently produced films, such as *Easy Rider,* in the sixties. Or the influence of *cinema verité* technology upon films. We see feature films, such as *Faces, Woman Under the Influence,* or *Battle of Algiers,* which directly show the influence of television and of *cinema verité* technology. Some periods of historical importance are related to particular countries, and I will come back to that in a moment, but the point is quite simple. One must give some attention to the watershed historical aspects of the motion picture, that is, the crucial times when the motion picture presented itself as a formidable, unique force in the history of twentieth century art forms.

PERIODS RELATED TO COUNTRIES

I spoke of selection by countries. There are certain particular countries which have, at one time or another, for one reason or another, risen to the forefront in the international cinema. The Italian, Scandinavian, French, and American cinema were of immense importance prior to World War II. The Italian cinema took years to recover from the effects of the War and other internal problems, but certainly until the coming of sound, the American, Scandinavian, German and Russian cinema were of worldwide importance. The Soviet revolution brought forth a torrent of ideas and important films which should be represented in every collection. Meanwhile, the Scandinavian cinema was moving to Germany, there to foster and reinforce a period known as German Expressionism which in turn became dissipated by the flight of directors, actors, and actresses to Hollywood. They, in turn, helped to make the American cinema of the late twenties and thirties extremely important worldwide. It was during the same period, however, that certain national cinemas in Europe were undergoing extreme change, first under the influence of an avant-garde movement in Europe, particularly in France, and then, in a reactionary sense, to Fascist governments. These were important films—those made in Italy between 1931 and 1940, for instance—for they tell much about how a political idea shapes and forms film.

Since World War II, there have been other important periods related to countries. First, the Neo-realist period in Italy. Second, the New Wave in France, and later another New Wave in Eastern Europe. Third, the flowering of the Japanese film industry and art which had its roots before the War. Fourth, the Film Noir movement in America. Fifth, the explosion of cinematic forms in the sixties throughout the world. Each of these situations has presented films in a new aesthetic and economic framework, thus recreating for us the idea of what a movie is. No collection would be complete until it tried to encompass these various aesthetic viewpoints.

INFLUENCES OF OTHER MEDIA

After selections based on history and country, I would hope for representation of the best in various film genres: the musical, the western, the gangster film, the detective film, the suspense film, the science-fiction film, the horror film, and comedy. Particularly, it seems to me, the western lends itself to study and to acquisition because it provides for Americans a particularly unique form. Many of the most entertaining western films, such as *The Wild Bunch*, lend themselves to the most intensive and detailed formal, sociological and psychological analysis. One can find in each of these genres, in fact, those works which stand out as exemplary, worthy of study and repeated viewing.

My own next category for selection would include films which are obviously related to other media, that is, films which are adaptations of novels or stage plays, films which are heavily influenced by movements in the arts—surrealism, as in Buñuel's *Viridiana*. One should look at both sides of the coin too. Which films might have influenced other artists in other media? Which films did Joyce, Fitzgerald, and Gertrude Stein see and like?

And when referring to films that were influenced by other media I would also consider films which were influenced by movement in politics, philosophy, economic, political, and social situations. Ophuls' *The Sorrow and the Pity* is a good example of a film in one of these categories. I also would certainly seek out those films made in the Third World, especially those which tended to deal directly with the problems of developing nations, countries under colonial control—Africa and South America particularly. By the same token, one would want to acquire films which were influenced by Marxist thought and certain aspects of phenomenology and structuralism. In these categories, one would want to include, among others, films by Vertov, Godard, Marker and Makavejev.

I would hope that any system of selection would also take into account the important directors in cinema. Many of these would be picked up by other criteria—country, history, genre—but they should still be considered. Certain of these filmmakers, Orson Welles and Alfred Hitchcock, for instance, are ideal for certain kinds of library situations because they offer first a fairly entertaining film which upon closer examination becomes a rich complex of ideas, thoughts, feelings, and cinematic virtuosity. Welles' *Touch of Evil* and Hitchcock's *Psycho,* for instance. But there are other directors: Ford, Fellini, Truffaut, Eisenstein, Bergman, Antonioni, Renoir.

And one of the most important criteria, which in many ways transcends all the others, is that of cinematic form. You select certain films because they represent the very best of cinema as an art form. Perhaps it is the camera movement (as in *Lola Montes*), the use of color (as in *Red Desert*), the editing (as in Eisenstein), the use of sound (as in Polonsky's *Force of Evil*), the use of space (as in Antonioni), the use of time (as in Renais) and unusual narrative form (such as the dream forms in Fellini's *8 1/2* or the structures used by Robbe-Grillet in his latest films). Whatever the criteria, one can point to the selection and justify it on the basis of form alone. And that criterion, by itself, is no more nor less justified than selecting films because they explore certain important humanistic themes in a new and fresh way, changing our sensibilities and our ideas. I'm sorry to learn that the National Project Center for Film and the Humanities is about to be abolished because it seemed to me that it was making a real inroad into the use of films for humanistic purposes in libraries, museums, and other continuing education centers.

A final suggestion, if you will. I hope you won't think of building a film library without at the same time considering the context. As you acquire films you should also acquire the supplementary written material which will help you and your audiences to understand the films. In some cases, for instance, you might be guided to acquire a certain film because an annotated script had been published. There are, for instance, several scripts, articles, and interviews with Fellini about the making of *Satyricon,* all compressed into several volumes. Or you may select a film because a single volume of analysis has been published, such as one of the texts in the Film Guide series produced by the University of Indiana Press. The March, 1975, issue of *Cinema Journal* has an article entitled "Reference Works for Film Study." Several people participated in putting that list together, and I personally know that it is ideally suited to help you select films and to help you find texts and articles which will support the viewing and the studying of those films. You can order a copy of that particular issue of *Cinema Journal* from Richard Dyer MacCaan, editior, *Cinema Journal,* TU Center, OA, University of Iowa, Iowa City, Iowa 52240.

The same general notion is applicable to the relation of films to film theory and criticism. The more your films can reflect certain theoretical positions, the more likely it is that you will want to study these positions. We teach several courses at NYU in which films are studied in the light of the theoretical statements made by the filmmakers themselves, and it seems to me that any library which wishes to acquire and select films must also consider the acquisition of the theoretical writings made by the filmmakers themselves. The point, of course, is that neither a film nor a book exists in a vacuum. Anything that can be done in order to help the viewer to understand his perceptions, or at least to articulate his own perceptions, by reading about the film, the more promising the film program will be at the library.

In summary, I think I'm merely asking you to select films from a number of different vantage points, not just entertainment and industry-dominated films, but rather those films which have pushed the art of the film forward, either in terms of form or content. I would imagine the criteria, in the most general sense, are not that different from selecting books for a library where one wants to provide the reader with a variety of excellent artifacts, which to the highest degree both reflect and inform our culture.

Programming Independent Film

by Peter Feinstein

Programming independent film has always been particularly problematical. Some very outspoken people have clear ideas of how the work of film artists should be shown; and audiences are often not as appreciative of one's efforts as one would wish. It is tempting to just show what the distributor is selling and avoid the wrath of both viewer and pundit, but the nature of the short film lends itself to imaginative selection and exhibition, and, though one might not find the massive audience that a time-proven feature may provide, the pleasures of introducing an audience to the very special joys of the short film is an enviable pursuit.

In programming the work of film artists, one should exercise the same care in selection as is expected by the exhibitors of the more traditional arts. Programming films by subject matter is commonplace. Very few people have seen more than a few short films, and the easiest aspect of a film to understand is its subject matter. Because of the general unsophistication, such programming is rarely questioned and I am sure, many are not aware that other options exist.

It is important for every programmer to develop a personalized view of film categories and definitions, groupings and sub-headings to fit one's designs. The great and true pleasure of programming independent films is to show an audience the wondrous discoveries that you have made, show how the pieces fit together, to share with them the joy of seeing an artist move further out into uncharted realms of creativity, or to reach for some particularly enigmatic passion.

The key to good programming is to have a grasp of the basic dimensions of the medium; to have placed what one has viewed in some order. It is not sufficient to show just what one likes, and showing films grouped by subject matter is the ignoblest form of programming.

DEFINITIONS

The term independent film refers to the characteristic that most all of the makers work outside of the commercial system. Many work alone like a painter, sculptor or poet; others work in small groups. One looks for work by individuals driven by more than the need of financial gain or public recognition.

The average independent filmmaker makes very little money from his or her craft. What little return is gained is usually absorbed by the next project. Of the 400 or so filmmakers listed in the Filmmakers Cooperative catalog, I would be willing to wager that fewer than ten make their livings as filmmakers. To characterize them as individuals awaiting the break into the big time is to do them the supreme disservice.

Other terms used to define independent films are "short" which is often misleading; "underground" which has the unfortunate connotation that the films are beneath some larger and more substantial body of work, which is totally untrue; "avant-garde" which has come to designate a small number of filmmakers working in a particular style and receiving the approval of a certain group of critics; "experimental" which connotes unfinished work or concepts produced to influence the popular medium, which is ridiculous; and "personal" which is my favorite, but frightens many people away.

What the work of these independent artists does have in common is a deep love of the medium as a means of expression; all work outside of the studio system or its vestiges; rarely are the films ever shown in commercial (theatrical) movie houses, and are therefore rarely seen by the general public. Most lack a didactic message such as we associate with text films.

SELECTION

It is essential for the programmer to divide independent films into some form of loose categories: "avant-garde" or "experimental" normally refer to structural and conceptual films. Though there is no clear consensus, this would include the work of Hollis Frampton, Tony Conrad, Peter Kubelka, Michael Snow, Ernie Gehr, Barry Gerson and a great many others. Though not clearly structural, the work of Stan Brakhage, George Landow, Bruce Baillie, Larry Jordan, Paul Sharits, Andy Warhol (not Morrissey) and many others may also be included. Jonas Mekas, P. Adams Sitney, and Annette Michaelson are the major critics of the school. Avant-garde film is generally associated with New York and the major showcases are the Anthology Film Archives and the Whitney Museum of Art.

A second style of filmmaking, sometimes called "West Coast," gained a great deal of attention in the sixties when words such as "acid" and "psychedelic" were in vogue. It is a more exuberant film style with direct visual pleasures clearly divergent from the more intellectual sensibilities of the East. Included in a list of such filmmakers would be Scott Bartlett, Freude Bartlett, Robert Nelson, Gunvor Nelson, Peter Hutton, Pat O'Neil, Lenny Lipton, the Whitneys, Jordan Belson, Curt McDowell, the Kuchars (despite their Bronx background), David Rimmer, etc. Gene Youngblood and David Curtis have written books that pay special attention to the West Coast filmmakers. The films often make use of mechanical devices such as optical printers, video synthesizers and computers.

The boundaries of both of these two categories are extremely vague. The above listings are not meant to be either inclusive or definitive, but as examples of the more generally accepted categories of film. Each programmer should develop his own lists. The process is not meant as a means of definition, but as a device for adding structure and substance to program groupings.

Certain styles of documentaries are normally included in the lists of independent films. It is even intellectually feasible to argue that the vast majority of independent films, including the work of Brakhage, Kubelka, Warhol, Baillie and others is in fact, documentary film. One of the most pleasing programs is to develop this notion.

In the category of documentary, we immediately dismiss all the commercial pap such as the National Geographic films and their ilk. Included are sensitive records by filmmakers of the world about them and their own lives. Most of these films are made in the cinema verite tradition, but many beautiful examples use montage techniques. A relatively recent development is the autobiographical film, films made on an intimate aspect of the filmmaker's own life or about individuals of special relevance such as siblings, parents, spouse or child. Well known filmmakers in the cinema verite tradition include Richard Leacock, D. A. Pennebaker, the Maysles brothers, Ed Pincus, Fred Wiseman and a great many other both inferior and superior filmmakers. Autobiographical filmmakers include Joyce Chopra, Martha Coolidge, Miriam Weinstein, Lenny Lipton and Peter Hutton as well as many others.

Particularly well made anthropological films, especially the films of John Marshal, are also to be included in programs, though it is at times hard to decide when such films are works of creativity or scientific records. It is particularly pleasant and satisfying, especially for the neophyte programmer, to develop programs comparing the various styles of documentary films. Unfortunately, documentary films have long been viewed as educational tools and are particularly susceptible to selection by subject matter. Films about the ghetto, or films of changing social values, are all well and good if the programmer and the audience are primarily interested in social values and ghettoes. If film as an art is the primary interest, I suggest the alternative of tracing the development of the cinematic techniques used to depict ghetto life or social values. On the other hand, if one is attempting to seek acceptance of film use by libraries or schools which are skeptical of its value, one is almost forced to concentrate on secondary or topical usage. But, that is a compromise and must be regarded as such.

Animation has always been a particular problem. Unlike the other areas of film, almost all animators, both commercial and personal, have similar work habits and there is a great deal of movement between the commercial and non-commercial worlds. Animated films will also attract the largest audience with the least effort, a severe temptation.

When sorting out animated films, I normally look for some special aspect of the work that is particularly creative or expressive. Economy of technique is especially important. Creative does not refer to nice drawings or complicated effects (I find very little interest in cell animation) or a cute story. Part of the problem is that I long ago overcame the fascination with the mysteries of animation and am no longer charmed by pictures that move and speak platitudes. This does not mean I do not like cartoons. I also like MacDonald's hamburgers, but I do not confuse them with the fare I serve to guests.

I look for the animator who explores the limits of the medium, touches some particularly fine area of the imagination or expresses with great clarity some infinite enigma. I do not find animated films about peace on earth or man's struggle with technology of particular interest. They remind me of something particularly unhappy in my youth.

Many other categories exist. It is up to each programmer to develop definitions particularly suited to one's own tastes and interests. It is not important that one's divisions match the generally accepted aesthetic, but they must work when applied to the selection of films and the structure of those films within a program.

FORMAT

The other major question in programming is format. Film programs range from a single, one-hour evening, to weekly screenings over long periods, to a single week of extensive screenings. The time slot is of primary importance. Will you have the audience's attention for just a moment, or will you have time to carefully build and cultivate their attention? The one night affairs are the hardest to conceptualize. Most audiences are not overly sophisticated, so it is necessary to put the program in perspective. One also wants to give a taste of the sublime, yet it is important not to lose the viewer in the first ten minutes.

There are three basic types of programs: guest filmmakers, one artist shows, and group shows. Each is to be approached differently and each has its particular positive and negative aspects. Guest filmmakers provide added interest and tend to draw a larger audience; one artist shows when done carefully provide the purest look at an artist's work, and group shows allow the programmer to put film in perspective, provide elemental interpretation and develop the audience's sophistication.

Unfortunately, most independent film is shown in the single program format. Someone will suggest the screening of short films, someone will pick them, they will be shown and everyone goes home none the wiser. Even more unfortunate are the screening programs that may span an entire season of many screenings and have absolutely no coherence. Not even the concept of showing good short films for the entire period. No point of view. It is the difference between a rainbow and a brown smudge. Both contain all the colors in the crayola box. The result of such lack of care is a different and indifferent audience each night—no continuity, no synergy, no energy and no memory.

The guest filmmaker is a highly popular form of film exhibition that reduces programming to administrative questions (how to get the filmmaker into the hall and how to fill the hall with people) rather than artistic choices (which films to show). A good deal of the popularity of this form of programming is the star factor. It is pleasant to hear an artist speak, or more accurately, comment on his or her own work. Unfortunately, few competent speakers exist on the topic of the independent film, so the filmmakers are burdened with the yoke of interpreting their own work. Like everyone else, I find this type of programming particularly pleasurable. Especially if I have dinner with the filmmaker before or drinks afterward.

But it has several inherent problems that make it a dubious practice. After a point, it becomes vaudeville. Artists are not particularly gifted at explaining their own work. Being gifted at making should be enough. Nor do I believe that their interpretation is inherently more valid than mine or anyone else's. Unfortunately, the income of a filmmaker often has more to do with the quality of the floorshow (not to mention the dinner and drinks, and cocktails with the local art patrons, programmer and literati) than the quality of the films.

The next obvious variation is the one artist screening. In this format, one retains the pleasure of viewing a substantial body of work by a single artist, but the programmer is able to select films so as to give a specific interpretation. Recent work may be shown, or early work, or contrasts among the body may be drawn, or the highest quality work may be shown. This places the burden on the programmer of having to know something about the filmmaker's work. The productivity of some filmmakers is so rich that I think I could program for months without ever leaving it. Brakhage, for instance: first a retrospective of everything; then tracing various developments through the entire body; then comparing the extremes; then screening the best work of each period; then showing the filmmakers who influenced Brakhage along with the films of Brakhage; then screening the filmmakers who were influenced by Brakhage, along with selected films by Brakhage. It could take years.

And Brakhage is not alone. Though he has been more prolific than most with a vast body of work spanning two decades, it is possible to use the same techniques with any artist. Sometimes I watch my father's home movies and think of how I would program them.

The group show is the programmer's greatest test. The amount of work involved in group programs increases geometrically. Easy roads present themselves constantly. Humorous films. Women's films. Films about social change. Erotic films. Even the best programmer must, on occasion, take the path of least resistance. But know it for what it is!

The selection of films in some coherent fashion is clearly the most rewarding approach for the programmer. Some would deny this pleasure in seeking a purer communication between artist and audience—no programming. Show everything or nothing. But few filmmakers are of sufficient strength and few audiences of sufficient patience.

Of special satisfaction in the group show is the building of an audience over many weeks. Leading an audience through the various realms of films. Tempting them with candy. Then asking for a little patience. Showing how it is done in an obvious film, then showing how it is done well in a truly sublime film.

If a programmer is a neophyte, then more research is necessary. I am amazed at the number of people who are content to show the films they like. "Critics Choice" is every programmer's dream. But such narcissism does not make for substantive programs. It is dangerous and for experts only. The intellect must come into play, and the intellect must be developed. That means work.

Risk is especially important. Programmers should take chances. I am still haunted by a program I put together at the Film Forum that I was sure everyone would like. It played for six nights. I doubt if twenty people came. Some four years later, a friend recalled that program and again chastised me for the lapse into laziness.

The only asset an individual needs to do high-quality programming is the energy to do the work. Not just to do the work, but to think about what one is doing. To sit up at night and wonder how the pieces will fit together. If one is a beginner, then it is necessary to do more research, contact more people, draw on the experience of others, go to every possible screening and then to sit alone and make up one's mind. If films are put together with a deft hand, even the people who walk out will come back next time.

It is absolutely necessary to make a statement about the films one shows. It is necessary to tell the audience of your own joys of discovery and your own love of film. I do not mean in the program notes, but in the choice of films. Just as we expect the artist to explore the outer limits of his creativity, we must expect film programmers to push their programming ability to the limit.

TECHNIQUES

When putting together a group show, I normally begin with a film that has some special point that I wish to reinforce. If that special point is particularly esoteric, I try to combine the film with others that open up the esoterica. If the film is sublimely simple, I try to show less economic attempts on the same theme. If the film is unusually successful, it is obvious to combine it with less successful attempts at the same goal. And if the programmer believes the film to be a seminal work, then the point should be proven by the context in which the film is shown.

Unlike the exhibitors of the plastic arts, film programmers have the ability to hold an audience for a specific length of time, and to select the exact order in which the works of art are presented. The programmer can ask all sorts of logical and aesthetic questions, make all kinds of explanations, tell stories and jokes and open in infinite detail the varied facets of the art form, all in the choice of films.

A program can ask the audience, "If you liked Brakhage's *Window Water Baby Moving* (1959, 12 min), can you reach out a little farther to *Dog Star Man* (Brakhage, 1961–64, 78 min)?" for a full program of ninety minutes. Or explain to them: If you show *Meshes of the Afternoon* (Maya Deren and Alexander Hamid, 1943, 14 min) and *Un Chien Andalou* (Bunuel and Dali, 1928, 20 min) and *Castro Street* (Bruce Baillie, 1966, 10 min) and *Offon* (Scott Bartlett, 1968, 9 min) then George Landow's *Remedial Reading Comprehension* (1971, 5 min) and *What's Wrong With This Picture, Parts I and II* (1971, 10.5 min) can be added for a total program time of 68.5 min. The above examples are given because the films are relatively well known, but I find the greatest pleasure in linking the known to the unknown, showing a highly regarded film as a benchmark, and then surpassing the mark with the work of an unknown artist.

I did one program at the Film Forum of which I am particularly proud. I was interested in the work of filmmakers who were involved with surfaces and the illusions of dimension. I called the program Window Films because when one looks at a window the eye can focus either on the surface of the glass, the image behind the glass, or the image reflected in the glass. The analogy parallels the relationship between the filmmaker, his art and the audience—one can view the image on the screen, one can search the image for details about the creative process, or one can search the image for information about oneself. I showed the work of Michael Snow, Barry Gerson and Andrew Noren. I would have liked also to have included Ernie Gehr and George Herbert. The program lasted just over one hour. It was very full and I was particularly pleased each time I viewed the program (six screenings) and continued to find new insight into the work, the artist, and my relationship to them. And I found that the audience, including the unsophisticated viewer, was able to grasp this fairly subliminal effect.

Of greatest pleasure to the programmer is to do a series combining all of the above formats. I was once asked to put together a week-long program at the Annenberg School in Philadelphia. I decided to wander through the world of the independent film, not making any definitive statements, but contrasting and tasting as an innocent and leaving a great deal of choice to the audience. The problem was how to accomplish this without being insubstantial. As the screenings were to take place on seven nights during an eight day span, I could expect a fairly high degree of audience continuity and sold series tickets at a discount to encourage series attendance.

I decided to have guest filmmakers each of the seven nights. They would show films, but not necessarily their own work. The first two speakers would concentrate on background and perspective. On the first night, P. Adams Sitney lectured, provided introductory material and showed basic work. Stan Lawder followed on the second night, providing a differing interpretation of the avant-garde film. Stan Vanderbeek showed his own work on the third night. Vanderbeek and his films are one. I did not ask him to show the works of others. Both he and his films suffer in the absence of the other, but together they are a phenomenon that is particularly interesting and provides unusual insight into the artist and the mood of independent film. Hollis Frampton followed showing his own work and films by Brakhage. Pat O'Neil the next night showed West Coast films and examples of his own work. On the last two evenings, Jonas Mekas and Ricky Leacock showed programs of their own work. Like Vanderbeek, they are so much a part of film history that they put a great deal of what is being done in perspective. Though both make what can be broadly called documentary films, and both are powerful and influential personalities, they are very different men, make very different film and aesthetic statements. They were also able to provide answers to many of the questions that had accumulated during the week. Often, two different answers.

Unfortunately, few libraries have facilities or time for programs of this breadth. But the concepts remain the same whether one is screening work by local filmmakers, ghetto children, or the big names of the avant-garde. Quality in programming is based on the interest of the programmer to impart some understanding of the films being screened to the audience. This understanding may be a deep intellectual concern or just the joy of discovery on the part of the programmer, but it is more than a simple image on a screen. I am one of those people who still choose to learn from the printed word rather than from a film whenever possible. I find it a much more economical use of my time and a process much more under my control. If I can gain the same information in the same amount of time from either a book or a film, I will invariably choose the printed word. But, I love film. I love film because it says things that can never be said in print. It has creative possibilities unlike any other art form. It is a very special medium. When programming film, it is primary that this specialness be the focus of all attention.

ADDENDA

Program notes are absolutely essential. People should have at least a printed list of what they see, the names of the filmmakers, running time, and where the films can be obtained. One supposes that in a perfect world, further explanation would not be necessary, but few of us are so skilled in programming as to be crystal clear and most audiences are not so comfortable with independent film that they do not appreciate guidance. If the muse is unavailable when it comes time to write the notes, quote from a book, or someone else's program notes, or something the filmmaker has written, or at least a poem or essay that has some special bearing on the films.

*   *   *

Boredom seems to be the greatest fear of most programmers. It should be hostility. I have always believed that excessive fear of boring an audience is a fault among both filmmakers and film programmers. More than any visual medium, film exists in time. It is a temporary experience that is more devoted to the memory than any other sense. One must remember each frame to see motion, one must remember each shot for continuity, and one must remember the film for later reference. Therefore, it is an ultimate test of the filmmakers' skill to manipulate time so as to draw us in and out of the film as a creative act. Slow portions may be no more than a chance to regroup one's senses. A moment of tedium is not a cardinal sin. Unfortunately, Hollywood has taught us that when the lights dim and the screen begins to flicker that no more is to be asked of us than to keep our eyes open for the remainder of the experience. Pandering to this convention is patronizing to an audience. If an audience is carefully guided, it learns to be discerning. They learn to consider what you offer.

Both excessive boredom and excessive excitement can be acts of hostility. There is a time and a place for sandbagging, but one is suspect of those who enjoy it too often. Among my pet peeves are people who show two hours of the most difficult of films to the uninitiated. They are the same people who destroy poetry by starting with Milton. I have equal dislike for the individuals who show an hour of children in playgrounds, pans of the sun and women in leotards, and tell us that that is art.

* * * *

Paying filmmakers, for some ungodly reason, is still in question. I was once asked whether it was necessary to pay filmmakers since they would gain by the exposure. I do not work for nothing, you do not work for nothing, they do not work for nothing.

* * * *

Where to see independent film continues to be a problem. New York has many showcases, almost all of which are listed in the *Village Voice, The Soho Weekly News,* and *The New Yorker.* If one cannot go, at least write and request programs. Film festivals vary in quality but are a good chance to see films outside of New York. The University Film Study Center has a listing of film festivals and the *Filmmaker's Newsletter* carries more current monthly listings. A good solid week at the Ann Arbor Film Festival, can put a lot of films into one's journal in a very short period of time. (Incidentally, when I was actively programming films, I kept a careful journal listing everything I saw. If I did not show the film, someone else might want it.) Seminars such as International Film Seminars are extremely valuable. In addition, many colleges and universities have film programs (usually not the film society) or seminars devoted to the independent film. Once one gets on a mailing list or two, a good deal of this information comes in unsolicited.

* * * *

Where to get independent films is a perennial question. The Filmmakers Coop in New York and Canyon Cinema in Sausalito, California, are good places to start. Beyond that, many films are in commercial distribution with the Serious Business Company in Berkeley, California.

Eight Millimeter Circulation Policies and Ranganathan's First Law

by Joseph W. Palmer

Remember Ranganathan's First Law of Library Science? It goes like this: BOOKS ARE FOR USE. This is a simple yet profound principle that we too often forget. It means that the library does not exist for itself but for the use that is made of its resources. If our resources aren't used, we are failing in our basic purpose. For this reason, all of our energies must be directed towards making our resources available, accessible, and used. We must make our materials and services known to the patron, make it easy to use them, and actively promote their use. This concept should be forever borne in mind by every library employee. It should underlie every single aspect of library service.

Too often it doesn't. We adopt thoughtless policies and practices that defeat our purpose, that hide materials from patrons and make it difficult for them to be used.

I wholeheartedly endorse this as the fundamental principle of librarianship. I also believe in the contribution 8mm films can make to library service.

Because they are inexpensive, because many patrons own 8mm projectors, because they make available those historic early films about which many books have been and continue to be written, because the films of the great silent comedians still have the power to delight and amuse, and because a variety of other popular materials are available in this format, I feel 8mm reel films can be unique and valuable library resources.

Because I believe in these things, I have been disturbed by some of the practices I have observed in public libraries. On the one hand, I suspect Ranganathan would approve of the way Fullerton (Calif.) Public Library handles its 8mm films. They are displayed on open shelf, circulate for two weeks and overdues of 5¢ a day are charged. Films, unlike books, are not browsable. Therefore a special card catalog is provided which gives an annotation for each film.

On the other hand, Ranganathan would probably not be pleased with the way 8mm films are handled in another library I've visited. This library is admirable in many ways—it has a fine, vital book collection, liberal book circulation policies, comfortable and attractive facilities, and a large staff of warm, friendly, helpful reference librarians. However, 8mm films are hidden in an office. If one asks if such materials are available an un-annotated list is produced from a desk drawer. Eight mm films, like expensive 16 mm films, are to be picked up between 2 p.m. and 6 p.m., and returned before noon on the following day. While the library is open until 9 p.m. most days, films are not accepted after 6 p.m. Overdue fines of 25¢ an hour are indicated.

These policies seem inappropriate. They do not facilitate the use of 8mm films, but—in effect—discourage their use. And to what purpose? I suspected the majority of the 8mm films were languishing unused on the shelf. However, even if there were heavy use, these circulation regulations would seem inappropriate. For Ranganathan has a second law: BOOKS ARE FOR ALL. Since only those persons whose schedules are so flexible they can comply with this rigid circulation period may use the films, the majority of the community is denied easy access to these materials.

I began to wonder about the entire question of 8mm reel films and their treatment in public libraries. Which library was most representative of the policies being pursued? I decided to find out. I sent a questionnaire to 186 California public libraries listed in the annual directory issue of *News Notes of California Libraries* seeking answers to the following questions:

1. How many California public libraries owned 8mm reel films?
2. What circulation regulations were in effect? For how long did 8mm films circulate? Were fees charged for their use? What overdue charges were imposed?
3. What proportion of the films owned remained uncirculated during an average week? Were rigid circulation policies being pursued while the bulk of the collection lay inactive on the shelves?

The shortcomings of this study are obvious. It only investigates two factors—the circulation policies and the estimated portion of films owned circulating in an average week. Factors other than the circulation policies certainly affect the amount of circulation. For instance: public awareness of the existence of the collection; open shelf versus closed shelf; types of films owned; provision of catalogs and descriptive annotations; provisions for the placing of reserves on titles in circulation. Also, libraries could only "estimate" the number of films circulating in an "average" week. Having visited a number of responding libraries, I suspect there sometimes was a tendency to overestimate volume of circulation.

One hundred and fifty-three libraries (i.e. 82%) answered the questionnaire. The number of 8mm reel films owned can be summarized as follows:

CIRCULATION POLICIES IN THE TWENTY-FIVE CALIFORNIA PUBLIC LIBRARIES WITH THE LARGEST 8 MM COLLECTIONS

8mm Films Owned	Fee for Use	Circulation Period	Overdue Charges	Percent Uncirculated in an Average Week	16mm Films Owned[1]	Are Policies for 8mm and 16mm Films the Same?
627	—	1 week	6¢/day	25 to 49%	204+70	No
477	—	1 day	none	50 to 75%	275	No information
450	—	1 week	5¢/day	over 75%	11	Yes
400	—	1 week	5¢/day	25 to 49%	50	Yes
373	—	1 week	no info.	below 25%	149+30	No
281	—	1 day	25¢/hr.	below 25%	146+125	Yes
279	—	1 day	50¢/day	below 25%	0+90	No
271	—	1 day	50¢/day	25 to 49%	1+24	No
253	—	1 week	5¢/day	50 to 74%	1500+100	No
250	—	1 week	5¢/day	50 to 74%	250+35	No
240	—	2 days	5¢/day	over 75%	63+57	No
200	25¢	1 day	25¢/hr.	over 75%	90+98	No
194	10–50¢ a day	1 week	same as fee	over 75%	no info.	
185	—	3 days	5¢/day	over 75%	20+30	No
185	—	1 day	5¢/hr.	over 75%	237	No
168	—	no info.	5¢/day	over 75%	373	No
165	—	1 day	25¢/hr.	over 75%	451+30	Yes
165	—	3 days	10¢/day	over 75%	324+70	No
154	—	1 week	none	over 75%	no info.	
150	—	1 week	25¢/week	50 to 74%	6+7	No
150	—	1 week	25¢/day	50 to 74%	98+450	No
150	—	2 days	$1/day	50 to 74%	600+35	No
141	—	2 weeks	none	over 75%	1+18	Yes
140	—	3 days	25¢/day	25 to 49%	300+150	No
137	—	1 week	5¢/day	50 to 74%	307+35	No

[1]The number following the "+" represents films on deposit from film circuits.

No 8mm reel films owned = 80 libraries (52%)
1 to 49 8mm reel films owned = 18 libraries (12%)
50 to 99 8mm reel films owned = 21 libraries (14%)
100 or more 8mm reel films owned = 34 libraries (22%)

For the purpose of this study, I felt it would be most useful to restrict my analysis to the 55 libraries owning 50 or more films. In order to provide the reader with an idea of how circulation policies vary in individual libraries, Table 1 describes the circulation policies of the 25 libraries reporting the largest 8mm collections.

Only three of the libraries owning 50 or more films charged fees for their use. One library charged 25¢ per title; another charged 10¢ per title; a third had a variable scale ranging from 10¢ to 50¢ per day per title. The remaining 52 libraries made no charge for 8mm reel films.

The circulation period varied from less than one day to three weeks. Thirty-three libraries had circulation periods of three days or more. Seventeen libraries had circulation periods of one day or less.

Circulation Period:

$$
\begin{array}{rcl}
3 \text{ weeks} &=& 1 \text{ library} \\
2 \text{ weeks} &=& 5 \text{ libraries} \\
1 \text{ week} &=& 23 \text{ libraries} \\
3 \text{ days} &=& 4 \text{ libraries} \\
2 \text{ days} &=& 3 \text{ libraries} \\
1 \text{ day or less} &=& 17 \text{ libraries} \\
\text{Varies} &=& 1 \text{ library} \\
\text{No information} &=& 1 \text{ library}
\end{array}
$$

Overdue fees varied greatly with 5¢ per day being the most widespread choice.

Overdue Fines:

$$
\begin{array}{rcl}
50¢ \text{ per hour} &=& 2 \text{ libraries} \\
25¢ \text{ per hour} &=& 4 \text{ libraries} \\
5¢ \text{ per hour} &=& 1 \text{ library} \\
\$1.00 \text{ per day} &=& 1 \text{ library} \\
50¢ \text{ per day} &=& 4 \text{ libraries} \\
25¢ \text{ per day} &=& 7 \text{ libraries} \\
10¢ \text{ per day} &=& 4 \text{ libraries} \\
6¢ \text{ per day} &=& 1 \text{ library} \\
5¢ \text{ per day} &=& 21 \text{ libraries} \\
25¢ \text{ per week} &=& 1 \text{ library} \\
\text{No charge} &=& 4 \text{ libraries} \\
\text{No information} &=& 5 \text{ libraries}
\end{array}
$$

PERCENTAGE OF 8mm FILMS OWNED THAT REMAIN UNCIRCULATED IN AN AVERAGE WEEK:

$$
\begin{array}{rcl}
\text{Many (75\% or more) uncirculated} &=& 24 \text{ libraries (43\%)} \\
50 \text{ to } 74\% \text{ uncirculated} &=& 17 \text{ libraries (31\%)} \\
25 \text{ to } 49\% \text{ uncirculated} &=& 6 \text{ libraries (11\%)} \\
\text{Few (25\% or less) uncirculated} &=& 6 \text{ libraries (11\%)} \\
\text{No information} &=& 2 \text{ libraries (4\%)}
\end{array}
$$

If we limit ourselves to those libraries with circulation periods of 1 day or less, we find:

$$
\begin{array}{rcl}
\text{Many (75\% or more) uncirculated} &=& 9 \text{ libraries (53\%)} \\
50 \text{ to } 74\% \text{ uncirculated} &=& 4 \text{ libraries (23\%)} \\
25 \text{ to } 49\% \text{ uncirculated} &=& 2 \text{ libraries (12\%)} \\
\text{Few (25\% or less) uncirculated} &=& 2 \text{ libraries (12\%)}
\end{array}
$$

Libraries were asked to estimate the percentage of 8mm films that circulate each week. Responses indicated that in 41 of the 55 libraries it was customary for 50% or more of the collection to remain uncirculated in an average week. Bear in mind, however, that a circulation of even 25% per week would still constitute substantial use. For these 41 libraries, however, circulation periods of 1 day or less appear to be indefensible.

What then does the survey show? It indicates almost half the public libraries in California own some 8mm reel films, and about one fourth have fairly large collections. It is unusual for circulation or insurance fees to be charged. The most common circulation period is one week, but more than a third of the libraries owning 50 or more films have a circulation period of one day or less. This stringent circulation policy does not appear to be justified in view of the proportion of the collection which generally is not circulated in an average week. Overdue fines can be as high as 50¢ an hour, but 5¢ a day is the mode.

This then is the current situation. What would the ideal situation be? Obviously, this must vary according to the particular library. But I will make the following recommendations:

1. Depending on the amount of use, the circulation period for 8mm films should be for a minimum of 3 days to one week. This will give the patron adequate time for use of the materials while insuring an adequate selection of materials for the would-be borrower to choose from.
2. An annotated catalog listing and describing all 8mm films should be prominently displayed in the library. It should clearly indicate that 8mm films, like books, may be reserved, and should encourage users to reserve titles they wish which are currently in circulation.
3. Ideally 8mm films should be placed on open shelf where patrons can peruse available titles. In this case, annotations should not only appear in the catalog but be affixed to the film container as well. A patron who would pass over *Conquest of the North Pole* thinking it to be a documentary probably would not bother to check with the catalog to determine the true nature of this marvelous Jules Verne-type fantasy. With the annotation on the container, he would know immediately.

Many librarians will protest that, due to theft, open shelves for 8mm films are not feasible. This will depend on the library. If closed shelves are deemed necessary, I would suggest the library adopt the procedure used by the Orange County (Calif.) Public Library for its 16mm films. For each title a jumbo sized index card is prepared which describes the film in detail. A box containing these cards is kept on top of the film desk. When a film is checked out, the card is removed. Thus, even with closed shelves, the patron is able to browse through the selection of titles available for immediate circulation.

These are relatively simple innovations. Libraries that adopt them will be encouraging full use of their 8mm resources. Remember— BOOKS ARE FOR USE means 8mm films too.

CATV: Visual Library Service

by Brigitte L. Kenney
and Frank W. Norwood

Community Antenna Television (CATV)—just another acronym? A way for those of us who live in remote areas to receive our favorite program? A way for enterprising businessmen to make money by bringing a service we want into our homes, for a fee? CATV is all of these, but it can become much more. It can become a powerful new tool by which librarians may reach both their "regular" library clients and those presently unserved, with special programming tailored to their needs. More importantly, it can become the means of interconnecting libraries for better delivery of information and documents.

What is CATV? Some of us, living in areas where television reception is poor because of our distance from the nearest station, or because of the mountains and valleys between station and receiver know all about how it works; others, living in mostly urban areas, may not. A brief explanation is in order. Television signals travel in a straight line and do not follow the curvature of the earth. TV signals may be blocked by tall buildings, hills, or other physical obstructions. The CATV industry has come into being because many people could receive only one or two channels, and sometimes those suffered from interference, or "snow." CATV operators erect high masts with sensitive antennas to pick up signals off the air, amplify them, and distribute them by cable to the receivers of customers who pay a modest fee, usually about five dollars per month. This allows a far broader choice of programs and brings in strong, clear signals where only weak signals, or none at all, were available before.

While CATV began in remote areas, usually in small hill-locked communities, it now serves virtually every state; more than 2,700 systems in the United States now transmit programs into 5,500,000 homes.[1] Some of the older systems are able to carry only a few channels in the lower portion of the VHF (Very High Frequency) band, while most modern systems can use all of the VHF channels, 2 through 13. Some systems are now being constructed which will carry more than twelve channels either by using dual cables so that the set can be switched from channel 2 to 13 on cable A, to channel 2 to 13 on cable B; or by carrying TV signals at other frequencies on the cable and "retrieving them" by the use of convertors mounted atop the homeowner's set. At the present state of the art, the cable will not carry UHF signals, so UHF stations are received and converted to a vacant VHF channel.

What makes CATV so different from television broadcasting (both commercial and educational)? One important factor is that more TV signals can be carried over the cable than can be made available over the air. In broadcasting, TV signals can and do interfere with one another so that in any given city no more than seven VHF channels can be assigned. Further, there are VHF frequencies suitable for TV below channel 2, between channels 6 and 7, and above channel 13, but these cannot be used for television broadcasting because those portions of the electromagnetic spectrum are assigned for other over-the-air services. On a CATV cable, however, the signals are enclosed, as water is in a pipe, and can be transmitted without interfering with other receivers not connected to the cable. Another important difference, the full value of which is yet to be exploited, is that cable holds the technical potential of being a two-way device. Given the proper amplifiers and terminal gear, messages could be sent both to and from the home.

Another important factor is that until recently CATV was strictly under local control; franchises are awarded by local government authorities to CATV operators. Each franchise is negotiated individually between the two parties; conditions laid down are usually binding for the length of the franchise. The Federal Communications Commission, under whose jurisdiction falls all broadcasting (i.e., use of the electromagnetic spectrum, which is considered belonging to the people), has recently begun to take a long, hard look at CATV, because of its effect on broadcast TV stations. There is concern that commercial TV audiences may become diluted because of a wider availability of channel (and therefore program) choices via CATV. For example, under present FCC rules, TV signals from distant cities may not be imported by cable into the hundred largest markets in the United States.

Hearings are presently in progress before the FCC, which will influence the development of CATV to a considerable extent. Testimony has been given by many interested parties, asking that the FCC require CATV operators to set aside some of their distribution capacity for educational and instructional purposes. The Joint Council of Educational Telecommunications, and others, have suggested that 20 percent of the spectrum space on CATV systems, old and new, large and small, should be made available without charge for broadly educational uses, including not only television but eventually computer assisted instruction, facsimile transmission, and the like. In a number of cities and towns, educational interests already have free access to one or more channels on the local CATV system and CATV operators have, often as a matter of course, provided free "drops" (connection from trunk cable to receiver) to schools and other public institutions. Some CATV operators and school systems are generating new, local programming on otherwise unused channels on the cable. CATV has become not only a medium distributing existing television signals but an opportunity for providing entirely new program services. A recent ruling by the FCC encourages such "cable-casting," and will soon require that all CATV systems serving more than 3,500 subscribers engage in a substantial amount of local cable originated programming. Much of this is expected to be public service in character, including coverage of high school sports, city council meetings, and discussion of local issues. Cable systems may, if they choose, support such programming with commercial advertising.

As schools are now taking advantage of present and potential applications in their planning, so could librarians include CATV in their activities. Let us take a look at what could be done right now by and for libraries and with existing technology.

If a library had a channel set aside for its exclusive use or shared one with a school system, it could bring children's story hours, book talks, local programs taking place in the library (such as discussion groups, chamber music, adult education activities) into each home connected to the cable system. It could generate special programs for specialized audiences, such as the disadvantaged, teenagers, church and community groups, and the like. With videotape equipment becoming quite inexpensive, such program generation is within the reach of most medium-sized libraries or systems.

This is only the beginning, however, and a quite traditional view of library use of CATV. The true application lies in the future. The inherent quality of a sharp, clear picture via cable, which can carry all kinds of data on a very wide band, and therefore very fast, opens up possibilities for libraries hitherto thought impossible.

We believe that CATV will become perhaps *the* most important means for interconnecting libraries, as well as for connecting users to libraries. All kinds of information can be transmitted, from facsimile of the printed page to microfilm, from pictures to drawings, and from maps to voice communication. The possibility of two-way communication which is technically feasible now would allow an almost infinite number of applications. The Federal Communications Commission suggested some services in one of its documents:

> It has been suggested that the expanding multichannel capacity of cable systems could be utilized to provide a variety of new communications services to homes and businesses within a community, in addition to services now commonly offered such as time, weather, news, stock exchange ticker, etc. While we shall not attempt an all-inclusive listing, some of the predicted services include: *facsimile reproduction of newspapers, magazines, documents, etc.;* electronic mail delivery; merchandising; *business concern links to branch offices,* primary customers, or suppliers; *access to computers: e.g. man-to-computer communications in the nature of inquiry and response* (credit checks, airlines reservations, branch banking, etc.) *information retrieval (library and other reference material, etc.)* and *computer-to-computer communications: the furtherance of various governmental programs on a federal, state and municipal level, e.g., employment services and manpower utilization, special communications systems to reach particular neighborhoods or ethnic groups within a community,* and for municipal surveillance of public areas for protection against crime, fire detection, control of air

pollution and traffic; *various educational and training programs,* e.g., job and literacy training, preschool programs in the nature of "Project Headstart," and to *enable professional groups such as doctors to keep abreast of developments in their fields;* and the provision of a low-cost outlet for political candidates, advertisers, *amateur expression (e.g., community drama groups)* and for other moderately funded organizations or persons desiring access to the community or a particular segment of the community.[2] [Italics added.]

It is easy to see that if we conceive of a multipurpose multitype of library network, many or all the italicized passages in the above statement could apply. If we are indeed convinced that the public library should become *the* community information center, backed up by other types of libraries with their specialized resources, we can then selectively distribute needed information wherever and whenever needed—perhaps becoming a modern version of "the right book to the right man at the right time." Conversely, this would hold true for the scholar who has need of a document or a piece of information located elsewhere; rapid transmission of the needed document will indeed speed his research. We can envision large microform storage libraries located in a few selected places, from whose vast stores desired documents may be distributed to someone needing them.

Inherent in this concept is the two-way communication referred to above. With relatively modest investment, both on the part of the home viewer—who would need a talk-back device (a telephone would do)—and the CATV operator—who would need to install equipment allowing him to distribute selectively rather than to the entire community—this two-way communication could soon become a reality. With somewhat more sophisticated equipment, including a device providing hard copy (but costing considerably more, and therefore perhaps to be located only in the library at first) the user could have his document in hand, instead of projected on the screen. He might also install a small videotape recorder near his home set and record for replay whenever convenient. The ability to store and "hold" still pictures for reading exists now; this would be another necessary part of such a system.

Ultimately, the user would be able to interact with the network directly, similar to the kind of interaction now possible with computer-stored information via terminal. He could request, read, respond, and even alter information with the aid of a light pen, which transmits a signal a TV screen can "read."

Not all of this is possible right now, of course, but there is no question that such a system will gradually evolve as time and money permit. It should be pointed out that the cost of a CATV-based network would be far less than one based on existing telephone lines, where lines at present are far too costly to allow most libraries the use of even such simple devices as telefacsimile.

While the technical and economic parameters are likely to become considerably more favorable in the future, problems of equal or greater significance will have to be solved in the area of copyright lest we find that what is technically possible and fiscally feasible is also—regrettably— illegal. Long-overdue revision of the 1909 copyright statute has been hung up on the complex questions of present-day CATV and how the proprietary rights in the television programs of local and distant stations are to be accommodated when a CATV system brings the programs of Los Angeles stations to San Antonio, Texas. How much more complex, then, will be the vexing issues to be solved before a page of copyrighted text can be delivered to the user in ephemeral or hard copy form? This is not to say that our present dreams are doomed to disaster, but that if we wish to see them come true, we shall need to keep an eye upon copyright as well as upon cable.

If we believe that the future does indeed hold this kind of promise and if we accept the vastly increased user services possible with a CATV network as desirable, then what can we do right now to be sure that libraries will be entitled to their rightful share of the system? As we said before, franchises are awarded locally. This means that city fathers nego- tiate with a CATV company; whoever offers the most attractive "deal" to the city or town usually wins out. In the past, this was often a matter of money. We have seen countless CATV systems going in with little thought being given to educational or informational use, with little knowledge of technological developments. City fathers are usually not expected to be television engineers; therefore we have many cases where CATV can only distribute a limited number of channels and cannot expand to include two-way communication and other, newer developments. The educa- tional community has only recently realized the potential of cable televi- sion, and often did not plead its case early enough to see to it that certain channels were set aside for its use. Lack of information has prevented open-ended franchises allowing for expansion; many run for a given number of years and terms cannot be changed.

There are certain steps librarians can take right now to inform them- selves about the local situation and to convince other interested parties that libraries do indeed have a stake in CATV systems. The first step might be to find out where your community is in the development of CATV. Do you presently have such a system? Who holds the franchise? What are its provisions? For how long does it run? Who is the manager? Get to know him and show him that you are truly interested. Is the system owned by a small company or by a corporation which operates a number of other systems (a "multiple system owner")? What kind of a record does the company have, in your town and in other towns? Have channels already been set aside for educational purposes?

If there is no CATV system in your town, what are the plans for the future? Has the city government been approached by prospective oper- ators? And most important, are members of the city government properly informed of all technical and social aspects of cable television? Are hear- ings being held? Who has presented testimony? What did it say?

The second, and very important step, is to find out who else is interested in educational and instructional uses of CATV in your commu- nity. Have you talked with your local school administration? How about the educational television station? Do you have closed-circuit television in the schools already? How about the local college or university? The YMCA? Other groups engaged in educational programs? Why not form a planning group of all interested parties? By discussing common goals and objectives, and then presenting a united front to city government in the pursuance of these, much more can be achieved than when we go it alone. Too, librarians are not likely to be ready with a full-fledged program of their own, and in some areas they may always wish to share channels rather than have one allocated solely to library purposes; in this way they can combine forces with others having mutual interests right now, and make their voice heard. Early creation of a planning group would serve another purpose; it could prevent needless duplication of services, given by various community agencies, and may have the added benefit for the library of making other agencies aware of the library's present and potential services via CATV, as well as its more traditional ones.

Another goal of a planning group should be to keep its members continuously informed about technical developments and results of FCC rulemaking so that they can present city government with the necessary technical information, as well as means of achieving stated goals of local programs. Some suggested readings are appended; there is a vast literature on the subject, much of it written in layman's language, which the librarian can read and provide to other interested parties.

There are those among us who say that before we plead our case for CATV, we must decide "what to put on the channel." They say that we are so enamored of technology that we forget the many problems yet to be solved before we can take full advantage of all that is available now. We agree—in principle. In practice, we must make our case now. There are only so many channels; and many, many interested parties are clamoring for them. If we don't participate in franchise negotiations, we are sure to be left out, probably forever. An analogy might be to say that we cannot support the funding of the "Networks for Knowledge Act" (1968) because we do not yet know what types of networks we want, or what we want to put on them. The time to act is now; planning must proceed apace, but it must not deter us from doing what has to be done.

To quote from a recent paper:

> Enlightened self-interest of those who plan communications networks requires, as does the public interest, that parochialism give way to broader vision, and that acute specialization be tempered with cooperation. Each new development in communications—new technology; new policy decisions . . . offer[s] an increasingly favorable climate for the development of library communications and other information networks. Library and information specialists can help themselves, and others, if they will seek to pool their interests and cooperate fully in the pursuit of the new opportunities which are now increasingly within our common grasp.

REFERENCES

1. Unpublished estimate provided by Research Department, National Cable Television Association, Washington, D.C.

2. Federal Communications Commission Docket No. 18397, *Notice of Proposed Rule Making and Notice of Inquiry*, (FCC 68-1175), p. 5.

3. Frank W. Norwood, *Telecommunications Programs Affecting Network Development*, paper presented for the *Conference on Interlibrary Communications and Information Networks*, Warrenton, Va., Sept.28–Oct. 2, 1970, p. 38.

BIBLIOGRAPHY

Joint Council on Educational Telecommunications. 1969. What Every Educational Media Specialist Ought to Know about CATV. *Audiovisual Instruction* 14(8):67-75.

Joint Council on Educational Telecommunications. 1968. *CATV: Data Base.* Washington: The Council, 1126 16th St., N.W. 4 pp.

Kemeny, John G. et al. 1962. A Library for 2000 A.D. Martin Greenberger, ed. *Computers and the World of the Future.* Cambridge: M.I.T. Press. Pp. 134-178.

Licklider, J. C. R. 1967. Televistas: Looking Ahead Through Side Windows. *Public Television: A Program for Action.* The Report and Recommendations of the Carnegie Commission on Educational Televison. New York: Harper & Row. Pp. 201-225.

National Education Association. 1971. *Schools and Cable Television.* Washington: NEA, Division of Educational Technology. 66 pp. $2.25.

Norwood, Frank W. CATV and Educational TV. *Audiovisual Instruction* 13(2): 1058-1061.

Programming Video

by Seth Feldman

After a half decade of optimistic expansion, the video movement has reached a point where an organized effort must be undertaken to establish the most efficient methods of viewing and distributing the products of the medium. Enormous sums have been spent on small gauge video facilities, yet these facilities are notoriously underused. The artists, documentarians and social scientists who have used video seldom issue catalogs or contribute to the books and journals on the uses of video. At the same time, the large commercial distribution systems being set up by the entertainment and education material industries threaten to, in the McLuhanesque sense, force the products of the old media onto the new (that is transfer existing films onto videotape).

It will be the video programmer's job to wade through the avalanche of commercial material becoming available to find those works which best demonstrate video's unique artistic, documentary and social interaction potentials. To aid in this pursuit, this article will: present a few basic guidelines to the acquisition of video equipment and trends in equipment development; give some sources of the more interesting work in the medium; and suggest some options for video presentation. While any such information is as vulnerable to obsolescence as the medium's equipment, it is my hope that enough interest and energy may be generated to save a large body of valuable work from a fatal neglect.

VIDEOTAPE FORMATS

While large institutions may be able to allocate funds to purchase and experiment with the many types of video equipment available, the best advice that can be given to a video programmer at a medium size or small institution is to borrow rather than buy equipment. It should not be too difficult for a library to borrow equipment from other institutions. The audio visual department of a large university might be able to lend video equipment itself or provide some ideas as to where such equipment may be obtained in the community.

Should rental or loans of equipment be impossible, the choice faced by anyone in the market for small gauge video is basically between the half-inch reel to reel and the three-quarter inch cassette formats. From the outset, the video consumer should be warned that the quarter-inch format, introduced during the first years of the video movement, is no longer used in the United States. The one-inch format, which has enjoyed some popularity as an institutional standard, has never been popular among video artists and documentarians because the different systems manufactured by different companies are nearly all incompatible.

The video work done in one inch formats as well as the work done on two-inch tape by those video artists with access to commercial and NET television studios, may be transferred to the more popular formats. The best possible transfer is between two-inch and three-quarter inch tape. Generally, transfers between half-inch and three-quarter inch tapes produce satisfactory results.

The choice between the half-inch and three-quarter inch formats is an important one in determining the direction in which any video program will go. The advantage of the half-inch reel to reel system is that it has been the closest thing to a universal standard that the video movement has known in its first half decade. With the exception of the CV format equipment (discontinued in 1971), all half-inch video equipment is compatible with each other, or can be made compatible with connecting cables. In addition, almost all documentary video has been done on half-inch and much of the work done by small documentary independent video artists exists only on half-inch. Half-inch has another advantage in that tapes on this format are easier to study than cassettes as the reels themselves may be moved manually, while referring back to an earlier portion of a cassette involves the careful manipulation of a motorized system. (This may change within the next few years when cassette decks, now in the design stage, appear with fast forward devices that will let the viewer instantly move to any spot on the tape being viewed.)

The major advantage of half-inch video at the present time is that it is the most useful production format. Compact, lightweight half-inch equipment has proven its versatility in millions of hours of field work. Thus, any video program incorporating viewer-generated images must, at least for the next two or three years, be designed around half-inch tape decks. At the same time, it should be noted that half-inch video cameras, with the proper connecting cables, are compatible with three-quarter inch recording equipment. When portable three-quarter inch decks become available, the only investment necessary will be the deck itself and the cables necessary to connect it with previously purchased cameras and monitors.

In its favor, the three-quarter inch cassette has been widely agreed upon as the future standard for pre-packaged software. At least one major manufacturer of video equipment is, over the vigorous objections of half-inch users, beginning to phase out half-inch in favor of the three-quarter inch cassette. Commercial distributors have already invested millions of dollars putting theatrical and educational film material on three-quarter inch. Both hardware and software manufacturers claim that the three-quarter inch image is superior to that of half-inch. While not everyone who has compared the two formats has been able to discern a difference in visual quality, it is generally agreed that the extra sound channel provided on the cassettes greatly enhances the audio potential of the medium.

Perhaps the greatest advantage of three-quarter inch is the ease in handling inherent in the cassette. Half-inch users point out that no tape deck made was ever as difficult to thread as even the simplest manually-threaded movie projector. Nevertheless, the psychological advantage of presenting the viewer with a book-like package which need only be put in the appropriate slot makes video as a whole that much more attractive to millions of people who are otherwise shy of what they believe to be a complex technology. Some of the library systems in New York State have solved the dilemma of whether to go with half-inch reel to reel or three-quarter inch cassette by acquiring both types of equipment.

THE VIDEO DISC

Within the next two or three years, video disc systems will probably be competing with the tape formats. While not necessarily replacing tapes (in the same way that the long playing audio record has not replaced audio tape), the video disc will represent the most efficient way of storing video information. Systems being tested now store up to an hour of video on twelve-inch discs that are just slightly thicker than audio records. Some systems allow the disc to be fed into the deck while still in its jacket, thus providing the ease in handling of a cassette.

Video discs have two major disadvantages. Most of the disc systems now under study are designed for playback only, a factor which will restrict production in this format to large commercial studios. This disadvantage will be somewhat mitigated by interfacing tape with discs in the same way that present day music lovers record LP's onto tape systems. The second disadvantage of discs is the number of incompatible systems that are scheduled to flood the market during the first years of disc use. The types of video discs under study range from comparatively simple modifications of audio systems to highly sophisticated devices using laser beams to read tiny bits of binary information. As there appears to be no attempt to agree upon a standard for all video disc production, the video disc consumer may look forward to a repetition of the half decade of technological chaos that accompanied the introduction of video tape.

Finally, whatever hardware format is chosen by the video programmer now or in the future, the deck (and, of course, the monitor) to be used should be capable of color reproduction. While black and white images were the rule in early documentary video, the increasing use of portable color equipment as well as the large body of work in color produced by video artists, makes color presentation a necessity. Surprisingly, the difference in cost between color and black and white decks is, depending on the particular equipment in question, seldom more than the difference in cost between color and black and white monitors.

SOFTWARE

In the beginning there were simply video and video makers. Those involved with the medium experimented with the various possibilities of it without thought of specialization. Tapes were distributed by word of mouth and sometimes through the galleries that grew out of living room screenings. Out of this situation, however, there has evolved a split between those interested in video's use as a documentary tool and those interested in its artistic potential. There has also evolved the beginnings of an attempt to organize video distribution through both documentary groups and art galleries.

The following is a beginner's list, an invitation to further exploration rather than a guarantee of inclusiveness. The organizations and individuals represent a far from complete spectrum of video. As video organizations and individual artists are a far from sedentary lot, some of the information listed may already be out of date. To compensate for this particular kind of software obsolescence, I can only suggest that the video programmer refer to the periodicals listed on page 173 for changes in available material and addresses.

DOCUMENTARY TAPES

The following groups have been selected to illustrate the diversity of interests, size and geographic location of those involved in using video to document social reality and change. It is hoped that contacting these groups will yield not only tapes for programming but also information and ideas on setting up local video production.

Alternate Media Center, School of the Arts, New York University, 144 Bleecker St., New York, NY 10012
> —a well organized program for the study and encouragement of video production, AMC has set up video apprenticeships at cable stations around the nation as well as publishing information on the movement.

April Video Collective, Box 77, Rte. 375, Woodstock, NY 12498
> —produces tapes on natural farming and Indian lore and is a good source of information concerning video activity.

Ant Farm, 994 Union Street, San Francisco, Cal
> —one of the most successful West Coast video collectives.

Antioch-Baltimore, 805 North Charles St., Baltimore, Md. 21202
> —produces and distributes excellent community tapes.

Vince Brown, Big Valley Cablevision, Stockton, Cal.
—sponsored partly by AMC and the University of the Pacific, has produced tapes on community culture.

Charis Horton, Broadside TV, 204 East Watauga Ave., Johnson City, Tenn. 37601
—tapes on Indians, miners and health clinics in rural Tennessee. Partly sponsored by AMC.

Diane Bockrath, Inner City Office, Buffalo and Erie County Library, Lafayette Square, Buffalo, NY 14203
—tapes made through a library system and used in conjunction with a mobil media van to meet urban problems.

Andy Beecher, Comax Telcom, 850 Elk St., Buffalo, NY 14210
—has used video in conjunction with a library program and to document local events. Partly sponsored by AMC.

Challenge for Change, National Film Board of Canada, Box 6100, Montreal, Quebec H3C 3H5, Canada
—perhaps the largest single video program to date, Challenge for Change has been responsible for the production of tapes throughout Canada.

Communications for Change, 1453 West Addison St., Chicago, Ill. 60613

Community Media Inc., P. O. Box 24272, St. Louis, Missouri 63130

Community Service Inc., Local Channel 10, 321 West Main St., Frankfort, Kentucky 40601

Gary Knowles, Complete Channel TV, 5723 Tokay Blvd., Madison, Wisconsin 53711
—tapes on religious and community activities. Partly sponsored by AMC.

Grant Masland, Communication Workshop, University of Nebraska at Omaha, Omaha, Neb. 68101

Kim Beaman and Nancy Hauser, Continental Cablevision of Michigan, 2000 Cooper St., Jackson, Michigan 49202

James Ludwig, Flathead Valley Community College, Kalispell, Montana

Global Village, 454 Broome St., New York, NY 10012
—distributes a large collection of well made and provocative tapes.

Hum Video, 5811 South Ellis, Chicago, Ill. 60637

Lance Wisniewski, Innervision, Box 35, Syracuse, NY 14850

Ithaca Video Project, 509 West Clinton, Ithaca, NY

Chuck Anderson, Faculty Project Advisor, Longwood High School, Middle Island, NY
—one of the most ambitious uses of video in the public schools.

Los Angeles Public Access Project, 1802 Berkeley St., Santa Monica, Cal. 90404
   —conducts workshops and distributes tapes on local problems and events.

Jeff Ullman, Community Access Center, Monroe County Public Library, 303 East Kirkwood, Bloomington, Ind. 47401
   —has used tape to interface library and community activities with cable. Partly sponsored by AMC.

David Korte, Public Access Coordinator, National Cable Company, P.O. Box 918, East Lansing, Michigan 48823

Tom Klinkowstein, Neighborhood Project, 416 West Onondaga St., Syracuse, NY 13202

Village Neighborhood Television, New School for Social Research, Room 408, 66 West 12th St., New York, NY 10011

Tom Germano, New York Letter Carrier's Union, 255 West 43rd St., New York, NY 10036
   —video used in union work.

George Story, Media Consultant, Office for the Aging, 250 Broadway, New York, NY 10017

Bill Stephens, People's Communication Network, 191 Claremont Ave., Apt. 32, New York, NY 10027

Glenn Silber, People's Video, 953 Jennifer St., Madison, Wisconsin 53703

Portable Channel, 8 Prince St., Rochester, NY 14607
   —distributes a large collection of tapes.

Edward de Sciora, Port Washington Library, Green Hays, Port Washington, NY 11050
   —The Port Washington Library has done extensive work with video.

Project Accountability, 1424 K St. NW, Washington, D.C.

Debi Amos, Workshop Coordinator, Public Access Workshop, 111 Virginia Drive, Orlando, Florida 32803

Bill Werner, Program Manager, Racine Telecable, 2081 South Greenbay Road, Racine, Wisconsin 53406

Survival Arts, 455 Broadway, New York, NY 10012

Kathy Bogle, Telecable Inc., Concord, N.H.
   —has used video in high schools. Partly sponsored by AMC.

Sue Miller, Telepromter of Dubuque, Dubuque, Iowa
   —has produced children's tapes and tapes about local culture. Partly sponsored by AMC.

Top Value Television, Box 630, San Francisco, Cal. 94101
   —a large, well organized group attempting to produce and distribute video documentaries on a commercial basis.

True View Trenton, 2 Rogers Ave., Trenton, NJ 08618
—tapes on community problems.

Bill Koenig, Video Access Center, P.O. Box 146, Columbus, Ind. 47201

Videocrafts, 14H Barrett Drive, Kendall Park, NJ 08824

Video Free America, Arthur Ginsberg, 1948 Fell St., San Francisco, Cal. 95018
—distributes a large collection of video.

Videofreex, Maple Tree Farm, Lanesville, NY 12450
—a good source of both tapes and information.

Videographe, 1604 St. Dennis, Montreal 129 Quebec
—tapes in both English and French on community use of video.

Videopolis, 4200 Marine Drive, Chicago, Ill, 60613

Jean Rice, Viking Media, Monoa, Wisconsin
—tapes on the Youth Corps, state government and community organization. Partly sponsored by AMC.

Rodger C. Prois, Vision Cable Television Co., Fort Lee, NJ
—children's tapes, local news, cultural and historical events. Partly sponsored by AMC.

Washington Community Video Center, 2414 18th St. NW, Washington, D.C. 20009
—a good source of tapes and information on community organizing.

Carol Lynn Yellin, Women in Cable Inc., Suite 2217, Sterick Building, Memphis, Tenn. 38103

VIDEO ART

Because the distribution of video art is in its infancy, the video programmer will, for some time to come, have to depend on a variety of sources for information about individual pieces and where to obtain them. Once again, the programmer is directed to the references in Appendix One. He may also contact local video documentarians who are aware of video activity in the area. Given the current state of distribution, advertising that the library is interested in displaying video art may be one of the more effective ways of learning about interesting video pieces.

Video programmers in the New York City area are, as will be seen below, at a distinct advantage when it comes to programming video art. While video art is going on all over the country, only a handful of New York art galleries have taken it upon themselves to set up distribution systems along the lines of film rental organizations. New York area programmers may not only preview tapes at these galleries but also have access to the regular video art programming at the Museum of Modern Art and at the several video showcases advertised in publications such as the *Village Voice*.

Hopefully, by the time this is being read, the following list of video galleries will be far from complete:

Castelli/Sonnabend Video and Film Corporation, 420 West Broadway, New York, NY 10012
>—distributes works by Lynda Benglis, Hermine Freed, Frank Gillette, Nancy Holt, Joan Jonas, Paul Kos, Richard Landry, Andy Mann, Robert Morris, Bruce Nauman, Richard Serra, Keith Sonnier and William Wegman. The gallery also rents a series of videotapes made by Hermine Freed about plastic artists.

Electronic Arts Intermix, 84 Fifth Avenue, New York, NY 10011
>—distributes tapes by Peter Campus, Peter Crown, Ed Emshwiller, Bill and Louise Etra and Nam June Paik and others. Electronic Arts Intermix is also distributing many of the experimental videotapes made at the television laboratories at WGBH (Boston), WNET (New York) and the National Center for Experiments in Television (affiliated with KQED in San Francisco).

Ronald Feldman Gallery, 33 West 74th Street, New York, NY 10021
>—distributes tapes by Agnetti, Joseph Beuys, Chris Burden and Hannah Wilke.

Stephanotty Gallery, 50 West 57th Street, New York, NY 10019
>—distributes tapes by video artists Eleanor Antin, Douglas Davis, Hans Haacke, Take Iimura, Allan Kaprow, Akira Kokubo, Fred Krughoff, Les Levine, Munroe-Schwartz, Dennis Oppenheim, Charlemagne Palestine and Roger Welch. Also distributes tapes by plastic artists: K. H. Hodicke, Al Hansen, Ulrike Rosenbach, Colette, Richard Landry, Gene Highstein, Robert Kushner and James Dearing.

Visual Resources Inc., 1 Lincoln Plaza, New York, NY 10023
>—publishes *Art and Cinema,* a journal of reviews of film and video art distributed by the galleries.

The following video artists distribute their own works. They are singled out for the reasons indicated:

Shirley Clarke, Hotel Chelsea, 222 West 23rd St., New York, NY 10011
>—Ms. Clarke and her troupe have developed a set of video interaction pieces based on audience participation and multi-camera and monitor input and display. Because the presence of her and her assistants is integral to Ms. Clarke's use of video, the programmer faces a major logistical task in booking her work.

Eric Seigal, Apt. 2K, 1620 Ocean Ave., Brooklyn, NY 11230
>—Mr. Seigel has been responsible for important innovations in synthesizing and colorizing images. His work includes both abstract and documentary pieces.

Woody and Steina Vasulka, 257 Franklin St., Buffalo, NY 14202
>—The Vasulkas have experimented with all varieties of video experience. While running the Kitchen Video Gallery in New York, they

played an important role in organizing the video movement. Both Woody and Steina have extensive teaching experience and are excellent lecturers both on the mechanics of their own work and on the dynamics of video art.

Walter Wright, 207 North Avenue, New Rochelle, NY 10801
—Mr. Wright has continued to produce some of the most technologically sophisticated video works. His early pieces rank among the classics of the movement.

PRESENTING VIDEO

Once hardware and software have been arranged for, video offers a tremendous potential for creative programming and presentation. While, as may be seen above, establishing a situation in which a small group of people watch one monitor being fed by one tape deck is no small accomplishment, it is, nevertheless, only a beginning.

If at all possible, the video tape maker or group of makers should be present at the screening of his or their work.

Whether or not the tape's maker is present, the video programmer should make every effort to duplicate the environment for which the tape's maker might have designed his work. If this is impossible, or if (as will be the case with most video documentary) there is no particular environment best suited for the work, the programmer is free to experiment with the most effective means of presentation. With the help of a distribution amplifier, a single tape deck can feed a larger number of monitors than is ever likely to be available. This should encourage the programmer to try to obtain as many monitors as possible—a task which becomes easier if the tape to be shown is in black and white.

If no particular arrangement of monitors is specified by a tape's maker, then the goal of the video programmer should be to provide the greatest degree of intimacy possible between individual spectators and monitors. Monitors should be spread around a room so that large groups of spectators are not forced to cluster around one set. The programmer may wish to place single monitors in confined spaces so that viewers may take turns having a one to one relationship with the images being screened. Or he may wish to arrange monitors in a circle facing inward so that a sense of simultaneously experiencing a communal event may be generated. Other configurations of monitor placements may be suggested by the shape of a particular room, the nature of a particular audience or by the nature of the material to be viewed.

Video projectors are another option open to the programmer. There are presently two video projectors on the market, priced at about $3000, which have color capability. Both machines are fed directly by a tape deck (though the deck can also simultaneously feed monitors). Both machines will throw an image that can be viewed comfortably by 50 to 100 people. In practice, the video projector when used alone converts video exhibition into film exhibition, concentrating everyone's gaze to the front of the room where one large image is filling a screen.

Even without the advent of the video projector, the video environment represents a transitory phase in video presentation. Video is, ultimately, a private experience. The proliferation of television sets to the point where there is more than one per individual in the United States seems to indicate that we want to be alone with our images. It will, of course, be some time—if ever—before the products of the video movement become available on these millions of individual sets. Nevertheless, the video programmer may wish to set up small areas in which individuals can show themselves video tapes the same way they look at slides, family albums or read a book.

A creative and eclectic video program is one step toward democratization of the electronic image. A second, complementary step is the demystification of electronic media through the encouragement of individual and community video production. If a video program is to demonstrate the full range of the medium's potential, it should include tapes made by members of the community concerning images familiar to those in the audience. An evening's video programming could also usefully be consumed with the making of an interaction tape in which members of an audience might be taped interacting with a tape of themselves made moments before. The resulting experience would demonstrate the effects of social feedback far better than any pre-packaged software.

Anything that can be done with video equipment can be interfaced with local cable stations. Thus the above mentioned series on community events could be cablecast as could story hours, tapes of guest speakers and video bulletins of upcoming library events. Librarians could even enhance these events with the creative use of graphic techniques. Speakers, for instance, might be encouraged to bring visual aids of any size or type. Similarly, the illustrations in children's books might be part of a taped story hour.

Beyond these hints of the potential of video production in the library, it is not the purpose of this article to outline a program of video production. It is appropriate, however, to point out that video cameras are becoming less expensive and will, in the near future, offer a color capability at less than present black and white prices. Instant color, sound synch production can and should be made available to anyone wishing to use it. That so few of the close to 100 libraries supplied with video equipment make this potential available to their patrons is perhaps one of the greatest failings of both the libraries and the video movement. For more than any of its spectacular hardware and software products, this enormous potential for personal, cultural and social development is what video is all about.

VIDEO BOOKS AND PERIODICALS

Books

Anderson, Chuck, *The Electronic Journalist: An Introduction to Video* (Praeger, 1973)

—a reasonably clear, well written and up to date manual for the use of small gauge video equipment.

Aspen Notebooks on Communications and Society (Praeger, 1973)

—this excellent series of anthologies on video and television includes: *Aspen Notebook: Cable and Continuing Education* (ed. Richard Adler); *Aspen Notebook on Government And The Media* (ed. William L. Rivers and Michael J. Nyhan); *Getting to Sesame Street* (Richard M. Polsky); *Cable Television USA* (Martin H. Seiden); *Television Programming for News and Public Affairs* (Frank Wolf); and *Children and the Urban Environment; A Learning Experience* (ed. Marshall Kaplan et al). In 1974, Praeger published another Aspen study, *The Electronic Box Office; Humanities and Arts on the Cable* (ed. Richard Adler and Walter Baer), containing an excellent piece by Kas Kalba on the video movement ("The Video Implosion: Models for Reinventing Television").

Aspen Handbook on the Media; Research, Publications, Organizations (available: Aspen Program on Communications and Society, Palo Alto Office, 770 Welch Road, Palo Alto, Cal. 94304)

—describes nearly 200 publications, organizations, university programs and other endeavors in communications research.

Catalogs, Everson Museum of Art, Syracuse, NY

—the Everson Museum has published catalogs on the work of video artists Nam June Paik, Juan Downey, Douglas Davidson, Frank Gillette and Peter Campus.

Center for Understanding Media, *Doing the Media: A Portfolio Of Activities and Resources* (available: Center for Understanding Media, 72 Horatio St., New York, NY)

—uses of video and other media with children.

Cooperstown TV is a Museum (available: Videofreex, Maple Tree Farm, Lanesville, NY 12450)

—the proceedings of an historical society conference on the uses of video for documentation.

Howard, Brice, *Videospace* (available: National Center for Experiments in Television, 288 7th St., San Francisco, Cal. 94103)

—a personal philosophic analysis of the basics and meaning of video.

The Network Project Reports (available: The Network Project, 101 Earl Hall, Columbia University, New York, NY 10027)

—a series of political analyses of telecommunications issues. Pamphlets published so far include: *Domestic Communications Satellites; Directory of the Networks; Control of Information; Office of Tele-*

communications Policy; Cable Television; Down Sesame Street; and *The Case Against Satellites.*

Price, Monroe and Wicklein, John, *Cable Television; A Guide For Citizen Action* (Pilgrim Press, 1972)
—explanation of cable services and requirements with a good bibliography of information on cable.

Shamberg, Michael, *Guerilla Television* (Holt, Rinehart and Winston, 1971)
—a guide to the uses and politics of portable video equipment. Provides comprehensive, though dated, analysis of the use of video as a social tool.

Sloan Commission on Cable Communications, *On the Cable: The Television of Abundance* (McGraw Hill, 1971)
—a thorough report on the history, politics and potential of cable.

Smith, Ralph Lee, *The Wired Nation* (Harper and Row, 1972)
—a perceptive essay on why cable often fails to meet its potential.

Stroh, Thomas F., *The Uses of Videotape in Training and Development* (American Management Association, 1969)
—an interesting insight into the uses of video for training and behavior modification in the business world.

Tate, Charles, *Cable Television in the Cities: Community Control, Public Access and Minority Ownership* (The Urban Institute, 2100 M St. NW, Washington, D.C. 20037)
—suggests strategies for using cable to affect social change in cities.

Telecommunications Reports (available: Abt Associates Inc., 55 Wheeler St., Cambridge, Mass, 02138)
—commissioned by HEW, the Abt pamphlets include: *Telecommunications Technologies; Telecommunications and Community Services; Telecommunications and Municipal Management; Telecommunications and Health Services; Telecommunications and Education.*

TV as Art, ed. Patric D. Hazard (available: National Council of Teachers of English, 508 South 6th St., Champaign, Ill, 61820)
—essays on the use of video in elementary schools.

TVTV, *The Prime Time Survey* (available: TVTV, Box 630, San Francisco, Cal. 94101)
—TVTV's report on new developments in video hardware and in its own software.

Video Exchange Directory (available: Video Exchange Directory, 358 Powell St., Vancouver 4, British Columbia)
—a guide to the whereabouts and activities of video groups in the U.S. and Canada.

Videofreex, *The Spaghetti City Video Manual* (Praeger, 1973)
—an accurate, flippant guide to small gauge video equipment.

Video Production (available: Petersen Publishing Co., 8490 Sunset Blvd., Los Angeles, Cal. 90069)
   —a little known though excellent guide to video equipment.

Video Research Directory (available: New York State Council on The Arts, 20 West 57th St., New York, NY 10019)
   —when available in late 1974, the Directory should represent the most complete and up to date guide to software in North America.

Videotapes in Psychiatric Training and Treatment, Milton M. Berger, ed. (Brunner/Manzel Inc., 1970)
   —a collection of articles on the early application of video as a mental health tool. Contains a good, though dated, bibliography.

Youngblood, Gene, *Expanded Cinema* (E. P. Dutton, 1970)
   —a collection of reviews of some of the first works of video art amid reviews of other film and multi-media works. *Expanded Cinema* is particularly valuable for its overview of the interface of technology, art and society.

Periodicals

Arts Canada (129 Adelaide W., Suite 400, Toronto, Ontario)
   —publishes occasional video articles. Vol. 30, no. 4 was devoted entirely to video.

Avalanche Magazine and *Avalanche Newspaper* (93 Grand St., New York, NY 10013)
   —both publications have frequent articles on video art. A special May/June, 1974 issue of the magazine dealt entirely with video.

Challenge for Change (available: Challenge for Change, National Film Board of Canada, Box 6100, Montreal, Quebec H3C 3H5)
   —progress reports on various aspects of the largest single ongoing video enterprise.

Community Access Video (Apt. E, 695 30th Ave., Santa Cruz, Cal.)
   —published irregularly to deal with social issues of video and cable.

Community Video Report (Washington Community Center, 2414 18th St, NW, Washington, D.C. 20009)
   —a quarterly review of developments in community video and hardware.

Educational And Industrial Television (C. S. Tepfer Publishing, 607 Main St., Ridgefield, Conn.)
   —technical information on video tools.

National Center for Experiments in Television Reports (288 7th St., San Francisco, Cal. 94103)
   —an irregularly issued collection of mimeographed papers on video topics.

Publications Program (Alternate Media Center, New York University School of the Arts, 144 Bleecker St., New York, NY 10012)
    —assorted information on video and cable, including excellent bibliographies and addresses of individuals and organizations.

Radical Software (Gordon and Breach, One Park Ave., New York, NY 10016)
    —the mainstay publication of the video movement, *Radical Software* now publishes thematic issues while continuing to provide up to date information on the activities of video artists and documentarians.

Urban Telecommunications Forum (267 Riverside Drive, New York, NY)
    —a monthly review of information concerning the use of video in the cities.

Videoscope (Gordon and Breach, One Park Ave., New York, NY 10016)
    —a new publication promising to devote itself to "all aspects of video."

Note: For assistance in preparing this report, the author wishes to thank the Alternate Media Center, Sandy Rockowitz *of Portable Channel, and the April Video Collective. Special thanks to* Woody Vasulka, *without whose obstinate argumentativeness this article could not have been written.*

Guerrilla Television in the Public Library

by Jay R. Peyser

We are living in the middle of a myth, the myth of an information explosion. Rather, there is a mass communications explosion, a plethora of media to transport broad-based information from area to area. But, there is still a dearth of local community information in any given area. This information, possibly the most vital of all, is usually not available in any of these mass communications formats, and therefore cannot be supplied *on an individual demand* by the public library or any other agency in the community. The traditional library only supplies passive use of mass-produced resources: periodicals, books, records, et al, and these resources do not facilitate the dissemination of community information. The library, if it is to be a community information resource, has to change from its old staid role to an active one; creating information, giving a voice to the community, and helping it learn about itself. If the informational needs of the community are not being filled by traditional libraries, then what has to be created is a library geared toward local production of community information resources, helping people understand the dynamics of their community.

The Huntington Public Library, in recognition of this need, and utilizing a $10,000 gift from its Board of Trustees and a $5000 grant from the New York State Council on the Arts, opened up its Video Project in May 1972, with the goal of creating an interchange of ideas within Huntington by making locally relevant information—produced by community groups and individuals—available.

WHY VIDEOTAPE?

Television is the most powerful medium in society today. It's part of the average American's environment. The tube is on for hours on end, regardless of programming. So far, libraries have not exploited this made-to-order information box, quite possibly because librarians, as others, have been awed by the aura of commercial television. But, the aura is being shattered. Portable television cameras and recorders are here to stay and Everyman is now a walkin', talkin', shoot-from-the-hip television producer. And children, who are now weaned on *Sesame Street, The Electric Company,* and *Sonny and Cher,* will no longer shun the monochromatic, two-dimensional library who does not acknowledge the existence of Oscar the Grouch, for they, and their parents and grandparents, can now create their own shows about themselves and about the community and play them back on any television set.

Through videotape the library can become a production center of local information, a training and production base for community resources. At the Huntington Public Library we train any community individual, group, or agency in the use of the Sony Porta-Pak videotape cameras and then lend them the equipment and blank television (½") tapes. They can then go into the community and shoot the piece of information that concerns them, be it a Consumer Protection Board Meeting or a creative, original film being worked on by teenagers. When the raw footage has been shot, they come back to the library, are trained in editing and sound-dubbing, if necessary, so that they can edit the tapes into a final, presentable production. The library exercises no direct supervision as to what goes on the tapes—it's community-based information, not *library*-based information. We act only as the catalyst in the production, without censorial prerogative. Previously a group had no way of letting people know of its work—it can now use the library's facilities to make the community aware of its contributions. If the group who produced a tape, or any other individual or agency, would like to borrow a tape, a duplicate copy is made from the videocassette and, along with the necessary equipment for playback, is lent out; thereby, serving all the community's group and individual needs. The borrowing of tapes is encouraged so as to facilitate the free interchange of ideas. Thus, the library, who foots the total cost of any production is the owner of the tapes. They are available for free.

INDIVIDUAL ACCESS

The ease and accessibility of playback facilities are of the utmost importance to any videotape project, for any information should be readily available to the individual. Though the library will loan out equipment for group showings in the community on demand, this does not answer the need for individual interest in information. If a patron enters a library he has free and immediate access to any book, periodical, or filmstrip. But, if he is to be expected to thread a reel-to-reel videotape machine to watch a tape produced by the Department of Environmental Protection, then the information will go unseen. Who has the time? To overcome this difficulty, the Huntington Public Library invested in videocassette equipment (Sony ¾" videocassette), as an extension of its video services. Located in the main reading room of the library is a 17" television monitor with color capabilities and a videocassette player. When a tape is finalized on ½" reel-to-reel tape it is transferred to ¾" videocassette and placed on a shelf next to the television. (The cassettes can be labeled and shelved as books.)

Now, when a patron enters the library in search of information on Walt Whitman, who was born in Huntington, he can take a videocassette off the shelf, drop it into the player, and watch it on television. The information is as accessible as any other piece of library material. The library has also invested in a dozen wireless headsets and a 12-channel transmitter, so there is no possibility that the audio portion of the television production will disturb other patrons. The entire main floor is wired for sound and the audio portion of the television show is channeled through the transmitter. Only a patron wearing a headset can hear the soundtrack. One side benefit of the wireless system is that the video-cassette only uses one of 12 channels, thus allowing the other 11 to be used for FM radio, music programs of different types and other television monitors when expanded. A user can look at the weekly program listing posted, select a classical music channel if he so desires, place the headset on and listen to his heart's content while reading or studying. Without constricting wires, he can get up and browse in the stacks, still wearing the headset and still listening to his program.

Of course the whole thrust of any library videotape project should be geared toward Cable Television (CATV)—here in some places but in the immediate future for all. If a community is not visually literate, i.e. trained in videotape work, then it cannot produce its own programming, which is essential for CATV. CATV should devote time to local programming, but the FCC has only given minimal guidelines. It's up to every community library to be in the forefront of efforts to have as much time devoted to local programming as possible. Then the library cannot only be the production center of local information, but it can also be instrumental in working on and with the CATV franchise in its area. Public access television will not work without trained community people, or interested community libraries. A visually literate community is one which can translate its needs into a video format for public access television.

The response at the Huntington Public Library has been over-whelming; the equipment is in constant use.

ECOLOGY AND THE ARTS

The Huntington Department of Environmental Protection was the first group to use our video equipment. After banning certain pesticides for sale in Huntington, the department was brought to court by a group who wanted the ban lifted. The Environmental Protection Agency contacted the library, was trained in the use of video equipment, and produced a tape showing the effect of these pesticides on mammals rather than simply stating that a particular chemical attacked the nervous system when given in small doses (such as could be consumed during spraying). The tape actually illustrated the effects to the court. *Seeing is believing.* They borrowed playback equipment from the library, played the tape, and had it admitted as legal evidence. Now the Department and the Huntington Ecological Union are involved in shooting and editing a major work on the ecology of Huntington—a tape that could be of the utmost importance in this north shore of Long Island community. This latter project illustrates another aspect of the library's videotape project. We are in a natural position to coordinate the activities and goals of different groups working towards the same end. The library arranged and held a meeting between the Department and the Union (a student-based group). The two organizations had never met before. Out of their discussion arose a joint project to co-produce a major videotape on the complete ecological picture of Huntington.

Huntington's Performing Arts Foundation Playhouse is a year-round professional theater in Huntington which puts on productions and teaches acting and improvisational theater. More important, it conducts an "Actor in the Classroom" program where each professional actor is assigned to a local school to work with teachers and students in solving multitudes of educational problems. For example, the actors help children to understand the concept of graphs by clearing off a classroom floor and using the tiles as the squares of the graph. The children stand as points on the graph. This unique program was, for all informational purposes, unknown in Huntington at large. The PAF Playhouse contacted the Huntington Public Library and produced a tape on this "Actor in the Classroom" program. This tape is now on the main floor of the library and has achieved wide exposure in Huntington.

One of the most creative and interesting uses of the video equipment has been with the Orlando Ballet, a company and school located in the town. For the last few months the company has been choreographing original ballets especially for the videotape cameras. This continuing project will result in a series of ballet tapes, produced and edited by Huntington artists and danced by Huntington ballet dancers, thus creating a complete informational cycle—ballet of, by, and for the Huntington community—all made possible by the videotape facilities at the library.

The Consumer Protection Board has been working with the videotape project in producing consumer education tapes, while the Association of American University Women (AAUW) is taping book reviews and preparing a videotaped cooking course, developed for the project by a local gourmet cook.

CHILDREN'S VIDEO

Quite possibly, the most rewarding aspect of the videotape project is our Videotape Workshop for children aged nine to 12. Schools sometimes tend to stifle individual creativity in children, so on an experimental basis the library offered a creative television workshop. The kids would write an original script, act it out, be trained on the video equipment, shoot the production, edit and finalize it—all with minimal supervision.

The small group sat around for two sessions (one 1½ hour session per week), batting around ideas until they formulated a preliminary script. They decided to do a tape about how all the characters in Fairyland were kidnapped, but with a twist . . . Mother Goose was the culprit, kidnapping them for the insurance money. The format chosen to present the idea was a Walter Cronkite newscast, complete with headline stories (Jack and Jill Murders), news flashes (the kidnapping), sports (the three pigs against the two wolves), and commercials (Rapunzel doing a shampoo commercial and Rumpelstiltskin advertising elevator shoes). After the news program we follow Detective Dumbo and Police Sargeant Sunday on the trail of the kidnapped characters until the resolution of the case.

After the finalization of the script, the kids were trained in the use of the videotape equipment and then videotaped auditions for parts. These tapes were later played back to the group at large and actors and director were elected. Everyone got a chance to try out and everyone had his/her turn at the camera.

At present the workshop is acting out the production, developing the acting, shooting for angles, and videotaping in a raw state. Following this step, which utilizes all the children at the camera for one scene or another, editors will be selected by the group after everyone has used the equipment, and the tape will be finalized.

The result of this workshop will be not only a finalized tape which will be added to the collection, but a nucleus of children trained and experienced in expressing themselves in a television format—no longer awed by commercial television. They will not only work in other workshops, to train and work with other children, but will also go out on their own with library video to produce their own tapes or work with adults and groups in the community in producing more information.

These children, now in a learning role, will eventually become teachers and producers in their own right, utilizing library materials and resources, experiencing a library not just as a building but as a creative and vital force in their lives.

Realizing that the library building can only reach a small number of children in such a workshop, HPL is now using community volunteers, trained in the use of videotape by the library, and having them hold similar children's workshops in their homes, in schools, in stores, etc. In this manner, more and more children can be trained, thus extending the library service directly into the community, without necessarily restricting itself to a building.

DOCUMENTARIES

Videotape also has an archival and documentary aspect to it, as exemplified by the tape of a George Plimpton speech at the Huntington Public Library. Those who missed the talk can now come to the library and see it on television. The Lions Club Annual Antique Auto Show as well as the Huntington Heritage Festival are also preserved. Local craftsmen have been contracted and have agreed to produce tapes on their arts for the project. One of them, the Chip Fyn Woodcarving Shop, is one of the only places in the United States that produces Cigar Store Indians and other 19th Century figures, carved by hand from logs, sometimes weighing upwards of 400 pounds. A tape of their work is now available for community people interested in this lost art.

Videotape is so simple (one button and instant replay) and versatile that new uses are presenting themselves every day at the library. A woman, whose husband is a mentalist who performs around Long Island, is now producing a videotape on her husband's work, a subject of great interest in our occult-oriented world.

The Youth Development Association of Huntington is using the equipment in the community with teenagers, producing a videotape on the realities of Hope House, a drug rehabilitation center. Young filmmakers from Huntington are borrowing the videotape equipment for experimental and original film work. A library orientation tape has been produced and placed in videocassette so that a new patron entering the library can plug in the cassette and, in a ten-minute span, become familiar with the layout and services of the Huntington Public Library. The Huntington Tennis Association, having trouble finding a good instructional tennis film, produced their own. In the spring, it will have a professional player who will give instruction once or twice a week at local courts. The videotape cameras will be on the spot so that the community person who is taking the instruction can see himself on tape and see his mistakes. A local golf pro—member of the Professional Golfers Association, who travels around the country playing tournaments—has contacted the library and offered to make golf instructional tapes for free, as a community informational service. Church groups and scouting groups have all used the project, as well as teachers and town officials, and the Knights of Columbus are producing a tape on their drum and bugle corps.

In the spring of 1973 Huntington will undertake a new concept. In preparation for the U.S. Bicentennial Celebration, an hour-long videotape will be produced jointly by the Library, the Town Historian, the Huntington Historical Society, the Sons of the American Revolution (SAR) and the Daughters of the American Revolution (DAR) on "Huntington in the Revolution." Taping will be done in Huntington in 18th Century houses and inns that still have their 1750's furnishings. SAR, DAR, and Historical Society members in costume will act out an original script prepared by the local historians. They will produce a major informational project of, by, and for the Huntington community.

If libraries and librarians allow themselves to adapt their roles, and become not only the collectors of informational materials but also the catalysts in the production of such materials, there need not be a dearth of local information in our communities. Don't let the two-dimensional cartoon-like libraries of yesteryear continue to crawl slowly up Gasoline Alley, for the 21st Century of Buck Rogers is upon us. Let's make the myth of the information explosion a reality.

PART

IV

PRODUCTION

Filmstrips— How to Make Your Own

by William Cloke

Most of you reading this are perhaps looking with a skeptical eye at the mere prospect of writing and making your own filmstrips. Well, it's not as difficult as it might seem. To make simple (for your own use) filmstrips, is not out of the question. They may not be quite the same quality as large companies can produce, but they can be made to tailor themselves to your specific needs.

The main expenses in making a decent quality filmstrip are the original costs to get yourself set up with the materials you need. After that, you can make literally endless numbers of filmstrips or slide shows on every conceivable subject, so the possibilities *are* worth looking into.

What you need to get started: A 35mm camera, close-up lens covers, photocopy stand with lights, viewfinder, carousel slide projector and film, originally. Later, you may want a cassette tape recorder and some stencils for titles. Many companies and/or school districts have available many of these items. Otherwise, for a good shopper the total cost could be as low as $150, which will certainly pay for itself through the value of a relevant up-to-date and original filmstrip. Who knows, this may be the beginning of a whole new adventure in life, adding new avenues for creative expression.

Cameras: Almost any 35mm camera with a lens for attaching filters and close-up lens covers is fine for your needs. Some good makes are: Minolta, Nikon, Nikkormat, Pentax, Fujica, Canon, Konica and Olympus, to name but a few of the better models. The best shooting speeds are from 1/60th of a second to 1/500th of a second. The best f. stop or lens setting is between 8, 5.6, 4, and 2.8. Otherwise, with the more extreme settings the chances of good quality photographs are diminished somewhat.

Film: For indoor shooting and for photocopy work you need a tungsten based film with 3200 Kelvin lights of about 100 watts. (Kelvin refers to the color temperature of the lights.) If you are planning to work indoors and outdoors, there is a film for both called ECO, and it can be purchased at special stores dealing exclusively with film. This type of film was developed by Consolidated Film Industries in Los Angeles. It can be used outdoors with a #85 filter and indoors without a filter. It is actually motion picture film put into rolls for still cameras. When you go shopping for film and filters be sure to bring your camera along, because the lens covers will vary according to the type of camera you are using. The ASA of ECO film is 50, which should cover most normal shooting conditions. ASA refers to the speed of the film which affects the speed at which you can shoot. The higher the ASA the less light you need, the reverse being true when you lower the ASA. If you are shooting outdoors in extreme shade, you might want to push your film. That is, you set your ASA dial higher, say from the normal of 50 to 500 ASA, then let the processor know and he can develop it at a higher speed. This does not hold true for the ECO film and be sure to ask first and shoot later. You may want to buy higher ASA color film such as HIGH SPEED EKTACHROME 160 ASA outdoor film, or HIGH SPEED EKTACHROME Tungsten 3200K indoor 125 ASA. When shooting outdoors a #85 filter is recommended because it cuts the blue rays of the sun and brings the earth tones out more.

Lenses: A normal 55mm lens is all that is usually needed to attain high quality slides. The close-up lens covers will help with photocopy work for they give various degrees of close-up shots for maximum efficiency. If you get carried away or are already a photography buff, you might want to buy a close-up lens or an 80mm to 150mm zoom lens for outside shots. You must always remember, however, that it is good composition which makes for high quality slide photographs. Take your time to get the shot you need. You may not get a better shot after you see that in your haste a telephone pole mars an otherwise beautiful shot. Make them neat and uncluttered, for the best photographs show only what is necessary and nothing more.

Title and theme: For the highest quality work, a working script or theme idea is of extreme importance. It not only saves time and film, but gives your project continuity from the start, which will heighten your creativity to the limits. Without a working outline you are literally fishing without a pole. First, find out if what you want to shoot is already available for purchase. Look in all the latest filmstrip catalogues and if you come up bland or blank you should proceed with a working outline of your ideas, which will in the end save you many hours of wasted energy. Start with a title and an idea. You will probably change everything as you go, but that is good, for the final product is a process of elimination and experimentation, ending in a creation of your own.

Photocopy stand: You can purchase one for very little money. They are easy to operate and have endless uses for copy work from magazines, stories, slide shows and the production of teaching aid filmstrips. Be sure that your lights are on 45° angle to what you are shooting, to eliminate glare and shadows.

Titles and inserts: Here the variations are quite numerous. Art supply stores carry a wide variety of colored stencils and you can even make your own or have some children make them. The main thing to remember, is to make your titles and insert prints or whatever in nonglare matte finish materials and with bright bold colors which will stand out. Try several different f. stop settings to make sure you have the right light for the maximum continuity with the rest of your filmstrip. You can even purchase photographer's press-on letter boards for a very professional looking product. It is the purpose for which the slides are intended that should determine the actual titles to be used.

Arrangement of slides: A carousel of 80 slides will cover approximately 2 filmstrips. There are new commercial filmstrips which contain 80 to 120 photographs. However, for your own purposes 3 to 8 carousels will serve all your needs very well. After you have your film processed, pull out your view finder and if luck is with you, there will be enough slides to follow the logical sequence of your outline. Arrange them in order, which will take some sorting and fussing with different arrangements, but a clear picture should emerge as a final sequence. Put your titles in and shazam! you are done with the visual aspects of your filmstrip.

Sound or narration: Many of you will prefer to narrate your filmstrip yourself as you go, but you can make a cassette tape that will fit your ideas verbally to the slides in the filmstrip. This can be done with a clicker or beep tone, to let the person who is working the projector know when to turn the frame. Music is another way to represent your ideas. Your narration should be as brief as possible, allowing the pictures to tell the main part of the story or idea, with the titles providing pertinent details. Again, the style in which you complete the narration will depend on the purposes and aesthetic tastes of the individual producing the filmstrip.

Commercial Filmstrips: Once you have gained confidence in your ability to make filmstrips you may want to hit the big time and sell your brain child. Well, it's not real easy, but then again, it is not a stone wall either. If you find a gap in the available data in the field you are specializing in, there just may be a chance for you to become a part of the filmstrip business. Professional companies want a fully developed proposal, stating objectives and costs. They will review your proposal and let you know if your budget has been approved. They do pay good prices for interesting ideas. You may want to purchase an illuminated board to put your slides on for arranging purposes.

In conclusion, filmstrips and slide shows can be of enormous importance towards a more complete sensory learning experience and can add an exciting, interesting and creative touch to any professional program.

Production of Slide-Tape Programs

by Carl F. Orgren

INTRODUCTION

Slide-tape programs are a convenient method of preparing instruction for repeated use in the classroom, in independent study, and for continuing and in-service education. This outline will serve as a guideline for the production and presentation of such programs.

CHOICE OF MEDIUM

Is a slide-tape program the best medium for your message? Considerations:

1. Can only simulate motion—so if motion is essential at all, use film.
2. Length of program—not much beyond half an hour, shorter is better.
3. Do you really need visual element? Maybe audio tape is all you need.
4. Does your message need to be "in the can"? Such programs can be repeated with little effort, but can be revised and updated less easily than a live presentation.
5. Slide-tape shows have the advantage over other AV media of *relatively* easy production with simple, available equipment and expertise either already at hand or readily developed. Students and faculty can see their achievements within a few weeks.
6. How about video-tape? Unless you have rather expensive VTR equipment, editing is somewhat difficult, but otherwise, much of what can be done with slide-tape programs could be equally well done with video tape. Color, too, may be easier with slide-tape.

If you still think your message might be best delivered with a slide-tape program, what next?

PURPOSE

I'm sure the idea of behavioral objectives need not be expanded upon here. However, because of the novelty and "fun" aspects of AV work, it is worth noting that the temptation arises to start a program before your objectives are really clear. Therefore ask yourself all the old questions:

What is the subject?

Who will be in the audience?

In what ways do you want them to be different as a result of your program?

As every talk show host asks every person connected with musicals—"which comes first—the music or the words?" or in our case, the audio or the visual? Unless you have a very unusual task or message, the answer is "words," or "audio!" The reason for this is twofold: organization on the one hand, and relevance of the video to the audio.

In order to retain the attention of the audience, and in order to keep it centered on one idea at a time, it is necessary that there be a direct relationship between what's going on on the screen and what is coming out of the speaker. It is much easier to accomplish this coordination if the audio portion is done first. Simply listen, trying to identify what visuals you need to clarify, depict, or expand on the audio portion. If you attempt to take the pictures first and then select things for the sound track, the result is choppy.

The other reason for this sequence of operations is organization. The attention of the audience and the profit they receive from the program is heavily dependent on the organization. Surrealistic media presentations are fun, and in extremely professional hands can be very effective and informative but the rest of us need obvious organization. Tight organization is most easily achieved if the sound track is done first.

PLANNING THE SOUND TRACK

1. Behavioral objectives—enough said.
2. Outline. Draw up the major segments of the program. In a 25 minute program perhaps you are going to make 5-8 major points—what are these points? In similar fashion, try to identify several factors to be treated for each of these major points. A planning board made up of cards is a convenient method of organization. Cards can be added as the program is more fully developed and may also be rearranged as needed. Sketches of visuals needed may be included on the cards.

   Parenthetical observations: at this point it is necessary to violate, at least partially, recommendations given above. Look over your major points and sub-points. Are you going to be able to find visuals for them. If some of your points are very abstract you may have difficulty visually illustrating them. Sure, you can always use slides of printed material, "title" slides, but if a very large part of the program is going to rely on these, you're in trouble.
3. Varieties of audio material. It is after all the spice of life.

   A. Narration—hand someone a microphone and have her/him read a script.

B. Live taping of interviews, discussion, conversations, lecture, any spoken communication.

C. Music—live or from records or tapes (don't forget copyright regulations).

D. Sound effects: special effects are available on record, or you can do your own.

TECHNICAL CONSIDERATIONS IN THE PREPARATION OF THE SOUND TRACK

A clean tape of sufficient and consistent volume level is not as easily produced as you might think. This is especially true when there is an attempt to provide a variety of sound sources. Following are some suggestions that should help in achieving a good sound track.

1. Taping with microphones, although essential to most programs, is one of the most difficult technical problems you will face. Even in the simple narration of a script it is often difficult to get good quality. Interviews, especially when more than one person is talking are even more difficult. Therefore, for all taping with microphones, you should:

A. Choose a room that will be free of interruptions. The room should have no forced air outlets, as microphones pick up the noise of air movement and exaggerate it. Also, the noise of transformers connected to fluorescent lighting fixtures is sometimes bothersome.

B. Place microphones within a few inches of person speaking. This is extremely critical. There is a strong temptation to ignore this rule because it might inhibit spontaneity, and if there are several people speaking it requires numerous microphones, or the shifting of one microphone. Nevertheless, always keep the microphone close to the speaker.

C. Do not place microphones on a table that holds the tape recorder or other motorized equipment. Again, noises will be recorded.

D. Do not hand-hold the microphones: sounds of any motion are easily picked up and are distracting. Use microphone stands, however simple, to avoid this movement of the microphone.

E. Do not use a microphone in the same room with a speaker connected to other audio equipment, as this will cause "feedback" with most moderately priced equipment.

F. The most effective way to achieve good sound when several people are being taped is to use several microphones connected to the tape recorder through a "mixer." This allows each microphone to be placed near the speaker, and allows individual volume control for each person. This is important since there are significant differences in speaking levels among people. See the section on equipment for information on mixers.

2. Taping from previously recorded sources such as other tapes, records, and radio or television can add much to your program.

A. If you are taping several selections from various sources in addition to narration or interviews it is important that each selection be recorded at the same volume level.

B. Transitions from one segment to the next should be smooth. One simple way to do this with the most basic equipment is simply to start and end the taping of the selection at zero volume level. If blank space is left between each portion, these can be cut and spliced in any order you wish. Such taping also removes any noises that might have been added by switching the machine on and off.

C. If you wish to have two sound sources heard at the same time, such as music behind narration, or one musical selection blending into another, it is necessary to have a "mixer" or a tape recorder with built in mixing capabilities. Again, be sure that the final taping volume is consistent for all sources. It is quite difficult to achieve background music for narration by playing a record player near the person speaking, hoping to catch the music with the microphone. The speaker for the record player is likely to interact with the microphone, causing feedback.

PLANNING THE SLIDES

Now that the audio portion has been completed, or at the very least the script written, it is possible to determine what slides will be needed to clarify, explain, or add to the sound track. Some of the factors that should be considered in choosing slides are:

1. How many? A long period of narration accompanied by a single slide might lose the attention of the audience. On the other hand, a rapid sequence of slides is often distracting and even disturbing to the viewer. The length of time a slide may remain on the screen is determined by several things:

A. How much information does the slide contain?

B. Is it competing with something quite demanding on the tape?

C. How rapidly will your equipment change slides?

D. How many slides will your budget allow?

2. What sources of slides exist? There are many commercial sources of already prepared slides which might be used in your program. Catalogs of these services, as well as standard AV bibliographies should be checked. Local collections of slides might also be available for use or duplication. However, when new slides need to be produced the following suggestions may help.

A. With the use of a copy stand and lights, slides may be made from illustrations in books, periodicals and other such materials. Record jackets make fine visuals. Of course you must consider the use to be made of the presentation to avoid copyright violation. With limited photographic expertise this type of copy work is the easiest and will produce the highest quality of slides. Once proper exposure is determined for your lighting set-up, you can consistently make good slides. Also the content and composition of the photographs may be of better quality than amateurs can obtain.

 B. Original art work and title slides may also be prepared. These, too, are best made into slides with the use of a copy stand and camera. Art work can be as simple or sophisticated as available time and talent dictate. At its simplest, titling can be done by typing the material on white or colored cards and photographing these cards. Colored cellophane or other clear plastics can be used between lens and art work to add interest.

 C. Regular photography is an important source of slides. Here your imagination and availability of subject matter are the only limitations to what can be obtained. In many instances such photographic work is essential in achieving a relevant series of slides. Of course the better the photographer, the better the results. An adequate ability with a 35mm camera is not beyond the reach of most interested people, however.

3. Sequencing the slides is determined not only by the need for relevance to the audio tape, but also by visual considerations. Scenes viewed from some distance should not be immediately adjacent to extreme close-ups. In other words, there should be a visual logic to the sequence of the slides.

TECHNICAL CONSIDERATIONS IN THE PREPARATION OF THE SLIDES

It is not necessary to obtain elaborate equipment for the production of slides. Cartridge loaded cameras accepting size 126 film are quite useful, and handled properly can produce beautiful results. However, if much local production is planned certain equipment and a few types of film make effective slides more easily achieved.

1. Choice of camera and lenses is important. A 35mm single lens reflex with through-the-lens light metering is by far the most convenient. With such a camera good results can be obtained with a minimum of training. The standard lens suits most picture taking, but might be supplemented with a wide angle lens (28mm or 35mm) for indoor or other close quarters shooting, and with a telephoto lens for long range work.

2. When copy work forms a very large proportion of the photography, some additional equipment is needed.

 A. A copy stand with photoflood lights can be purchased rather inexpensively, or one can be made.

B. Copy work requires special attachments or lenses to allow the camera to focus at close range, even a very few inches. Although a rather large investment, the macro lens is by far the most convenient arrangement. Such a lens can be purchased with the camera *instead* of the regular lens, as the macro acts not only as a close-up lens, but can also be used for regular photography. Close-ups and copy work can also be accomplished with attachments to the regular lens such as extension tubes, extension bellows, or filter like "plus" lenses. All of these will give fine results, but the macro lens requires the least expertise in use and the least switching back and forth from one piece of equipment to another.

3. Choice of films should be carefully made. It is best to limit the different types of film used as much as possible. This will enable the photographer to become well acquainted with the characteristics of the films.

A. For general outdoor and indoor photography Kodak Ektachrome X, ASA 64, daylight type, is quite satisfactory. Color rendition is accurate, even with fluorescent lights, electronic flash or blue flash bulbs. If the light meter indicates that shutter speeds of slower than 1/125 of a second are needed for proper exposure, a tripod should be used. If a more sensitive film is needed, High Speed Ektachrome is a good choice, especially for use indoors with fluorescent lighting.

B. For work on the copy stand, the best combination is the use of inexpensive #2 photofloods, or any photographic lights of 3200 to 3400 K color temperature, along with Kodak Kodachrome II Professional Type A film, ASA 40. Although available only in 36 exposure rolls, this film gives consistently good slides copied from illustrative and art work. If lighting is that described above, the color rendition will be very good. Copy lights should be placed at either side of the material to be copied, and strike the surface of the copy material at a 45° angle to avoid glare. With the lights turned on, the camera's light meter will read the proper exposure. With such an arrangement of film and lighting it is not unusual to get 36 perfect slides on a roll.

4. Processing and mounting are best handled commercially. For programs intended for long-term use, glass mounts might be considered. However, the standard cardboard mounts are usually quite satisfactory. Also, if a 140 slide tray is required, many glass mounts will not fit in the narrow slots provided.

SYNCHRONIZATION OF THE TAPE AND SLIDES

The major choice to be made here is whether the synchronization is to be manual or automatic.

1. A program that uses manual synchronization has certain advantages. Simple equipment may be used. A regular monaural tape recorder is

all that is required. As the audio portion of the tape is made, simply add an audible signal of some kind to indicate the slide changes. Experimentation will show what "noise" best announces a new slide without being distracting. We have found the little "crickets" of childhood memory effective, as well as a guitar string plucked about the nut of the guitar.

The audible signal also has the advantage that the program may be loaned to other users with limited equipment.

Many slide projectors have a provision for changing slides automatically every few seconds. If the sound track is planned to match a regular change cycle, this method can be used for synchronizing the tape with the slides.

2. With more elaborate equipment other alternatives are possible. If a stereo tape recorder is available, an audible signal might be placed on the second channel. This channel might be connected to earphones rather than a speaker, so that only the operator of the program needs to hear the change signals.

   Even more automatically synchronized playback of sound slide shows is possible with the use of a cassette programmable recorder. Using standard tape cassettes, such a recorder employs one channel of the tape for the audio portion of the program, and the other channel for impulses which silently signal any Carousel or Ektagraphic projector of required slide changes. Since the two channels can be recorded independently, the synchronization can be altered at any time without destroying the completed audio portion of the program.

3. In synchronizing the show it is best to use an opaque slide both at the beginning and at the end of the slide tray. This avoids the bright-white screen, which can be visually disturbing.

4. The length of the program may result in need for additional equipment. Slide trays are available for the Kodak Carousel that will hold up to 140 slides. If the program requires more than this it is necessary to use two projectors and additional equipment to coordinate them. Most dissolve units, priced from about $200 and up, will coordinate at least two projectors and add the function of visually dissolving one slide into the next—a very pleasing effect.

EQUIPMENT

Tape recorder:
> Quality shows—the better the records the better the program. For automatically run shows, use the Wollensak 2570 slide sync recorder or equivalent.

Microphone(s):
> Again, quality makes a difference, but first be sure microphone is compatible to the tape recorder being used.

Record player or turntable:
  If records are to be used as sound source.
AM-FM radio or tuner, television:
  If these are to be sound sources.
Mixer:
  A unit such as the Sony MX 6S is most useful in coordinating sound inputs.
Slide projector(s):
  The Kodak Carousel and Ektagraphic are among several good brands, and have the advantage of compatibility with much accessory equipment produced by Kodak and other manufacturers.
Slide trays.
Dissolve unit:
  For connecting more than one slide projector.
Camera:
  35mm single lens reflex, thru-the-lens metering. Many good brands exist. Macro lens is most desirable (or Micro Nikkor Auto in the case of Nikon). Wide angle and telephoto lenses to fit camera are also useful.
Copy stand:
  Many available, from $30 to $1300. Any fairly sturdy model will serve well.
Lights for copy stand:
  Many copy stands come equipped with lights. If not, attachments may be purchased, or photographic portrait lights may be used.
Materials:
  Recording tape—any good quality mylar tape splicing tape, if using ¼″ reel to reel machine.
Film:
  Kodachrome II Professional Type A KPA-135. Ektachrome X daylight EX 135.
Extra cardboard mounts.
Additional equipment and materials will be needed if extensive original art work is to be used as a source for slides.

BASIC EQUIPMENT

Effective slide-tape programs can be produced with very simple equipment. If synchronization is to be manual, and if all recording is done by microphone, minimum equipment is needed. A monaural tape recorder—even a cassette recorder will suffice, with its microphone. A slide projector and an inexpensive camera complete the basic list of equipment needed for production and presentation of the program.

CONCLUSION

The slide-tape program may be an effective method of presenting instructional material. If students are involved in the production of these programs there are added benefits. As in any creation of materials there is learning in the production. It appears that the effort and organization required in producing a slide-tape program is more instructive than for the usual term paper. This is also a good opportunity for independent study, or for group projects. The instructional benefits include, then, both the media and the message.

Do-It-Yourself Videotape for Library Orientation Based on a Term Paper Project

by Barbara Foster

After several conferences and workshops, it happened; I contracted media fever! I vowed to enrich my library instruction lectures from then on with some type of media production.

My job since 1969 has been to design innovative library lessons for students "catching up" through the special *SEEK* Program (Search for Education, Elevation and Knowledge) at Hunter College in New York. After due reflection, I narrowed my options down to a sound-slide project, film, or videotape venture. My eventual choice of videotape format was influenced by the conviviality and expertise of Hunter's videotape division, as well as the adaptability of videotape to student use without benefit of librarian or instructor. Ultimately, the tape would be available in a lab situation on request. The production had to be geared toward "disadvantaged" freshmen—those lacking library awareness because their previous exposure had been negative or non-existent. Moreover, I swore to bypass patronizing attitudes and flashy gimmicks designed to titillate without providing basic information.

WORTHLESS CONCOCTIONS

I previewed a generous sampling of commercial concoctions marketed as library instruction; these glossy creations were not only woefully deficient in originality and content—especially meaningless to *SEEKs*—but they reinforced those undesirable library stereotypes. Such packaged ephemera lacked the verve to capture the imagination of turned-off youth. For some months, I evaluated proposals that would: be compatible with videotape requirements; provide library research techniques; and still hold viewers with modest attention spans.

But what exactly to tape? A broadcast of two or three hours in library instruction would be a lethal dose for the unsuspecting freshman. I decided to pare down to manageable proportions a one-hour library tour, in-library experience, and term-paper lesson. The term-paper approach seemed most useable since it summed up and unified, in a meaningful way, the other two elements. In his first term at Hunter, the entering *SEEK* tours the research network to dispel fears and uncertainties. He is introduced to circulation procedures and general library policy and given appropriate hand-outs. Next hour, each freshman investigates a specific topic to reinforce research skills with practice. Finally, the term-paper lesson covers: outline, footnotes, bibliography, theme, conclusion, etc. During the hour, students sit in rapt attention: term-paper deadlines are imminent. I focus on a specific topic such as "air pollution" to make the lecture concrete; step by step, a logical system is set down for the listener to follow. A general exposition, without strict subject focus, would be hopelessly diffuse.

GLOSSY MELANGE

To get opinions on the feasibility of a TV tape, I invited two members of the videotape division to observe my "stand-up" term-paper lesson; it was clear from their reactions that the bibliographic and media mentality diverged radically. The TV crew was bent on a glossy visual mélange, totally disregarding content. I realized I would need to write my own script to achieve a balance between facts and frosting, between a turned-off student and a turned-on librarian, between scholarly credibility and popular appeal, using language with which the urban *SEEK* could freely identify.

The script evolved from my own library contacts with the *SEEK* students. Usually our newcomers are wary, hesitant to approach what they suspect to be stereotyped library and librarian. In the script, the protagonist enters confused and hostile; but shortly, he is led to a new library awareness by a sympathetic librarian (myself). He is brought to realize the reward and satisfactions of solving a challenging research problem.

Our hero enters the library faced with a term paper on "air pollution," not knowing where to turn and in a mild state of shock. After his guided tour and association with a considerate librarian, he begins to master library rudiments and procedures. A rapport develops between the librarian and her initiate as they discuss the books, magazines, and newspaper indexes. My pupil eventually exudes such positive vibrations that a female friend comes rushing up to him for term-paper advice. Finally, the librarian becomes superfluous as the confident classmates go off on their own tour.

Some two weeks of writing 9 to 5 yielded what I considered a manageable script; it was pronounced feasible by the videotapers shortly after. My next step was to cast the Bewildered Student. I would have preferred a professional actor; but with my paltry $25 budget, it seemed more realistic to engage someone already on the payroll. A salaried library employee seemed the answer, and by sheer good fortune I discovered an acting major behind the circulation desk, thrilled by a "starring role."

My co-actor had to quiz me in a structured way so that term-paper information could be transferred to the viewer, but his delivery had to appear natural, not stiff or forced. We didn't want to present a dull-witted under-achiever confronting an establishment stereotype. We lacked the assurance of practiced troupers, but three relaxed intersession weeks allowed us some extra time for memorizing lines and rehearsing. The performance was buoyed up by a student director who blocked our positions and coached us in technical matters.

THE SCENARIO

The action opens in front of the card catalog; enter librarian, and the puzzled freshman is shown the subject arrangement, cross references, and how to narrow down a topic. When he sees the advantage of a more specific topic over a large, unwieldy one, he limits his from pollution to air pollution—and even further, to air pollution, New York City. He is introduced to the benefits of a term-paper handbook and note-cards. By the time he fills out a call slip and masters the circulation procedure, a new note of confidence sets in. Transition to the periodicals section as the freshman, on his own, realizes that his term-paper is incomplete and mentions the need for more current data. The scene shifts to the periodicals room.

The librarian helps him locate current magazine literature by using periodical indexes. *Reader's Guide to Periodical Literature* supplies him with abundant references to air pollution, New York City. After he is familiar with magazine information, he is steered to newspaper sources. He is overwhelmed by the variety of newspaper accounts on microfilm in the *New York Times Index,* intrigued by the possibility of reading these actual accounts, and positively exhilarated when he absorbs the scope of the *Times Index*—information dating back to 1898. He comments on the value of magazines and newspapers to the harried researcher, especially when book material is unavailable or not yet published. By now, he is eager for a respite from the library and librarians; instead, he is gently propelled to the reference room, where the librarian explains outline preparation, footnotes, and bibliography. Now the student better understands the earlier insistence on term-paper handbook and note cards.

The awkward pupil has subtly become library master, and he is approached by a female colleague. The friends have a humorous exchange on women's lib and go off to tour the library, the hero passing on his new-found knowledge with just a touch of superiority.

SHOOTING IT

The actual "shoot" took one frenetic day—from 8:30 to 4:30. We were forced to adhere to a rigid schedule since classes were beginning the next day and once patrons filled the library shooting would be impossible. As the deadline approached, I felt dreadful anxiety at the thought of facing a dispassionate TV camera; but two practice run-throughs for each recorded shot dispelled my nervousness. Ultimately, we loved being TV stars-for-a-day.

The crew consisted of five persons: two on the cameras, two more for audio, special effects, and lighting, while the fifth supervised the total operation. They were young and enthusiastic, unruffled in the face of blown fuses and other minor disasters. They lent confidence to both of us. We could watch our performances on two nine-inch playback monitors to see if re-doing was merited. The recording was on one-half-inch video-tape for reproduction on the Sony AV 3600 series, widely available in any respectable AV hook-up.

My $25 budget, which merely paid for the tape, was one limitation in achieving what was originally conceived. With such finances, I could hardly insist on embellishments. The videotapers supplied their labor and expertise gratis, which again limited my editorial control: every suggestion I made took on a tentative ring. My script might have profited from some comic aspects of air pollution. For example, the camera could have followed the student as he wheezed around New York City in a gas mask. Another regret was not being able to employ a first-rate graphic designer for visuals. In a two-actor situation, imaginative graphics can provide sophisticated relief and contrast.

After all the performing and coordinating, my energy supply evaporated. I was delighted to devote a few days to neglected library tasks, without videotape deadlines. But because of my lassitude, the videotapers took full charge of editing and tape, and after a full day of editing a severely truncated version of my original emerged. At first, I had imagined a one-hour tape, which was later reduced to one-half hour—and now further shrunk to sixteen minutes.

Many pauses and transitions had been edited out, which made the presentation seem rapid and jerky to me. I should have followed the tape to the cutting room floor. Fortunately, all the basic information was intact, and its brevity makes it more appealing to a less-motivated viewer.

Recently, my effort was previewed at a Library Association of the City University institute, "Media Integration in the Academic Library." My colleagues responded well to the humor of the tape, and were able to identify with the situation presented. Various other exhibitions are scheduled, and a note in the library press brought a flood of requests for information. In fact, the response has been so encouraging that tapes are being made available to other institutions for a $15 rental fee.

In library instruction, the full potential of media as a message is yet to be explored. We as librarians can take part in this exploration; it requires not a huge sum of money, but a great willingness to learn.

Note: In the September 1973 WLB, there appeared on page 7 a small notice calling attention to a "Videotape on the 'Term Paper.'" It said: " 'Designed for library instruction purposes, especially with disadvantaged students,' *The Term Paper; Getting It Together* was produced by Barbara Foster, Hunter College Library . . . One-half inch, 16mm., Sony AV 3600 series, $15 rental."

Since that notice appeared, Ms. Foster has been flooded not only with orders, but with hundreds of requests from librarians for information on how she did design and produce the tape. This article attempts to present that information. The tape is still for rent as above, but from the Educational Technology Department, Room 619, Hunter College, 695 Park Ave., New York 10021. Checks should be payable to that department.

PART
V

AUDIOVISUAL EQUIPMENT

The Selection of Audiovisual Equipment: A Few Basics

by Kenyon C. Rosenberg

Frequently, we get calls and letters at the Media Equipment Testing Service (METS) of the Kent State University Center for Library Studies requesting information about audiovisual equipment appropriate to the requester's institution. Such petitions usually begin something like, "I've just been made the AV librarian and have $---- to purchase new equipment, what do you recommend?" Obviously, it is virtually impossible to make specific, or even meaningful, recommendations without first knowing a range of facts regarding the institution. Such data as the size and type of population to be served, the size and type of physical plant, the number and makeup of staff, and the goals and policies of the institution are all determinants. Future plans, budget constraints, facilities in proximity, and the time frame in which all these operate are also important considerations.

Ergo, we often have to suggest that the requester try to find knowledgeable consultants or colleagues, close at hand, with whom to discuss these problems. But, there is one other initial piece of advice we can offer, and that is: try to find a reputable and reliable dealer. These people can provide a huge amount of assistance and usually do so without charge. The problem then becomes one of finding such a person or firm. We recommend consulting with local colleagues to discover their experiences and the resultant choices they have made. A few things to look for which aid selection are: National Audio-Visual Association membership; the stocking and offering of equipment by various well-known manufacturers (hopefully, indicative of the dealer's selection of the best products of these manufacturers); and the willingness to provide equipment "on approval" for a brief, but reasonable, trial period (at least 30 days). Things to avoid in dealers are: "pushing" of specific manufacturers; the stocking of but one manufacturer's products; being loath either to provide equipment "on approval" or to exchange improper or faulty items. Any good dealer also should be able, on request, to provide references from satisfied customers in libraries and/or schools. It is preferable, too, to find a dealer who is prepared and able to offer service and parts for the items he sells—and to provide these in a reasonable amount of time at reasonable prices. With a satisfactory selection of dealers, the librarian or media specialist will be considerably more self-assured and comfortable in the performance of her or his job.

As a final preliminary, I would like to briefly mention the quality of audiovisual equipment, generally. In the course of operating METS, the staff and I have found that there seems to be a discernible relationship between the intentions of a manufacturer and the quality of his products. This may seem a fatuously obvious observation, but it is one frequently overlooked by prospective customers. It can be summarized thus: those items specifically intended for institutional use (as opposed to general consumer use) usually tend to be more rugged and long lived. Frequently, however, those items intended for general consumer use have better specifications of fidelity (e.g., a projector may have greater powers of resolution, or a turntable greater speed accuracy, etc.). Occasionally, a manufacturer will produce equipment which embodies the best of both. When this is so, however, the price is probably prohibitive. Therefore, the person charged with the responsibility for audiovisual purchasing decisions should keep in mind the ancient Chinese principle of duality which has, inherent in it, the aspect of giving something up for getting something. Or, win a few, lose a few.

One *caveat* to the *emptor:* never purchase any electrical or electronic equipment which is not: tested and approved by the Underwriters' Laboratory (such equipment will carry the UL seal to indicate that a sample of the equipment was tested by UL and found to be electrically safe), and possessed of a three-wire/three-prong-plug, grounded power cord. When such a plug is inserted into a properly grounded outlet, the device is electrically grounded and, in most instances, will not constitute a shock hazard.

MOTION PICTURE PROJECTORS

In almost all schools, libraries, and media centers in the U.S., the choice of motion picture projectors is based on the size of the film to be used. These sizes are essentially two: 16mm (the most popular) and Super 8mm. The size designation of each film relates to its width. Super 8 is so called because Kodak, in 1965-66, devised this system which offers 50% larger frame size than the old 8mm, while utilizing the same width film. Both types of film are sprocketed. Since silent projectors are becoming scarce in institutional use, the general description that follows is appropriate to all motion picture sound projectors. These units are made up of three distinct, but related systems.

The function of the mechanical system is the actual movement of the film from one reel to another. To do this well, it must move the film at a pre-determined rate, which is expressed as frames-per second (fps), and do so with a minimum of inconsistency. The film speed is determined by the camera in which it was exposed. For example, in a 16mm sound camera, the rate of film travel as it is being exposed ("shot") is 24 fps. Once processed ("developed"), in order to be accurately projected, the film must be placed on a projector which is also capable of moving it at 24 fps. The hallmarks of a good mechanical system are consistency of speed, quiet operation and gentle film handling (i.e., does not damage sprocket holes or break the film). Naturally, there will be some noise created by a mechanical system which has many things to accomplish at once. Therefore, a good test of the mechanical system is to operate the projector, in a quiet room, with the sound turned off and sit close to the device as it runs. If it is objectionably loud under these conditions try turning up the sound and see if, at a normal listening level, the sound sufficiently masks the noise produced by the mechanical system. The mechanical system of a good projector will not damage the film. Some good projectors do not use sprocketed (geared or toothed) wheels, but instead use rubber rollers which grip the edges of the film and drive it frictionally. Unfortunately, many of the projectors of this type do not drive the film with the consistency of speed as do those which employ sprockets.

The second system is the optical one. The components of this portion of the projector are usually a light source or bulb, a lens (or lenses), a "framing" device, a fan to cool the light source (driven by the motor of the mechanical system), and a shutter which "blacks out" the screen between frames. It is the function of this system to direct a focused beam of light through the film as it passes and then to pass this image through the lens in order to enlarge the image to a viewable size when cast upon a screen. The critical aspects of the optical system are: the light source should be such that it does not overheat (and burn) the film; the shutter should operate properly and, as far as possible, quietly; the lens should cast a sharp and clear image of an appropriate size. The cooler the light source is kept, the less chance of damaging the film and, as a by product, the longer the bulb will last. When selecting a projector, check the projected image not only in the center, but also at its edges and corners. All should be in focus and equally sharp. Some projectors are equipped with, or have as an option, a zoom lens. These can be very handy from the standpoint of projecting an appropriately sized image at various distances from the screen, as in different rooms. However, when the intention is to use the projector in one room, at a fixed distance, the zoom lens is not needed. The best type of fan for cooling the light source seems to be that type called the "squirrel cage." It moves considerably more air (and is usually quieter) than the bladed type. A quick and simple check of the fan's efficiency is to run the projector for about ten minutes and then place one's hand near the ventilation grill. Air being expelled should be noticeably warmer than the ambient air in the room. This means that heat is being lost effectively by the bulb. If the projector has the capability of "freeze framing," that is, stop-motion, there should be some apparatus (usually a glass plate) interposed between the bulb and the lens to prevent the film from burning. Try this function for about three or four minutes to check for any noticeable degradation of either the film or the image. Most modern sound projectors should have a resolving power (clarity of the image projected) of between 50 to 80 lines-per-millimeter. Less than 50 lines-per-millimeter and the image will be markedly fuzzy.

RUNNING TIME: SUPER 8mm FILM

Reel Size	S8 Sound at 24 fps	S8 Silent at 18 fps
50' reel	2.17 min.	3.25 min.
100' reel	4.34 min.	6.50 min.
200' reel	8.68 min.	13.00 min.
400' reel	17.36 min.	26.00 min.
800' reel	34.72 min.	52.00 min.
1200' reel	52.08 min.	88.00 min.
1600' reel	69.44 min.	104.00 min.
2000' reel	138.88 min.	208.00 min.

RUNNING TIME: 16mm SOUND FILM

Feet of Film	Reel(s)	Minutes
200	½	5½
400	1	11
600	1½	16½
800	2	22
1200	3	33
1600	4	44
2000	5	55

The sound system is the last of the three. In older projectors, this was exclusively an optical sound system. The sound was converted into optical impulses and laid down, as a "sound track," alongside the frames. In the projector, the film passes a light beam from the "exciter lamp" which beam is projected onto a photoelectric cell in the sound drum (on which the film is moving). This cell changes the varying light energy to electrical energy which is then amplified and, finally, activates the projector's speaker system. Now, although most 16mm sound projectors utilize optically recorded sound, virtually all 8mm sound projectors use magnetic sound recording (which is exactly the same system used in all tape recording). This system presupposes the use of magnetically striped film. Many newer 16mm sound projectors are equipped to handle both types of sound recording, while some offer only the magnetic type. Not all projectors which can use magnetically recorded sound, however, can also record. Some have playback devices only, while the more flexible ones allow for recording also. These are more flexible in that one can change the sound track at one's pleasure. The most sophisticated of the projectors using magnetic recording not only permit simple recording from a microphone, but also allow for "line and mike mixing." This means that the microphone and another sound source (phonograph or tape recorder, etc.) can be mixed together in a controlled volume blend to produce both sources on the film. Thus, a travel film may have both a narration plus appropriate background music to add greater interest. The magnetic recording system, generally, when used properly, produces better and cleaner sound. Its major disadvantage lies in the possibility that one may inadvertently erase the existing recording.

S8 LOOP PROJECTORS

The 1960's also saw the development of the Super 8mm continuous-loop film cartridge. In this type of system, one simply inserts the cartridge into a slot in the projector and the machine is turned on. This approach requires no threading or rewinding. Some such projectors even are pre-focused and, when the film has been shown, turn themselves off, leaving the cartridge rewound for the next showing. Other manufacturers incorporate other niceties such as: built-in projection screens, zoom lenses, and recording capability. Among the problems sometimes encountered in these devices are: difficulty in retrieving either broken film or film pulled off the cartridge hub, bulb changing, and film jamming. The only way to preclude these is to test the device for a number of hours (at least 15) using different films—some short and some long—to see how well these varying lengths are handled. Lastly, there are fewer films, as yet, available in cartridge format.

Remember, the more conveniences and options, the greater the potential for breakdown or failure, and greater the price. Judiciousness of choice is the watchword: buy only those options or accessories which are really needed.

SLIDE PROJECTORS

In general use today is the "miniature" or 2″ × 2″ slide in which is mounted a single frame of transparent 35mm film. These are termed "miniature" because, earlier in this century, the "regular" lantern slide had dimensions of 3¼″ × 4″. Since the advent of the popularity of the 35mm camera, the 2″ × 2″ slide has virtually supplanted the older size.

The motion picture projector and the slide projector have an optical system whose purpose is the same. In addition, there is a mechanical system intended to move the slide from its container (either a circular or cube-like tray) to a position in the optical system whence it may be projected. The optical system of the slide projector has similar characteristics to those of the motion picture projector. If anything, the lens of the slide projector should have greater resolving power (60-100 lines-per-millimeter) than that of a movie projector.

The mechanical system that moves the slides (and whose motor drives a fan to cool the bulb) may be one of two basic types. The older method is the "mechanical feed" one. Here the slide is pushed or pulled into the optical system by some mechanical device. In the newer system, the so-called "gravity feed" (developed by Kodak in its Carousel projectors), the slide is allowed to drop (hence "gravity") into the optical system from its tray and, when the viewing time has elapsed, is mechanically pushed back into the tray. Both systems have their advantages and drawbacks. By and large, in that mechanical handling is reduced by half in the gravity system, slides seem to suffer a little less wear and the mechanism, being a little simpler, seems to offer a bit more efficiency. The major problem with gravity systems occurs when the projector is tilted, sometimes causing the slide not to drop.

Once again, zoom lenses are available for these devices. But here, I feel, they are somewhat more useful in that, even though the projector may be used at a fixed distance from the screen and always in the same room, one can "blow-up" an interesting portion of the slide for closer examination. Again, too, the fan should be sufficiently effective that the bulb remains relatively cool.

One of the more useful options available with currently produced slide projectors is a unit which allows for control (both forward and reverse, plus focus) of the projector remotely. This allows the projectionist some freedom either of movement or position.

Unless the slides to be projected are mounted between glass plates, they will "pop" when placed in the optical system. This is caused by the heat of the bulb and is nothing more than the slides' expanding within its mount and bulging at the center. This will cause the projected image to go slightly out of focus. Some projectors ameliorate this phenomenon somewhat by "pre-warming" the three or four slides closest to the optical system so that, once the first slide is properly focused, the next slide (assuming that they are in the "pre-warming" section long enough) will also be, for the most part, focused. Some of the newer projectors have, as an option, an "automatic" focusing device. Here, again, once the first slide is focused, the rest are too, but not necessarily by "pre-warming." Rather, an additional optical device compensates for the "popping" by comparing the clarity of the focus for the first slide to succeeding slides' clarity. This is useful, particularly when the projector has no operator in attendance and is being run continuously by a timing device (which some projectors have as a built-in option).

SLIDE AND AUDIO PROJECTORS

A few manufacturers have recently begun to market 2″ × 2″ slide projectors which are capable of more than just slide projection. The slide (and, usually, its cardboard mount) are mounted in variously designed frames, which frames are possessed of magnetic stripping, etc. (depending on the manufacturer's system) upon which can be recorded (usually through a recorder/player built into the projector) a brief message varying in length from ten to thirty seconds. At the end of the message, a pulse can be added so that, in actual use, the audience views the projected image and simultaneously hears the recorded message, at the conclusion of which the next slide is automatically advanced, etc. Once more, the projection portion of the device should be the equal of regular projectors, while the recorder/player—since, more often than not, it will only be used for spoken rather than musical material—need not have the frequency response capabilities of good, separate audio equipment.

FILMSTRIP PROJECTORS

Filmstrips, until recently, were called slide films in that they are, essentially, a group of 35mm transparent frames on one piece of film. Filmstrips are frequently differentiated as being either "silent" or "sound." This is, actually, a fatuous differentiation since filmstrips don't have an optical or magnetic sound track on the film itself. "Sound" filmstrips are intended to be used with a recorded program, usually on disc or cassette tape. "Silent" filmstrips are not used with a recording and often have an explanatory or narrative caption on each frame.

The projectors for "silent" filmstrips vary greatly in design but can be divided into two basic groups. The first are what may be termed "semi-automatic" framing projectors. These advance the film, one frame at a time, by means of a mechanism which is pulled, depressed or otherwise manually caused to function. The second type of filmstrip projector could be called the "manual framing" type. With this type, the operator usually rotates a knob which advances the film and said operator determines proper framing. In some very inexpensive (read "cheap") projectors, the film, rather than being advanced by a rotating-knob-controlled mechanism, is pulled by the operator's fingers through the projector. This last type is objectionable for various reasons and should be avoided.

Among the two basic types of projectors, there are a variety of internal devices which actually move the film. In some there are sprocket wheels (gears) which mesh with the sprocket holes on the film and act as a driving system. In others, a pawl (a pivoted, finger-like projection which engages a sprocket hole) advances the film. My own favorite type of mechanism for driving the filmstrip is the rubber roller type which gently grasps the edges of the film. Further, although a properly acting "semi-automatic" framing device is desirable, many have a tendency to go "out of frame" or "half-frame" after a few advances. This means that the operator has to reframe the film every so often. Also, these "semi-automatic" types tend to rely on either the pawl mechanism, or the sprocketed wheels, or a combination of both. Improperly inserted film, then, may become damaged. Not only is manual framing more positive, it can also be gentler on what is potentially an expensive piece of software.

Besides the above ideas about projector choice, the projector should have a fan to cool the bulb and, as with all such devices, be constructed of high impact plastic or sufficiently heavy gauge metal that firm finger pressure does not cause permanent deformation. The cooling fan, once more, may be tested simply by holding one's hand close to the vent, etc.

FILMSTRIP AND AUDIO PROJECTORS

Currently, manufacturers are making available two methods of "sound" filmstrips. One is the coupled cassette recorder and filmstrip projector, the other is the coupled disc player and filmstrip projector. The idea in both is to provide an appropriate, and "canned," narration to the frames of the filmstrip and, in many instances—equipment permitting—to advance the frames in automatic synchronization with the recording. This is done with a pulsed signal, or beep, which may be audible on discs, or inaudible, as in the instance of cassettes. These units should have, essentially, the same kinds of desirable characteristics they would have if they were not coupled and were to be purchased as separate units. The only exception to this is that since the audio portions will hardly, if ever, be used simply as music playback systems, their frequency responses need only be in the 100 Hz to 10kHz ± 4dB. What does need testing in such units is their ability to move the filmstrip properly and to maintain the framing so that partial framing does not occur, and that they do not damage the film through rough handling. Also, it is advantageous when the projection portion of these units can be used as simple, manual filmstrip projectors when needed.

MAGNETIC VIDEO RECORDING

Magnetic video recording, more commonly known as video tape recording (VTR) was invented by the Ampex Corp. a few decades ago. This process, similar to the magnetic tape recording of sound, enables one to record visual images (plus sound) on magnetic tape rather than on regular film. Although such tape is more expensive than film, it offers some obvious advantages. First, the tape, just as with sound tape recordings, can be "erased" and re-recorded. Secondly, editing is relatively simple. Thirdly, the tape requires no processing. Once the program is recorded, it can be played back immediately. Lastly, when used with a monitor, the program can be viewed simultaneously as it is being recorded. This means that some editing "in the camera" can be made during the recording process.

There are two basic approaches to VTR. The original method is called "open-reel" and the initialism VTR is used almost exclusively with the open-reel system, ergo, we shall use it here in that fashion. VTR, as in open-reel sound tape recording (and similar to "regular" movies as opposed to cartridge formats) uses two individually accessible reels—one designated "supply," the other "take-up." In VTR, the tape width varies from ¼", ½", to 1" or 2", depending on the equipment manufacturer. Unfortunately, tapes made on the equipment of one manufacturer are usually not compatible with the equipment of another. The larger the width, generally, the better the visual image.

The equipment necessary to create a VTR consists of a video camera, a video tape recorder and (optionally) a monitor (which is built into most VTR cameras). Many VTR systems include all three of the aforementioned, or just the first two, or the three items available separately. In any system, even though it may be mentioned as an option, the monitor is desirable for reasons mentioned earlier. For playback of a VTR, all that is necessary is the monitor and the video tape recorder which functions like an ordinary sound tape recorder in this way. There are some video tape players (i.e., they can not record but simply playback), but obviously these offer considerably less flexibility.

The most critical parts of a VTR system are the camera and the heads. The camera should be sufficiently light sensitive to be useful in the ambient lighting of the institution for which it is intended. Regardless of the statements of some salesmen, there are modestly priced (approximately $1,000.00) cameras available which can produce a very decent picture, even under incandescent lights.

The heads of the VTR system should be so stable as to cause little necessity for realignment. By this I mean realignment shouldn't be necessary more often than once a year with average (five to ten hours a day) use. Because of the necessary design of VTR heads, they must be kept very clean, otherwise poor tape-to-head contact will cause visible "drop-outs." These usually take the appearance of momentary picture lapses or briefly visible scanning lines intruding on the picture. "Drop-outs" may be caused by things other than dirt on the heads (e.g., unevenly formulated tape or poor maintenance of pressure on the tape to insure good head contact), but more often than not, dirt is the culprit.

Gaining in popularity now is the video cassette recording (VCR) system. This approach is analogous to tape recording cassettes. VCR cassettes are available in varying widths (depending on manufacturer) and playing time lengths. A common width now is ¾" (as in the Sony "U-matic" cassette) and in 20 minutes, half hour, and one hour lengths, etc. The components of a VCR system are the same as for a VTR one, except that the videotape recorder, instead of accepting open reels, accepts a cassette. As with VTR, VCR may be either in black-and-white or color, the former being the less expensive approach. In use, the VCR is almost as simple as sound cassette recording and many institutions are converting films and videotapes to video cassettes.

A few of the important things to consider when deciding upon a VTR or VCR are:

1. Wow and flutter: These are objectionable motions imparted to the tape by the device while either recording or playing back. Wow and flutter are expressed as a percentage of deviation from perfect speed and, therefore, the lower this figure, the better. Taken together, wow and flutter should be no more than .25%, and hopefully, less than .2%.
2. Interlocking recording controls: These will tend to preclude the inadvertent erasure of recorded tapes.
3. Portability: VTRs and VCRs should be able to be moved easily from site to site unless they are intended for use in a specific place.
4. The ability to accept a remote loudspeaker by means of a jack: The loudspeakers built into most monitors are, more often than not,

unable to reproduce sound with any real quality because of their necessarily small size.

5. Ease of operation: Some of these units can be hopelessly confusing to the novice, and they really needn't be. Be sure to try both recording and playing back on these units before making a purchase decision. After all, these are some of the most expensive ($1,500.00 +) units to be found in most institutions.

TURNTABLES

Turntables have been around too long to need a full description here. However, they may be divided into three basic types: rim or "puck" driven; directly driven from the motor; belt driven. By far the most common (and least satisfactory) is the rim drive. They are unsatisfactory in that, ultimately, the driving wheel ("puck") may develop flattened portions of its circumference (which cause erratic platter speed and/or an audible "thumping"), or the "puck" (whose outer rim is rubber) may suffer shrinkage or glazing of its outer rim. Either of these two conditions can cause insufficient torque to turn the platter (with whose inner rim the puck must be in intimate contact and maintain sufficient friction to transmit its torque) properly, or even at all.

The direct drive turntable is driven directly by the motor, no intermediary device is interposed between the motor and the platter. This type is the most reliable and accurate turntable.

In the belt drive, a rubber (or other elastomer) belt provides the rotation from the motor to the platter. This method is almost as reliable and accurate as direct drive but is ordinarily less expensive. Further, the belts are usually easily (and inexpensively) replaced when necessary.

The only turntable speeds necessary are 33 ⅓ rpm and 45 rpm. The much vaunted 16 rpm for spoken material never has proven useful due to the paucity of discs at this speed, and 78 rpm discs are, for the most part, a thing of the past.

One of the most useful options to be found on turntables is a speed adjustment control. This is particularly useful in those situations where the table may be used by music students for "play-or-sing along." Many such recordings are available and, in order to be used properly, require that the table be able to be "tuned" to an "A" (440 Hertz) given at the beginning of the disc. This, of course, is accomplished by adjusting the platter speed so that the "A" on the disc and that of a tuning fork (or an instrument) coincide. In order for the speed adjustment to be truly useful, it should be capable of at least ±4% change.

Associated with the turntable is the tonearm, a pivoted device in which, at one end (opposite the pivot), is located the cartridge which contains the stylus. Most institutional turntables are supplied with a tonearm already mounted, and, usually, with a cartridge. Ordinarily, the cartridge supplied is of the piezoelectric type (i.e., ceramic or crystal). These are used because, first, they are less expensive than magnetic cartridges and, second, because they emit a louder signal than magnetic ones. Actually, however, the magnetic cartridge offers substantial comparative benefits. It is lighter in the tracking force (or pressure) it requires, usually between 1.5 and 3 grams, which means less wear for both stylus and disc. The piezoelectric cartridge ordinarily requires from 2 to 5 grams. Further, the magnetic cartridge is not anywhere near as sensitive to temperature and humidity change as the piezoelectric. Quite often climatic conditions alone may cause a piezoelectric cartridge to malfunction or even break. And, too, piezoelectric cartridges are more subject to breakage caused by rough handling than the magnetic kind. Also, a word about stereo and quadraphonic cartridges. Both magnetic and piezoelectric cartridges are available for stereophonic (and naturally, monophonic) and matrix quadraphonic recordings. To date, only magnetic cartridges are being manufactured for the CD-4, "discrete" type, quadraphonic disc. Without going into a lengthy discussion of quadraphony, the CD-4 discs require a cartridge capable of reproducing signals on the disc which are considerably higher than those of human hearing (e.g., 30-40 kHz) and, preferably, which are attached to the amplifier by quite low-capacitance cables. The stylus which is normally used with the CD-4 disc is of a Japanese design and is termed the Shibata, after its designer.

Most institutions have avoided using automatic "changer" turntables, and with good reason. Most often the user only wishes to listen to one or two sides of a disc. The added cost of a changer vs. a "manual" turntable is not supportable in such an instance. Then, too, changers are far more prone to break-downs (given rough handling) than manual turntables.

AMPLIFIERS AND RECEIVERS

An amplifier is a device which takes a very small electrical impulse (usually in millivolts) and amplifies that impulse (or signal) several hundred or thousand times. The amplifier usually contains a pre-amplification section which enables it to accept the very small signal of a magnetic cartridge and it usually has a set of controls by which means the operator can choose from a variety of inputs (e.g., tape recorder, radio-tuner, phonograph, etc.) plus such other controls as volume, tone, etc. The amplifiers which are usually encountered in institutions combine the functions of pre-amplification and amplification and are sometimes termed "integrated amplifiers." Those which are not of this type ordinarily have no controls and must be connected with a pre-amplifier.

The more input devices which can be operated through a given amplifier, the more flexible it is. Also, the more varied the controls, the more useful. Tone and volume controls are imperatives. But such refinements as a "loudness" compensation switch are helpful. In normal hearing, there is an apparent loss of low frequency audibility as volume decreases. That is, as the volume is made lower, there seems to be a proportional decrease in the "bass" one hears. This occurs even when there is no real loss of bass frequencies. In order to compensate for this, many manufacturers have included, in their amplifiers, a switch which, when activated at low listening levels, boosts the bass frequencies commensurately with the hearing loss. This, then, provides fuller sound when listening to the device at lower than normal volume settings. Another handy thing included in many amplifiers is the "monitor" switch. This allows one, when making recordings with recorders compatibly equipped (i.e., with monitor outputs), to compare the signal being recorded with the original. Thus, a radio broadcast being recorded can be "monitored" against the actual radio broadcast being received. Hence, the recording can, if necessary, be adjusted while the process is ongoing.

Another helpful switch is the stereo-mono, which allows the user to combine the sound emanating from the two sides of a stereo source into one signal fed to both speakers. This is, obviously, most useful for reproducing monaural recordings.

Some specifications (and the minimally acceptable figures) are:

1. Signal-to-Noise Ratio (S/N): This is indicative of the inherent amplifier noise (usually hissy) when listening to a given signal (usually a single tone). The S/N is always expressed as a minus number in deciBels (dB). The higher the number the better, e.g., –80dB is better than –40dB. The minimum S/N should be at least –55dB. Some manufacturers combine "Hum and Noise" as a specification and offer that figure in lieu of S/N. This should also be at least –55dB or better.

2. Harmonic distortion is the production of spurious frequencies which are created by adding actual signal frequencies. For instance, an amplifier may add 200 Hz and 1000 Hz and produce the spurious tone of 1200 Hz. Harmonic distortion (HD) is expressed as a percentage and, here, the lower the percentage, the better. Minimal HD should be under .5%.

3. Power output is an ostensible measure, in watts, of the power the amplifier makes available to the speakers. There is much technical controversy at present as to how this should be measured. Nonetheless, there is general agreement that the most meaningful way to describe the power output is in terms of "Root-Mean-Square" (RMS) or continuously available power. The RMS or continuous power rating, to be more meaningful, should be coupled with the impedance of the load (taking the place of the speakers), given in ohms plus the frequency which was used to obtain this figure. A complete power output specification should read something like: 50 watts (RMS) into 8 ohms at 1 kHz (most tests are done at 1 kHz). Most speakers have a nominal impedance of either 4 or 8 ohms. When reading power output specifications, remember that power (in wattage) tends to increase as impedance drops, so that 50 watts (RMS) into 8 ohms may well be 70 or 80 watts (RMS) into 4 ohms. Finally, the power output should be given per channel (for stereo or quadraphonic amplifiers) with both (or all) channels being driven.

4. Frequency response is one of the most often cited and misunderstood of almost all specifications. Simply, frequency response is an indi-

cation of the sound spectrum which a device is capable of re-producing. Human hearing covers a range of from about 40 Hz (Hertz, abbreviated "hz," is the common, but technical, term which means "cycles-per-second") to about 17,000 Hz (properly, 17,000 Hz should be written 17 kHz, the "k" being a multiplication factor of 1,000). Despite the limits of human hearing, devices whose frequency responses are in excess, at both ends of the spectrum, of those limits are preferable to those whose frequency responses are either at those limits or within them. This is true for a variety of reasons. One of the problems with the use of the frequency response as an indication of quality is that, given a good pair of numbers for the ends of the response (for example, 20 Hz to 25 kHz), these numbers alone do not tell how *well* this range of frequencies is being reproduced. There-fore, a full statement of the frequency response must include a qualitative factor, which is always given in deciBels. Minimal fre-quency response for an amplifier should be 20 Hz to 20 kHz ±3dB.

A receiver is an integrated stereo amplifier plus an AM or FM or AM/FM tuner, all on one chassis. This means that with the addition of speakers one has, in effect, a radio which is also capable of using whatever other inputs the amplifier can accept. Most modern receivers are AM/FM stereo (or multiplex) and can demodulate an FM stereo broadcast and re-produce it stereophonically. Many manufacturers are now producing quadraphonic receivers which are capable of handling either matrix or discrete discs (or both), quadraphonic discs, plus quadraphonic tapes.

Among the FM tuner section's most important specifications are:

1. Sensitivity, which is the minimum input signal required with a given S/N. Minimum sensitivity should be at least 2 microvolts or lower.
2. Selectivity, which is the measure of the receiver to accept the signal of the station to which it is tuned while rejecting the signals of adjacent stations. This is given in deciBels and the higher the figure, the better the selectivity. A minimum of selectivity should be 60dB.
3. Frequency response should minimally be 35 Hz to 14 kHz ±2.5dB.
4. A receiver should have, at least, a tuning meter to indicate when the desired station has been properly tuned.

LOUDSPEAKERS

Loudspeakers are devices which transform electrical energy into acoustical energy into the air. Loudspeakers (or, sometimes, speakers) are occasionally called transducers. A transducer is any device which receives energy from one system (or device) and transmits it to another, usually different, system (or device). Often this energy becomes changed in the process.

There are two types of loudspeakers in general use now. The most common is the piston (or cone) type. In this type the electrical energy is fed to a "voice coil" of wire which is attached to the small end of the loudspeaker cone, or diaphragm. The coil is suspended in a magnetic field and this coil acts like a pulsating piston when the electrical energy is fed to it. Naturally, the coil then drives the cone itself, thus causing the acoustical energy which is radiated into the air. This kind of loudspeaker works well, generally, with lower frequencies (from about 20 Hz to about 500 Hz) and reasonably well with middle frequencies (about 500 Hz to 3 kHz). Problems arise in the middle frequencies and increase in the upper ones (3 kHz to 18 or 20 kHz). This is why, in many loudspeaker systems, specially designed speaker units are used to handle specific portions of the frequency spectrum. The "woofer" takes care of low frequency sounds. The "mid-range" is self-explanatory, and the "tweeter" "tweets" out the higher frequency sonics. These units are coupled by a "crossover network" which divides up the incoming electrical energy into "bands" appropriate to each of the speaker units involved and feeds that specific "band" to each of the particular speakers.

The other variety of speaker is termed electrostatic. Here there is nothing like the cone-piston. The diaphragm of the electrostatic speaker is a virtually flat material (perhaps mylar, or some other metalized plastic sheet) which is suspended between two acoustically transparent metal plates. Instead of a magnetic field activating the diaphragm, a static electric field is employed. This field activates the entire diaphragm, rather than just a portion of it. In the piston type, only the apex of the cone is activated. The electrostatic system tends to avoid unwanted "breakup" and the consequent creation of unwanted sounds. But the electrostatic has difficulty in reproducing tones below 500 Hz. For this reason many manufacturers suggest the use of an electrostatic loudspeaker *with* a woofer in order to provide a fuller range of sound. Regardless of the type of speaker on which one decides (and, at present, the best bet is the piston type), there are some things one should look for. Speakers should be well built for sturdiness especially in those institutions where they must be moved from site to site. The grille cloth should be acoustically transparent but tough. And there should be crossover (or "brilliance") controls to accommodate the "brightness" to the listening room conditions. There are many types of speaker systems and their quality may vary within one type. What is important is that, in listening tests, the speaker *sounds* good.

Some specifications applicable to speakers are:

1. Frequency response should be at least 60 Hz to 14 kHz ±4dB.
2. Resonant frequency is the specific frequency at which a given system vibrates with maximum amplitude. In other words, when a speaker, or speaker system, is busy reproducing music, there are often low tones which correspond to the resonant frequency of the speaker (or system) and which cause it to vibrate with some amplitude—in less than good systems, audibly. The better speakers have relatively low resonant frequencies. The lower the resonant frequency the less the possibility of the resonance being audible. A resonant frequency of 50 Hz or lower is acceptable.
3. Power handling is a measure of the maximal power a speaker can handle. What is acceptable will depend on the power output of the amplifier. The speaker should have at least a 20 to 25 watt power

handling figure greater than the amplifier for low to moderate powered amplifiers (10 to 30 watts).

4. Dispersion is the ability of the speaker to "spread" sound in an arc and is given in degrees. The greater the dispersion, the larger the area which will receive sound. Therefore, the larger the figure the better, and a minimum number these days should be at least 115 degrees.

5. Colorlessness or flatness. A good speaker adds no frequencies to the program it is reproducing. Further it does not accentuate any specific part of the frequency response. The "tuning" of a speaker to create artificial peaks which may make a speaker sound "brighter" or more "alive" is a bow to the people who appreciate rock music and want to hear the ostensible brightness of the guitar and cymbals, etc. Although there are no simple specifications for a lack of "coloration," a good test is to try a disc with which one is familiar, particularly chamber music, piano, and organ.

6. Transient response. Every sharp attack of certain instruments (tympani, cymbals, other percussion particularly) causes an abrupt pulsation and, what should be, an abrupt decay without any ringing (or "after image"). Drum sounds should be sharp and fade quickly. Cymbals should clash and not sound "sandpapery" or otherwise distorted.

7. Minimum power handling. A basic distinction between piston type speaker systems is that of "low efficiency" and those that are "efficient" or "highly efficient." The low efficiency systems require a greater amount of amplifier power output than other kinds, often this means at least 20 watts minimum. Therefore, low efficiency speaker systems need more power than more efficient speaker systems and they, and amplifiers, should be matched accordingly.

FREQUENCY BALANCING EQUIPMENT

Almost every receiver or integrated amplifier has tone controls for bass and treble. These controls are continuous and non-discriminatory, so that, in order to lower the treble to cut out some hiss, one cuts off all the top frequencies, too. For example, suppose the hiss occurs at 12 kHz, then all frequencies above 12 kHz are cut off. And for bass rumble, say at 70 Hz in order to alleviate the rumble. With a frequency balancing device (known by various names) one is capable of selecting a specific portion of the audio frequency spectrum (many of these are designed to select a certain octave) and reduce (or increase) the volume in that band. Most of the better frequency balancers are capable of selecting from any of ten octaves (per stereo channel) and varying the volume for each. Not only will these accommodate the ear to given equipment, but also the equipment to a given listening environment.

Frequency balancing devices have another use, too. When copying old discs or tapes onto tapes, the frequency balancer can "clean up" the sound of the older recordings in the dubbing process. Hissiness, rumble and any other specific frequency problems can be filtered out, for the most part, by adjusting the frequency balancer appropriately. Besides this, the frequency balancer can also synthesize an artificial stereo sound from monaural recordings rather nicely.

By and large, this type of device is one of the handiest for all of the above purposes—and they are not horribly expensive, tending to run from $125 to $300. And this kind of equipment is not difficult to use. We suggest, in choosing a piece of equipment of this type, that the eight- or ten-octave-band variety be considered over those with fewer bands in that they tend to be more versatile and, ultimately, useful.

MISCELLANEOUS PERIPHERAL DEVICES

On the market now are a number of time saving and clever gadgets which can either make larger pieces of equipment more useful or protect those items from damage. One of these is a switching box which interconnects up to three tape recorders of any kind (cassette, open reel, etc.) with one amplifier. Using this item, one can record onto the three recorders simultaneously from one source (phonograph, radio, etc.), or onto two of the recorders from one of them. One can also playback from one, or two, or all three of them—simultaneously.

Another item is a speaker switch box which connects two stereo pairs of speakers to one stereo amplifier. With this device, the individual pairs are each volume-controllable from the device while the amplifier's volume control can be used as "master" volume control for all speakers at once. Such a unit is nice for the addition of "remote" speakers in a listening area other than the main one, and to provide a suitable individual volume in that area while a different volume level is used in the main listening area.

Quite new on the consumer market, but definitely applicable to any user of audio equipment, is the electronic "fuse" or speaker protector. These items are designed to protect speakers (particularly the vulnerable tweeter) from sudden surges of power which can destroy them. These units are very simple to connect into the system and are also simple in their setting (according to the speaker's power handling ability) and use. They are priced in the $25 range and can save easily more than twice their cost in speakers.

The last important item recently made available are "noise reduction" devices. In some ways these are the most important of all new devices. They have been incorporated into cassette recorders, open reel machines and receivers. Many manufacturers have designed their own noise reduction circuits, but the majority of American and Japanese manufacturers have incorporated (under license) the system invented by the Ray Dolby laboratories. There are two Dolby systems: "A" and "B." The "A" system is primarily intended for professional applications. The "B" system is the one generally found in consumer and institutional items and exemplifies a definite advance in the capabilities of new equipment.

Any user of tape recording equipment, particularly cassettes, has probably noticed that there is an inherent "hissiness" in tape which is only ameliorated by recording at very high volume levels in order to mask the background hiss. Unfortunately, recording at high volume levels may well lead to audible distortion. This hiss is technically known as "noise." It is particularly intrusive in quiet passages of music or other program material. When Dolby encoded recorded programs are played back on equipment capable of Dolby decoding, there is a dramatic reduction in audible noise. Many cassette recorders (and a few open reel machines), as noted above, incorporate both Dolby encoding and decoding. And some receivers have built-in Dolby decoders to better handle Dolby encoded FM broadcasts. But Dolby "B" noise reduction "boxes" are also available separately and can be employed with any older equipment. Many manufacturers of pre-recorded cassettes, cartridges, and open reel tapes are now offering these products Dolbyized so that, in order properly to play back these recordings, the playback devices should be possessed of Dolby decoding circuits. However, such Dolbyized recordings may be played back on non-Dolby equipment, but there has to be an adjustment of the treble control to compensate for the recording process. The sound to be derived thusly will not be the equal of playback through proper Dolbyized devices.

SYNCHRONIZING DEVICES

For institutions which already own slide projectors and tape or cassette recorders, there are devices which can be used to couple these units. Among the least expensive are those available from the Edmund Scientific Co. (624 Edscorp Bldg., Barrington, N.J., 08007), whose free catalog, by the way, is a browser's delight. One such unit can be used with either those Kodak Carousel or Airequipt slide projectors which are capable of being operated by remote control, assuming that these will be used with stereo cassette or open reel tape recorders. The Edmund unit is priced at less than $30, including the essential connecting cable for the projector.

Another Edmund device can couple the same types of slide projectors to monaural cassette or open reel recorders. Not only will this little cutie run such slide projectors, but also film strip projectors which can be operated by remote control. With cables, this item costs less than $60.00.

In summary, we have discussed some of the most important kinds of basic equipment to be found in media centers. For purposes of space and time, we have omitted any real mention of cassette and open reel tape recorders since these were covered at length in another article *(Previews,* October, 1972, pp. 5-11). Other kinds of equipment (e.g., high speed cassette duplicators, slide mounting devices, microphones, etc.) were deemed to be of less general importance. However, the Center for Library Studies at Kent State University would be pleased to answer brief inquiries regarding any equipment (of which it has cognizance) for any members of the profession. Further, the Center appreciates any recommendations regarding appropriate types of equipment for evaluation. Please send inquiries and recommendations directly to the Center for Library Studies, Kent State University, Kent, Ohio 44242.

Look Before You Leap
Tape Recorders:
Open Reel vs. Cassettes

by Kenyon C. Rosenberg

Anyone who likes either the sound of music or that of his own or other voices has probably been fascinated with the concept of recording and instantaneous replay offered by tape recording techniques. Today, with the proliferation of tape formats, and options and quality within those formats, the task of choosing a tape recorder or player has become a virtual Gordian knot. Finding a solution to this dilemma requires a bit of time and study—neither in great quantity.

Tape recording began in this country shortly after World War II, when Alexander M. Poniatoff, an engineer working in California, formed a company to construct and sell an improved version of the Magnetophon —an early type of tape recorder developed by the Germans. The company he founded, which took its name from his initials plus "ex" from "excellence," is now known as Ampex. John T. Mullin, a former WW II Signal Corps officer, also worked with Ampex in improving the German recorder. The machine Ampex first produced was and, essentially, still is the prototype of the "open reel" tape recorder. This is the common term employed to differentiate among the other two basic types of tape recorders, i.e., cassette and cartridge.

OPEN REEL TAPE RECORDERS

In the open reel machine (or just plain "tape recorder" hence), the tape is fed from the supply reel, past some interesting devices, to the take up reel. The most important of these "interesting" devices are the three types of tape heads. The erase head erases any magnetism on the tape. The record head converts an electrical signal into a magnetic field, thereby magnetizing the tape. The playback head "reads" the magnetism of the tape and converts it into an electrical signal. The better tape recorders have three heads, thus allowing the record head to function while the playback head is monitoring what is being placed on the tape. In less expensive recorders, the functions of record and playback are combined in one head. In open reel machines, the tape is usually moved past a given point at any of three speeds, all measured in inches per second (ips): 7½ ips, 3¾ ips, and 1⅞ ips. Professional machines use speeds of 30 ips and 15 ips since the faster the speed the better the fidelity, particularly in the upper portion of the sound spectrum. With the better tape recorders, not the professional type, one can now use the 7½ ips for excellent fidelity and the 3¾ ips for very good fidelity. The 1⅞ ips speed is still only useful for spoken recordings, since the fidelity here is only fair.

Some of the things a tape recorder should have in order to make it hardy and able to withstand abuse or much use while providing creditable fidelity are:

1. Three motors. One to propel the capstan (a shaft or spindle which rotates against the tape and propels it in either the play or record modes), one each to drive the take up and supply reels in the fast-forward or rewind modes. Machines with one motor have to utilize some sort of linkage system (e.g., belts, gears or pulleys), tend to require servicing more often, and usually are not as consistent or smooth in their operation.
2. Capstan drive. This means that the capstan itself moves the tape. Other types (e.g., reel drive) are not as even in the movement of the tape and, therefore, cause the pitch of the recorded sound to vary.
3. Tape lifters. A device to remove the tape from intimate contact with the heads during the fast forward and rewind modes. This prevents unnecessary abrasion and resultant wear of the heads.
4. Solid state electronics. Solid state devices (e.g., transistors, diodes, integrated circuits, etc.) are smaller than vacuum tubes, produce far less heat, and offer excellent reliability.
5. Bias adjustment. Needed to select the appropriate bias current for a given brand of tape, since the optimum "magnetizability" of tape varies from manufacturer to manufacturer.
6. Tone controls. Used to vary the upper and lower parts of the tonal range during playback.
7. Digital counter. Usually a three digit (better machines use four digits) device which can be set to "zero" at the beginning of a tape in order to index that tape.

CASSETTE RECORDERS

The cassette recorder was developed by the Netherlands firm of Philips and imported to the U.S. by Norelco. In essence, it is a miniature tape recorder with a few exceptions. The first of these is that the tape is completely enclosed in a plastic housing (the cassette) which contains two tiny reels on which the tape is stored. This eliminates the necessity for handling tape. When the cassette is placed in its receptacle in the machine, only the portion of tape necessary at any instant for recording or playback

playback is not enclosed. When the cassette recorder is placed in the record or playback mode, the head assembly and capstan are moved into contact with that small portion of tape. In the fast forward or rewind modes, the head assembly and capstan do not contact the tape at all, thus preventing excessive head wear.

Cassette tapes come in a variety of playing times (i.e., tape lengths)—30, 60 and 90 minutes are the most usual. The tape in cassette players is almost exactly half the width of that in open reel machines (i.e., ¼" vs. approx. ⅛"). Because of its slow tape speed and narrow tape width, the cassette recorder has, until recently, been unable to provide the frequency response or lack of speed eccentricities of its open reel competitors. Further, tape noise (or "hiss"), which is more noticeable in quiet passages of a recording, was quite apparent in cassette recordings because of the way such machines work. In order to explain this problem we must approach a subject which I have delayed in order to provide a little background first—the tape itself.

RECORDING TIME PER TRACK: ONE DIRECTION

Tape Speed	1200 Ft. Reel	1800 Ft. Reel	2400 Ft. Reel
1⅞ ips	128 min.	192 min.	384 min.
3¾ ips	64 min.	96 min.	192 min.
7½ ips	32 min.	48 min.	96 min.

Magnetic tape is comprised of three basic parts: oxide, binder, and base. The oxide (ordinarily a ferric oxide) is made up of tiny particles of a material similar to iron rust and is suspended in the binder. This oxide-binder combination is then applied to the base, dried (the binder acting as a kind of glue), and milled to a very thin flat surface. The material from which the base is made is usually a polyester (frequently mylar) or an acetate. The polyester, although stronger than acetate and better able to withstand changes in temperature and humidity, is prone to stretch more easily. Rather than stretch, acetate simply breaks. Some manufacturers offer "pre-stretched" polyester tape (usually termed "tensilized") at a somewhat higher cost.

Virtually all tape used in homes or schools for sound recording is ¼" wide. The length and thickness of such tape varies according to the use to which it will be put. The reel sizes available are 3", 5", and 7" (the most common) diameters. Some commercial machines can accept 10½" reels, but these are seldom encountered outside the professional recording studio. The most common tape thicknesses are 1 mil (.001") and ½ mil. The length of the tape, which can vary from about 300 feet to 3,600 feet, when taken into consideration with the tape speed used, will determine the playing time of the tape. A table of lengths and speeds which produce given playing times is to be found below.

One frequently hears such terms as quarter or eight track tape, or full or half track tape. These terms do not refer to the makeup of the tape itself but to the way in which it was (or will be) recorded. In other words, depending on the head characteristics of the machine to be used, the same ¼″ tape may be full track or quarter track, etc. Now, what are tracks? These are the lines of magnetism imposed upon the oxide of the tape by a recording head. Figure 1 is a representation of a tape which has been recorded by a half track recorder. There are two tracks which run in opposite directions, and in order to hear track 2 the tape must be turned over or played back in the opposite direction (some machines do this automatically). Figure 2 indicates how a typical quarter track (or 4 track) tape would appear. Tracks 1 and 3 are the left and right channels, respectively, or a stereo pair. Tracks 2 and 4 are the tracks which would be heard when the tape is turned over or played in the reverse direction. Figure 3 shows a stereo cassette tape (also 4 track) and how it differs from a 4 track tape made by a quarter track open reel machine. Here tracks 1 and 2 are a stereo pair (left and right) as are tracks 3 and 4 (also left and right). This system was decided upon so that either stereo or monaural cassette machines could play either stereo or monaural cassette tapes with complete compatibility.

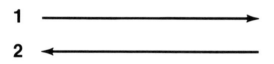

Figure 1: Tape recorded by a half track recorder

Getting back to cassette recorders, the narrowness of the tracks on a cassette stereo tape is the primary cause of hiss in this format. Also, the very slow speed at which all cassette machines move tape (1⅞″, remember?) tends to cause a narrow frequency response (i.e. from about 80 Hz to about 10,000 Hz). The "Dolby Noise-Reduction System," a technique invented by Dr. Ray Dolby, is used to overcome the "hissiness" of cassette recordings. The Dolby system has been successfully applied to cassette use and is now available for home, school, or professional use. It can be had either as a separate playback and/or record unit, or incorporated directly into various cassette machines. Another development, the use of chromium-dioxide tape instead of ferric oxide, has been pioneered by DuPont and allows cassette recorders to provide far better frequency responses.

Among the obvious advantages of the cassette recorder *vis à vis* the open reel recorder are:

1. Compactness and easier portability.
2. Ease of tape handling (inserting a cassette into the machine, or turning it over to hear or record the second side is considerably simpler than threading an open reel machine, or reversing the reels).
3. Prevention of accidentally erasing a valuable pre-recorded tape. Blank cassettes have two plastic tabs on the rear (one for each side). As long as these remain in place, the tape in the cassette may be erased and recorded upon any number of times. If they are removed, the cassette recorder cannot be put into the record mode, thus preventing erasure. All commercially available pre-recorded cassettes have already had these tabs removed to prevent such accidental erasure. No such precaution is possible, at present, with open reel tapes.
4. Compatibility of stereo and monaural cassette tapes with all stereo or monaural cassette machines.
5. Size of cassettes themselves make for easy storage and portability.

Although almost everything listed as desirable for open reel machines applies equally to cassette recorders (the main exception is tape lifters which are unnecessary here), below are a few other features which are peculiar to cassette machines:

1. Automatic shut off. Now a relatively common feature of cassette recorders which prevents undue wear of the motor and other parts.
2. Some sort of signal (preferably a light) to indicate that a side of the cassette has been completely played.
3. A clear window through which one may see the cassette while it is in the machine.
4. Having the heads and capstan easily accessible for cleaning and repair, since cassette tapes, particularly those thinner tape ones with playing times of 90 and 120 minutes, often can be torn from the cassette and wrapped about various internal components of the machine. This can occur when using too thin a tape (to obtain greater playing time) or a faultily constructed cassette.
5. If the cassette recorder is to be used for dictation or recording meetings, etc., then a remote-control microphone (by means of which the machine may be stopped or started in both the record and playback modes) and automatic volume (or level) control are recommended. This latter automatically raises or lowers the recording volume in accordance with the loudness of whatever is being recorded.

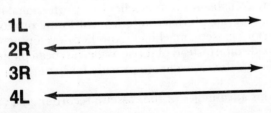

Figure 2: Tape recorded by a quarter track (four track) recorder

BEWARE

Things of which to be wary in recorders are:

1. Pressure pads. These are usually felt covered metal contrivances which press the tape firmly onto the heads, causing more than normal wear on the heads. Better machines don't need pressure pads.
2. Lack of some sort of loudness (volume) metering. The most useful of the various kinds of meters, particularly in recording music, is the "volume unit" (v.u.) meter. The machine is more useful if the meter operates when playing back a recorded tape since head alignment, among other corrective operations, is more easily accomplished. There should be a meter for each channel in stereo machines.
3. Confusing or misleading specifications in manufacturers' advertising. A few specifications to look for can be found listed here under Basic Specifications.

MAINTENANCE

Now, a few words about the maintenance of all tape machines. There are only two types of maintenance with which a tape machine owner should concern himself. The first of these is the cleaning of the heads and capstan. All tape, new and old, contains some loose oxide which is likely to be deposited upon the heads and the capstan. If left to accumulate, this material will clog the most important part of the heads—the narrow gaps —causing a marked decrease in frequency response. Also, this loose oxide can act as grains of sand and cause greater than normal head abrasion and wear. Therefore, the heads should be cleaned regularly, using a commercially available head cleaning solvent (or isopropyl alcohol) gently applied with cotton covered swabs.

The other maintenance procedure to be undertaken is that of demagnetizing (or "degaussing") the heads and capstan. After recording and playing back for a certain period (which varies from machine to machine), the heads and, ultimately, the capstan will build up a small magnetic charge which will interfere with proper record and playback. If allowed to remain, this magnetism may eventually make itself felt upon the tapes being used and, to varying degrees, spoil them. To demagnetize the heads and capstan, one should acquire what is usually called a "head demagnetizer"—there are various types made by a number of manufacturers. The demagnetizer tip should be held closely to, *but not touching,* in succession, the record and playback heads and capstan. The proper method is to wave the demagnetizer in a small circle about ⅛" from the surface to be acted upon for about 15 seconds for each head and the capstan. Both cleaning and demagnetizing should be performed as a regular regimen after about every ten hours of machine use. By following these measures, your machine should provide many thousands of hours of use. One word of caution—unless you are very knowledgeable, leave other repairs to bona fide service personnel.

BASIC SPECIFICATIONS

Look for these specifications when selecting an open reel or cassette recorder:

Crosstalk: the leakage of the information (i.e., music, speech, etc.) from one track into another one. This is undesirable and figures given in specifications usually express the amount of leakage in terms of negative decibels (db) at a given frequency (e.g., −40 db at 1,000 Hz). The lower the decibel rate of crosstalk the better. At any frequency, the acceptable crosstalk is in the vicinity of −35 to − 40 db. Any higher and the stereo effect will be watered down. These figures apply equally for cassette and open reel machines.

Flutter: rapid variations in the tape speed which, when pronounced, causes a wavering of pitch. The flutter specification is usually given as a percentage of deviation from a perfect specific speed. A cassette tape machine should provide no more than .10 percent, an open reel machine no more than .07 per cent at 7½ ips. Occasionally, manufacturers will combine flutter and wow (q.v.) percentages. For a cassette machine the total flutter and wow should not exceed .20 percent; for open reel tape machines, not greater than .15 percent at 7½ ips.

Frequency response: the measure of given equipment to reproduce a range of frequencies. To be considered "high fidelity," such equipment should handle at least 20 to 20,000 Hz. In order for a frequency response to be meaningful, it must also indicate to what extent this range deviates from uniformity. This is almost always done by giving the range and indicating that it varies from, plus or minus, so many decibels. The lower the number of decibels (db), the closer the machine reproduces its range of frequencies to perfection. For a good cassette machine, a playback frequency response of ±3 cb 50 to 10,000 Hz or better. An open reel machine's frequency response, at 7½ ips, should be 2.0 db 30 to 16,000 Hz or better.

Intermodulation (IM) distortion: the mixing (or modulation) of two frequencies to produce other (and unwanted) ones. Suppose a bass clarinet produced a given note with a frequency of 100 Hz, while simultaneously a violin produced one at 3,000 Hz. Intermodulation distortion would produce the new and spurious frequencies of 2,900 Hz and 3,100 Hz. Usually intermodulation distortion increases as the power (volume) is increased and, also, at the extremes of the frequency response. Intermodulation distortion, like flutter and wow, is expressed as a percentage of deviation—the lower the figure the better. Good intermodulation distortion for a cassette machine is about 2 percent when measured at − 10 on the VU meter. For a good open reel machine, the figure should be about 1 percent or 2 percent at 7½ ips and − 10 on the VU meter.

Power output: the amount of power (specified in watts) delivered by an amplifier to the speakers. If the power output of any tape recorder's amplifier is critical in relation to the speakers to be used with it, it is best to ask for the power to be given as "continuous power" (or "root-mean-square"). Ordinarily, in specifications this will be given as "x watts RMS."

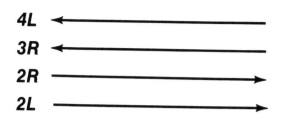

Figure 3: Tape recorded by a cassette recorder

This means that the amplifier of the equipment puts out so many watts *continuously* at 1,000 Hz. Such rating systems as "music power" or "dynamic power" only measure the power output for short bursts and can be very deceiving. Power output is important in determining both the type and number of loud speakers the amplifier can supply, and, similarly, the type and number of headphones. In other words, these components should be properly matched.

Signal-to-noise (S/N): the magnitude by which a signal (e.g., music, speech, etc.) is separated from unwanted noises (e.g, hiss). This is expressed in decibels, and the higher the number the better. The minimum S/N ratio for a cassette or open reel machine, at 0 VU, using a test tape, should be 50 db.

Wow: the result of slow, regular variations in tape speed. When pronounced, wow can produce quite audible, rather low toned, variations in pitch. Like flutter (see above), wow is usually given as a percentage deviation from a perfect specific speed. The same figures for flutter hold true for wow.

OPTIONS AND OTHER FEATURES

Automatic demagnetization (degaussing): consists of a special circuit in the tape recorder to remove unwanted magnetization of the record and playback heads.

Automatic reverse: any of a number of methods by means of which the tape, while in the record and/or playback mode, will be moved in the opposite direction when the supply reel is nearly exhausted of tape. Some machines offer both bi-directional playback and record, while others offer only bi-directional playback. Bi-directionality is not necessarily automatically accomplished—in some machines the direction is controlled manually. In any event, the bi-directionality of automatic or manual reverse does eliminate the necessity for physically reversing the reels in order to resume playback and/or recording.

Automatic shutoff: the means (often a switch) by which the reels (and in some machines, the motors) are stopped when the tape either breaks or runs out.

Digital counter: a mechanical device which counts and displays the number of rotations of the supply reel and is useful in indexing tapes.

Mixer: a device which can be built into a recorder which allows for the blending and balancing of more than one sound source, e.g., radio and microphone.

Monitoring: the process of hearing what the tape recorder is receiving or recording. There are two types of monitoring: "source" and "tape." The former permits one to hear the information as the recording amplifier "hears" it. "Tape" (or "off-the-tape") monitoring allows one to hear what has actually been recorded on the tape. This last can be accomplished only if the recorder has, minimally, separate record and playback heads. Usually, the only way to determine which type of monitoring a machine offers is by checking the specifications or the owner's manual.

Pause (or edit) control: a device which allows the tape recorder to be stopped instantaneously without disengaging it from either the record or playback mode.

Sound-on-sound: a type of recording procedure, sometimes called "over-dubbing," which permits material previously recorded on one track to be transferred to another track along with (and simultaneously) adding new material to it.

Sound-with-sound: a type of recording procedure which allows one to monitor (off-the-tape) one track of a tape while simultaneously and separately recording on another track of the same tape.

Tone control: control knobs or switches which vary the bass and treble output of a tape recorder. They function in most tape machines only in the playback mode.

GENERAL GLOSSARY

Bias: a high frequency (inaudible) alternating current which is fed to the record head along with the signal (q.v.) current to reduce distortion.

Bulk eraser: A device which erases an entire reel (or cassette) or tape without removing the tape from the reel (or cassette).

Cycles-per-second (cps): expression of a given frequency (e.g., the frequency of "A" to which an American orchestra tunes is at 440 cps). The term is obsolete and has been replaced by Hertz (Hz). e.g., "A" equals 440 Hz.

Deck, tape: a tape recorder (open reel, cassette, etc.) which usually contains a tape-transport (q.v.), recording amplifiers, and output pre-amplifiers but which requires, for playback, playback amplifiers and speakers.

Dropout: a momentary loss of signal (q.v.) in playing back a tape, usually caused by any physical imperfections in the tape itself.

Dub (or dubbing): used as a noun: a copy or a recording. As a verb: the process of copying a recording.

Editing: the alteration of a tape by either excising (i.e., cutting and splicing) or erasing portions.

Frequency: the rate of repetition of a given pitch, formerly in cycles-per-second (q.v.) now in Hertz.

Gap: the distance between the opposite poles of a magnetic head, usually measured in microns. Because they are small, gaps are easily clogged by oxide particles and require frequent cleaning.

Hertz: see "cycles-per-second."

Leader: tape which is spliced onto recording tape. Leader is not magnetic tape and cannot be recorded upon. It is usually tough and can withstand the strain of repeated threadings. Can also be of various colors for coding.

Low-noise tape: magnetic tape designed to be used for recording at relatively slow speeds since it offers less hiss than ordinary tape. Usually commensurately more expensive than regular tape.

Noise: unwanted sound, ordinarily in the form of hiss, caused by poorer quality tape or a poorly functioning record head.

Pre-echo: see print-through.

Print-through: the unwanted transfer of a recorded signal (q.v.) from one layer of tape to another. This usually takes the form of "pre-echo"—a passage is heard faintly just before that same passage is heard at a normal level. Primarily caused by using a tape with too thin a base (less than 1 mil.) or by the machine winding the tape tightly, or by recording at too high a level.

Reel-to-reel: another term for "open reel" machines.

Tape-transport: as part of a tape recorder, it is the combination of mechanical and electrical parts which moves the tape from reel to reel. As a specific device, it is a mechanical and electrical device which moves tape but contains none of the electronic equipment necessary for recording or playing back (i.e., no record or playback preamplifiers, amplifiers or speakers).

Signal: the physical embodiment of a message, i.e., usually the electrical or magnetic impulse which is ultimately convertible, in tape recording into a sound, or the sound itself. Usually, signal is taken to be a desideratum in contra-distinction to noise (q.v.).

SUGGESTED READINGS

General

1. Kubiak, Leonard P. "Selecting a Tape Recorder," *Electronics World,* May 1969, p. 39.

2. "Library Technology Reports," *ALA Bulletin,* January 1969.

3. Long, Robert & Norman Eisenberg, "Tape Recording at Twenty-Five," *High Fidelity Magazine,* August 1970, p. 40–50.

4. Petras, Fred. "How to Buy a Tape Recorder," *Radio-Electronics*, October 1968, p. 92–95.

5. Ragosine, Victor E. "Magnetic Recording," *Scientific American,*November 1969, p. 71+.

6. Shatavsky, Sam. "The Best Tape System for You," *Popular Science,* February 1969, p. 126–129.

Cassette Machines

1. Allen, Larry. "Stereo Cassettes: The Electronic Side," *Radio-Electronics,* March 1971, p. 29–43.

2. "Cassette Recorders," *Consumer Bulletin,* January 1971, p. 31–35.

3. "Cassette Tape Recorders," *Consumer Reports,* May 1971, p. 279–283.

4. Hirsch, Julian D. "New Dolby-ized Cassette Decks," *Electronics World.* March 1971, p. 25+.

5. Hodges, Ralph. "What Causes Cassette Malfunction?," *Stereo Review,* September 1971, p. 63–65.

6. Lincoln, Charles, "Cassettes: Not Either/Or, But And!," *Popular Electronics,* June 1969, p. 65–68.

7. "Stereo Cassette Tape Players with Automatic Changers," *Consumer Bulletin,* September 1969, p. 29–32.

8. Zide, Larry. "Are Cassettes Fulfilling Their Promise?," *High Fidelity Magazine,* November 1970, p. 73–77.

Magnetic Tapes

1. Dodson, Charles H. "Magnetic Tape: Handle With Care," *Popular Electronics,* February 1970, p. 85+

2. Hirsch, Julian D. "Hirsch-Houk Laboratory Tests of Cassette Tapes," *Stereo Review,* September 1971, p. 58+.

3. Kipnis, Igor. "Cassette Packaging," *Stereo Review,* September 1971, p. 61.

4. Madden, William H. "Recording Tape: A Short Primer," *Hi-Fi/Stereo Review,* March 1968, p. 71–74.

5. Salm, Walter G. "New in Stereo Cassettes '70," *Radio-Electronics,* December 1969, p. 37–39.

6. Zide, Larry. "Tape Up to Date," *High Fidelity Magazine,* August 1971, p. 42–47.

The Dolby System

1. Berger, Ivan. "Dolby and Four Channel: Two Interim Reports," *Saturday Review,* April 25, 1970, p. 73.

2. Salm, Walter G. "The Dolby System: How It Works," *Radio-Electronics,* October 1969, p. 53+.

One-On-One AV: The User's Point of View

by H. Michael Eisler

The fan's blowing hot air in my face. There's a burn blister on my arm from the lamp housing. I can't reach the focus knob without covering the lens with my arm. The gate opens against the carrel wall, so it's very hard to thread the projector. This framing knob's on that side too. The picture, when I'm lucky enough to get one, is too small because the projector's lens is wrong for the short throw. These are the kinds of problems we run into when we try to use projectors in situations for which they were not designed.

Very little audiovisual equipment was designed for individual viewing or carrel use. The basic designs were well established long before anybody had thought of carrels or heard of individualized instruction. Even the few machines which have been designed for individual or small group use often take up too much room in the average carrel, and may not have all the controls up front where they should be.

So how close can we get to the right projector for today's instructional styles? Since so many audiovisual materials are now used in one-on-one situations, let's take a look at playback equipment from the user's point of view.

WHAT'S AVAILABLE?

There is one comprehensive catalog of available equipment. It gives basic specifications, capabilities, and costs of practically every type of playback and projection equipment. There are also sections on carrels, screens, language labs, control devices, etc. It's specifically designed for users, not producers. If you don't have a copy of *The Audio-Visual Equipment Directory,* it's available from the National Audio-Visual Association, Inc., 3150 Spring Street, Fairfax, Virginia 22030, price: $10. It's an excellent way to begin to survey the field.

HOW GOOD IS IT?

Reliability is the single most important characteristic of any projector or player. Will it work, and will it last? There have been very few attempts to rate audiovisual equipment for reliability and longevity. The most recent is being made by the Educational Products Information Exchange Institute (EPIE), 386 Park Avenue South, New York, N.Y. 10016. This is a continuing and expanding effort. Super 8mm motion picture projectors, overhead projectors, and filmstrip viewers have already been covered. Audio cassette players are now being surveyed. The results are published in the *EPIE Reports* which appear nine times a year covering specific classes of instructional products, materials, and methods. Five are "in-depth" and four "in-brief." Current bulletins of interest appear in the twice-monthly *EPIEGRAM,* an educational consumer's newsletter.

Obviously, the life of any piece of equipment depends on how well it is maintained and whether the user knows how to use it. Proper maintenance and use also safeguard the films and tapes played on the equipment.

MAINTENANCE

Manufacturers seem to be reluctant to spell out the full care and maintenance their machines deserve. But maintenance is one of the two most important factors in reliability and long life. The second most important factor is that the user knows how to use the machine and when to call for help. It follows that projectors which are difficult to maintain and too tricky to load, unload, and use will probably be less reliable than those easy to use and care for, no matter how expensive and well-built they may be. Even a projector which needs only "simple" maintenance may not get the care it needs if that simple maintenance is surrounded by complications—like having to undo three tiny screws to get at a dirty lens. By the same token, a projector which is awkward to use is likely to be abused. The only way to find out is to try it out. Get your hands on the machine. Clean the gate, change a bulb, do everything the manufacturer recommends. Don't watch the salesman do it. Try it yourself. And keep track of how many times you find yourself cursing, or feeling like it.

OPERATION

Then sit down with the machine as a user would. If it's going to be used in a carrel, try it out in one. Or simulate the walls with a couple of stacks of books. Load, unload, operate. Don't assume that the little head-aches like the gate that won't open wide enough will be cured with practice. They won't. Especially not when equipment is available to all comers, not just practiced projectionists.

VIEWABILITY

If you're looking at projectors with built-in screens, make sure that the screen is adequately shaded to avoid reflections. Is there a lens available which will give the correct size of picture for the type of carrel or size of screen you will be using?

SCREENS

Screens are often not needed. Any light colored, smooth surface will do. For extremely bright areas, special screens are available. But check for possible problems. Some give a poor picture when viewed from an angle. Others are easily damaged and hard to clean.

CRITERIA

Hazards: Hot surfaces, sharp corners, electrical shocks. If the projector is to be attached to other devices or controls, make sure that the connectors do not touch metal if misinserted.

Inconveniences: Are all controls for loading, focusing, volume, and other adjustments readily accessible to the user when the machine is in operating position? Does the device have to be moved out of position for any of these functions?

Maintenance: Can lamps be replaced, heads and optics cleaned by someone who is not an experienced ambidextrous technician with special tools and infinite patience?

Nuisances: Is it quiet in operation of motors, fans, frame changing mechanisms?

Simplicity: If you can't put the key operating instructions and cautions on a 3×5 card, consider a different machine!

Economy: Projection lamps are expensive. Will it work with longer-lived, lower wattage bulbs for short-throw situations like carrel use?

A WORD ON CARRELS

If you already have carrels, be sure the projectors you buy will fit. Don't forget to allow room for books, models, test-tubes, etc. Consider whether students will be working in pairs. If you're thinking about installing carrels, ask yourself if they are really necessary. The major function of a carrel is to assign and organize space. They also provide a measure of privacy and freedom from distractions. But with av materials, these considerations may not be too important. Earphones create an effective feeling of privacy, and attention focused on a screen is hard to distract. Before you take the plunge, try using plain tables. Mark off the space for each carrel or viewing area with tape. Set up the equipment and try it out. This will quickly tell you whether you need carrels at all, and if you decide you do, how big they should be and where they should be located. An av carrel should at least have its own electrical outlets and built-in master electrical switch. Multimedia carrels need to be arranged so that projectors don't get in each other's and the user's way. Some carrels are available with a shelf big enough for several pieces of av equipment. Their images are projected through one built-in mirror to the back wall of the carrel. Others provide for separate mirror systems which direct the image to a screen, or shelves situated so that you can project directly. When such carrels are being considered, be particularly careful to be sure that all projector controls are accessible.

AUTOMATION

Many pieces of audiovisual equipment are available with features such as cartridge loading and self-threading. A reasonable rule of thumb is to assume that the more automatic a device is, the more difficult it will be to maintain and repair. And since automation usually means more parts, the chances of breakdown may be increased. If you are considering an automatic version of a machine, try the maintenance and cleaning. If possible, compare it to the same jobs done on a simpler version of the same machine. And don't be afraid to ask (and try) how to get a broken or jammed tape, slide, or film, out of the machine. With audio cassette devices with compartments which pop up, or trap doors or slots into which the cassette disappears, find out how you can get a misbehaving cassette back out. Remember, regardless of the type of projector, try it. You mightn't like it.

CARTRIDGES AND CASSETTES

Film cartridges (motion and still) do protect their contents from unnecessary handling when loading and unloading. All devices which use cartridges or cassettes are self-threading. But there are some disadvantages. Compatibility is one. Most cartridges will work only in the projector they were designed for (*Previews,* September 1972, p. 5). In the most common types of cartridges for visuals, the film is spliced into a continuous loop. This means that it will only project forwards at projection speed. This can be a nuisance when one wants to repeat a portion of the program. You have to let it play until it gets back to that point. Cartridges which use looped film are usually impossible for the user to repair if something goes wrong with the cartridge. If the contents need help, like cleaning or splicing, the whole thing usually has to be sent back to the manufacturer.

Cassettes for film and tape (audio and video) contain two hubs. The film winds from one to the other, rather than turning on itself as in the loop format. Cassettes will go backwards and forwards, at slow, normal, and high speeds if the projector or player has those features. Some cassettes can be opened to remove the medium, but it's tricky.

A third type of cartridge is simply a container which holds a reel. This type is available for several different brands of Super 8mm motion picture projectors. Some will work in more than one brand of projector. These projectors are self-threading, reaching into the cartridge and pulling the film through the machine and onto a take-up reel. Since the film goes from reel to reel, it will go fast forward and reverse. Some of the projectors using these cartridges will also accept films on reels. These cartridge-containers can easily be opened and the film removed for cleaning, repair, or replacement. One caution with this type of projector: find out how to remove the film should trouble develop during projection or rewinding.

MULTI-PURPOSE MACHINES

Some projectors will do more than one job—for example, projectors with built-in screens which will also project onto an external screen. Others can, or have attachments, which allow the use of slides on filmstrip machines and vice versa. There are movie projectors which let you look at one frame at a time plus a range of speeds from "slow-motion" to super fast. Others provide for both optical and magnetic sound. True slow motion, by the way, is created by filming action at much higher speeds than usual, and then playing it back at normal speeds.

If you're considering a multi-purpose machine keep in mind that it may not do any one of its several jobs as well as a machine designed to do just one of them. Or, it will do one function well and the other only marginally. How often you need the extra feature is an important consideration. If you will need it often, consider getting the right machine for each job. Remember that having one dual-purpose machine is not the same as having two! It can only do one job at a time.

THE MOST IMPORTANT CONSIDERATION

Before making any decision about projectors and players, take a long, careful look at the media you use the most. What mix of films (16mm, 8mm Super Standard, sound or silent) do you have, or want to be able to use? How about records vs. cassettes, audio tapes (at what speeds), filmstrips (single or double frame), videotapes (size, speed, type). Let the materials determine the machines, because the materials do the teaching, not the machines.

Where to Kick: A Troubleshooter's Guide for Teachers Who Don't Need Trouble

by Phyllis Ward

This article is intended as a troubleshooter's aid, not as an instruction in how to use these machines. Only if you are familiar with the equipment will the remedies make sense.

A FEW GENERAL RULES

Never force a machine. If you have to apply pressure you are doing something wrong. The "strong arm" technique of making equipment work is lousy—repeat—lousy.

All about light bulbs. Replacement bulbs are very sensitive to skin oils and should always be handled with a cloth. Picking bulbs up with your fingers will often cause the bulb to blow and at approximately $7.00 apiece, it is worth rounding up a hankie.

Report any malfunction or damage to the media center *before* it deteriorates to an unrepairable condition.

These items are particularly vulnerable to the lure of the open road and must be constantly guarded to prevent disappearance:

tape recorder microphones
detachable power cords
portable cassette recorders
heavy duty extension cords (will they *ever* return?)
VTR cables—if these escape you are in serious trouble
tape recorder patch cords & adapters
headsets and earphones

Always handle film, filmstrips, slides, records, etc. on the edges. Fingerprints hurt!

Memorize the following hints or sleep with them under your pillow every night for a month.

OVERHEAD PROJECTORS

Symptom: Transparency will not focus.
Remedy: Adjust focus knob or if that fails move overhead projector closer to screen until focusing is possible.
Symptom: No light.
Remedy: About the only equipment failure possible is a burned out bulb or failure to plug in the machine. In the first instance refer to general rules and in the second—stop blushing.

FILMSTRIP PROJECTORS

Symptom: Can't focus correctly.
Remedy: Usually filmstrip is somehow not in the track correctly. Check feed and try focusing again.
Symptom: Still can't focus.
Remedy: If still no luck, check to see if lens is in correctly. Sometimes these are accidentally shoved in or pulled out too far, causing no end of confusion.
Symptom: Image is too large or too small to fit screen.
Remedy: Adjust lens. Remember DO NOT FORCE.
Hint: Before putting projector away, run the fan a few minutes after the lamp is turned off—until the exhaust flow of air is cool. This will lengthen the life of the bulb considerably and earn you the gratitude of the Media Center.

SLIDE PROJECTORS

Symptom: Slide projects wrong way on screen.
Remedy: Face the screen. Hold the slide so it reads correctly. Invert slide, so that image is upside down and insert slide into tray.
Symptom: Slide won't fit into tray.
Remedy: Loosen safety lock.
Symptom: Slides fell all over the parking lot on way to school.
Remedy: Next time tighten safety lock.
Symptom: Tray won't fit onto projector.
Remedy: Line up "O" in tray setting with notch on projector. If tray still will not sit down on projector check the tray spring—you may have a bum tray.
Symptom: Tray won't come off projector.
Remedy: Press "select" button and rotate tray to "O." Lift off.
Symptom: A warped slide is stuck in projector and will not reject.
Remedy: Take off tray and carefully—oh so care-carefully—remove slide.

OPAQUE PROJECTORS

Symptom: Light is on but no image is projected.
Remedy: Lift lens cover.

Symptom: Wrinkled, singed pictures.
Remedy: Too much heat. Watch the picture closely next time. (Too long an exposure will affect some pictures, especially colored ones, so avoid showing pages that are part of expensive or irreplaceable books.)

RECORD PLAYER

Symptom: Turntable will not rotate.
Remedy: Check speed adjustments. If not properly aligned on speed often the turntable is inoperable.

Symptom: Lousy sound.
Remedy: Check needle and record for dust and scratches. Also check tone controls on record player.
Hint: Always lock the playing arm securely on its rest to avoid needle damage.

TAPE RECORDERS

Instruction sheet usually available from Media Center. Lots of symptoms can be avoided if you thoroughly understand the operation manual.

Symptom: Distorted sound on playback.
Remedy: Volume control was set too high when recording. Next time make a trial recording to check this. (Tone control could also be at fault.)

Many tape recorder symptoms are irrelevant with simple classroom tape recorders. Now is the time to conquer these easy, limited-use tape recorders so you will be ready and anxious to understand the subtleties of a more complex machine.

8MM FILM LOOP PROJECTORS

Operation is very simple. Just remember—do not force cartridge into projector.

Symptom: Cartridge does not fit into projector.

Remedy: It may be the wrong cartridge container. See Media Center for further evaluation and help. Also check to make sure you have the proper projector—we have two types—one for *sound* film loops and one for *silent* film loops.

16MM PROJECTORS

Instruction manuals are available from the Media Center. Biggest problem is need for familiarity with EACH machine—they have separate personalities and demand individual attention. Stop by for a personal introduction.

MANUAL LOAD PROJECTORS

Symptom: Projector is turned on but lamp does not go on.
Remedy: Check to see that switch is set all the way to LAMP, not just at run. If it is and *still* no lamp then suspect a blown bulb.

Symptom: Picture will not focus with the use of the focus knob.
Remedy: Check position of projector to screen—it may be too close. Also check to be sure lens is properly in casing—not too far in or out.
Check to be sure projector does not have a wide angle lens by mistake (1.5 inch for example). The wide angle lens is necessary for showing films with the movie mover but will not project picture on normal wall.

Symptom: There are parts of two pictures on screen.
Remedy: Adjust FRAME knob.

Symptom: Film is fluttering.
Remedy: STOP PROJECTOR. There is no excuse for a badly torn film. Stop projector at first sign of trouble and correct it. Usual cause of film flutter is in the loops. If loops check out OK then check to see that film is properly on sprocket holes.

Symptom: By some strange fluke film damage occurs.
Remedy: Please inform Media Center promptly.

Symptom: Sound is mushy.
Remedy: STOP PROJECTOR. Check to make sure film is taut around sound drum. If it is then check tone controls, 99 out of 100 times, however, the problem is with the sound drum.

Symptom: Projector is running but there is no sound.
Remedy: Check to see that sound is turned on. It takes a minute or so to warm up so be patient.

AUTOMATIC PROJECTORS

Symptom: Film will not feed into projector.
Remedy: Be sure threading lever is in AUTO-LOAD position and that film is undamaged and free of tape or obstructions. Film can be trimmed in film cutter. Projector should be turned to forward position and film should be guided onto sprocket holes.

Note: Automatic projectors are notorious for not accepting film for any minor flaw. Check film condition carefully when threading.

Symptom: Film flutter.
Remedy: STOP PROJECTOR. Push "system restorer" lever to correct loop placement.

Other symptoms and remedies are the same as manual projectors. Just remember when in doubt STOP THE PROJECTOR to avoid film damage.

VIDEOTAPE RECORDERS

Manual available from Media Center. A MUST for VTR users.

Important Points to Remember

Never point the camera directly at the sun or other source of bright light. Avoid continuous shooting at a subject in strong light, especially when the picture has high contrast. If the camera is used for a long time in this way, the sensitivity of the vidicon tube will decrease. When aiming the camera at a bright subject, pan the camera from side to side occasionally, so that the image on the vidicon does not remain fixed.

AVOID UNNECESSARY EXPOSURE TO LIGHT. Keep the lens cap in place or set the power switch to STANDBY or to OFF when the camera is not being used.

AVOID ROUGH HANDLING OR MECHANICAL SHOCK to the camera, especially when the lens faces downward.

When the camera is not used for a long period of time, be sure to turn off the power and keep the camera in a horizontal plane.

KEEP slack in tape while machine is idling to reduce recording head wear. (Coaches take note.)

It is always wise to play back a short recorded sequence immediately before doing a complete recording to be sure all is well and operating properly.

RETURN and carefully check all cables, reels, etc. It is very easy to drop one in the hall or on the football field.

CAREFULLY label tapes to prevent someone else wiping them out.

Rule of Life: If someone else can possibly erase them, they will.

ALWAYS return or store the VTR with cover and lens cap in place. The VTR is very sensitive to dust and should be protected as much as possible.

Whatever Happened to Videodisc?

by Deirdre Boyle

Eight years ago announcements that videodiscs were just around the corner caught the public imagination. But that "imminent" arrival is still in the wings. Diverse problems—from resolving technical wrinkles to deciding on the initial target audiences and selecting suitable programming—continue to stall the advent of the videodisc.

Libraries have been among the most enthusiastic fans of the videodisc, anticipating a video system as easy to operate as a phonograph, with the capability of recording an encyclopedia or an entire slide library or several million catalog cards on one or more discs. Though the possibilities inherent in the new technology are exciting, some practical realities cloud this rosy picture.

WHEN WILL VIDEODISC BE READY?

Last November AEG-Telefunken announced that their videodisc player, *TeD*, would be on the market in the United States this year. *TeD* has been on sale in West Germany since March 1975, but before it arrives here, Telefunken must find licensees ready to venture into the as-yet-risky videodisc market.

Philips/MCA promises that *Disco-Vision* will begin regional marketing in the Los Angeles area this spring. RCA, in its 1976 report to stockholders, forecast that *Selecta Vision* would be marketed in less than two years. But a recent U.S. Navy report on videodisc systems suggests that RCA will never market its system and that Philips/MCA's laser system—the best to date—is only the best of unsatisfactory systems. Interestingly, neither RCA nor Philips/MCA was willing to demonstrate its system publicly at a videodisc conference held in New York City in November of 1976.

The videodisc formats being developed by Philips/MCA, RCA, Telefunken, and Thomson CFS (France)—to name a few—are not compatible with one another. Each system employs a different technology with varying potentials for educational uses.

- Philips/MCA's *Disco-Vision* uses a laser beam which reads light reflected off the underside of its rigid plastic disc. The life of the laser pick-up is an impressive 10,000 hours of playing time; the disc's life is unlimited. A protective plastic coating prevents dust and scratch damage to the disc, and there is no disc wear and tear because the laser beam never touches it. Each disc contains 54,000 frames and plays for 30 minutes. The player offers variable slow motion, fast forward and backward, instant replay, and freeze-frame capabilities. Especially important to libraries is the capacity, by means of adding equipment, to turn the player into a pushbutton system for locating individual frames. Thus, any form of indexed information—from encyclopedias to catalog cards—could be easily accessed. At a planned $499 purchase price for the player, with discs selling for $2 to $10, *Disco-Vision* is the best bet for education and information uses.

- RCA's *Selecta Vision* uses a sapphire-tipped stylus which senses changes in the electric capacitance in each groove of the disc. *Selecta Vision* most closely resembles the familiar phonograph. The stylus has a life of 300–500 hours and can be replaced for under $10; the player is expected to sell for $400. Each disc, made of soft plastic, has a life of 300–500 plays, after which the image deteriorates. Since four frames are recorded on each revolution of the disc, it is difficult to display a freeze frame on this machine. Furthermore, even if it *were* possible to obtain a freeze frame, the image would be erased after two minutes of viewing, so in effect *Selecta Vision* has no freeze frame capability of use to the educational consumer. Discs with a playing time of 60 minutes (30 minutes on each side) should retail for $10 to $15. This system is aimed at a mass market audience.

- Telefunken's *TeD* uses a mechanical pressure pick-up with an expensive diamond stylus that plays for only 80 hours. Each paper-thin plastic foil disc plays a 10-minute program, with a life of 100–200 plays. The player offers manual rapid selection and a replay programmed to last 10 seconds. As with *Selecta Vision*, *TeD*'s image deteriorates and would not stand up to repeated educational uses. Telefunken has developed a changer which permits playing up to 12 discs (2 hours) with a four-second delay between discs, but the changer is not yet on the market. The short life of the stylus and disc coupled with a disc's short playing time severely limit *TeD*.

Since no decision to standardize formats appears to be forthcoming, consumers will have to experiment with incompatible systems until a superior format dominates. Pleasing educators is not a high industry priority now that the big-dollar education market of the '60s has shifted to the more conservative '70s market.

While there is no consensus in the video industry, a mass market seems to be the initial target audience, followed by industrial and professional training. After having been burned by the short-lived *Cartravision* and *EVR* ventures of the late '60s, education and industry are wary of untried video technologies.

Libraries have a vested interest in the outcome of the format battles. To date, only Philips/MCA *Disco-Vision*, with its capacity for high-density, long-term information storage, offers real potential for educational use. Concerned individuals, such as Professor Lee Wilcox, a physicist at SUNY/Stony Brook, are recommending a public policy against decisions which could rule out a compatible entertainment *and* educational video system.

Even if *Disco-Vision* wins out over other formats, delays in television technology may mask the advantages offered by the disc. The current U.S. video standard for image resolution is 525 lines of information scanned in a single frame (that is, the TV image is made up of 525 lines scanned light and dark by a light beam). At 525 lines, the clarity of a printed page from the *Encyclopaedia Britannica* would be unsatisfactory, barely an improvement over the fuzzy image produced by micro-readers. The European standard is 625 lines, and we could double our standard to 1,050 lines by 1980. But there's no word yet on whether this advance is in the works.

Videodiscs also offer enhanced sound fidelity over existing phonodisc and tape recording, but with present TV sound equipment still in the dark ages, such advances will never be heard. We can only hope that videodisc technology will finally spur TV manufacturers to update and improve equipment.

WHAT DO YOU PUT ON THE DISC?

With technology more or less perfected, the main videodisc problem is programming. No one seems to know what kind of audio and video information will command repeated viewings. Some say audio *and* video music concerts will be first on the disc. Examples of programming from *TeD* disc producer Teldec leave much to be desired. Philips/MCA has acquired Universal's film library of 11,000 films and is seeking to acquire other film libraries. Their current catalog lists 2,000 movie titles on disc.

But how many people will want to view and review "All Quiet on the Western Front"? The videodisc is a new medium and it will take some time to discover what new kinds of programming will evolve because of it.

The cost of producing a master disc of a video program is high. Teldec requires a minimum run of 500 discs, and other industry people concerned with profits are talking in larger terms. For instance, a run of 10,000 to 50,000 would make sales of half-hour discs possible at $2–15.

Although the state of the art of video, computer, and laser technologies would allow for storage of high-density information such as slide libraries or card catalogs, the costs involved in producing such discs would be phenomenal. It is very clear that videodisc is a business venture, and in this highly competitive atmosphere prospects are bad for high-cost, low-profit library tapes. Willocks suggested that charitable grants might help finance library recordings, but that possibility looks unlikely in an industry where there is even talk of making videodisc into an advertising medium to outstrip commercial TV.

VIDEODISC VS. VIDEOCASSETTE

The breakthrough in mass market video systems may not be on disc, but rather, on tape. That prediction was made recently by Gunnar Bergvahl, a Swedish economist and video specialist for the Bonniers Leisure Groups.

Half-inch video cassettes for the home arrived on the market last February with Sony's Betamax, which was expected to sell over 30,000 units last year, according to Sony Corporation of America President Harvey Schein. Sony remains sanguine about Betamax's future, despite a lawsuit filed in November by Universal Studios and Walt Disney Productions alleging copyright infringement by Sony, its outlets, advertising agency, and even one consumer. Home audiotaping of off-air programs has never prompted copyright controversy, and it is unlikely that Sony will lose the suit. At any rate, this case applies to home use and has little bearing on the question of off-air taping in more public situations, such as libraries.

There are two main advantages of tape over the disc: tape systems—unlike discs—can be used to record programs off-air or to create new programs with a camera; and, tape is reusable, intrinsically offering more value for the money. At present, a ½″ U cassette tape costs $15.95 for a half-hour. Right now the Betamax retails for about $1,300, but predictions are that a streamlined version without such deluxe features as a digital timer will soon put Betamax into a more affordable price range.

As with videodisc, the question of how to use videotape arises. Betamax's initial pitch has been for off-air recording of TV programs, but Sony is interested in developing prerecorded ½″ cassettes to fill the gap when the novelty of taping TV shows wears off. And with a lawsuit pending, now is a good time for Sony to switch gears and emphasize other uses of the home Betamax system.

Plans are under way to construct U.S. plants to manufacture the new ½″ tape, which costs half the price of ¾″ tape. Sony is also planning to make transfers of Super-8mm film onto tape at costs of from $11 for 10 minutes to $33 for a 30-minute tape, excluding tape and program costs, and is working on a changer attachment to allow for playing 10-hour-long cassettes.

Competition among Sony, Sanyo, Matsushita (Panasonic), and Japan Victor (JVC) may lead to the emergence of a single, inter-manufacturer standard for ½″ cassette tapes, similar to the EIAJ standard for ½″ video tape arrived at in the late 60s. Uniformity might be prompted by the

Japanese firms' need to compete more effectively with American and European disc developments.

It seems likely that some form of disc and tape will coexist, since each system offers certain features not provided by the other. Half-inch cassette tape is here to stay and should, in time, be within the price range of most TV consumers. Though videodisc player costs—as supplied by their producers—are lower than Betamax, videodisc has yet to appear in dealer showrooms. And when it does arrive, its success will be limited by the quality and scope of the prerecorded programming available.

Prognosticators vary in their predictions of how long it will take before the videodisc has established itself; predictions range anywhere from three to ten years, or longer. With a laser system we can hope for high-density, long-term information storage systems which could revolutionize libraries and their relationships to patrons. But that is still a long way off.

PART

VI

STANDARDS AND CATALOGING

Thoughts on Media Programs: District and School

by William E. Hug

Both the Association for Educational Communications and Technology (AECT) and the American Association of School Librarians (AASL) have historically played key roles in formulating and promoting criteria for building strong media programs. *Media Programs: District and School,* like the 1969 *Standards for School Media Programs* it replaces, is a cooperative effort by these associations. I believe it is safe to say that the majority of the members of the various task forces and of the editorial committee view a publication such as this as a working document rather than as the final word even though it does represent a wide consensus. During this period of rapid change, a continual program for revision is necessary—any standards published at this point in time are a kind of interim report that needs to be revised periodically to provide direction for the field.

Media Programs: District and School is of value only to the extent that it is used to help create better educational programs for individual students. It is a tool that practitioners can learn to use. *Media Programs: District and School* is neither a how-to-do-it text nor a solution to the problems educators face in any definitive sense. Rather, the document is but one of many forces that can help improve education. Its power rests in the hands of media professionals who understand the document well enough to make it work for them. With intelligent use *Media Programs: District and School* can help move programs forward, but it can also be ignored, and it could even block program improvement, especially if it is flaunted in the faces of administrators as some kind of bible.

Media Programs: District and School is organized into eight chapters. Chapter one presents the general purpose of the document and introduces the reader to the next seven chapters. Chapter eight, the last chapter, attempts to summarize the general thrust of the document.

Chapter two discusses the nature and purposes of school media programs, identifying many observable activities that characterize quality media programs. Throughout the document, an attempt is made to encourage professionals to identify and develop quality activities. In other words, the emphasis is on what users are doing. A number of lists have been generated to put the focus on the media program user in the center. For example, in quality media programs users are observed finding needed information on an appropriate level and in an acceptable format, users are seen utilizing instructional sequences of tested effectiveness to reach personal and program objectives, and users may be seen receiving assistance, both formally and informally, in the use and production of learning resources.

Chapter two also suggests four general functions—design, consultation, information, and administration—that cut across operations such as planning, budgeting, accessing, and evaluating. Typical activities associated with the design, consultation, information, and administration functions are also listed. The attempt is to identify broad functions that relate to each of the operations.

Chapter three, "Program Patterns and Relationships," describes differences and similarities between and among school media programs, district media programs, regional media programs, state media programs, networks, and telecommunications. Typical responsibilities of the school, district, regional, and state media programs are listed. Making generalized statements that apply nationally is difficult. Obviously the state media program affects the kind of district program needed. Or, to work from the other end, the nature of the school media program determines many of the operations of the district media program. The presence or absence of a regional program again affects what is provided at the state and the district level. Nevertheless, there seem to be certain activities that are best associated with each of these levels. These are identified and discussed.

Chapter four, "Personnel"; chapter five, "Operations of the Media Program"; chapter six, "Collections"; and chapter seven, "Facilities" present points to consider in building programs, and principles to apply in making decisions in each area. The keynote is flexibility for purpose. Each chapter raises many questions to be considered as a particular media program emerges as a part of an individual curriculum, but answers are not given, only possibilities to consider before decisions are made.

TOWARD MORE PURPOSEFUL PROGRAMS

I hope that *Media Programs: District and School* will cause people to wonder why they are doing what they are doing. I hope the document stresses *why* media as much as *how* media and *what* media. Consequently, I would like to try to set the tone for looking at the standards and try to reflect the intent of those who worked on this document. From this point on I will refer to specifics only as they are needed to illustrate why the task forces and the editorial committee did what they did.

Before we begin to use the standards, we should ask ourselves: What are our commitments? What is our vision of education? Of the future? What are we determined to have, come hell or high water? If, for example, we are determined to have things, to build collections, the document provides numbers. If we are determined to have more power, more control, the document implies a role, the implications of which should make any superintendent blink. If we are looking for a safe place to hide, then we can dismiss the standards as impractical or use only those parts that help us mend our walls; or we can condemn the standards for using jargon—this is an excellent excuse for ignoring anything.

On the other hand, if we are committed to promoting a rich and variegated curriculum, the document suggests ways and means for accomplishing this. If we believe in the power of communication, the document promotes the use of a wide variety of media. If we believe the media program should provide assistance in the instructional development process, we can use the document to support this position. Or, if we support the humanistic movement, we can use the document to promote media programs that directly relate to the intellectual, emotional, social, physical, aesthetic, and spiritual growth of users.

Regardless of the document's intent, it will probably be used only to the extent that it can serve individual ends. Consequently, before any of us uses this document as an authority, we must do a little soul searching. We must determine what our priorities are and then look at the document to see how it can be used to develop that which we feel is of paramount importance.

DEFINITIONS

To understand what the document is saying, to understand its power, and to overcome its limitations, we must understand how certain terms are used.

The document defines a number of terms under three general headings: personnel, program, process. The definitions are not meant to be conclusive. Rather, the definitions establish usage within the standards. The editorial committee attempted to bring the terms into focus, to apply them practically, and to avoid the controversy that surrounds many of the terms. The intent was to communicate, not to settle the theoretical issues in the field. To use the definitions as the ultimate authority would be to accept half-truths, oversimplifications, and incomplete concepts. The editorial committee is well aware that groups such as information scientists, communication theorists, academic librarians, administrators, programmers, and curriculum theorists would bring a different set of meanings to these terms. It is for this reason that I will make my remarks in order to clarify and justify the terms defined under the three headings.

Understanding the use of the terms media specialist and media professional is basic to the understanding of the document. The media specialist is defined as the basic professional prepared at the master's degree level in discreet competencies that enable him to build and manage a comprehensive school media program. This is the professional that most of us think of when we refer to the merged role of the school librarian, audiovisual specialist, and instructional product developer. He is a specialist in building school media programs in the same sense that a teacher is a specialist, that a counselor is a specialist, and that a principal is a specialist. The broad generic category employed is the media professional. Media professionals are all personnel qualified by education and experience in areas such as television, programmed instruction, instructional product design and development, technical processing, and so forth. The media specialist is one type of media professional.

At this point we could stop and argue over individual perceptions of and preferences for the terms media specialist and media generalist, or over what constitutes professional and nonprofessional. I suspect we could likewise spend time trying to determine the role of the teacher. I personally find a certain amount of this kind of dialogue fun, sometimes even productive. But, for the purpose of understanding the standards, one simply has to read the document in light of the way words are used in it.

In the consideration of a media program, the new standards move beyond a curriculum guide, beyond an audiovisual support system, and beyond a school library. The move is toward systematically establishing relationships between and among people, materials, machines, and facilities that interface to form the program. If this is jargon to some, or mind boggling to others, let's say it in another way. It is not what you have that makes the program; it is the way resources are used. It is the way things work together that tells you what's going on. Components only suggest a potential for program development. What all this means to me is that any media program can improve and that genuine improvement results in establishing more productive, more comfortable relationships between and among program elements, as well as establishing needed functions that didn't exist before.

The various task forces and the editorial committee all seemed to agree that the document should continually stress the importance of the quality of contact between the student and media personnel, between the student and materials, and between the student and the environment. The term interface is therefore employed to describe these all-important points of contact. Since teachers, administrators, students, and community people benefit from the school media program, these groups are collectively called users. These terms underlie the document's definition of a media program. The media program is a pattern of interfacings among program components such as users, materials, machines, facilities, and environments. It then becomes the media professional's duty to establish and improve the interfacings between and among users and the universe of information.

In this sense, those responsible for writing the document believe that some new language is necessary for people to think differently about media programs. For this reason the word services is never used to describe the relationship between the media program and the educational program. Rather, the media program, like the educational program, provides students with essential information and activities leading to the achievement of both individual and curricular objectives.

The last group of definitions relates to process. Process is defined as a series of steps formulated for achieving some purpose. A group of generalized steps is presented as each relates to educational technology, instructional technology, instructional design, instructional development, and instructional product design. Unfortunately, in the literature, these terms tend to blend, one into the other. The document attempts to separate them by identifying a central thrust or purpose and to arrange them in hierarchical order from the most general to the most specific.

I want to stress again that the purpose of defining these particular terms is simply to clarify to the reader the intent of the document. The point of agreement that I hope all of us have relates to what one must do in order to identify quality media programs. This, I believe, is a central concern of the authors. Consequently, the document continually underscores the necessity of observing what the media program is doing *for* students as well as *to* students. All of the fancy facilities and materials that one too frequently associates with quality media programs are useless unless users are doing what they need to do and experiencing a certain amount of joy in the adventure. To this end, I hope the standards will help focus the media program on the user and overcome the obstacles that programs experience as they attempt to penetrate all aspects of the curriculum. Above all else, we must continually remind ourselves that media programs should not simply be a collection of stuff in response to some artificial need. Media programs must be built on real, not perceived, needs of human beings. And, somehow, someway, differing needs must be accommodated or reconciled.

PROBLEMS AND CONSIDERATIONS

Building educational programs and media programs will continue to depend to a large degree on best guess, political expedience, and personal prejudice as much as on know-how. The shape of the media programs will be influenced by the values and beliefs held by those in control. They will reflect the determination of the powers that be. Media programs of the future will spend a great deal of their energies justifying what they are doing in terms of the assumptions they are making since little hard data exist that tell us, in any definitive sense, what knowledge is of most value, where people learn best, or how people learn. And so, if administrators are going to change priorities in favor of the media program, they must be convinced that the assumptions made about teaching and learning that are supported by the media program are simply better than those in common practice. Supporting just one strategy is probably dangerous. For example, the current thrust of competency-based curricula gives the impression that this thrust is the only answer. Yet, one is hard put to find a clear-cut consensus as to the definition of competency-based curricula. In short, we are not sure what we are supporting when we back the competency-based movement since those on the bandwagon are defining it in so many different ways.

A much safer and effective position is to sell media programs because they provide better ways and means for a wide range of teaching and learning strategies and fit many philosophical frames. I believe the building of strong media programs is facilitated when media professionals use a softer, more thoughtful approach to building programs that continually strive to establish a sound, empirical base. In other words, we should make our decisions on the best information and research available and avoid being associated with any one camp.

Along this same line I would like to draw to your attention some research that has been collected on the ordering of values, a process which we are all up against. Let us suppose that *Media Programs: District and School* provided for a totally rational methodology for building stronger media programs and that this rationale was accepted by the field at large. Granted, this is a wild assumption. Nevertheless, even though we were to provide this united front, we still have to sell others on the value of a media program, which is, in my estimation, more difficult than selling ourselves. So, when we talk to accrediting agencies, boards of education, and administrators, we have to be aware of how they order their values.

In 1968 the National Opinion Research Center conducted a value inventory sampling various sectors of the American population. Eighteen values were identified. It is important here to note that the supporters of the seven 1968 presidential candidates placed intellectual and logical fifteenth and sixteenth out of eighteen in their value statements. In other words, most qualities were placed above rational attributes by people looking for leadership. What this, as well as other research, says to me concerning values is that we, as individuals, are not going to sell media programs to everyone simply by convincing them of the logic we employ.

The message that comes through to me is that the logical and rational processes employed by the standards must be used differently by individuals and must relate to their individual settings. The standards must, in addition to providing better ways, also stress the quality of individual life that has to be central to decision making. This is the reason why I have continually stressed the necessity for identifying our priorities and commitments, and the reason I believe that the power of the standards resides in the individual and how he integrates them with his system of values in order to use them most effectively.

In closing let me quote from *Curriculum for the Seventies: An Agenda for Invention* by Arthur Foshay: "If the world is a long array of splits, then it is the individual who must find the means of sanity, and he has to find those means within himself. Society is schizoid; only the individual can be whole. If urbanization produces a new need for individual identity, it is not society that will confer it; each man must do that for himself. If new means for relating to other people must be found . . . then the means must be based on individual integrity." We are now challenged to bring *Media Programs: District and School* into the context of our individual worlds and to make it a part of the whole in our own individual ways.

Note

Dr. Hug served on Task Force I and the AASL/AECT Joint Committee on Standards Revision convened to bring together the work of Task Force I (school standards) and Task Force II (district standards) into one document.

A New Version of Chapter 12 of the *Anglo-American Cataloging Rules*

by B. R. Tucker

The American Library Association (ALA), the Canadian Library Association, and the Library of Congress (LC) are presently engaged in rewriting chapter 12 of the *Anglo-American Cataloging Rules (AACR)* in order to provide revised rules for the nonbook works presently covered in this chapter and to provide new rules for instructional materials not presently covered in any chapter of the *AACR*. This rewritten chapter will become part of the North American text of the rules. In New York at the 1974 Annual Conference of the American Library Association, The Library of Congress presented to the Catalog Code Revision Committee a first draft of this revision of chapter 12. In making the presentation, LC pointed out the differences found in comparing the most important of the recently published standards and rules relating to nonbook material and indicated also the way in which the draft revision differed from each of the items noted below. The remarks made on that occasion have formed the basis of the text of this article, but changes made in later versions of the draft have been taken into account and the present text reflects the situation as of May 1975, following approval of the final draft by the Catalog Code Revision Committee at its meeting of 18–19 April 1975. Publication of the revised chapter 12 is anticipated in summer of this year.

The draft revision of chapter 12 of the *AACR* is intended insofar as possible to exploit the results of extensive earlier work reflected in four documents: *Non-book Materials Cataloguing Rules,* prepared by the Media Cataloguing Rules Committee of the Library Association ("British rules"), *Nonbook Materials: The Organization of Integrated Collections,* prepared by Jean Riddle Weihs, Shirley Lewis, and Janet Macdonald ("Canadian rules"), *Nonprint Media Guidelines,* prepared by a task force of librarians and audiovisual specialists under the chairmanship of Pearce S. Grove, and *Standards for Cataloging Nonprint Materials,* prepared by the Association for Educational Communications and Technology ("AECT standards").[1]

The library began work on this draft with no prejudices relative to positions which might be termed "American," "Canadian," or "British" as shown in the publications cited above or in other articles, correspondence, etc. However, a study of the deliberations held since 1967 soon made it clear the LC was committed to reflecting a consensus of "North American" opinion on at least one item—the medium designator, namely that (1) every catalog entry for a nonbook item should include a medium designator, (2) the medium designator should be generic rather than specific, whenever there was such a choice, and (3) the medium designator should be positioned directly after the title. In fact the terms to be used to designate the various media had already been determined by LC in June 1972 in close consultation with the Joint Advisory Committee on Nonbook Materials. Another matter already settled was the coverage of the draft. A wholesale revision of Part III of the *AACR* will be included in the preparation of the second edition (scheduled to be undertaken in January 1975), thus precluding a total revision at this time of rules for materials covered in chapters 10 (manuscripts), 11 (maps, atlases, etc.), 13 (music), 14 (phonorecords), and 15 (pictures, designs, and other two-dimensional representations). Thus the revised draft of chapter 12 will differ from the other published rules and standards in that the latter are intended to cover all nonbook materials, while the scope of the draft is limited to motion pictures, filmstrips, videorecordings, slides and transparencies, and special instructional materials not previously covered in *AACR*.

An initial decision was made to write an entirely new chapter instead of revising rule by rule the existing one. Chapter 12 is strongly influenced by concepts derived from theatrical films, and it does not seem possible to fit within its framework such widely differing works as non-theatrical films, slides, transparencies, videorecordings, and a wide variety of instructional materials, including charts, dioramas, flash cards, games, kits, models, and realia. The comprehensive revision was managed by adopting a format generally in agreement with the several existing codes, i.e., general rules covering all nonbook materials, followed by special rules concentrating to a large extent on physical description for each medium.

An examination of the codes made it immediately apparent that there was a great similarity both in general philosophy and in many details of description. The major points of divergence were (1) the British placement of the medium designator in the collation area and (2) the AECT rule for arbitrary title main entry in all cases. There is of course a superficial appearance of disagreement on every page of the several codes because of great differences in approach, in wording, in details of structure, and in general style. But disagreement is not apparent in the substance of the rules. It seems necessary to say this in order to put into perspective the remainder of these remarks which concentrate on how the present draft and existing codes differ in the matters of structure, coverage, main entry, medium designators, imprint, and physical description.

The following comparison concentrates on the publications identified as British rules, Canadian rules, and AECT standards. *Nonprint Media Guidelines,* cited earlier as a fourth source on which the draft of chapter 12 depends, is a document of six leaves which, as its title indicates, is too restricted in scope to figure in the comparison as often as the other three publications. No criticism of any of the publications is intended by statements in this article. All were invaluable in the writing of the draft and will continue to be so as work progresses toward the completion of the new chapter 12.

STRUCTURE

The AECT standards consist of two sections: the first is devoted to general cataloging rules, applicable to all media; the second consists of specialized rules for individual media, providing for each, information on the source and choice of title and on physical description. Examples and definitions are also provided for each medium.

The Canadian rules include general rules intended to cover all media, with individual media covered in detail by individual supplements devoted to definitions, additions, and exceptions to the general rules. These supplements always cover collation but otherwise vary from medium to medium; they may also give special directions for main entry, imprint, etc. The special rules include many examples showing complete catalog records.

The British rules also include general rules followed by special rules. The special rules are divided into three sections: "Graphics and three-dimensional representations," "Motion pictures," and "Sound recordings." Each of these sections includes rules general to that section as well as special provisions for physical description, all of which constitute exceptions to or amplifications of the main section of general rules. The special provisions include some definitions. Complete catalog entries are not used as examples; portions of examples are given illustrating specific points throughout the rules.

The LC draft has one set of rules covering entry and all aspects of description. Some of these are subdivided into special rules dealing with certain of the media; the rules for physical description include particularly extensive and specialized treatment for each medium. Portions of catalog records, rather than complete entries, are provided as examples throughout the draft, and definitions are provided in a separate glossary.

COVERAGE

As already indicated, the American, British, and Canadian rules all include rules or standards for all types of nonbook materials and are therefore more comprehensive than the draft inasmuch as they cover materials such as microreproductions, maps, pictures, and sound recordings, all of which are covered in sections other than chapter 12 of *AACR*. For nonbook material which falls within the predetermined scope of the revised chapter 12, the American, British, and Canadian rules cover virtually the same items. Of the many media included in one or more of the sets of rules, the draft omits only machine-readable files (included in AECT and Canadian rules and *Nonprint Media Guidelines*) and laboratory kits and radiographs (included in the British rules). Conversely, all of the media treated by the draft are included in each of the sets of rules with the single exception that the British rules do not include "flash cards."

MAIN ENTRY

The AECT standards specify that "the entry for all audiovisual materials will be by title," but also provide that "if an audiovisual work is an exact reproduction of another work . . . it may be entered in the same manner as the original work."[2]

In the British rules main entry is determined by the criteria for a "statement of primary intellectual responsibility." Here a person or corporate body's overall responsibility for the whole of the intellectual or artistic content of the work must be "both 1) clearly attributed as such in the work or other authoritative source, and 2) such that the name has a primary significance in the identification of the work."[3] It should also be noted that the "Motion pictures" section of the British rules includes this provision: "Primary intellectual responsibility is not normally attributed in motion pictures, and the General Rule is consequently not used."[4]

The Canadian rules follow the principles of main entry found in Part I of *AACR*, which are intended to be applied to all media, but observe that "entry under title will occur more frequently for nonbook materials because authorship cannot be established as readily for many nonbook items."[5] The Canadian special rule for motion pictures prescribes title main entry with few exceptions.

The general principles of authorship of *AACR* have been applied in the draft with the single exception that main entry under the name of a commercial firm is expressly forbidden.

MEDIUM DESIGNATORS

As already indicated, the draft prescribes that the medium designator be a generic term applying to the medium rather than to the specific item being cataloged and that it be placed directly after the title. (A more specific designator may be indicated in the physical description or in the notes area.) The following terms are used as medium designators in the draft:

chart	model
diorama	motion picture
filmstrip	realia
flash card	slide
game	transparency
kit	videorecording
microscope slide	

Only the British rules place the medium designator as the first element in the physical description area, rather than following the title. The British medium designators tend to be specific rather than generic, e.g., "EVR," "videodisc," "videotape," "flipchart," "wallchart," "laboratory kit," "relief model." This accords well with placing the designator in the area which includes other specific elements of description pertaining not to the medium generally but to the example of it in hand. In the section labeled "Graphics and three-dimensional representations," the British rules also specify adding the word "set" when a group of items is cataloged as a single unit. The only other points of variance are differences in terminology: the British "cinefilm" for "motion picture" and "specimen" for "realia."

The Canadian rules agree with the medium designators used in the draft with a single exception: "videorecord" rather than "video-recording."

Nonprint Media Guidelines agree except that the word "slide" is used in the *Guidelines* to designate both microscope and diapositive slides, whereas the draft, considering these as two different media, uses the terms "microscope slide" and "slide."

The AECT standards agree with the draft except for the following points:

1. "Mock-up" and "model" are given separate designators, but provision is made for using "model" for both media when it is not necessary to distinguish between the two.
2. "Slide" is used for both microscope and diapositive slides.
3. "Specimen" is used instead of "realia."
4. "Videorecord" is used instead of "videorecording," although the single AECT example shows "videorecording" as the word used.
5. "Videotape" is provided as a separate designator in addition to "videorecord" (the draft uses one designator "videorecording" to cover all videorecordings, whether on film, tape, or disc).

IMPRINT

The AECT standards provide for a statement which may include the following items: producer, sponsor, and releasing agent. The location of an entity is excluded from this statement. The date of release is added at the end of the statement with a copyright date being equated with the release date and being transcribed with the copyright symbol omitted. A significantly different date of production may also be given.

In the British rules the name given to the area in question is "imprint," and the following elements are given in the order indicated: place of publication, publisher or manufacturer, sponsor, date of publication, place of distribution, and distributor. The absence of any imprint data is shown in a note; there is no provision for indicating lack of a place of publication or lack of publisher or for an imprecise date of publication such as 19—?. The special rule for motion pictures (excluding loops and original videorecordings) provides for giving the name of the country of the production company as the place, the name of the production company, the name of the sponsor, the date of release or exact date of first transmission, the place where the distributor is located, and the name of the distributor. The provision for date allows the date of production if the date of release is not available but does not provide for giving both when they are different. Copyright dates are not mentioned.

The Canadian rules also use the term "imprint." This consists of the following elements:

1. place, which is the location of the producer—but place need be given only if the body is obscure, has a common name, or is a government printer;
2. the producer or manufacturer;
3. the distributor and releasing agent, if significant; and
4. date.

The special motion picture rule for "imprint" agrees with the unrevised chapter 12, providing for sponsor, producer, releasing agent, and date of release.

All three publications retain in the one statement the varied activities of sponsoring, producing, and releasing or distributing. The draft has attempted to separate out and retain in an imprint-like statement called "release/publication area" the activities of publication, release, and distribution, with activities relating to initiation of production placed in the first area of the cataloging record as a "statement of responsibility." Place is given in the release/publication area. Dates of publication, release, or distribution are given and there are provisions for copyright dates, approximate dates, and production dates for appropriate materials, with provision also for the absence of a date similar to that of the ISBD for monographs.

PHYSICAL DESCRIPTION

The rules or standards for physical description are remarkably similar to the American, British, and Canadian rules used in preparing the draft. This similarity is attested by the following brief list of variations, which constitute the totality of major variations over a very broad range of media.

AECT Standards

1. The word "color" is not abbreviated when used in the physical description; the draft uses the abbreviation "col."
2. Under "chart," there is no mention of "flipchart," and specifications for charts include a description of the mounting; the draft provides for "flipchart" under "chart" and ignores mounting for charts.
3. The provision for filmstrips does not include any explanation for counting the number of frames; the draft includes specific directions for counting unnumbered frames.
4. For kits, the physical description is usually omitted in favor of a note; the draft provides for an explicit physical description area in all cases.
5. For slides, "(Glass)" is shown in an example of a microscope slide, although the standard does not specify this qualification; the draft omits any specification of the transparent material.
6. For transparencies, the overlays are specified in a note rather than as part of the collation area; the draft relates information about overlays parenthetically in the physical description area.

British Rules

The British rules for the physical description of slides, transparencies, and all instructional materials largely agree with the draft. However, it is difficult to compare the rules for motion pictures, because the British rules give a multiplicity of specifications with the following permissive statement: "the listing of [descriptive data] . . . contains more elements than are likely to be needed in a non-specialist catalogue or bibliography, and fewer than may be needed in a highly specialized one. Some suggestions are made, but these are neither mandatory nor exhaustive."[6] For the "extent" of a work, length of film, number of reels, cassettes, or loops, and playing time are mentioned with the implication in an explanatory note that depending on the institution for which the cataloging is being done, only one of these several indications of "extent" would be given, e.g., for a lending library, the number of reels. For videotape also, the British rules include a multitude of date elements listed under the headings "qualifiers," "extent," and "enrichment." It is presumed that as for motion pictures, not all would be prescribed in a particular case. For both motion pictures and videorecordings the draft prescribes definite specifications for the physical description area, with others, only partly enumerated, given in the notes area. For filmstrips the British rule prescribes a separate count of title frames, to be included parenthetically after the total number of frames; the draft counts only content frames.

Canadian Rules

1. For charts, the size of the mount is prescribed; the draft ignores the mount.

2. For dioramas, only the number of pieces (or "various pieces") and color are prescribed; the draft provides for size, number of figures, etc., material, or any other specification as appropriate.

3. For filmstrips, the term "filmstrip" is used as appropriate in the collation (but not as a medium designator). If the frames of a filmstrip are unnumbered, the extent is expressed as "1 role," "1 filmstrip," or "1 filmslip," but an optional rule for counting agrees with the draft. The draft does not include "filmslip" as a specific term to be used in the physical description area; it provides for counting unnumbered frames "if practical."

4. For flash cards, the size of the mount is prescribed; the draft ignores the mount.

5. For microscope slides, the type of mount is given parenthetically, e.g., "(Glass)"; the draft ignores type of mount.

6. For slides, "stereograph" is used as a specific indicator instead of the draft's "stereoscopic."

7. For videorecords, there is somewhat detailed treatment for the three formats of film, tape, and disc, with recording mode and playback speed indicated in the collation area in some cases, and "line, field, and colour standards" indicated in notes in some cases. The draft's rule for videorecordings confines the physical description area to form (reel, cassette, cartridge, or disc), number of physical units, running time, sound and color statements, and dimensions of physical units; other specifications are not enumerated although it is assumed that those which are necessary would appear in the notes area.

SPECIAL FEATURES

The text as published will include (1) examples of complete catalog entries for each medium; (2) a table summarizing the provisions for physical description of each medium, similar to the table provided in the Appendix of the AECT standards; (3) a glossary of terms; and (4) an index. It is hoped that inclusion of these items will expedite the introduction and acceptance of the new practices.

REFERENCES

1. Library Association. Media Cataloguing Rules Committee, *Non-book Materials Cataloguing Rules* (N.C.E.T. Working Paper no. 11 [London: National Council for Educational Technology with the Library Association, 1973]). Jean Riddle Weihs, Shirley Lewis, and Janet Macdonald, *Nonbook Materials: The Organization of Integrated Collections* (1st ed.; Ottawa: Canadian Library Association, 1973).
Nonprint Media Guidelines. Unpublished, distributed in 1973 by Pearce

S. Grove. Association for Educational Communications and Technology, *Standards for Cataloging Nonprint Materials* (3rd ed.; Washington, D.C.: Association for Educational Communications and Technology, 1972). A new edition is scheduled to be published in the summer of 1975.

2. Association for Educational Communications and Technology, *Standards for Cataloging Nonprint Materials*, p. 1.

3. Library Association, *Non-book Materials Cataloguing Rules*, p. 21.

4. Ibid., p. 46.

5. Weihs, Lewis, and Macdonald, *Nonbook Materials: The Organization of Integrated Collections*, p. 13.

6. *Non-book Materials Cataloguing Rules*, p. 49.

Rules for Cataloging Audio-Visual Materials at Hennepin County Library

by Sanford Berman

These rules have been in operation since mid-February, so far without any major "bugs" developing. They almost fully coincide, except for *specific* rather than generic media-statements, to the proposed ALA standards.

1. *Basic Principles/Objectives*
   —All formalized communication formats are potentially valuable to library users and accordingly demand the attention and interest of librarians.
   —Audio-visual materials and services should enjoy among library administrators and staff a weight, concern, familiarity and support equal to those accorded printed materials.
   —All audio-visual materials should be fully cataloged, essentially on the same basis as books, and completely represented in the official Shelflist, Headquarters catalog, and HCL book-form catalog.
   —Given the premise of parity in processing and user-access for both print and A/V materials, the goal must be an integrated, multi-media catalog through which a user can readily determine the availability of material on any medium on a particular subject or of various editions or representations of a specific work.

2. *Cataloging elements*
   —call number
   —main entry
   —title (if not main entry)/medium statement
   —imprint
   —collation/series' statement
   —notes
   —tracings

3. *Call numbers* (3-line for non-fiction, 2-line for juvenile fiction, 1-line for adult fiction) are composed of: one of the symbols shown below, representing specific type of medium; a Dewey number (non-fiction only) indicating subject-class; and the initial main-entry letter (non-

fiction) or juvenalia-symbol. Two or more interdependent media are cataloged by the dominant medium, with the subordinate medium listed in the collation or in a note. For music, Dewey numbers are selected from the special HCL classification scheme devised for phonograph records. Exclusively and consistently employing DDC will ensure that one classification system prevails throughout the system, properly emphasize content rather than form, and enhance user-familiarity with the system-wide arrangement of library materials.

Media-symbols (adapted from *NAVE* and the DAVI *Standards,* in H&T, p. 67):

Art original	PO	Motion picture cartridge	MR
Art print	PA	Motion picture cassette	MC
Art reproduction	PR	Motion picture film—16mm	MP
Audio cartridge	RR	Motion picture film—8mm	MQ
Audio cassette	RC	Motion picture film—	
Audio roll	RO	Super 8mm	MS
Audio tape	RT	Motion picture loop	ML
Chart	PC	Phonodisc	R
Diorama	DD	Photograph	PP
Filmslip	FL	Picture	PI
Filmstrip	FS	Poster	PT
Flash card	PL	Realia	DR
Flip chart	PF	Slide	SL
Game	DA	Stereoscopic slide	SS
Globe	DL	Study print	PS
Kinescope	MK	Transparency,	
Kit	KT	Overhead	TR
Map	PM	Video cartridge	VR
Microaperture card	NC	Video cassette	VC
Microfiche	NF	Video cube	VQ
Microfilm	NM	Video disc	VD
Micro-opaque	NO	Video tape	VT
Models	DM	Wall chart	PW

For definitions, see ALA, p. 3–8; CLA, p. 87–8; H&T, *passim;* WASL, *passim.*

4. *Main entry* is under title, except when the creator is of primary importance or the material is totally or largely a reproduction of printed material, in which case—as with microfilms—the work is cataloged under the entry which would be chosen for the original.

5. *Title* should be determined from the material itself, or secondarily from the container, accompanying data, etc. Immediately following the title, identify the type of medium with the singular form of the descriptive word, enclosed in parentheses; e.g., (Filmslip), (Kit), (Realia).

6. The *imprint* statement consists of the producer or manufacturer's name (using abbreviations solely for well-known names; e.g., RCA), succeeded by date of issue as given on the material itself, or secondarily determined from other sources like producers' catalogs. For phonodiscs, cite the record company and record number or serial identification as shown on the disc-label, then the release date, as ascertained from album itself, Schwann Catalog, or authoritative review source. For films, specify the film-making organization and releasing agent (if different from producer) immediately after the producer's name; e.g., Salem Productions and Dover Productions. Released by Paramount Pictures, 1962.

7. The *collation* physically describes the material, variously encompassing form of reproduction, length of time or amount of information included, color, size/dimensions, speed, and any other necessary data (e.g., for phonodiscs, whether nonaural, stereophonic, or quadrisonic; for films, whether sound or silent). If applicable, a series' statement in parentheses follows the physical description. For motion pictures, filmstrips, and pictures, observe the AACR collation rules (except that picture sizes will be shown in inches, rather than centimeters); for all other media, the CLA instructions.

8. *Notes* may be of four types, appearing in this order:
   —Additional description; e.g., for prints or flash cards:
      Text on verso.
      Notes by James Tierney on container.
   —Specification of accompanying, auxiliary material; e.g.,
      Includes 26 p. teacher's manual
      With lecture notes.
   —Designation of persons or groups responsible for or associated with the work (e.g., film credits), whether an adaptation from another medium, relationship to other works, etc. e.g.,
      Based on James Hilton's novel of the same title.
      After the painting by Gilbert Stuart.
      Issued also as a filmstrip under title: Primary treatment plants.
      Narrated by George Rose.
   —Indication of contents by means of a complete, "partial," or "with" note when the material includes several distinct and significant items or selections, *or* an either quoted or composed "summary" to reveal scope and nature when the title and/or series statement inadequately express these aspects. Composed summaries should describe subject matter both succinctly and objectively.

9. *Tracings* are assigned in the same manner as for printed matter:
   —Subject headings, derived from the LC scheme.
   —Added entries or analytics, as appropriate, for author/composer/performer/photographer, narrator, producer, title (if not main entry), and series. No arbitrary limit applies to the permissible number of author/title analytics, this decision being best left to the cataloger's discretion or the judgment of subject/media specialists.

10. *Circulation cards,* in order to minimize confusion and error in the checkout/return process, must include call number, copy letter, main entry, title, record number (for phonodiscs), and all format and quantitative details in the collation and notes (e.g., 30 slides col. 2×2 in., with 20-p. booklet).

11. *Authorized abbreviations*

b&w	black and white	min.	minutes
col.	color	mono.	monaural
fr.	frames	quad.	quadrisonic
in.	inches	rpm.	revolutions per minute
ips.	inches per second	s.	side
l.	leaves	sd.	sound
mm.	millimeters	si.	silent
		stereo	stereophonic

12. As a logical application of the "parity-principle," no catalog card sets are sent to branches with new A/V material. Instead, such material is to be processed in the same fashion as books. However, as an immediate, short-term means of bibliographic control and user information, single main entry cards will accompany A/V material in the interim period until media titles begin to appear in the book-form catalog. While recognizing in principle that printed material should be designated by a call number symbol as simply one among several media, this change cannot yet be introduced because of the enormity of reclassifying and relabeling the existing, largely book-type collection. Further, the usually recommended symbol, "B," would conflict with the same, currently employed juvenalia tag, producing undue confusion.

13. *Typing formats*
    Author main entry:

```
SYMBOL    SUBJECT HEADING or added entry
Class #   Author . . .
Letter      Title (Medium statement) Producer, date.

          Physical description: form, time, color, size, etc. (Series)

          Accompanying material.
Notes . . . . . . . . . . . . . . . . . . . . . . . . . . . . . . . . . . . . . . . . . . . . . .
. . . . . . . . . . . . . . . . . . . . . . . . . . . . . . . . . . . . . . . . . . . . . . . . . .

          Tracings
```

Title main entry:

SYMBOL   SUBJECT HEADING or added entry . . .
Class #   Title (Medium statement) Producer, date.
Letter

        Physical description: form, time, color, size, etc.
(Series)

        Accompanying material.
Notes . . . .
. . . .

        Tracings

---

14. *Sample catalog cards*

KT
629.2   Radlauer, Edward
R   Motorcycles (Kit) Bowmar, 1967.

        1 filmstrip, 1 phonodisc, 1 booklet (Reading
incentive program)

        With teacher's guide.

        1. Motorcycles. I. Title

KT
428.4   Sounds I can hear (Kit) Scott, Foresman, 1966.
S

        4 phonodiscs, 4 charts, 42 flash cards

        Pamphlets attached.
        CONTENTS: v. 1. House.-v. 2. Farm in the
zoo.-v. 3. Neighborhood.-v. 4. School.

        1. Reading. 2. Sounds

DA
511   Kiddiscales (Game) Kiddicraft, 1962
K

    9 pieces. col.

     1. Arithmetic.

ML
541   The Diffraction of x-rays by crystals (Motion picture
D   loop) Longmans, 1969.

     1 cartridge 4 min. si. b&w 8mm.
(Chemistry)

    Notes on cartridge case.

     1. Chemistry, physical and theoretical.

MP
362.4   It's good to be back (Motion picture) Canadian
I   National Institute for the Blind. Made by the
Motion Picture Centre. Released by the
National Film Board, 1966.

    24 min. sd. col. 16mm.

     1. Blind. I. Canadian National Institute for
the Blind.

PS
917.2   Mexico, the cities (Study print) Tuttle, 1968.
M
    8 prints col. 13 × 18 in.

     1. Cities and towns—Mexico. 2. Mexico—
description and travel.

```
FS
332.1      Seggie, Alexander Pringle.
S              The story of a draft (Filmstrip) Canadian
           Bankers Assn., 1970.

           41 fr. b&w 35mm.

           1. Banks and banking. 2. Business. I. Title.
```

15. *Sample circulation cards*

```
KT         Radlauer, Edward
629.2
R -a           Motorcycles (Kit: 1
           filmstrip, 1 phonodisc,
           1 booklet, teacher's
           guide)
```

```
KT             Sounds I can hear (Kit: 4
428.4      phonodiscs, 4 charts,
S -s       42 flash cards, attached
           pamphlets)
```

```
DA         Kiddiscales (Game: 9
551        pieces col.)
K -a
```

```
ML             The Diffraction of x-rays
541        by crystals (Motion
D -a       picture loop: 1 cartridge
           4 min. si. b&w 8mm)
```

```
MP         It's good to be back (Motion
362.4      picture: 24 min.
I -a       sd. col. 16mm.)
```

```
PS             Mexico, the cities (Study
917.2      print: 8 prints col.
M -a       13 × 8 in.)
```

```
FS         Seggie, Alexander Pringle
332.1      The story of a draft
S -a       (Filmstrip: 41 fr. b&w
           35 mm.)
```

16. *Book-form catalog.* Once input commences for A/V items, the catalog "introduction" should be revised to indicate the expanded scope. Also useful would be prefatory tables for call number symbols and collation abbreviations.

17. *Statistics* are to be maintained for the broad category, "Audio-Visual Materials," which will encompass phonodiscs, kits, tapes, films, etc. Each discretely cataloged unit is to be considered a "title," while various interdependent but physically unique materials within such units (e.g., individual phonodiscs, cassettes, cartridges, reels) are to be regarded as processed "items" (instead of "volumes").

18. *Miscellanea*
    —Strictly ephemeral, disposable items often included in kits—e.g., buttons, club membership cards, ditto stencils, and coloring books— are *not* to be cataloged. The cataloger will remove such material from kits and separately forward it to either the Adult or Juvenile Book Selection Librarian (RSD) for programming or other use.
    —When several, identical copies of a pamphlet, booklet, or manual accompany any other medium, only *one* such copy is cataloged with the whole unit, the remainder being labelled and forwarded to the receiving agency for storage as replacements or employment in library-conducted programs.
    —When two audio-vehicles (most commonly cassettes and phonodiscs) appear in the same media unit, *both* will be cataloged with the unit and processed together.
    —Multi-topic slide sets are not to be cataloged; rather, these will be transmitted directly to the A/V Librarian for processing and storage.
    —When a cataloged slide set is to be permanently fitted into a carousel tray, the tray will be cited in either the collation or a note, as well as on the circulation card.

19. *Sources consulted and cited*
    —ALA, American Library Association. Audio-Visual Committee: *Guidelines materials & services for public libraries* (Chicago: A.L.A., 1970).
    —AACR, *Anglo-American cataloging rules.* North American text. (Chicago: A.L.A., 1967).
    —AECT, Association for Educational Communications & Technology. Information Systems Division: *Nonprint media cataloging, classification and designation* (1973).
    —H&T, Hicks, Warren B. and Alma M. Tillin: *Developing multi-media libraries* (N.Y.: Bowker, 1970).
    —NAVC, National Audiovisual Center: *Basic media designation and codes* (1973). Mimeo.
    —CLA, Weihs, Jean Riddle, and others: *Non-book materials; the organization of integrated collections.* 1st ed. (Ottawa: Canadian L. Assn., 1973).
    —WASL, Wisconsin Association of School Librarians: *Cataloging, processing, administering AV materials; a model for Wisconsin schools* (Madison: 1972).

The Mystery of Ips and Mono
Or, Do Students Understand
AV Card Catalog Terms?

by Jane Schlueter
and Robert D. Little

Ostensibly catalog cards are designed to aid the user by providing information relevant to his search for materials. Thus, the terminology used on these cards needs to be self-explanatory. Unfortunately, users are not always able to interpret the abbreviations and symbols commonly used on audiovisual catalog cards. A survey of university and high school students was conducted to prove that for maximum reader accessibility the abbreviations should be spelled out and the terms be ones that the most inexperienced user is able to comprehend.

The library user's understanding of the audiovisual materials described and their location in the library is a necessity. Hopefully the results of the survey are significant enough to indicate improvements and revisions that can be made in audiovisual catalog card terminology.

Two questionnaires were prepared using the commonly used manuals and standards for audiovisual materials. Two volunteers were given the questionnaires in preliminary form so that possible problems could be anticipated and mistakes corrected. It was found that one questionnaire could bias the other; therefore, in the testing process, no one volunteer was given both questionnaires. A total of 100 volunteers took part in the survey.

Over a three-day period, 25 university students and 25 high school students were given the questionnaire individually. The university students surveyed were selected from users of the Cunningham Memorial Library at Indiana State University. High school students surveyed were selected from summer school English classes held at the Laboratory School of Indiana State University. The high school students were taken from remedial classes because there were no other groups attending summer school that were large enough for the researcher's purposes.

Questionnaire I was prepared to test 1) the user's ability to identify terms, 2) the user's ability to identify abbreviations, 3) the user's ability to understand the use of color codes and 4) the user's ability to understand symbols above the call number on audiovisual catalog cards.

The abbreviations used were taken from Jean Riddle's *Non-Book Materials; The Organization of Integrated Collections,* Ottawa, Canadian Library Association, 1971. Since this is the closest to a standard method for preparing audiovisual materials on catalog cards, the researcher felt that using only one accepted authority *(Non-Book Materials)* for the terms and abbreviations would be the only valid method of research. All the abbreviations listed on page 51 of *Non-Book Materials* were used. The cards containing the abbreviations and terms were placed in alphabetical order. The volunteer was given a sheet for answers and the cards and asked to give the meanings of circled abbreviations and terms. There was one circled item to be identified on each card. The volunteer thus was asked the questions in context.

The abbreviations were:

b&w, black and white	mono., monaural
col., colour	n.d., no date
fr., frames	rpm, revolutions per minute
in., inches	s., side
ips., inches per second	sd., sound
l., leaves	si., silent
mm., millimetres	stereo., stereophonic
min., minutes	

The sample color codes were cards taken from *Non-Book Materials* with arbitrary color codes added to them as examples. Sample symbols (FS, RD) above the call numbers on Questionnaire I, Part III, were taken from Warren Hicks' *Developing Multimedia Libraries,* New York, Bowker, 1970, since *Non-Book Materials* did not employ such symbols. The cards themselves again were taken from *Non-Book Materials.* The researcher indicated that the volunteer was not expected to know the answers to all the questions and that he could leave blank any that he was not able to answer.

In Questionnaire I the university students did consistently better than the high school students, but both groups missed a high number of the terms and abbreviations. This might be caused by the fact that of the 25 university students filling out Questionnaire I, 20 were graduate students while the high school students consisted of slow students ranging from sophomore to senior.

Fifteen of the 18 terms and abbreviations were missed repeatedly. Only questions five, eight, and nine (abbreviations in., mm., and min.) were answered correctly on the questionnaire a high percentage of the time. At any rate one can conclude that only the abbreviations for inches, millimeters, and minutes can be used on catalog cards with confidence. Even such commonly used library abbreviations as the *c* for copyright was misunderstood by 20 of the 50 people or 40 percent of them.

In testing the terms "phonodisc" and "phonotape" it was concluded that these terms are not commonly understood.

In testing student understanding of color codes and location symbols, the answer was considered correct if the student gave either location or media designation as the answer. Even so, it can be concluded that high school and university students did not understand the meaning of color codes or symbols above the call number on audiovisual catalog cards.

Questionnaire II was designed to compare audiovisual catalog cards which employ abbreviations and unfamiliar terms with those that spell out words instead of employing abbreviations and commonly used terms. Ten questions were prepared. The first five contained questions about cards taken from *Non-Book Materials* and the second five contained corresponding questions taken from the Wisconsin Association of School Librarians' *Cataloging, Processing, Administering AV Materials.*

For example, in question one the student was asked whether the material was in black and white or color and shown a catalog card which employed abbreviations. In question six, the student was asked the same question and shown a catalog card which used complete words. The other questions were also paired.

The volunteer was given the same directions as those given to volunteers filling out Questionnaire I. In addition, these volunteers were instructed to answer the questions in sequence and not to change anything after going on to the next question. This instruction was given because the volunteer could have figured out some of the more difficult abbreviations after seeing those questions in which no abbreviations were used. Questionnaire II was passed out randomly to university students using the Cunningham Memorial Library at Indiana State University and high school students from the Laboratory School at Indiana State University.

In Questionnaire II, the university students did consistently better than the high school students. Even so, the university students still missed a number of the questions one to five which employed abbreviations and terms not commonly used in everyday situations. Questions one to five were missed by a greater number of people than questions six to ten which used complete words and commonly used terms. The cards without abbreviations and with popularly used terminology proved easier to understand. For example, the terms phonodisc and phonotape were not understood as frequently as the terms tape and record. Because Questionnaire II worded the questions in such a way as to indicate the type of information desired, a greater percentage of the respondents were able to figure out the meaning of the abbreviations.

This survey of high school and university students indicates that abbreviations and unfamiliar terminology are not understood as frequently as when the words are spelled out and popular terminology is used. From the results of both questionnaires, one can easily see that the catalog cards eliminating abbreviations and unfamiliar terms are better understood by students than those which employ them. If the library user's ability to understand the audiovisual materials described on catalog cards as well as their location in the library or media center is of primary concern, then catalog cards need to eliminate unfamiliar abbreviations, terms, color codes and symbols.

PART

VII

EDUCATION

Library Education and Non-Print Media: Where It's At

by Herman L. Totten

Non-print media and materials as teaching devices have made a very significant impact on education programs, whether private, public, or commercial. Through usage and experimentation, educational institutions have attempted to increase the utility and effectiveness of these materials. By contrast, the library profession in general has ignored these materials or even resisted the emergence of these tools as viable aids in the communication of information. Not only have professional library organizations been lax in formulating standards and guidelines for these new tools, but also individual librarians have opposed the new media in their libraries. Lastly, and perhaps most importantly, library science educational programs offer few courses in non-print media, and very few curricula, if any, require students to obtain even an elementary background in this area.

Library educators involved with non-print media have suggested many reasons for this inertia in the profession. These reasons, for purposes of discussion, may be grouped into three major problem areas: (1) lack of commitment of library science schools and their faculties, resulting in shortsighted content of library science media courses; (2) negative attitudes of practicing librarians; and (3) lack of concern of the professional organizations.

It is apparent that the major reason for the failure of a non-print media impact on the library profession lies with the indifferent treatment these programs receive in library schools. And this indifference is generated from the top down; that is, at the administrative level little or no concern exists. In this situation, then, a non-print media program simply is not going to command the financial support essential to its basic implementation and solid continuation. From this primary lack, the rest follows: space and equipment will be inadequate at best; technical staff to assist instructors cannot be hired; recognition of faculty participation will be insubstantial and unrewarding, thereby providing no stimulation to increased faculty interest in improving the quality of instruction.

Unless the individuals responsible for administering the media are convinced of the benefits to be derived from these materials, they will do little to support the program. It is of great importance to have the operation initiated by someone at a high enough level in the organization to gain unquestioned administrative and professional sanction from the beginning. At present too few individuals in positions of such authority possess the expertise or, more importantly, the desire to implement a non-print media program. In short, no hope of permanent improvement in the use of new media will occur without a substantial institutional commitment.

The importance of the library school as a whole in breaking down the attitudes of ignorance and distrust toward the non-print media is matched by the importance of faculty enthusiasm toward non-print media. Unfortunately, most instructors are not at all supportive; they neither employ new media in the teaching of courses nor advocate its use in library institutions. It is given only a cursory acknowledgment, if any. The problem is further compounded by the fact that, as of yet, library schools have not produced enough capable people to lead the field, and they offer little indication that they will do so in the near future.

The present is not completely dark; a few library school programs have initiated non-print media programs, at least to a limited extent. The University of Pittsburgh, one bright spot, has set up a special laboratory which offers full television and videotape recording services to introduce students to new instructional programs featuring analysis of the communication and learning process. At Kent State University videotape has been effectively used in the teaching of reference service. Furthermore, a self-study course for basic cataloging students has been developed which includes the use of computer-aided instruction and a miracode information retrieval machine. At most institutions, however, innovations have originated mostly with individuals rather than from whole departments. These individual projects, though, do not benefit from the full support of the department. This is a sad situation, for while it is not the responsibility of the library school to provide "media specialists," individuals graduating from library schools should acquire competence in the selection and processing of non-print media materials as well as book form material, since all means of communicating information should be of concern to the library profession.

The new non-print media courses offered by library schools have come under heavy attack from library educators. Their major objection has to do with the present emphasis placed on the methodology and practical application rather than on theory and professional considerations; they feel research and experimentation should be stressed as prime elements. If the library profession plans to play a vital role in the newer modes of communication and education, it must consider the development of communication theory as an essential element, and it must make every effort to avoid the preoccupation with hardware that prevails in the audio-visual and information science professions.

What guidelines should we follow in implementing a non-print media program? The following are basic:

1. an attitude of openmindedness in reviewing present programs and the setting of specific goals and objectives for new, less rigidly oriented programs;
2. content related to communication theory and research must be included, along with a provision for constant interaction between theory about the use of devices and actual use;
3. a skills laboratory with adequate equipment to achieve faculty and student proficiency in the manipulation of hardware.

The skills laboratory would have the beneficial side effect of encouraging other library school instructors to use these non-print media as teaching aids in non-media courses, for we all know that equipment set up and ready to use is much more conducive to media utilization. This effect might well be one of the most important long-run gains, because until the library school instructors themselves are convinced of the importance of media, they are not going to generate attitudes of change in practicing librarians.

It should come as no surprise that a lack of exposure to non-print materials in the graduate program has made the majority of practicing librarians ill-informed in this area, and left them with all the prejudices and misconceptions that accompany a lack of information. Moreover, librarians so far have been conveniently able to avoid the use of multimedia materials. The most common excuses given for the low priority assigned these materials are: lack of funds, difficulty of operating the equipment, inaccessibility of software, and indecision over what role the library should play in administering these materials. And these are accompanied by a major cause of resistance to non-print media, the inability of librarians to deal with non-print materials. Almost without exception, public and academic librarians come to the administration of multi-media resources unprepared to treat them as library materials, for these materials present unique problems in terms of processing and storage which cannot be dealt with by traditional library procedures. In this case the all-too-prevalent solution to these problems is simply not to get involved with non-print media, not to accept the challenge.

Another reason for resistance stems from the educational background of librarians, who by accident or design have avoided contact with applied science and technology. Schooled in the social sciences and the humanities, they have been conditioned to believe they cannot gain technical or mechanical competence even if they try, with the result that such lack of and even distaste for technological knowledge has seriously thwarted multi-media use. Although attitudes are beginning to change, enough of this sentiment still lingers on to delay the acceptance of new non-print materials. The end-product of all this is that librarians resist having the responsibility of these media without a technician to advise them, yet when face to face with the audio-visual specialist (usually male and better paid), they resent him immensely. He is an outsider, not sensitive to the unique, ever-present, ever-pressuring problems of librarianship. Furthermore, he intimidates librarians with his technical jargon and exuberant behavior. It is better not to bother with media at all thinks the practicing librarian. And so it goes.

Already three times squelched, non-print media receives little better attention from the professional organizations. Thus far, professional organizations (especially the American Library Association) have moved slowly to accommodate the new media needs and help librarians in the day-to-day handling of materials. In 1955, the American Library Association made its first attempt to deal with the organization of media, when it sponsored a committee to survey librarians who were at that time organizing audio-visual materials. The recommendations and conclusions of that study were:

1. standardizing essential elements in cataloging audio-visual materials;
2. considering the possibility of having the Library of Congress catalog audio-visual materials;
3. determining whether subject heading lists are adequate for audio-visual materials;
4. standardizing a manual of procedure for handling materials;
5. encouraging research on the approach of audio-visual catalog users.

Since 1955, the American Library Association has contributed insignificantly to multi-media matters. None of the recommendations from that first study has been carried any further by the sponsorship of this association. Concern with and study of multi-media since then has originated from other sources, such as the United States Office of Education, or the Association for Educational Communications and Technology. Even with these efforts, however, in 1972, approximately 16 years later, the suggestions of the 1955 study have still not been adequately followed, and so librarians must contend with the same old problems on an even larger scale.

Library educators concerned with media agree that to overcome these barriers, professional organizations and agencies must take a more active part in developing multi-media resources. Standards, bibliographic control, guides and reviews, training sessions, and display services are vitally needed to encourage more favorable attitudes and to promote media usage. A national information system on audio-visual materials would give a major boost to media. At present it is difficult to find out what is available and where it is located. A national information center, perhaps in cooperation with regional centers, would permit quick and easy access to materials. And, of utmost importance is cooperation through joint statements, proposals, and recommendations for the control of media by the American Library Association, American Association of School Libraries, and the Association for Educational Communications and Technology.

The following facts summarize the plight of non-print media: most library educators are not committed to learning about, much less using, multi-media materials; the few multi-media courses which do exist are not adequate in intellectual content or in technological preparation, as a result, practicing librarians are both ill-informed about and resistant to new media; furthermore, the American Library Association has failed to lead the way or even attempt to fill some gaps. The vicious cycle returns back to the hands of library educators, who, like it or not, must shoulder the responsibility for raising multi-media to a level of importance. They will be held accountable for the success or failure which media achieves within the profession.

LIST OF SOURCES

American Library Association and National Educational Association. *Standards for School Media Programs.* Chicago, American Library Association, 1969.

Bixler, Paul: The Media-Source of a Library Neurosis. *The Rub-Off,* 21:42–46, Sept.–Oct. 1970.

Clement, Evelyn, and Totten, H. L.: Organization and Administration of Multi-Media Resources. *Wilson Library Bulletin,* 43:360–362, Dec. 1968.

Evans, Roy: Specialization in Educational Media at the University of Missouri. *Illinois Libraries,* 52:678–679, Sept. 1970.

Geller, Evelyn: Matter of Media. *Library Journal,* 96:2048–2053, June 15, 1971.

Goldstein, Harold: Media Standards and Education for Media Specialists. *Illinois Libraries,* 52:661–664, Sept. 1970.

Goldstein, Harold: The Importance of Newer Media in Library Training and the Education of Professional Personnel. *Library Trends,* 16:157–265, Oct. 1967.

Grove, Pearce, and Totten, H. L.: Bibliographic Control of Media: The Librarian's Excedrin Headache. *Wilson Library Bulletin,* 44:299–311, Nov. 1969.

Hart, T. L.: Media for the 70's. *Focus on Indiana Libraries,* 25:11–15, 34, March 1971.

Immroth, J. P.: I'm a Media Freak. *Library Journal,* 96:1935–1936, June 1971.

Kittilson, Bruce: Librarians, Audiovisualists, and School Media Programs. *Illinois Libraries,* 53:522–526, Sept. 1971.

Lieberman, Irving: Use of Nonprint Media in Library School Instruction. *International Conference on Education for Librarianship.* Edited by Larry Earl Bone. Urbana, University of Illinois Graduate School of Library Science, 1967.

McGuire, Ora: The Age of Media. *Focus on Indiana Libraries,* 25:44, 47, March 1971.

Penland, Patrick: Toward the Competencies of a Media Communicator. *Illinois Libraries*, 52:665–677, Sept. 1970.

Ramey, J. W.: The Human Element: Why Non Print Managers Turn Gray. *Drexel Library Quarterly, 7:91–106, April 1971.*

Roberts, Don: Libraries to the (Electric) People. *Wilson Library Bulletin*, 44:288–289, Nov. 1969.

Rogers, Robert: The Shock of Recognition: An Experiment with Videotape. *Ohio Library Association Bulletin*, 41:1012–1013, April 1971.

Stone, C. W.: The Library Function Redefined. *Library Trends*, 16:181–195, Oct. 1967.

Stone, C. W.: AV Report Card for Librarianship. *Wilson Library Bulletin*, 44:290–293, Nov. 1969.

Sullivan, Marjorie: The Media Specialist and Disciplined Curriculum. *Journal of Education for Librarianship*, 10:286–295, Spring 1970.

Totten, H. L. "An Analysis and Evaluation of the Use of Educational Media in the Teaching of Library Science in Accredited American Graduate Library Schools." Unpublished Ph.D. dissertation, University of Oklahoma, 1966.

Scope and Content of Non-Print Media Courses Taught in Graduate Library Schools

by Herman L. Totten
and Martin L. Mitchell

Ever since Marshall MuLuhan shook the world awake to the mystique of non-print, millions of words have been printed and spoken on that subject. Education, on all levels, has either embraced, in fact, or has adopted the stance of embracing, if only in fancy, the new phenomenon. Although the subject of non-print media—especially courses relating to non-print media—is of direct relevance to library schools, it was found that not enough was known about the status of non-print courses in the library science curriculum. As a consequence, a study was undertaken in 1972 by the authors to assess the current scope and content of non-print media courses in American graduate library schools.

There were two major questions the study sought to answer: (1) To what extent are non-print media courses made available to the current library science student? and (2) To what degree is non-print course work integrated into the general curriculum of graduate library schools? Tangential to these questions, a decision was made to obtain data that would (a) classify the types of non-print courses to which library science students are being exposed, (b) reveal profiles of the staff teaching such courses, and (c) isolate the basic textbooks being used in the teaching of such courses.

The study design involved the administration of a seventeen point mail questionnaire. The survey format was chosen not only because of its ease of administration and convenience, but because a review of the literature on the same subject revealed the questionnaire method to be a successful and valid means of obtaining the type of information needed.

A thorough investigation of library literature from 1940 to 1972 indicates that there have been four important studies made on the subject of non-print media instruction in the education of librarians: one by

Irving Lieberman in 1955;[1] a second by E. T. Schofield in 1957;[2] a third by Herman L. Totten in 1966;[3] and a fourth by Frederic R. Hartz in 1967.[4] The fact that no study has been published since that of Hartz constituted a further reason for making an assessment of the current situation regarding this subject.

Drawing from both studies, Hartz concluded that library schools are simply not offering the training necessary to support the field of instructional media. Hartz cites Lieberman's study which indicated that only 11 per cent of the subjects in his survey offered independent audio-visual courses. Schofield's study, completed five years after Lieberman's, indicated that only 48 per cent of the respondents offered independent audio-visual courses.

Hartz's own study, concluded in 1966, showed the situation had not changed radically: he found that only 47 per cent of the accredited library schools responding to his survey offered separate audio-visual courses.

The universe of schools being surveyed was limited to the 51 American graduate library schools which were listed as being accredited by the American Library Association at the time the present study was undertaken. The decision to exclude the Canadian library schools was made because it was the authors' intent to reflect the current situation in the United States alone. It should be noted that although the universe queried by Totten and Mitchell was unsurprisingly larger than that of two of the previous studies (Schofield and Hartz), it was more selective than that of Lieberman who did not specify accreditation to be a criterion for receiving his questionnaire.

The response to Totten's and Mitchell's survey was gratifying. Of the 51 schools surveyed, 90 per cent completed and returned the questionnaires—a significantly larger proportion of responses than were reflected in any of the earlier studies. In general, the data is treated in the aggregate only as the main objective is to assess the national picture of non-print instruction. In only a few cases was it necessary to mention individual schools because of some particular aspect. The usual pattern of response was one questionnaire per school, but in the case of three institutions, multiple responses were received. Pratt Institute and Columbia University each replied with three questionnaires, and Rutgers with two. Columbia University is also singled out later in the text of this study because of the nature of the program described by one of the respondents.

The first question dealt with the titles of non-print media courses. On the basis of the responses received, it was possible to divide the titles of non-print media courses into four general classifications. The first classification was specified as *General*—those titles whose content represent an introduction to media or a survey type of course. Nearly 65 per cent of the 52 course titles dealt with could be subsumed in this category. The second classification was specified as *Technical Service* or *Production*—a classification derived from the content of the course indicating specific technically oriented types of activities, such as acquisition, evaluation, processing of, or production of non-print media items. This group accounted for 18.24 per cent of the 52 course titles. The third classification was specified as *School Library*—titles whose content indicated special applicability to those training for service in school libraries or media centers. Of this group, 11.20 per cent were represented within the 52 titles. The fourth classification was specified as *Special Problems*—a classification given to those courses whose content did not fall within the scope of one of the other classifications and those courses which dealt with narrow content such as cartography or film history. This group represented 5.56 per cent of the 52 titles. In summary, the 52 titles represent those courses which are directly listed as library science curricula but are not integrated within the Schools of Education or within another discipline.

The second question required the respondents to state whether the media courses in their curricula were required courses. Of the 52 courses reported, 23 per cent were required by the schools of library science for either school librarians or school library certification. In one instance a media course was required by the program for special librarians; otherwise, the courses described were elective.

Questions three through seven probed for the physical details and descriptive data concerning the media courses. Specifically, this section of the questionnaire attempted to ascertain the common characteristics of non-print media courses in terms of the number of hours of credit given; the frequency of class meetings; the elapsed interval, if any, before the course would be offered again; the richness of course offerings for night school students; the availability of facilities to teach media courses within library school buildings; and the average projected enrollment per course.

In terms of average hours of credit given per course, the data revealed that 38.5 per cent of the courses offered are on a semester basis, offering three credit hours per semester. On a quarterly basis, it was found that 11 per cent of the courses offered three quarter hours credit. The remaining courses, 50.5 per cent, varied between two and four semester hours and four and five quarter hours. In terms of the time of day in which the courses were offered, 33.87 per cent of the respondents indicated that the times classes were scheduled varied widely, 45.16 per cent of the respondents indicated that classes were offered during the day only, while 20.97 per cent of the respondents said more options were available to them.

Concerning regularity of offering, 53.19 per cent of the respondents indicated that their courses were available every term. Another 27.66 per cent listed courses as available once a year, while 19.15 per cent indicated their courses were offered twice a year.

It can be seen that both in terms of time of offering and frequency, the student was generally given adequate opportunity to take a media course. In terms of the physical location where the courses would be offered, one would not necessarily expect that the media courses would be taught within the facilities of the library school due to the need often times for special equipment to conduct such courses; yet it was found that 34 per cent of the courses offered are taught in the physical plant of the library schools. Although no attempt was made in the questionnaire to ascertain where such courses were being taught other than in the library school, in at least one instance (i.e., the University of Washington) all of the non-print courses carry a library science number, but are conducted by and within the facilities of the College of Education. At the University of Kentucky, however, this is only partially true. The College of Library Science and the College of Education each conduct one course within its facility, and both courses carry a library science number.

The scope and content of the non-print media courses which was examined in question eight was found to follow closely the percentage breakdown given in question one. In general, respondents to this question were not precise in their descriptions, other than to label the content as being "a survey" or "an introduction." From the course syllabi submitted it is possible to ascertain that most of the courses classified in question one as being "general" are confined to that. In most instances, the basic concerns of the instruction are with orienting print librarians to issues of the non-print field. Technical processing kinds of courses deal largely with production of visuals and aurals for use in school and university media centers. School library type courses tend to relate the Standards for Media Programs of the American Library Association and the National Education Association to the current state of educational philosophy in American public schools. To some degree these courses appear to attempt to be all things to all people, dealing as they do with philosophy, technical services, selection and evaluation, administration, and all other aspects relative to the microcosm that is the school media center.

On the other hand, the courses categorized as being "special" in response to question one are very narrow in scope. For example, one course deals with maps and cartography as they affect the job of the librarian coming in contact with these non-print media while another probes the history, in depth, of the film industry and its products.

Question nine concerned itself with the titles of required textbooks. Fifty-three per cent of the respondents revealed there were no required texts, while nine per cent of the respondents disclosed they had texts in preparation at the time of the survey. Of the titles listed, the following ten were named as being required:

Bobker, Lee R. *Elements of Film*. New York: Harcourt, Brace and World, 1969.

Brown, James W., Richard B. Lewis, and Fred Harcleroad. *Audiovisual Materials and Methods*. 3rd ed. New York: McGraw-Hill, 1969.

Emery, Edwin, Phillip H. Ault, and Warren K. Agee. *Introduction to Mass Communications*. 3rd ed. New York: Dodd, Mead, 1970.

Erickson, Carlton W. *Administering Instructional Media Programs*. New York: Macmillan, 1968.

Gambee, Budd L. *Non-Book Materials as Library Resources*. Chapel Hill, North Carolina: Student Stores, University of North Carolina, 1967.

Hicks, Warren B. and Alma M. Tillin. *Developing Multi-Media Libraries.* New York: R. R. Bowker Company, 1970.

Kemp, Jerrold E., et al. *Planning and Producing Audiovisual Materials.* 2nd ed. San Francisco, California: Chandler Publishing Company; distributors: Science Research Associates, Chicago, 1968.

Knight, Arthur. *The Liveliest Art: A Panoramic History of the Movies.* New York: Macmillan, 1957.

Prince, George M. *The Practice of Creativity: A Manual for Dynamic Group Problem Solving.* 1st ed. New York: Harper & Row, 1970.

Rufsvold, Margaret I. and Carolyn Guss. *Guides to Newer Educational Media: Films, Filmstrips, Kinescopes, Phonodiscs, Phonotapes, Programmed Instruction Materials, Slides, Transparencies, Videotapes.* 3rd ed. Chicago: American Library Association, 1971.

The most commonly used text (12 per cent of the responses) is Hicks and Tillin's *Developing Multi-Media Libraries.* Brown, Lewis and Harcleroad's *Audio-Visual Media and Materials* was cited 9 per cent of the time, while Knight's *The Liveliest Art* was cited 6 per cent of the time.

Question ten required the respondent to list any supplemental bibliographies used in their course and to forward copies to this researcher. Sixty-six per cent of the respondents indicated that they did make use of supplemental bibliographies, while 34 per cent said they did not use bibliographies at all or did not answer the question. Of those using supplemental bibliographies, nearly 13 per cent indicated they had bibliographies which they use but were unwilling to send; and 30.12 per cent sent copies of listed titles on the back of the questionnaire.

Course availability to special non-library science students was the essence of question eleven. It would appear that library schools are not terribly exclusive concerning who may take their courses since 86 per cent responded that non-library science graduate students were permitted to enroll in the non-print media courses.

As for the availability of media courses to undergraduates, as examined by question twelve, it was found that non-print media courses are for the most part a graduate level specialty. Fifty-nine per cent of the responses indicated that undergraduates are excluded from taking non-print media courses in the library school.

Question thirteen attempted to secure data concerning the sequential nature of media courses by asking whether related courses were made available to students studying non-print media (i.e., cataloging, acquisition, and evaluation of non-print media). An analysis of the responses revealed that within the library school curriculum correlative courses are available in 64.37 per cent of the schools. Another 6.90 per cent of the responses indicated that correlative course work is available but not within the library curriculum, while 28.73 per cent of the responses indicated no related course work available.

Question fourteen concerned the integration of non-print media into the general library science curricula. It was difficult to tally the responses to this question and to put them into a definable format, pointing perhaps to weakness in the survey instrument's design. The respondents might better have been asked to place their response on some sort of a sliding scale of −5 to +5. As it was, the responses tended to be vague and undescriptive. At best, the authors have attempted to classify them in terms of "extensive" integration, "little" integration, and "unknown"— descriptions which tended to appear in the responses the most often. Thus, 39.53 per cent of the respondents claim the degree of integration of nonprint media into the subject matter of other library science courses to be on an "extensive" level; a larger percentage—50 per cent— claimed no integration of non-print media into the general library science curricula; and another 10.47 per cent claimed they could not answer the question.

Question fifteen attempted to gauge the availability of non-print media courses outside of the library science curriculum. As suspected, the data showed that if one cannot get training in non-print media in the library school, it is available in quantity in other departments of instruction. Seventy-eight per cent of the schools responding reported that non-print media courses are offered in another discipline. Other than one reference to a drama department, all of the course work available was through colleges of education. In one instance, that of the University of Washington, all non-print instruction is given through the College of Education under the title of Library Media Programs. Credit is given in library science for courses carrying education titles and numbers. Some of the responses indicated a cross listing of courses by the departments of education and library science, but the University of Washington program appears to be the only one which places all of the instruction for a library science program area into the facilities and supervision of another discipline.

The professional qualification of the teacher and years of teaching experience were the concerns of question sixteen and seventeen. The purpose was to obtain a profile of the persons teaching non-print media courses. The assumption was made that the person answering the questionnaire would be the person filling in this section of the data requested. If that assumption is valid non-print media courses are taught by holders of either the Ph.D. or D.L.S. degrees 7.26 per cent of the time. Another 28.74 per cent reported holding either the M.A. or M.S. in library science but not a doctoral level degree, while 64 per cent were in the process of working on or were near completion of the doctor's degree. The average number of years of experience for the teachers of non-print media courses was slightly more than nine years. Thus, it can be seen that students taking work in this area are not being assigned to faculty who have inferior backgrounds or lack experience.

There has been an apparent increase in the amount of attention given non-print media in American graduate library schools since 1966. There is also an obvious progression from Lieberman's study of 1955 to this study carried out in 1972. The finding that there was not a greater degree of integration of non-print into the general library science curricula was not totally unexpected. But the authors are somewhat perplexed by the fact that library schools do not seem to be making use of the availability of non-print media courses on their campuses in other disciplines when they do not offer such work within their own structure. Another source of concern is that a library school would offer an introductory course to non-print media but would take no steps to supplement technical services types of courses to augment the knowledge gained in the introductory course. For, what good is knowing about non-print media conceptually if the practicalities of the problem of selecting, evaluating, cataloging, and retrieving non-print information remains a mystery?

Although the instrument did solicit the type of data wanted, in retrospect, a more open ended questionnaire might have yielded more precise data, allowing the institution to respond according to its own idiosyncracies. Nevertheless, it can be concluded, on the basis of this study that although library schools have come a long way in terms of their non-print media programs they are still merely at the beginning of their work in dealing with this problem.

REFERENCES

1. Lieberman, Irving: *Audio-Visual Instruction in Library Education.* New York, School of Library Service, Columbia University, 1955, p. 85.

2. Schofield, E. T.: Basically a Library Service; Audio-Visual Aids in the Modern Library Program, *School Libraries,* 5:5–6, 27, January 1956.

3. Totten, H. L.: The Use of Educational Media in the Teaching of Library Science. *Oklahoma Librarian,* 16:107, October 1966.

4. Hartz, Frederic: Curriculum Implications for Training Instructional Materials Center Librarians. *Journal of Education for Librarianship,* 4:232, Spring 1967.

ADDITIONAL REFERENCES

Goldstein, Harold: The Importance of Newer Media in Library Training and the Education of Professional Personnel. *Library Trends,* 16:259–265, October 1967.

Lieberman, Irving: The Use of Non-print Media in Library School Instruction. *In:* Bone, L. E., ed.: *Library Education: An International Survey.* Urbana, University of Illinois Graduate School of Library Science, 1968.

QUESTIONNAIRE

A Survey of Non-Print Media Courses
Taught in Graduate Library Schools
by
Herman L. Totten and Martin L. Mitchell
College of Library Science
The University of Kentucky
Lexington, Kentucky

1. Title of non-print media course taught:

2. Course required?:

3. Number of credit hours _____ semester _____ quarter

4. Time course usually offered _____ hour _____ day _____ night.

5. How often course offered (i.e., every semester, summers, etc.):

6. Is classroom in library school or facilities of another discipline:

7. Approximate enrollment per course:

8. Scope and content of course:

9. Title of text, if any, used in the course:

10. Supplemental bibliographies used with the course (Please include a copy if possible):

11. Is course available to special students not enrolled in library school?:

12. Is course available to undergraduates?:

13. Are related courses available to students studying non-print media, i.e., cataloging of non-print media, acquisition and evaluation of non-print media, etc.?:

14. To what extent are non-print media discussed in other library science courses?:

15. Are non-print media courses available in another discipline such as Education or Medicine? (If so, please give as much information as you can about the offerings):

16. Professional qualifications of teacher:
    Undergraduate degree(s):
    Library Science degree(s):
    Other Graduate degree(s):
    Other courses taught:

17. Years of teaching experience:

A Systematic Examination and Analysis of Non-Print Media Courses in Library Schools

by Karen S. Munday
and John W. Ellison

Some students planning to enter graduate library schools seem extremely sophisticated in their selection of library schools and areas of library specialization. In part this is dictated by the current economic situation and counseling regarding job openings in various aspects of librarianship. There also seems an awareness on the part of some students as to their personal interests and abilities as they relate to library type positions. The interest expressed by many prospective students in non-print media appears to be based on a belief that valuable information is contained in a variety of material formats and libraries should actively involve themselves in information irrespective of format.

There are few studies published regarding graduate library school course offerings in the area of non-print media. The five major studies completed to date are: Irving Lieberman in 1955, E. T. Schofield in 1957, Herman L. Totten in 1966, Frederic R. Hartz in 1967 and Herman L. Totten and Martin L. Mitchell in 1972. This 1973 study, when appropriate, is intended to corroborate the findings in the Totten and Mitchell study of 1972.

This study was a systematic examination of the current course offerings in the 51 graduate library school programs in the United States accredited by the American Library Association as reflected in catalog course descriptions. It sought to answer several questions: (1) How many non-print media courses are offered? (2) Are these courses designed for all library school students or just those preparing for certification in school librarianship? (3) How many of the courses are cross-listed and/or offered outside graduate library schools? (4) Who are the library school faculty responsible for non-print media courses? (5) Which courses other than those designated as exclusive non-print media courses refer to media in their catalog descriptions? (6) How many non-print media courses are required in graduate library schools? (7) Are non-print laboratories available to students? (8) Is there a direct mention of nonprint media in the library schools' objective, goal or purpose statements? and (9) Will the answers to the above questions aid prospective library students interested in non-print media in their selection of a library school?

Use of an objective methodology to gather data would have been more valid if every library school had consistently used the terms "media," "non-print," and "non-book." No guarantee exists for such usage, however, this study used these terms synonymously.

Data for this study were obtained from graduate library school catalogs and bulletins which were obtained under the guise of a prospective student inquiring directly to the library school for application information. It was felt this method would produce the materials prospective students would have available when selecting library schools and the types of programs offered.

Of the 51 schools surveyed, only 43 (84.31%) responded with catalogs, bulletins, and application forms. An additional five schools (9.80%) replied, but did not forward catalogs or bulletins within 63 days after the initial request. Three library schools (5.88%) failed to acknowledge the request for application information. The over-all response was similar to that reported in the 1972 Totten and Mitchell study, which showed 47 schools (90%) responding to their questionnaire.

Totten and Mitchell reported 52 non-print media courses being offered in the 47 accredited United States library school programs responding in 1972. This investigation identified 146 non-print media courses listed in 41 library school catalogs in 1973. Only Northern Illinois and Maryland do not identify non-print media courses. Of the 146 courses, 66 (45.20%) are school library oriented while 80 (54.79%) do not specify a type of library in the title or course description. For the purpose of this study, these 80 courses are considered exclusively non-print media courses. Case Western Reserve (7), Wayne State (7), and Catholic (6) had the largest number of school non-print media courses. Thirty-five (81.40%) library schools offer exclusive non-print media courses. Buffalo (5), Texas Women's (5), Long Island (4), and Rosary (4) rank highest in number of such courses offered. Catholic offers a total of nine school, exclusive, and cross-listed non-print media courses. Buffalo, Case Western Reserve, Long Island, Michigan, and Wayne State each offer seven. These results indicate a dramatic increase in the number of non-print media courses since the Totten and Mitchell study in 1972.

A serious question immediately surfaces upon examining the above results. Each graduate library school averages 1.53 non-print media courses designed for school library students, while only 1.86 non-print media courses per school remain to serve public, academic (especially community college), and special (especially medical) librarians combined.

The integration of non-print media concepts into the general library school curricula since the Totten and Mitchell study is dramatic. They reported nineteen (39.53%) schools integrate non-print media into the subject matter of other library science courses. This study shows that a total of 85 courses representing 29 (67.44%) library schools mention non-print, non-book, and media. Buffalo, Columbia, Geneseo, and Kent State offer the largest number of courses (6) indicating emphasis on non-print media. Combining these courses with the 146 exclusive and school library oriented non-print media courses reveals 231 courses which directly or indirectly discuss aspects of non-print media in their course descriptions in the 43 library schools. These 231 courses represent 13.07 per cent of the total 1,767 course offerings in the library schools used in this study.

There are 13 Children's Literature and Acquisition of Library Materials courses each which make direct reference to non-print, non-book or media in their course descriptions. Twelve advanced cataloging and nine young adult courses make similar references in their course descriptions as well as two courses in medical librarianship.

School library students will be deluged with non-print media cataloging on the job. To acquire the necessary information to properly organize nonprint media, they are forced in 12 (27.90%) library schools to take two cataloging courses. School library students have a large percentage of their required course load fixed in many instances because of state certification requirements. Only four (9.30%) library schools make references to non-print media in their basic cataloging course descriptions. Only one of five (11.62%) library schools with special non-print media cataloging courses make reference to non-print media in their basic cataloging course. This means 22 (51.17%) library schools, according to their catalogs, do not teach cataloging of non-print media in any context.

Nearly every library school requires one or two non-print media courses for school library specialization due to certification requirements in their particular state. However, this examination of library school catalogs shows that not one non-print media course is required by other library school students. Only in a few cases are non-print media courses suggested for areas of study in academic, public, and special libraries. This finding is disturbing since so many small four-year and community college libraries are becoming heavily involved in non-print media. The same is true with medical and large urban public libraries. The listing of job openings for non-print media librarians in professional journals is another indication of the need for persons with an adequate background in both library science and non-print media.

Four (9.30%) library school catalogs list 23 non-print media courses offered by other departments. San Jose alone lists 13 offered in cooperation with the Department of Instructional Technology on their campus. None of these courses, according to the San Jose catalog, is cross-listed with the library school.

Only four (9.30%) library schools cross-list seven non-print media courses, all with departments of education. Of these, Wayne State lists four. Thirty-four (81.39%) of the library schools permit students to take courses outside the library school and credit these hours toward the M.L.S. degree. However, eight (18.60%) of the library school catalogs examined do not mention transfer credit. The Totten and Mitchell study showed that 37 (78%) library schools offer non-print media courses in other disciplines.

Four (9.30%) library school catalogs give specific information regarding five instructors of exclusive non-print media courses. Buffalo, Kentucky, and Rutgers list one while Illinois lists two. This information was ascertained through those catalogs which provided instructors' degrees and special areas of competencies in media. This study did not tabulate those instructors named with a course title and description unless additional degrees and competencies were provided in the catalog. Thirty-one (70.46%) of the catalogs surveyed do not list instructor names by course titles.

Eight (18.60%) library schools have non-print media laboratories within and operated by their staff. Three (6.89%) library schools have similar laboratories available to them, but operated by departments and personnel outside their jurisdiction. Thirty-two (74.41%) of the library schools do not indicate the availability of a non-print media laboratory. An average of 5.37 exclusive or related non-print media courses are offered in each library school.

Only eight (18.60%) of the library school catalogs directly or indirectly make reference to the terms media, non-print, or non-book in their objective, goal, or purpose statements. Interestingly, 23 (53.48%) library schools make reference to information science. No library school uses the term "media" in its title while seven (16.27%) use "information."

Some significant references are made regarding non-print media in objective, goal, and purpose statements taken from library school catalogs. The following are examples:

> The ability to evaluate, interpret, and stimulate use of all types of materials, print and non-print. (Catholic)
> Knowledge of the basic materials of the major subject fields, and the selection and use of non-book materials. (Emporia)
> New Media—film, audiotape, videotape, and computer memories—are ways of representing information, ways that approach re-creation of original discovery; they offer new modes of transmitting and preserving thoughts, ideas, and records of our society. (Buffalo)

Several possible reasons exist for the inconsistencies between this study and the 1972 Totten and Mitchell study. First, even though course titles and descriptions refer to media, respondents to the Totten and Mitchell study may have known more accurately the course content and responded accordingly. Second, course content may have changed considerably over the past two years. Third, the use of the terms media, non-print, and non-book were not used consistently by all library schools. Fourth, library school catalogs may contain some inaccuracies. Finally, the two methodologies used in collecting the data may account for dramatic differences in the results.

In conclusion, it appears that the number of non-print media courses offered in library schools, at least as indicated in catalogs, has increased dramatically over the past few years. This does not mean these courses serve the current and future media needs of libraries. Even though library schools are beginning to recognize non-print media as legitimate and valuable information for librarians, many are not communicating this clearly through their catalogs.

Some recommendations can be made regarding the results of this study:

- Students planning careers in academic, public and special libraries should be formally introduced to non-print media.
- Non-print media courses (Basic Media Utilization; Media Production; Selection, Acquisition and Management of Media, etc.) should not be oriented to a type of library (school, academic, public, or special) program.
- Cataloging of non-print media should be in the basic cataloging courses rather than in advanced cataloging courses.
- Non-print media laboratories should be made available to students. Ideally, this laboratory should be an integral part of the library school library.
- Library school objective, goal and purpose statements, when appropriate, should reflect non-print media.
- Library school catalogs should identify faculty competencies and areas of specialization.
- Prospective students should be privy to all information regarding non-print media through library school catalogs.
- Non-print media courses taught in or outside library schools should reflect non-print media in the library context.

BIBLIOGRAPHY

Hartz, Frederic: "Curriculum Implications for Training Instructional Materials Center Librarians." *Journal of Education for Librarianship,* 7:232–236, Spring 1967.

Lieberman, Irving: *Audio-Visual Instruction in Library Education.* New York, School of Library Service, Columbia University, 1955.

Schofield, E. T.: Basically a Library Service; Audio-Visual Aids in the Modern Library Program. *School Libraries,* 5:5–6, Jan. 1956.

Totten, H. L.: The Use of Educational Media in the Teaching of Library Science. *Oklahoma Librarian,* 16:107, Oct. 1966.

Totten, H. L., and Mitchell, M. L.: Scope and Content of Non-Print Media Courses Taught in Graduate Library Schools. *Journal of Education for Librarianship* 14:58–66, Summer 1973.

PART

VIII

MEDIA POLITICS

Ivory Tower Ghettoes

by Bill Hinchliff

Every one of us is involved to some extent in converting the world into one vast "Auschwitz." Like Eichmann, we execute antihuman orders from above. Being aware of fiendish phenomena, observing but not protesting, is comparable to the attitudes which prevailed while the Nazis were gassing and incinerating millions of Jews. Sane scientists—there are many —give us less than a 50-50 chance of surviving to the year 2000 unless we alter our death-dealing course.

Our nation has become a war-lubricated techno-corporate state. Universities, financial institutions, and labor unions have joined the military-industrial "cosa nostra." Deluges of death-dealing dollars have radically altered our national economy. War industry has plenty of money with which to "influence public policy." The same suicidal syndrome has seized other "major powers" and is spreading to all industrialized nations. It means war after war after war. It means one, two, three, four, five, six lobbyists per politician. It means socially irresponsible associations out-working us on Capitol Hill.

In each of the world's "great cities" and each of the world's major universities the problems are compounding. Smoldering discontent has given way to blind rage. Peaceful leaders have been displaced by ruthless ones.

As media distributors we must try to understand our media-polluted, war-prone, pseudo-civilization. We must try to understand the tyranny of television which haunts our children; makes actors and politicians interchangeable; prevents us from thinking about the real world. Truth needed for survival is buried under piles of . . . ugh!

The human race will go down the drain unless librarians and other responsible knowledge distributors help citizens to cut the media fog and focus knowledge on crucial problems in ways that will lead to effective remedies. The Social Responsibilities movement and the new Congress for Change represent American librarians' perhaps last opportunity to use their knowledge and leadership talents for human survival.

As Buell Gallagher put it: "A society that does not correct its own ills cannot expect peace." Can we expect our hungry, rottenly-housed, poorly clothed, intermittently employed, education-deprived, police-abused brothers, and our war-forced sons to be "socially responsible"? If you had to endure those conditions, would you be socially responsible? Yet they are often far more socially responsible than we comfortable librarians.

Our democracy is an unfinished experiment. It is late. The clock moves faster. Are we too timid, too obsessed with trivia? Shouldn't we join our impatient black brothers and our restless students to wake the people up? Including our fellow librarians?

Our most notable failure is in the realm of human relations: recruiting and developing librarians able to serve all students, including black students, effectively. We attend to *things* better than we attend to *people*. Many of us minimize human contacts and some of us avoid them altogether. Some of us concentrate on serving faculty, graduate students, and undergraduate elite students. How many of us would care to canvass our respective student populations for their criticisms and suggestions, and then discuss the results with student leaders, and follow through with corrective action?

Conventional library philosophy, like so much of our conventional wisdom, has lost its power. A L A standards for college and university libraries are obsolete. The Standards Committee does not meet often enough. It needs new members, fresh ideas.

The time has come to publicize the best, most innovative university and college libraries as the Knapp Project publicized the best school libraries; to facilitate much heavier use of the most important, most socially relevant media; to involve faculty and students who are not reached by conventional practices.

What might a team of economists say about college libraries? That costs are rising, efficiency falling, staff and users' time being wasted, backlogs higher, productivity lower, cost controls lacking, quality controls nonexistent, busy-work abundant, mechanization stalled, obsolete activities maintained? That most college libraries are weak, bogged down, underutilized?

What might a team of psychologists and sociologists say about attitudes toward college libraries? That faculty and students feel their resources are inaccessible; librarians unknowable; that librarians' efforts to gain understanding are feeble; that some teachers view the library staff as rivals, exposers of teachers' limitations, potential diverters of students' interest? Would the psychologists and the sociologists agree that bored, frustrated librarians create their own emotional ghettoes?

Might they not suggest that psychologists and sociologists be added to college library staffs, that they study faculty attitudes toward media and toward independent study; discover how some teachers motivate their students to read a great deal; help involve faculty and students in reorganizing the library for greater effectiveness?

Large-scale behavioral research would probably not only confirm the findings of Shores, Jordan, Knapp, Gaver, Monroe, Wasserman, and Bundy on the failures of conventional libraries, but might result in a recommendation for a million-dollar filmed "master course" in media utilization. Such a filmed course, while not a panacea, could multiply public understanding and use of libraries.

The quality of the college library depends not only on able, socially responsible staff members, but also upon the leadership, social commitment, and media sophistication of the faculty, the top-level college administration, and its governing board.

Is the college's "governing establishment" sensitive to human needs and willing to commit the college to the pursuit of a less destructive, more just, society? To focus the college's available knowledge and skill upon the removal of obstacles to the advancement of the people of the community? Do the college's policy-makers and leaders read and discuss the most authoritative sources on war and peace; racism; urban problems; the student rebellion; the social effects of the mass media? Do they favor a less regimented curriculum and more independent study? Do they recognize the fundamental importance of media utilization?

Is the purpose of education to stimulate independent thinking or is it to condition young people to submit, to obey, and to kowtow? If the latter is the case, college libraries should be abolished. Required textbooks will suffice. To the extent that students do not realize the liberating power of their libraries, college librarians have failed.

So let's attend closely to the young men and women for whom the college library exists. Unlike their forefathers, they refuse to submit to boredom, intimidation, indoctrination, and exploitation. Increasingly they refuse to be ignored, mistreated, or subjected to unreasonable, capricious, discriminatory military and educational compulsion. They are bitter toward bureaucracies that retard progress and degrade people. They want less emphasis on hardware, more emphasis on human beings.

A measure of the effectiveness of a college library is the quality and quantity of two-way communication between librarians and students. Do the librarians know how students feel about their college library? Are students' impressions, opinions, and suggestions for library improvement actively solicited, respected, acted on? Do most students feel that their library is irresistible or do they feel it is *unattractive?*

The movement toward student published course and teacher evaluation is spreading. Perhaps student evaluation of college libraries and librarians will come next. Some successful college libraries, anticipating this development, have placed suggestion boxes at heavy traffic points and have promptly posted "action taken" answers and explanations. Many progressive college libraries have student-faculty library committees which consider library problems, recommend solutions, and participate in planning better policies, services, and resources.

What responses could your college library administrators offer to a delegation of faculty members and students asking such questions as these: What major improvements in service has the library made recently? What service improvements are scheduled? What are you doing to increase faculty and student media sophistication and use?

Do you have accurate records of complaints? Books and other media requested but not supplied? Reference queries not answered? Waiting time for books to be retrieved from closed stacks? Photocopying service? Faculty members who do *not* use the library? Students who do *not* use the library? Cataloged titles lost, strayed, or stolen? Average time elapsed from selection of a new title to its availability on the shelf and in the catalog? Based on this information, what actions are taken?

College library collections: What proportion of them will never be used? How many college libraries have aggressive acquisition programs on racism; militarism; urban rot; sex; drugs; crime; political, bureaucratic, and police corruption; mental illness; capital punishment; and world government? How many have respectable holdings on Africa, Asia, and Latin America? When will college libraries begin to supply new books as fast as bookstores do, and receive the same discount?

Are most college libraries hopelessly behind with respect to the flood of non-print media: phonograph records, tapes, films, slides? How many college libraries are acquiring some of the interesting experimental motion pictures which are being produced by college students?

When will cataloging arrearages become a nightmare of the past? What would the hypothetical team of consulting psychologists say about the depressing effects of card catalogs upon those who must use them? Might they recommend that our new book catalogs become motivational as well as informational devices? That they use illustrations, photographs, cartoons, excerpts, and quotations, with color, style, and flair? Publishers' catalogs: Bantam, Grove, Doubleday, New American Library, Ballantine, Simon & Schuster, and of course, the New York Graphic Society catalogs are irresistible. We should learn from them.

How about our bibliographies? Do we confine them to "safe" subjects? What results do they produce? Would they be more effective if they dealt with major issues and were printed in the college newspaper? What if an urban college library cooperated with the public library, the leading newspapers, and the leading T V broadcasters in promoting selective, annotated bibliographies of paperbound books and other low-cost media on socially crucial subjects? A community resident would simply telephone the college library and receive by return mail a media-packet containing all of the items in the bibliography; he would thereby become an extension student.

Media utilization and educational effectiveness could be rapidly increased by providing "free" packets of course-required media to students at registration. At an estimated cost of less than $100 per student per year this measure would increase students' achievement, reduce their frustration, and raise morale very substantially. It would reduce strains on the library and on the bookstore. The cost of the proposed media packets would subsequently be repaid by the students themselves through taxation.

Prevailing book and media display practices fail somehow to uplift the human spirit. What if new multi-media shelving were designed which would attractively exhibit all types of media on a subject of major social importance? What if this multi-media display contained a special section for FREE materials: catalogs, lists, bibliographies, syllabi, reprints, reviews, guides, pictures, and pamphlets? Another special section for SALE materials: paperbacks, maps, posters, discs, kits, replicas, slides, and diagrams? Another section for the usual LOAN items? Another section for NONCIRCULATING REFERENCE works? These collections on subjects of greatest interest could be arranged in attractive bays with lounge chairs and "wet" carrels at hand. Although they would take up more space, much heavier media utilization would follow. Media-circulated-per-square-foot is a more relevant ratio than media-stored-per-square-foot.

A special exhibit version of the new model shelving loaded with media on a currently pressing social problem could be placed at the college's heaviest traffic point. An attractive "new image" librarian could be stationed there to explain it to students who have not yet been "hooked on the library." The new model media counselor would also engage in recruitment. She, or he, would probably talk with more unsuspecting potential librarians than would be possible in any other context. The library manpower crisis is no myth. Thousands of librarians are approaching, or have already passed retirement age, but they continue to fill key positions for which younger, more aggressive librarians are better qualified. Thousands are equipped neither by training nor by inclination to reach out with new, more effective media services to the poorly served black children and youth of the inner cities.

Recruitment: the most conspicuous disaster of contemporary library leadership! Who plans and directs recruitment for your library? Does he visit library schools and college placement offices, including that of your own college? What are his demonstrated recruitment skills? How effective are his interviews? Are group interviews conducted? Do students and subprofessionals participate? Are detailed records of interviews kept?

Does your library have a recruitment brochure or information kit? What is in it? Do you have position descriptions? Are they true? Do they describe the actual work? Do they sound as if Great Aunt "Bureaucratia" had written them? Your job offers: are they being accepted? Are your starting salaries and fringe benefits competitive? Do you pay, or share, costs of candidates' visits? Are such visits carefully planned? In your library are beginning librarians given challenging, diversified, growth-conducive work? Who appraises the recruitment program?

Does anyone analyze your library's staff turnover, especially the reasons why you may be losing your best younger librarians? What libraries are attracting them? Why? Has your library a well-budgeted staff development program and a well-understood promotional ladder by which an aide may become a technician, a technician an intern; an intern a librarian, media counselor or specialist, and on up to an administrator? Do black librarians have equal opportunities for promotion to administrative posts?

The nation needs at least 100,000 new librarians to meet minimum standards which are already obsolete, particularly with respect to inner-city media services. Of these at least 15,000 should be black, including at least 8000 males. The members of the American Library Association should hammer out an enlightened national library manpower policy and action program including definite specifications for recruitment of blacks, especially males. Black librarians communicate, inspire, and motivate young black people more effectively than presently available whites.

There is no surer way for librarians to help end racism in this country than to recruit large numbers of talented, warm-hearted, socially responsible young black men and women to become children's, school, college, public, special librarians, and library administrators. Prejudice takes root in the very young. It must be stopped there. Our libraries need thousands of black librarians, a few of whom, in addition to their "regular duties," may do for libraries what the Holts, Hentoffs, and Herndons, the Kozols, Kaufmans, and Kohls have done for ghetto schools. I don't mean that those authors were black, but they exposed horrible conditions.

Black males are needed for many powerful reasons, chief of which is their ability to encourage and to convince ghetto children, particularly boys and youth, that education, libraries, books, and media are respectable and necessary to survival and progress.

The members of the American Library Association should raise five million dollars for a ten-year program to recruit 1500 black graduates per year for preprofessional internships or for immediate entrance to accredited library schools. The job must be done even if it costs ten million dollars. This is like a mere trace of moisture in the bucket when compared with the social costs which result from the failure of city people to educate their heirs. It is less than *one millionth* of our total national warfare expenditures which are at a rate of *over a trillion dollars per decade.* Over $5000 of military spending for every man, woman, and child in the United States of America!

The cause of the relative failure of college libraries is not too few *ideas* for programs, but too few librarians willing to support them; too few librarians willing to agree on priorities; too few librarians with the leadership, guts, energy, and persistence to bring about desperately needed changes. Successful innovation requires vast cooperation, tremendous thought, unremitting effort.

Let's shoulder our share of responsibility for constructive concerted action on society's major problems. Ivory towers, like lilywhite suburbs, are ghettoes too.

Working at Federal City College has convinced me that whites will gain as much—personally, I believe more—from the complete emancipation of blacks as blacks will gain. Understanding, mutual respect, pride, and affection will replace ignorance, prejudice, fear, rage, and violence. Instead of sitting busily out of it, we will have been in there digging it.

Cable Television: Should Librarians Get into the Act?

by George C. Stoney

While investors are abandoning cable television on all sides and banks are charging up to 18% in interest for money needed to develop or to expand systems, librarians are becoming active in cable as never before.

This makes sense for two reasons: First, cable is still a good long-term investment in the one-third of the nation where you must have its kind of help to get a better TV signal. Second, cable will become a good investment in many more communities as we find better ways to use the services it can provide. Meanwhile, librarians should use this grace period afforded us by the money men—certainly not out of the goodness of their hearts—to test out what really ought to be done with this medium.

Librarians are in the information business and CATV should be thought of, first, as a mechanism for exchanging information. That it happens to be a "hot" investment in one place and time and a "dog" in another is something that we all have to care about, for without money no cable gets laid. But it is tragic that, once again in these United States, the immediate greed of investors rather than the needs of the people is shaping the media.

Congress set up the Federal Communications Commission to regulate radio, television and, now, cable for the public good. Not even its strongest defenders would dispute the fact that the FCC has become little more than the servant of the industries it was set up to govern, with cable having the least power of persuasion only because there is the least money invested in it. Insofar as cable television regulation is concerned, more effective efforts to gain benefits for viewers are being made on the local level. I am pleased to say that alert librarians are playing an important part in what has become a nationwide movement.

At least three years ago librarians in Wisconsin were gathering information about CATV. What started as a few "information shelves" grew into a statewide concern, supported by workshops, published guidelines, and finally, some active politicking. The Citizens Cable Council of Madison and Dane County was started in a library. It soon reorganized itself as a private civic body with the right to use the library's meeting facilities, and helped to shape one of the better municipal franchises. Now ex-librarian Merry Sue Smoller is Madison's Director of Cable Regulations.

In Port Washington, Long Island, at this writing, a group spawned in the local library is leading a campaign to delay the granting of a franchise for cable in one of the richest areas in the country—"a real goodie," according to the trade press—until substantial revisions are made in the basic document to guarantee channels for public access, municipal, and educational access and to provide facilities to use them. It is significant that the library's director, Edward De Sciora, has the support of his Board in leading this action. It is also significant that without the Port Washington Library group's action the franchise would have been approved by the commissioners with hardly a question being raised, for almost no one in any other of the several municipalities included in the franchise area was aware of the issues involved.

The thing that put this considerable body of Port Washington citizens in the know about cable was a video access center started by library associate Lillian Katz almost four years ago. Walter Dale, fresh from a training period with the National Film Board of Canada's "Challenge for Change" program, was chosen the video center's director. With basement quarters and a minimum of equipment, Walter Dale and Mark Bates, a Vista volunteer who now heads the workshop, began teaching people in Port Washington to use videotape in closed-circuit situations. Soon there were dozens of tapemakers and a handful of gifted and willing volunteer teachers to take the idea of homemade TV—TV with a purpose—into schools, civic organizations, nursing homes, youth clubs, and subsequently, into the meeting of governing bodies where decisions about the community's future were being made by men (yes, mostly men) who were not used to being watched, much less recorded.

Long before there was cable then, Port Washington learned that half-inch video could be a new and sometimes unwelcome recorder and disseminator of information. They have fought through this battle—a battle that every library that gets involved in the meaningful application of video will have to face sooner or later.

Trouble began in Port Washington with the first tape made by young people about drugs. Next there was an even bigger fuss when the workshop people asked to tape the almost unpublicized meetings of a municipal board that was deciding on the sale of a large body of public land. That's when video really hit the fan, bringing the library into true confrontation. The library found itself hip-deep in the kind of politics most tax-supported bodies try to avoid. Once any library gets into cable in a significant way it will find such situations almost impossible to avoid.

REALITY IS DIFFERENT

For several years now I have been one of those involved in cable who urge librarians to take an active part in establishing this new medium as a public information service. At first I assumed, naively, that the basic beliefs librarians share in "freedom of the press," "freedom to read," and the "right to information" would prepare them for the battle. Somehow reality is different.

For example, it is one thing to have the *Cantos* of Ezra Pound on a library shelf and quite another to have his often anti-Semitic verse read aloud on the cable. No library to my knowledge has had to face that choice, but the material appearing on citizen-generated cable channels around the country indicates that this is not a far-fetched hypothesis.

A couple of weeks ago in Johnson City, Tennessee, I saw tapes run by a citizens' group protesting the building of a modern, minimum-security prison in their county. It was a strong demonstration of the "Will of the People" being given voice. Unfortunately, in the process there were repeated statements about the dangers that might befall this community if "all those rapists got loose" or if prisoners on work release programs were permitted out "to take over our jobs at 80¢ an hour."

In Bloomington, Indiana, the county library has leased a channel for one dollar a year and has been operating it for the benefit of the public with impressive results. But before their first program went on cable this summer, the director, Bob Trinkle, was so concerned with the fact that they had not faced up to the problems of responsibility for content that he postponed the opening date by two full weeks to think things over. Finally he decided to assume "the role of censor" himself. Though this is not a decision that pleased all members of his staff or the officially appointed Telecommunications Council, so far all has gone well. Trinkle knew he had to worry about his conservative county governing body as well as about the far more radical one now controlling Bloomington itself.

Among the first tapes to be seen on Bloomington's library channel was an interview with a prominent Black minister who was to recount the history of his church. What could be less controversial? Yet, within minutes this minister was talking about Ku Klux Klan activity in downtown Bloomington as recently as four years ago that shaped his church's history quite directly. Interestingly enough, Bob Trinkle himself helped to shoot this tape and subsequently saw that it got cablecast.

Bloomington's library channel was organized and put into operation by a gifted young videomaker named Jeff Ullman, who was brought to Indiana from Berkeley on a matching grant from the National Endowment for the Arts, through a cable internship program directed by New York University's Alternate Media Center. The local cable operator supplied the matching grant, plus some equipment. More has come from the city. But, right from the beginning, the library faced the fact that this was to be a major investment. In all, about $20,000 worth of equipment was required for a quite unsophisticated black-and-white transmission system located in the library itself. (In Tulsa, the library has a "moderately professional" unit that cost several times as much.) Most programming is recorded on video rovers used on location. Important segments are recorded "live" in the library itself, using an open area lounge as a studio where anyone passing can watch and join in if they wish. Now that the channel is operating and gaining public acceptance, Bob Trinkle is consolidating the library's position in CATV by building the full salary of the cable coordinator into his regular budget.

STARTING SMALL

Few libraries will be able to find the funds or courage needed to support efforts like those being made in Bloomington perhaps, but dozens are finding themselves drawn into franchise hearings like the one in Port Washington. Literally hundreds of libraries are getting their feet wet in video by buying the odd portapak. Sometimes I wish they wouldn't—at least not until careful thought is given to *how* video will be used.

It takes no special skill as a prognosticator to guess that a lot of portapaks bought by librarians just because it's the fashionable thing to do these days will become scarcely remembered items on the inventory two years from now.

Video is too expensive to mess around with unless one has a purpose for doing so. After the initial capital investment is made, you need money for manpower (personpower?), money for maintenance, money for tape. Like cable itself, video can and should be a great deal more than a cheap substitute for film or on-air television. Our ideas about media have been so strongly fixed by commercial television, theatrical movies, and even 16mm non-theatrical formulas and customs, that almost everyone has to experience the difference for himself. This is why a community video center is an ideal precursor for community cable.

Libraries can provide the spark, as they did in Madison, or the main impetus as in Port Washington. Libraries can operate their own channels, as in Bloomington and Tulsa. Most will serve as one of many sources of locally made programming carried on cable, sharing channel space with the schools, city agencies, churches, and community organizations as they do now in West Seneca, New York; Columbus, Indiana; and dozens of other places.

By now I have seen so many Saturday morning story hours on tape made for cable that I wouldn't be able to recognize a good one if I was tied to a chair to watch it. On the other hand I have seen dozens of fascinating tapes about local history. I have enjoyed dozens of conversations with ordinary citizens that could be dismissed as "talking heads" only by media specialists with hearts of stone.

Last week in a school video room in Big Stone Gap, Virginia, I saw marvelous tapes about "Coon Dog Running," "Old Plain Baptist Singing," and "An Old Fashioned Grist Mill" taped by the local man who found and restored it. Unless some librarians take a hand, these tapes and hundreds like them being made all over the country may be destroyed or lost before they can be seen and enjoyed by a larger public.

I live in a neighborhood of New York City where the neighborhood branch library has decided that its role in video, at least for the time being, should be confined to setting up an archive for tape originals and a copying and playback service so people in the community can have access to what is being produced by dozens of people in the West Village who own their own half-inch equipment.

When Bob Pinto and I made a tape about the history of the church across the street from my apartment I found it heartening to know that Phil Gerrard at the Jefferson Market Branch would be interested in adding this to his collection. From now on, every tape I make about the neighborhood will be put together with considerably more care because I have the archive in mind. Of course I can—and often do—get these tapes run on the two public access channels the city's cable system offers, but there is something particularly satisfying in knowing that anybody can drop down to the library and see my work whenever it suits them. The church likes the idea, too.

The Jefferson Market Branch has a video playback deck, a three-quarter-inch cassette rig and monitors in a meeting room so video viewing can be made a part of community meetings. Soon a cable outlet will be added (a free drop is called for in the city's franchise), so TV viewing of all kinds can become a group experience. One of the least attractive things about most TV watching is that it is done in solitude. Maybe that's why most librarians are comfortable with the "Watch-A-Book" experiments in which programs originally run on educational television are offered to patrons in three-quarter-inch cassette form to be seen in tiny, individual viewing spaces. No doubt this will be the most widely used way of viewing video in libraries in the future. Even Ezra Pound's *Cantos* can be read aloud with little fear of offense if playback is through a single set of earphones.

Fortunately, I find a sizable number of librarians willing to take more of a chance on video these days. Some in the old "inner city" neighborhoods, where grand old Carnegie buildings are all but abandoned fortresses of the unread, are saying libraries have an obligation to make a fresh start with media rather than to press it into the "Watch-A-Book" mold, however comfortably familiar that might be. This past year, Bob Pinto of the Alternate Media Center staff and I helped sixteen Masters Degree candidates in Columbia University's Library School prepare for inner city work as media specialists. The experience made me realize that video—and certainly cable—is but one of many tools that should be used to help libraries serve this new constituency. However, there may be times when other media than video should get top priority. When you count the cost, a strong community development person with a cassette tape recorder, a 35mm camera, and a slide projector may be better armed for his/her work than if loaded down with $5,000 worth of video equipment.

This is the point: Before you get involved in video or cable, know that the costs to be measured may include more personal involvement than the usual professional is accustomed to making, more political involvement than most institutions are willing to risk. Obviously, a lot of libraries are going to wait a long time before they deal with video.

A Study in Censorship:
The Los Angeles "19"

by Ronald F. Sigler

The Los Angeles County Library serves 2 ½ million people within an area of 3000 square miles which includes 43 cities and county territory. The Audio-Visual Program emanates from eight regional libraries with a current film circulation of three to four thousand each month and an annual audience level of over one million. The Library presently sponsors more than 500 film programs in library buildings per month for children, young adults, adults and family groups. For further information see Film Library Quarterly, *Summer 1968, Vol. I, No. 3, "Working Together to Build a Unique System," pp. 11-14. The following study is an attempt to clarify the successful management of their recent film censorship problems that have come to the attention of all libraries. It will also clear up fragmentary information in past news releases, including the article in* Library Journal, *March 1, 1971.*

All is not quiet on the western front, that is at Los Angeles County Public Library, where in January, nineteen films from our collection were withheld from circulation for eight days. It was indeed unjustifiable that the "Los Angeles 19," as Chet Martin of Radio Station KFI referred to the films in a radio editorial on February 2, 1971, were removed. It was inevitable to see as Chet Martin said,

> The Los Angeles 19 finally have won a reprieve . . . after their conviction without a trial . . . and have been restored to society.

We agree with Harry Reasoner, of ABC News, who quoted President Eisenhower as follows,

> As it is an ancient truth that Freedom cannot be legislated into existence, so it is no less obvious that Freedom cannot be censored into existence.

as he introduced Dick Shoemaker in Los Angeles on the ABC TV network, reporting the withdrawal of the films. In a television network editorial immediately following the newscast, Harry Reasoner made another fitting and proper comment.

> There is something very wrong in raising political hell with art. It's a Communist not an American technique.

Eighteen of the titles were originally scheduled as a series of film programs between October and December, 1970 in suburban Hacienda

Heights, a bedroom community of about 35,000 people located about 20 miles east of Los Angeles and served by the Los Angeles County Library System. Audio-Visual Services, including the advisory services of an A-V Librarian, emanate locally from the Regional Library in West Covina, serving all the East San Gabriel Valley.

The original program entitled "Friday Flicks for High School Students," was planned by the librarian-in-charge of Hacienda Heights as a Young Adult Discussion series. In her own words she described her intent as follows:

> Being aware that I serve a conservative community, I made a conscious effort to avoid films which might be patently controversial. For example, an article in the *Claremont Courier* on September 10, 1969, entitled "What our Young People are Reading These Days" surveys opinions of various community librarians in the area. Mentioned are civil rights, drugs, the draft, marriage, hippie culture, Vietnam, witchcraft, abortion, and sex. I chose not to deal with most of those subjects. The films I chose generally related to personal or cultural values and interests, and seemed to permit or encourage varied interpretations which would lead to open-ended discussion. The themes of the six-program fall film series covered (1) education, (2) materialism, (3) the 21st Century, (4) war as a personal experience, (5) conformity and oppression and (6) the search for ethics and values.

The program as it was printed and distributed to the public looked like this. (The necessary filmographic information has been added in brackets.)

Oct. 2—Drop in or Out?
Chris Wood could see *No
Reason to Stay in School.*   (bw, 29 min., NFBC/Films Inc.)
Are you your own man?
Alan Arkin says *That's Me.*   (bw, 15 min., Stuart/McGraw-Hill)
Professor *Zuckerkandl* made
it big. Or did he?   (color, 14 min., Hubley/Grove Press)

Oct. 16—The American Way?
Little White Crimes can build   (bw, 28 min., NFBC/McGraw-Hill)
a big image.
Is the rat race won by ability
to *Run?*   (bw, 16 min., Kuper-CCM-Brandon)
The product won't work, or
*Help, My Snowman's Burning   (color, 9 min., Beaux Arts/ BFA)
Down [*Duet*]

Oct. 30—Your Future?
Welcome to the era of
Computer Revolution.   (color, 24 min., CBS/BFA)
Autos, Autos, Everywhere,   (color, 25 min., CBS/McGraw-Hill)
with drivers out of sight.
Your next date may be
Comput-Her Baby.   (color, 5 min., Pyramid)

*Carson Davidson's *Help My Snowman* . . . was not shown because of a scheduling problem. *Duet* was shown instead and was therefore included in the "19".

Nov. 13—What's in a War?
A strange thing happened at
Owl Creek Bridge.   (bw, 27 min., Enrico/Comtemp/McGraw-Hill)
The Magician plays at war, with (bw, 13 min., Poland/Sterling Educ.)
toy guns or real?
Let's dig *The Hole* to the   (color, 15 min., Hubley/CCM-Brandon)
bottom of the truth.
Nov. 27—Free to Choose
Can a *Musical Pig* triumph   (color, 9 min., Zagreb/Contemp/McGraw-Hill)
over pig fate?
Does it seem that *The Hand*   (color, 19 min., Trnka/Contemp/McGraw-Hill)
dominates your life?
From *"21-87"* automation   (bw, 10 min., NFBC/Contemp/McGraw-Hill)
carries you through.
Dec. 11—What's Right?
What's in a *Parable?* The   (color, 15 min., Forsberg/Cine. Cath.)
circus clown knows.
It's About This Carpenter   (bw, 14 min., Louis Teague/NYU)
in New York City.
Where would you place
The Rock in the Road?   (color, 6 min., Beaux Arts/BFA)

Young Adult Services ordinarily discourages adults and parents from attending the programs in order to encourage good discussion participation from the young people.

However, as the program progressed, two women from the community made their appearance and insisted on attending and disrupting the discussion. As a springboard for discussion, the librarian wore a peace symbol during one of the programs and had collected varying information on its background. (Earlier that week a young adult had asked her about it.) The women attacked her for displaying the symbol and rejected her attempt to offer the varying views on it. Following instructions, the librarian asked the two women if they would mind leaving and screening the films at another time convenient to them. The ladies completely refused to do so.

A telephone complaint was received early in October by the Young Adult Coordinator, Mrs. Harriett Covey, from Mrs. Jean Stratton, one of the ladies referred to earlier. The protest was aimed primarily at the "Communistic" leanings of the programs and the restrictions on adult attendance. Mrs. Covey encouraged Mrs. Stratton in her assumption of responsibility for her own children's activities but reminded her that this responsibility did not extend to other youngsters in the community. A complaint was subsequently filed with County Supervisor Bonnelli[1] who is the elected representative of the community involved as well as the chairman of the Library Department. After a call from one of the ladies, a local High School Principal then refused to circulate library fliers advertising the programs.

Noon preview showings were voluntarily offered by the library for all community adults interested in the programs scheduled for young adults in the late afternoon. At the request of the President of the Regional Advisory Council[2] for the East San Gabriel Valley Region, a community preview of six of the titles programmed was scheduled at 9 P. M. on November 4, 1970. Unfortunately, the only publicity was in the local community weekly newspaper appearing on the morning of the scheduled showing. Knowing of this evening preview showing in advance, the ladies formed a telephone committee, called all their friends, and the end result was one sided. Interestingly enough, the library staff recognized almost no one at this meeting as a library patron.

The program began at 9 P. M. and ran approximately 3½ hours. Both the Audio-Visual and Young Adult Coordinators were in attendance to speak to the group about selection and utilization of the films in question, since both services were affected. Films shown included *Parable, Little White Crimes, Duet, Run, Comput-Her Baby,* and *Autos, Autos, Everywhere.* The meeting, attended by 100-150 people, was disrupted and threatened to become completely disorganized and is best described in the words of a librarian who resides in the community and was observing in the audience:

> From the beginning there was a tangible hostility that robbed the meeting of any kind of ease of communication. Constant running comment during the film showings and rude invective rather than interchange of ideas between the films marked the entire meeting. The Coordinators and the Librarian-in-Charge were not given an opportunity to defend their program. . . . It was a case of "A man convinced against his will is of the same opinion still."

The group was asked to fill out film evaluation forms to be forwarded to the County Librarian's office. Although there were a few positive comments by people who happened to hear of this meeting at the last minute, the majority of comments were similar to the following excerpts:

> All the films shown have absolutely no redeeming value! Please quit trying to educate and get back to pushing books. . . . What a waste of tax dollars! I can't describe how terrible I think these films are. It's not up to the Library System to re-educate. *(Parable) Sick.* The public library should get out of religion unless it knows what it is talking about.

> All seen tonight are very poor—but the real damage is done during the discussion sessions.

> *(Little White Crimes)* A perfect complement to the socialist indoctrination in the public school system. It suggests a negative, immoral, picture of business and enforces this concept of free enterprise system taught by socialist teachers. A negative influence bordering on the subversive. . . . *(Parable)* Blasphemy! Part of the world wide communist effort to ridicule Christ and Christianity. . . . A bad film that should not be paid for with tax money. . . . The library appears to have been thoroughly infiltrated by the communist conspiracy!

> All films are negative and should not be shown to our young adults. I do not approve of this "Program for Stimulating Thought."

Comments were heard several times during the evening suggesting that
the evaluations not be turned in to the library but sent directly to Supervisor Bonelli's office. Some were sent directly to Mr. Bonelli's office along
with innumerable critical letters of complaint, nearly all with similar
wording. The library administration had been keeping Mr. Bonelli well-
informed of the situation. It was clear to the administration also at this
point that something had to be done to inform "the silent majority" of this
attempt to restrict its free access to library materials. The November 5,
1970 *San Gabriel Valley Tribune* carried a letter to the editor from Mrs. Jean
Stratton. She writes in part:

> Our library is showing propaganda films to the High School students while
> the librarian proudly wears a Peace symbol. These films are promoting
> socialism and are completely anti-American. . . . Another film, produced in a
> Communist country, shows the joy of communal living and how the world
> falls apart when you don't live this way. . . . The district attorney's office told
> me if I didn't like the films I should run for librarian and pick the kind of films
> I like.

In an effort to tell the story as it really is, Jim Donahue, a reporter from
the *San Gabriel Tribune,* contacted both the Young Adult and Audio-
Visual Coordinators and printed valid statements from both of them on
Friday, November 13, 1970.

> Mrs. Harriett Covey said one purpose of the film programs is to attract young
> adults to the library to make them aware of the resources available through
> the public libraries.

> Mrs. Covey added that the film programs, like similar Young Adult book
> discussions, are designed "to stimulate thought about all points of view . . .
> and to provide a forum where young adults can express their thoughts, ideas,
> and reactions in a relaxed, non-schoolroom atmosphere." She explained that
> an objective of the film programs is to "examine, not teach cultural and
> personal values. Thus each program offers different themes."

> "The choice of films shown has no relationship to the discussion leader's
> personal view, just as good library book selection cannot be limited by these
> but must reflect the total community," she said.

> Mrs. Covey noted that librarians are advised that "the discussion leader's
> personal views should not be reflected in the discussion; his job is to draw out
> all sides of an issue or question to present as many aspects of it as possible.

> The county library does not buy films specifically produced for school curric-
> ulum use, and titles from the film collection (there are 1,100) are not available
> for classroom, instructional use or for school assemblies. . . . According to
> Ronald Sigler . . . the popularity of the motion picture film program is
> increasing each year. The present countywide circulation is between three to
> four thousand films per month.

> "After a comprehensive screening and evaluation process by the audio-visual
> staff, including downtown and regional audio-visual librarians, Sigler selects
> films for inclusion in the library's collection."

"Films must be well organized cinematic presentations with good photography and sound which complements the visual. We insist on high creative and artistic quality. We try to avoid films with a strong bias," Sigler stated.

The staff also attempts to acquire films which will be of general public interest and suitable for use in any of the 500 library programs sponsored throughout the county each month.

The *San Gabriel Valley Tribune* also reported on a preview session it sponsored involving several businessmen and an educator. In addition, in late November, the library inadvertently discovered that a showing of several of the films had been scheduled in a West Covina Police Dept. meeting room by a gentleman who identified himself to a librarian as "The Watchdog of the American Legion."

For the second time, the library agreed to meet with the group in Hacienda Heights in the hope of coming to some reasonable understanding. William S. Geller, County Librarian, met with the group early in December and made an arduous and futile attempt to reason with them. He absolutely refused to remove the films in question. He also refused to provide lists of staff names, addresses, and position titles demanded by the group unless the demand was made in writing. No such demand was received. (County Counsel has ruled that this is public information; however, *only* this information about an employee is available, as a matter of public record.)

Attendance at the final program on December 11 at Hacienda Library was heavily populated with adults. *Parable* was shown and there was both pro and con participation by the group, including area ministers. Some adult interpretations of *Parable* and *Rock in the Road* were incredible in comparison with the refreshing comments from the valiantly participating young adults. In summation, a group of young people who were members of a confirmation class from a local church, attended the final program and made these comments in a letter published in the *Hacienda Highlander* on December 21, 1970:

> We enjoyed and appreciated the films and the opportunity for discussion. Unfortunately, we felt that the discussion was hampered by unnecessary and unhelpful adult comments and criticisms. It appeared to us from some of the adult comments that we youth are viewed as immature, unreliable, and incapable of forming intelligent and responsible opinions of what we see.

Just below this letter was one signed by W. J. Chapman, the husband of one of the original "two ladies" referred to earlier. He opens:

> If the several films I have seen so far are typical of the films that the County Library is actively encouraging young people of high school age to view through the Young Adult Film Program in the Hacienda Heights location as well as other locations in the county, then it appears as though those who would have us abandon the spiritual, moral and political heritage passed on to us by America's founding fathers have now achieved a position of controlling influence in our county library.

The move to spread those views of the library and incite public opinion throughout the county had begun earlier. The *Los Angeles Times* had reported on December 7, 1970, the leaders of the 8000 member conservative United Republicans of California (known as UROC) met in Los Angeles on December 6, 1970. The last paragraph of the *Times* article reads as follows:

> And they charged that the Los Angeles County Library has some films in the loan collection made in Poland and Czechoslovakia that "could result in the corruption of youths, causing young people to reject our way of life, our free enterprise system and religion."

Early in January, a member of the Republican Women's Club of Hacienda Heights, Leone Chapman (Mrs. W. J.) "researched" a two-page report on the Hacienda Heights programs. It was included under the heading "Education" in a newsletter from the club dated January 1971. The introduction states:

> Our Board is recommending this be sent to the Presidents of every Republican Women's Club in the Los Angeles County.

Mrs. Chapman indicts the library and its program with the following:

> The reaction of the great majority of the people viewing these films ranges from disbelief and shock to utter disgust, outrage, and anger. There are two primary concerns expressed by those who object to these films. They are: (1) What it may do to the young people's understanding of the theological, philosophical, and political values underlying our American heritage and (2) the appalling, shameful waste of tax money.

She reinforces her reasoning by pinpointing the "subject content of the films" as "un-American and appear to be based more on atheistic, socialistic philosophy of life." She goes on to say that "Many of the films were produced in Communist countries. . . . We all know that these countries which are under the complete subjugation of the USSR do not produce anything not designed to promote the Russian Communist goal of world revolution and Communist world domination." She then attacks the library by stating:

> In view of the communists' stated intentions, we do not understand how the county library can justify the purchase of films from communist countries to use in indoctrinating our young people.

Primary charges against specific titles include:

> . . . there is a film entitled *Little White Crimes* produced in Canada which implies, or gives the impression, that all businessmen are dishonest, immoral; they are blackmailers, cheaters, and all have mistresses supported by padded expense accounts. . . . Another film called *Duet,* produced in Communist Czechoslovakia, is a cartoon about two fictional neighbors. . . . The implication, or inference, in this film appears to be one of presenting advantages of communal living over that of the philosophy of free enterprise and the right to private property.

Her concluding paragraph most significantly states:

> We urge all you Federated members to initiate vigorous action to get these films out of the library system. They serve no constructive purpose, and can in fact do irreparable damage to our youth. In making this statement we refer to a particular segment of the library film inventory and are not condemning the entire film library. . . .

As a follow-up suggestion, these comments were added at the bottom of the page:

> If this is news to you and you would like to see a sample of these films that are shown to our young people, try to attend the showing of *Rock in the Road* and *The Hangman.* Both of these films will be shown at the Montebello Regional Library . . . on January 13 . . . On February 4, at the Huntington Park Library . . ., there will be a showing of **I Am Joaquín, Weapons of Gordon Parks, Black and White, Uptight,* and *Home of the Brave.*
>
> For further information call Leone Chapman, 300-6658.

The war on removal of the films was launched and spreading throughout the country. On Thursday, January 21, 1971, County Librarian William S. Geller was asked by Supervisor Frank Bonelli to attend a meeting the following morning. Supervisor Bonelli appeared convinced that the Mesdames Chapman & Stratton must be correct: the Library really must be showing lewd films. In a staff newsletter, Mr. Geller aptly describes the occurrence:

> After a somewhat heated discussion, I was asked by Mr. Bonelli if I would "review" the films complained against, taking them out of circulation during the process.
>
> Considering the ladies' arguments against the 19 films, I stated that, by their lights, something must be wrong with *all* of our 1,100 titles, therefore, I was taking all titles from circulation for review. This seemed to disturb all those present, when I said it would take us a year to accomplish this. We left the meeting at this point.
>
> On Monday morning, January 25, I met with our Administrative Council and discussed the situation. Its members supported me in my decision to withhold circulation of all films and instructions to all community libraries were so issued.

---

*I Am Joaquín (col. 20 min. Valdez/El Teatro Campesino, Canyon Cinema) A powerful and controversial film produced in Fresno by El Teatro Campesino, an independent Chicano theater company which grew out of the Delano grape strike. It is a filmic interpretation of the Corky Gonzales historical poem of the Chicano experience dramatized with an angry pride and a cry for justice. It was blamed by some California officials as one of the forces that helped to spark the East Los Angeles riots. It naturally became the "19th" film in the group to be indicted.

By noon my phone was ringing constantly with patrons calling in to protest my action. The gist of their complaint was: "How can two women dictate what anyone else wished to see?" (This was exactly what I anticipated.)

At a brief meeting with Mr. Bonelli, Mr. Geller decided to release all film titles for circulation except the 19 originally indicted. A re-evaluation would be arranged with the Chairmen of the Regional Library Councils and members of the staff. Mr. Geller goes on to say:

> The advice of the council members was sought, as you know I alone have the legal responsibility to acquire or discard library materials. . . . Mr. Bonelli has accepted my recommendation that we use this *modus operandi* as a means of releasing the 19 films.

Although the authority to acquire or remove library materials is delegated to members of his staff, Mr. Geller firmly believes that all library materials are subject to re-evaluation in order to insure that the material reflects the public's need to know. His request for re-evaluation is viewed as a positive re-inforcement rather than a question of the judgment or professional integrity of his staff.

It was also obvious to Mr. Geller that the public had to be informed. During the ensuing week, five television stations and four radio stations interviewed both Mr. Geller and Mrs. Stratton. Some of the TV coverage included film clips from *Duet, Rock in the Road,* and *I Am Joaquin.* The ABC News telecast with Harry Reasoner was network and provided national coverage.

Well over a hundred letters were received from local library patrons, and nationally from librarians, film distributors, and producers. Many letters to newpapers pro and con were published and editorials were written as well. The great majority (the ratio was 70:1) were supportive of the library and the films and programs in question. Many were critical of Mr. Geller's actions.

A letter was received by Mr. Bonelli from a disgruntled local pro-ducer-distributor whose "Americana" films failed to qualify for inclusion in the collection during evaluation by the A-V librarians and staff.

An ad hoc committee made up of the chairmen of the Regional Library Councils and the administrative staff met on January 29, 1971, to screen four of the most criticized titles, *Parable, I Am Joaquin, Little White Crimes,* and *Duet.* Mr. Geller briefly presented the background for the complaints against each film. I, in my role as A-V Coordinator, then explained in detail County Library film evaluation procedures, described the use of the evaluation form, the pre-screening process by the audio-visual librarians, and the evaluation meeting. Here, all the films are evaluated and discussed by audio-visual specialists and other librarians who may utilize them in programs. The group present was asked to fill out the same evaluation form regularly used by the library. I commented on the intent of the producer before each film was shown. After all of the films were screened, discussion time was devoted to each title. A motion by a Regional Council chairman was proposed and seconded that supported continued use of the nineteen films in question and their immediate return to circulation. Thus the eight day stay of the "Los Angeles 19" was over and the films were returned to service by Mr. Geller on February 2, 1971.

From a previously cited staff newsletter, Mr. Geller commented on the events:

> In essence, the public airing of this issue of intellectual freedom was salutary; I quickly learned of our support. It is necessary to take a stand in this increasingly colder climate, and I am hopeful that we shall emerge from this battle stronger than ever.

> I want to assure all of you that I support the basic reason for the Library—the presentation of information on all sides of an issue to the best of our ability to do so. We owe it to the citizenry we serve—that each one must be able to obtain the information he seeks without any consideration of what his beliefs are.

In a public newsletter released on February 2, 1971, Supervisor Frank Bonelli released the following statement. He said, in part:

> Some constituents in my district have lodged complaints against certain film titles being shown at discussion groups planned for young adults of high school age. It appears to me that there is a sincere and genuine belief by those who have complained about the films that the County Library Department is, perhaps unwittingly, promoting a particular point of view by these films and discussion groups.

> I believe that it is my responsibility as a member of the Board of Supervisors to investigate all complaints about County services in my district—whether it be a road matter, a flood control problem, or the activities of the County Library Department.

> In furtherance of this principle, I request William S. Geller, the County Librarian, to have the films in question re-evaluated by the chairman to the eight regional library councils. . . .

> Mr. Geller has advised me that he has accepted the recommendation of the regional library councils. In view of his responsibilities as County Librarian and the responsibility of the membership of the councils, this action appears reasonable.

> However, I would admonish the County Public Library Department to take all necessary steps to insure that no member of the staff promotes or tries to promote any doctrinal or partisan viewpoint in any of his job-related activities. It is the library's responsibility to provide information on all sides of socially significant issues so that individual patrons may arrive at their own decisions.

We are continuing to document this story (now in March) and we're still receiving letters. Mrs. Jean Stratton takes a different approach from her earlier letter in the *San Gabriel Valley Tribune* on March 3, 1971 and she writes in part:

> The Council Library is advertising and promoting film programs for the high school children. Each film deals with one aspect of our society. These films bring out only the negative side. The library has censored out anything

positive. In the discussion that follows the showing of each film the librarian asks leading questions bringing out any negativism that the student has missed. If in turn the student tries to bring out a positive issue, the librarian tries to prove the student wrong. This has been observed by many adults. The library is enforcing censorship by not allowing both sides of an issue to be presented. This is illegal according to the Library Bill of Rights.

The county library has many films which are of poor technical quality. In a letter to Supervisor Bonelli, one police chief stated that it was a waste of taxpayers' monies when it is spent on such poor quality material. They are poorly produced and have no educational value.

As taxpayers we feel that we have the right to request that our tax dollars are more wisely spent. We do not wish to censor what others may see, but neither should the library force censorship on us. The Public Library of Los Angeles County has been enforcing censorship for many years. We are going to continue our fight against our censorship and so will the hundreds of others who are concerned.

The "ladies" and others like them will continue to write and fight but the County Library and its professional staff will continue to provide film programs for all ages on any issue without bias of any kind as it has in the past. The library will also continue to provide the best in its professional judgement of the "new media" without fear of censorship for the ordeal of the "Los Angeles 19" is over, and as in all good public libraries throughout our nation, the words of President John F. Kennedy re-echo:

> If this nation is to be wise as well as strong, if we are to achieve our destiny, then we need more new ideas for more wise men reading more good books in more public libraries. These libraries should be open to all—except the censor. We must know all the facts and hear all the alternatives and listen to all the criticisms. Let us welcome controversial books and controversial authors. For the Bill of Rights is the guardian of our security as well as our Liberty.

REFERENCES

1. The County Librarian is responsible directly to the Board of Supervisors and specifically Supervisor Bonelli. There is no Library Board of Trustees.

2. The Regional Library Councils were established in 1959 by the Board of Supervisors to serve in an advisory capacity to the Board of Supervisors and the County Librarian in matters of policy and operation. There are representatives from each of the cities and communities served, appointed by the City Councils or County Board of Supervisors.

Radical Mediacy

by Don Roberts

Carrot and stick media is one of the public library's paradoxes. It is true there are many fine film and audio collections in libraries around the country, some even transcending the Disney world of second rate establishment values and conventional techniques. But the profession has steadfastly refused (even with some degree of clever flirtation) to face its shallow attitudes toward the more serious aspects of non-print development. "Primacy of Print" still rules our hearts, and the majority of library activity is dedicated to the furtherance of this rear-view mirror supremacy.

Not surprising then is the "radical/liberal" librarians' acceptance of this view. Library activists are still notoriously print-bound. For those of us who have fought to get the "alternative press" into libraries by competing for funds which would have otherwise gone to establishment, mass consumption print, it is disconcerting to see the newer media wipe out the small gains made in the acquisition of independent and radical press publications. In this period of soaring costs and budget cuts, the specter of another superficial, "establishment" competitor is a bit much!

Thus ALA's Social Responsibilities Roundtable and other liberal librarians have not been active in professional concerns about media: committee work, access (e.g., bibliographic/mediagraphic control), standards, education, communication theory, communication satellites, censorship, etc. One of my recent memories was the inability of some audio-visual committee members of ALA to decipher the acronym "SRRT"! No wonder, since the rank and file members of SRRT are still consistently preoccupied with tending ALA's voracious paper-maché machine.

The one exception to this has been the sidepocket issue of video, which has found its way away from SRRT into the Information Science and Automation Division. But my fear is that we may find the future of video in ALA dominated by apolitical, non-aesthetic types who will infect the most important communication medium of our time with a technological surrealism. A comparable example is the Association For Educational Communications and Technology (AECT), which is pervaded by a kind of hard-hat realism where technology reigns supreme and the most serious talk about censorship is centered on the copyright controversy.

Many of us in media have been alarmed by the NCLIS's ignorance and lack of concern for non-print and mass communications. The tenor of this group is so totally establishment that they ignore the manipulation of the profession by the publishing industry. Indeed, the Commission held hearings throughout the entire United States before they discovered the existence of the national media organization, AECT. Information Science (so called) seems to be their major concern, and one can foresee the computerization and compartmentalization of print into sprawling, OK cartels of approved information as a "reasonable" outcome of Gerald Ford's acceptance speech. White House Conference on Libraries? Sure thing, baby, and just wait 'til you meet the new Secretary of HEW and the Historian of the Library of Congress:

"And furthermore, we promise to recycle 50-55% of all your discards into new print. And I categorically deny that we will allow the total domination of your profession by the computerization of print."

"Thank you, Mr. President, but what about the domination of the information satellites by the military, police and big business?"

"I'm sorry, but time is up. Please await a further communication on this. In fact, we will send out a printout next week if you will leave your name and address."

The only counter I see to this is the growing concern librarians have for *community* information systems and their increasing cynicism about the incestuous relationship between the profession and big publishers. Support and participation in "alternative information nets" has grown to some extent. Although the candidates for high ALA offices still mouth the truisms of the last decade, there is a healthy skepticism of the status quo knowledge transfer empire. One thing which is certain is that both radical and mainline librarians are unwilling to face the issue of non-print. And it may be that they will refuse to do this until the extinction of their very jobs!

Librarians and other educators have done much to perpetuate disastrous standards for the populace by washing their elitist hands of the contemporary dilemmas of modern communication and insisting upon molds more appropriate to earlier communication grids.

A veritable "Pandora's box" is upon us if we open ourselves up to media. We have not begun to consider the patron's needs until we respond to the sensory learning experiences of the individual person. We have never known censorship problems to the extent that we will encounter them with the compelling power of film, video and audio to arouse response. We must broaden that old slogan Freedom-To-Read into FREEDOM TO KNOW. We won't have to tangle with the ultimate problems in information handling if we do not open the "box." Why not keep it closed?

Then, we will become more obsolete than we are, the dehumanization of our library environments will become more complete (even less sensory, certainly), and we will sell out the more crucial media to cartels and government agencies. And this will happen even with continued and insistent support for alternative publishers, the underground press, etc.

One way we can begin to turn this around (because to give primary support to establishment non-print producers is to parallel the mistakes made with the publishing/library complex in the past) is to support the alternative non-print producers. Listed below are alternative media producers whose materials can be previewed, purchased and supported.

If their films, audio cassettes, filmstrips, videotapes are not in your collection, check preview slips to see *why* they were rejected. If the reasons were political, moral, or in just plain ignorance of the medium, have them previewed again. If they're not there, send for catalogs. Remember, alternative media producers face the same problems as small presses; their transience is even more common. Please notify me of any address changes or recommendations for the list. It is still incomplete and I would like to update it if possible.

RADICAL MEDIACY

Altern. Environmental Futures
316 W. 88th St.
New York, NY 10024

Amer. Friends Service Comm.
112 South 16 St.
Philadelphia, PA 19102

Anargyros Film Library
1815 Fairburn Ave.
Los Angeles, CA 90025

Ant Farm
247 Gate 5 Road
Sausalito, CA 94965

Route 2 Box 41
Angleton, TX 77515

Anti-Defamation League of
B'nai B'rith
315 Lexington Ave.
New York, NY 10016

Antioch Television
Dept. Instructional Systems
Antioch College
Yellow Springs, OH 45387

Appalshop, Inc.
Box 743
Whitesburg, KY 41858

April Video Cooperative
Box AK
Downsville, NY 13755

Atlantis Productions
850 Thousand Oaks Blvd.
Thousand Oaks, CA 91360

Ballis Associates
4696 North Millbrook
Fresno, CA 93726

Black Box
1346 Connecticut Ave.
Room 817
Washington, D.C. 20036

Blue Ridge Films
9003 Glenbrook Rd.
Fairfax, VA 22030

Bowling Green Films
Box 384-D
Hudson, NY 12534

Stan and Jane Brakhage
Box 170
Rollinsville, CO 80474

CBC Learning Systems
P.O. Box 500, Terminal A
Toronto, Ontario, Canada

CRM Educational Films
Del Mar, CA 92014

Canyon Cinema Co-op
Room 220
Industrial Center Bldg.
Sausalito, CA 94965

Center For The Study of
Democratic Institutions
P.O. Box 4446
Santa Barbara, CA 93103

Chamba Educ. Film Service
P.O. Box U
Brooklyn, NY 11201

Circle One
1456 E. Magnolia Ave.#112
St. Paul, MN 55106

Community Video Center
Div. Community Education
Federal City College
1411 K St. N.W.
Washington, D.C. 20005

Current Affairs
24 Danbury Rd.
Wilton, CT 06897

Denoyer-Geppert
5235 Ravenswood Ave.
Chicago, IL 60640

Denver Comm. Video Center
1400 Lafayette St.
Denver, CO 80218

Earth News Service
24 California St.
Suite 400
San Francisco, CA 94111

Eccentric Circle Cinema
P.O. Box 1481
Evanston, IL 60204

Environmental Communications
62 Windward Ave.
Venice, CA 90291

Experimental TV Center Ltd.
164 Court St.
Binghamton, NY 13901

Feminist History Research
Project
P.O. Box 1156
Topanga, CA 90290

Filmmakers Cooperative
175 Lexington Ave.
New York, NY 10016

Flower Films
11305Q - Ranch Rd.
Austin TX 78757

Global Village
454 Broome St.
New York, NY 10012

Great Atlantic Radio
Conspiracy
2743 Maryland Ave.
Baltimore, MD 21218

Grove Press Films
53 E. 11th St.
New York, NY 10003

HAF/Alternatives on Film
311 Spruce St.
San Francisco, CA 94118

Hartley Productions, Inc.
Cat Rock Road
Cos Cob, CT 06807

Herstory Films
137 E. 13th St.
New York, NY 10003

Impact Films
144 Bleecker St.
New York, NY 10012

KVST - TV
1136 N. Highland Ave.
Hollywood, CA 90038

Kartemquin Films Ltd.
1901 W. Wellington
Chicago, IL 60657

Lindisfree
50 Fish Cove Rd.
Southampton, NY 11968

Living Library Corp.
P.O. Box 5405
Linden Hill Station
Flushing, NY 11354

Martha Stuart
Communications, Inc.
66 Bank St.
New York, NY 10014

Mass Media Ministries
2116 North Charles
Baltimore, MD 21218

Media Access Center
% Portola Institute
1115 Merrill St.
Menlo Park, CA 94025

Meditapes
Thomas More Association
180 North Wabash
Chicago, IL 60601

Mission Hill Video
41 Calumet St.
Mission Hill, MA 02120

Montage Distributors
152 W. 42nd St.
New York, NY 10036

Monument Film Corp.
43 West 16th St.
New York, NY 10011

Multi Media Resource Ctr.
540 Powell St.
San Francisco, CA 94108

Museum of Conceptual Art
75 Third St.
San Francisco, CA 94103

Nat. Council of Churches
Broadcasting & Film Comm.
475 Riverside Dr.
New York, NY 10027

Nat. Film Board of Canada
1 Lombard St.
Toronto, Ontario, Canada

Nat. Organization for
Women (NOW)
5 South Wabash, Suite 1615
Chicago, IL 60603

New Day Films
267 W. 25th St.
Franklin Lakes, NJ 07417

New Distribution Co.
Devensky
418 E. 9th St.
New York, NY 10009

New Film Co., Inc.
331 Newberry St.
Boston, MA 02115

New Line
% Video Free America
442 Shotwell St.
San Francisco, CA 94110

New Line Cinema
853 Broadway, 16th Floor
New York, NY 10003

New World Productions
Box 881
Lawrence, KS 66044

New Yorker Films
43 West 61st St.
New York, NY 10023

Newsreel
26 W. 20th St.
New York, NY 10011

4418 P. St. N.W.
Washington, D.C. 20007

Non Media Co.
Box 750
Port Chester, NY 10573

Odeon Films, Inc.
1619 Broadway
New York, NY 10019

Open Circle Cinema
P.O. Box 315
Franklin Lakes, NJ 07417

Open Circuit TV
Box 5463
Seattle, WA 98105

Pacific Street Films
280 Clinton St.
Brooklyn NY 11201

Pacifica Tape Library
5316 Venice Blvd.
Los Angeles, CA 90019

Pennebaker, Inc.
56 W. 45th St.
New York, NY 10036

People's Video Theater
544 Sixth Ave.
New York, NY 10011

Pictura Films
43 W. 16th St.
New York, NY 10011

Point Foundation
Box 99554
San Francisco, CA 94109

Public Service Video
New City School
400 Sibley St.
St. Paul, MN 55101

Queer Blue Light
Gay Revolution Video
Box 410
Old Chelsea Station
New York, NY 10011

Radio Free People
133 Mercer St.
New York, NY 10012

Raindance Radical Software
Box 630
San Francisco, CA 94101

Red Ball Films
Box 298
Village Station
New York, NY 10014

The Rest of the News
306 E. State St.
Ithaca, NY 14850

See Saw Films
P.O. Box 262
Palo Alto, CA 94302

Smith/Mattingly
Productions, Ltd.
310 South Fairfax St.
Alexandria, VA 22314

Source Coalition
2115 S. Street N.W.
Washington, D.C. 20008

Third World Newsreel
26 W. 20th St.
New York, NY 10011

Tricontinental Film Ctr.
333 Sixth Ave.
New York, NY 10014

Union Resource Exchange
Network
Antioch College
Yellow Springs, OH 45387

Univ. of Calif. Extension
Media Center
2223 Fulton St.
Berkeley, CA 94720

Vedo Films
85 Longview Rd.
Port Washington, NY 11050

Video Access Center
Box 8690, Station H
Vancouver, B.C., Canada

Video Access Center
5th Floor, Rarig Center
Studio A
Minneapolis, MN 55455

Video Free America
1948 Fell St.
San Francisco, CA 94117

Video Freex
Maple Tree Farm
Lanesville, NY 12450

Videomaker
132 S. Washington
Cookeville, TN 38501

Videopolis
% Anda Korstes
2550 N. Halsted
Chicago, IL 60614

Videotape Network
115 E. 62nd St.
New York, NY 10021

Video Women's Catalogue
Women & Video
C 109A Charles St. W.
Toronto, Ontario, Canada

Videoworks
Univ. of Arizona
Tucson, AZ 85721

Voodoo Video
Box 124
Manhattanville Station
New York, NY 10027

Washington Comm. Video Ctr.
Box 3157
Washington, D.C. 20010

Wombat Productions, Inc.
87 Main St.
Hastings-on-Hudson, NY 10706

Women History Project
Valentine Hertz/Open Studio
KQED
1011 Bryant St.
San Francisco, CA 94103

Women's Film Co-op
% Valley Women's Center
200 Main St.
Northampton, MA 01060

Women's Involvement
Programme/Suite 309
341 Bloor St.
Toronto, Ontario, Canada

Women's Oral Herstory Library
2325 Oak St.
Berkeley, CA 94708

Women's Radio Workshop
Station WDET
5035 Woodward
Detroit, MI 48202

Yellow Ball Workshop
62 Tarbell Ave.
Lexington, MA 02173

Young Director's Center
267 W. 25th St.
New York, NY 10011

Young Filmaker's Foundation
310 W. 53rd St.
New York, NY 10019

Zodiac News Service
950 Howard St.
San Francisco, CA 94103

"Printism" and Non-Print Censorship

by Don Roberts

Printism: The notion that the print medium is superior to other media. The printist unwittingly or overtly subjugates non-print media to print media.

I became interested in the subject of non-print censorship while teaching an intellectual freedom course in a library school in the late sixties. The students soon pointed out that there was nothing in the syllabus on non-print, and that the books and articles on the course bibliography didn't mention it. We started looking into this and found that there was practically nothing on the subject and the other library schools which devoted a course to the subject didn't mention it either!

Checking back into the history of the American Library Association it was discovered that the first awareness of audiovisuals occurred around the start of World War I, and there had been some attempts at committee activity in the mid-twenties. But it wasn't until after World War II that audiovisuals were given any real credence in the organization. In 1939 ALA (American Library Association) took an official stand on print censorship; but it was another twelve years before the Association added a footnote to the Library Bill of Rights to say that more than print was at stake. In 1967 this (slim) awareness was finally incorporated into the text of the document itself.

If you check back in the history of audiovisual committee activity you find no awareness of censorship issues (at least they are unrecorded). I have not found any record of audiovisual professionals pressuring ALA to incorporate the scanty footnote of 1951 into the Library Bill of Rights, for example. Nor do I find any pressure having been applied by audiovisual people to see that young adults and children have equal access to the minimal media materials which do exist in libraries. The non-activity aspect is equally true for the Division of Audiovisual Instruction and its successor the AECT did not have an official intellectual freedom committee until last year, and this was brought about largely through the consideration of copyright issues.

I am not saying that all professionals who have had concerns about this have remained silent. There are brief mentions here and there throughout the "literature," and several people have even taken some risks in their collections! But in crisscrossing the country as I do, and visiting libraries and school media centers, there is no doubt that prior censorship is very much with us in the selection of non-print, and that there is a double standard in the way professionals apply awareness of intellectual freedom.

My study last fall and in subsequent follow-up has proven that there is a strong disregard and lack of respect for non-print media in the profession. The awareness of censorship is so integral to the print mentality, so biased toward the "intellectual" as a print consumer, that the very definitions (OIF's *Intellectual Freedom Manual* and the "Intellectual Freedom Newsletter") and organizations (Freedom to Read Foundation) simply extend the problem of "printism" as a deterrent to openness toward the "newer" media.

If you check through the periodical literature you find five cases of non-print censorship mentioned in the last twenty years! Only one of the standard books on the subject has given any mention of this at all, and my suspicion is that this occurred because the author was on the Intellectual Freedom Committee at the time the first major case of film censorship surfaced in ALA. The fact of the matter is that non-print media is far more explosive (potentially) than print. The absence of cases in the literature and in intellectual freedom activities is extremely suspect to say the least.

There is no doubt in my mind why this is so. The censorship of non-book material is the 'bete noire' of intellectual freedom. All we have to do is look at the way libraries have dealt with print materials which have strong and frank illustrations, (e.g., the illustrated version of *Joy of Sex*, or some of the more explosive periodicals ("underground") on radical politics). Imagine films, videotapes and other materials being previewed (and purchased!) which would depict subjects which are all but forbidden if they are even visualized or made "suggestive" of their sensual or political impact in print!

I know all the rationalizations as well as anyone. I've been there, from the offices of ALA to the homeville public library: budget, (potential) damage, the Board, the this and that are always alluded to. Typically these rationalizations are based upon unexamined and unfair attitudes (fears), perpetrated by "printists" for reasons which they would rather not examine.

The majority of the population communicates verbally (or through electric electronic networks). Meanwhile libraries continue to spend ninety to ninety-nine per cent of their materials budget on print (the one to nine percent spent on non-print is typically spent on conservative, unimaginative material), while they expend much larger amounts of money (relative to non-print expenditures) on new forms of print (microfiche, computerized data bases), expensive technological processes to make print and new print "flow" (computerized technical services) or for technological surveillance (e.g., "Checkpoint" and closed circuit television). The Orwellian extension of keeping print dominant is staggering.

If we are going to arrest this domination and integrate media in the resources of our libraries and our profession these are the steps which I feel must be taken:

(1) Face the inherent "printism," the assumptions of which pervade our literature, job descriptions, library school education, policies, budgets, standards (guidelines) and basic attitudes; not to mention our intellectual freedom documents.

(2) Insist that bibliographic access be provided on an equal basis for all library materials.

(3) Parallel the richness, diversity and *controversy* of our print collections in non-print, and see to it that there is an equitable division of materials budgets to facilitate this.

(4) Defeat the double standard which now exists in the application of the Library Bill of Rights to library materials and facilities (e.g., individual access, age restrictions, special fees, etc.).

(5) Adopt technological standards to enable quality access (playback) of the media, and prevent the censorship through playback distortion of formats which depend upon equipment to disseminate the message faithfully.

(6) Plan our services and architectures to enable the present and future technological availability of the non-print formats in our buildings and in the surrounding community.

If we cannot face these issues then the discussions of "intellectual freedom" will continue to have a hollow ring, and libraries will avoid their prime responsibility in the late twentieth century. How can we have the gall to discuss "intellectual freedom" today without an honest appraisal of where the library stands in the communications spectrum?

INDEX

Index

Compiled by Miranda d'Ancona

Academy for Educational Development, 29
AEG-Telefunken, 241–2
Alternate Media Center (New York University), 9, 309, 311
American Association of School Librarians (AASL), 249, 282
American Film Festival: The Best of 19– (EFLA), 91
American Libraries, 29
American Library Association (ALA), 23, 77, 88, 90, 131, 256, 282–3, 286, 293, 306, 323, 324, 330–1
accreditation, 286
cataloging, 256, 265
standards, 23, 29, 288, 302
American Record Guide, 70
American Sign Language (Ameslan), 26
Ampex Corp., 210, 220
Anglo-American Cataloging Rules (AACR), 10, 256–64, 267
Anthology Film Archives, 140
Antonioni, Michelangelo, 137
Arlen, Michael J., 47
Arnheim, Rudolf, 106
Art and Education (Sir Herbert Read), 32
Art Libraries Society of North America (ARLIS/NA), 101
Art Libraries Society of the United Kingdom (ARLIS/UK), 101
Asheim, Lester, 41–51
Aslib, 101
Association for College and Research Libraries (ACRL), 29, 100
Association for Educational Communications and Technology (AECT), 249, 256–60, 262, 263, 282, 323–4, 330

Audio, 9, 73, 186
cassettes, 74, 111–8, 218–9, 221–4, 234, 325–9
equipment, 208–10, 212–9, 220–30
glossary of terms, 228–9
See also Oral history; Record players; Recordings; Slide-tape programs; Tape recorders
Audiovisual equipment, 49, 58–9, 62–3, 80, 162, 163, 169, 176–7, 203–19, 231–5
maintenance and operation, 232, 236–40
See also Audio; Film; Filmstrips; Slides; Tape recorders; Video
Audio-Visual Media and Materials (Brown, Lewis & Harcleroad), 289
Autos, Autos, Everywhere, 315

Baillie, Bruce, 140, 141, 145
Bancroft Library, The, 120–4
Banfield, Edward, 18
Bartlett, Freude, 140
Bartlett, Scott, 140, 145
Battle of Algiers (Gillo Pontecorvo), 135
Baum, Willa, 119–24
Belson, Jordan, 140
Bergen Community College, Library and Learning Resources Center, 73–4
Bergman, Ingmar, 137
Bergvahl, Gunnar, 244
Berman, Sanford, 265–72
Big Sur Audio Tape Catalog, 73
Black and White, 319
BOCES, 13
Bonelli, Frank, 314, 316, 319–21

Booklist, 70, 71, 74, 89, 90
Books, 8–11, 12–21, 23, 29, 31–2, 35,
    39, 42, 44–5, 46, 49–51, 56, 59,
    90, 101, 138, 149–50, 176
    paperback, 14, 16
    See also Print
Books in Print, 72, 88
Boston University, School of Public
    Communication, 106
Boyle, Deirdre, 3–11, 241–5
Bradbury, Ray, 36
Brakhage, Stan, 140, 141, 143, 145,
    146
Brawley, Paul, 90
Brown, James, 9, 289
Bruck, Jr., Jerry, 85
Buñuel, Luis, 145

Cable television (CATV), 154–60,
    177, 307–11
Caldecott Award, 90–1
Canadian Library Association (CLA),
    256
Carothers, J. C., 32, 36–7
Carpenter, Ted, 9
Carrels, 231, 233–4
Cartravision, 242
Case Western Reserve University,
    294
Cassette Information Services, 70
Castro Street (Bruce Baillie), 145
Cataloging, 52, 55, 149, 256–64,
    265–72, 273–5, 304
    American rules, 257, 258–61, 262
    audiocassettes, 115, 121–2
    British rules, 257, 258–61, 262
    Canadian rules, 257, 258–61, 262–3
    Dewey Decimal classification, 105,
        266
    Library of Congress, 74, 119, 267
    oral history collections, 121–2
    sample entries, 268–71
    slides, 103–5
*Cataloging, Processing, Administering
    AV Materials,* 275
Catholic University, 294
Cayard, Bruce, 131
Censorship, 10, 16, 308–9, 311, 323–5
    Los Angeles "19," 312–22
Center for Library Studies (Kent
    State University), 203, 219
Center for Understanding Media,
    130

Center for Visual Literacy (University
    of Rochester), 101
Chapman, Leone, 318–9
Chien Andalou, Un (Luis Buñuel), 145
Children's Film Theater, 130–1
Choice, 74
Chopra, Joyce, 141
Chronicle of Higher Education, 45
Churchill, Robert, 83
Cinema Journal, 138
Cleveland Museum of Art, 103
Cloke, William, 183–5
Cohen, Abraham, 14–5
Colleges. *See* Libraries; individual
    universities
Color Slide for Teaching Art History (Pa-
    tricia Sloane), 105
Columbia University, 286, 297, 311
Commission on Instructional Tech-
    nology, 12
Communication
    by audiovisual media, 4–7, 25–7,
        41–51, 69, 74–5, 99–107, 154–9,
        175, 251, 280, 324, 331
    by print, 4–5, 22–3, 25–7, 33–9, 46
    languages of, 4, 50
    libraries as centers of, 41, 175–80,
        324
    transportation theory of, 6
Community antenna television. *See*
    Cable television (CATV)
Comput-Her Baby, 315
Conrad, Tony, 140
Consortiums, 80–1
Contagious Imbecility (Jean Stafford),
    28, 31
Coolidge, Martha, 141
Copy Guard Encoder, 84
Copying, 14, 83–4, 116
Copyright, 102–3, 157–8, 323
Council for Basic Education, 28
Council of National Library Associ-
    ations, 101
Council on Library Resources, 10, 73,
    104
Covey, Harriett, 314, 316
*Curriculum for the Seventies: An Agenda
    for Invention* (Arthur Foshay),
    254–5
Curtis, David, 140

Dale, Walter, 308
Danish, Roy, 17

Danmarks Bibliotekskole (Copenhagen), 61
Dark Ghetto (Kenneth Clark), 18
Debasement of School Libraries, The (Harry Foster), 28
Debes, John L., 25–7
Deren, Maya, 145
DeSciora, Edward, 308
Developing Multimedia Libraries (Warren Hicks and Alma Tillin), 274, 289
Dewey Decimal classification system, 105, 266
Directory of Cassette Producers, 70
Directory of Spoken-Voice Audio Cassettes, 114
Dog Star Man (Stan Brakhage), 145
Dolby system, 113, 218–9, 223
Donnell Library, 148
Dreyer, Carl, 48
Duet, 315, 318, 320

Eastman Kodak, 105, 127, 128, 204, 207, 219
Easy Rider, 135
Edmund Scientific Co., 219
Education, 5, 12, 22–4, 25, 33–9, 46, 48–9, 53–65, 69–75, 80, 86–7, 99–100, 106–7, 155, 158–9, 195–9, 249–55, 279, 280
academic, 53–65, 69–75
cable in, 158–9
schools, 53–65, 249–55
slide-tape programs for, 186–94
video in, 195–9
See also Library schools; Schools; and individual universities
Education of Vision (Gyorgy Kepes), 106
Educational Film Library Association (EFLA), 90, 134
Educational Media Producers Council (EMPC), 85
Educational Products Information Exchange Institute (EPIE), 232
Educational Screen and AV Guide, 89
EFLA Review Cards, 70, 80, 91
Egan, Carol M., 111–8
Eisenstein, Sergei, 137
Eisler, H. Michael, 231–5
Electric Company, The, 176
Elementary School Library Collection (Mary Gaver), 70, 72

Ellison, John W., 293–7
Ellul, Jacques, 5
Emmens, Carol A., 80–5
Enzensberger, Hans Magnus, 5
ESEA Title II, 87
Eshelman, William R., 22–4, 28
EVR, 13, 243
Expanded Cinema (Gene Youngblood), 148
Experimental Cinema (David Curtis), 148

Faces (John Cassavetes), 135
Fahrenheit 451 (Ray Bradbury), 20–1, 36
Feature Films on 8mm and 16mm (James L. Limbacher), 70
Federal Communications Commission, The (FCC), 155, 156, 159, 177, 307
Feinstein, Peter, 139–48
Feldman, Gene, 80
Feldman, Seth, 161–74
Fellini, Federico, 137
Film, 4, 8, 9, 12–3, 17, 22–4, 30, 42–8, 50, 71, 304, 325
and children, 130–3
cartridges, 234–5
educational, 12, 43
8mm, 149–53, 204, 206, 207, 244
equipment, 204–7, 234–5, 238–40
evaluation and selection, 70–1, 76–9, 87, 89, 90, 134–7, 139, 312–22
feature, 134–8
independent, 12–3, 20, 139–48
library acquisition of, 80–5
programming, 134–8, 140–8, 312–22
16mm, 204, 206
sources, 80–5, 140, 147, 325–9
Film Culture Reader (P. Adams Sitney), 148
Film Guide Series (University of Indiana Press), 138
Film Library Information Council (FLIC), 134
Film Library Quarterly, 71, 312
Film News, 70, 71, 89, 90
Film Programmers Guide to 16mm Rental (Linda Artel and Kathleen Weaver), 147
Film Review Index, 70

Filmmaker's Newsletter, 147
Films Kids Like (Susan Rice), 131, 133
Filmstrips, 4, 22–4, 46, 71, 74, 176
    equipment, 183–4, 210, 237
    evaluation and selection, 86–97,
        185
    making of, 183–5
    sources, 325–9
Fogg Art Museum, 102, 103
Force of Evil (Abraham Polonsky), 137
Ford, John, 137
Foster, Barbara, 195–9
Foster, Harry, 28–30, 31, 32
Frampton, Hollis, 140, 146
French, Janet, 86–97
Freudenthal, Juan R., 99–108
Funding. *See* Libraries
Future of the Book, The (confer-
    ence), 50
Future Shock (Alvin Toffler), 7, 54

Gaines, Ervin, 19
Gallagher, Buell, 301
Gehr, Ernie, 140, 145
Geller, Evelyn, 12–21, 88–9
Geller, William S., 319–21
Gerhardt, Lillian N., 25
Gerrard, Phil, 311
Gerson, Barry, 140, 145
Godard, Jean-Luc, 137
Golden Fish, The (Jacques-Yves Cous-
    teau), 77, 130
Grade Teacher, The, 89
Great Gatsby, The, 45
Griffith, D. W., 135
*Guidelines for Two-Year College Learn-
    ing Resources Programs,* 29
Guides to Educational Media (Rusfvold
    & Guss), 70
Guides to Educational Technology
    (Frankle), 70
Gutenberg Galaxy (Marshall McLu-
    han), 35

*Handlist of Museum Sources for Slides
    and Photography* (Petrini and
    Bromberger), 102
Hangman, The, 319
Harrison Tape Catalogue, 113–4
Hartz, Frederic R., 286, 293

Henne, Frances, 49
Herbert, George, 145
Higgins, Karen Sayer, 81
Hinchliff, Bill, 301–6
*History of Photography from 1839 to the
    Present Day, The* (Beaumont New-
    hall), 106
*History of Photography from the Camera
    Obscura to the Beginning of the Mod-
    ern Era, The* (Helmut and Alison
    Gernsheim), 106
Hitchcock, Alfred, 137
Home of the Brave, 319
Hope Reports, 80, 84
Hsu, 25
Hug, William E., 249–55
Hunt Library (Carnegie-Mellon Uni-
    versity), 105
Hunter College, 195, 196
Huntington Public Library, 175, 180
Hutton, Peter, 140, 141
Huxley, Aldous, 36

I Am Joaquin (El Teatro Campesino),
    319, 320
Index of Literary Recordings, 70
Index to 35mm Filmstrips, 88
Indiana State University, 81, 273, 275
Instructor, The, 89
Intellectual Freedom Committee
    (ALA), 331
International Film Seminars, 147
*Introduction to the American Under-
    ground Film, An* (Sheldon Renan),
    148
Irvine, Richard H., 84

Japan Victor (JVC), 244
Joint Advisory Committee on Non-
    book Materials, 257
Joint Council of Educational Tele-
    communications, The, (JCET),
    155
Jones, Emily, 91–2, 93
Jordan, Larry, 140
Journey into Spring, 78
Jussim, Estelle, 7, 30–2, 33–41

Kael, Pauline, 28
Katz, Lillian, 308

Kennedy, John F., 322
Kenney, Brigitte L., 154–60
Kent State University, 280, 297
Kepes, Gyorgy, 106
Kirkegaard, Preben, 61
Kubelka, Peter, 140, 141
Kusnerz, Peggy Ann, 102

Lady or the Tiger?, 78
Landon, George, 140, 145
Language, 22–3, 31
  and literacy, 26–7, 38–9
Lawder, Stan, 145
Leacock, Richard, 141, 146
Learning Directory, 70
Learning Resources, 70
Learning Resources Centers, 104
LeClercq, Angie, 69–75
Lennox, Tom, 102
Librarians, 3, 4, 5, 6–7, 8, 10, 12, 13,
  20–1, 30–2, 41–51, 86, 88, 170
  academic, 55–64, 69–70, 72,
    249–55, 301–6
  and cable TV, 154–60, 307–11
  and censorship, 312–22, 323–5,
    330–2
  and film, 76–9, 80–5, 134–8,
    139–48, 312–22
  and technology, 6–7, 9, 280, 281
  art, 99–107
  black, 306
  media specialists, 3, 13, 15, 19, 25,
    36, 42, 72–5, 95–7, 99–107, 203,
    251–2, 281–2, 313, 315–7, 320
  public, 14, 15, 18–9, 24, 29, 76–9,
    148–53, 175–9, 307–11
  resistance to nonprint media, 4,
    6–8, 10–1, 55–6, 279–82, 323–5,
    331
  school, 13, 15, 19, 20, 23, 25, 29–30,
    32, 55–64, 249–55, 275, 287
  See also Libraries; Library schools
Libraries
  academic, 28, 29, 52–64, 69–75, 80,
    81, 100, 102, 104, 147, 249–55,
    273–7, 301–6
  administration, 52–65
  and cable TV, 154–60
  and censorship, 10, 16, 309, 311,
    312–22, 323–5, 330–2

cataloging, 52, 55, 74, 103–5, 119,
    121–2, 149, 256–64, 265–72,
    273–5
  cooperation among, 8–9, 154
  funding for media, 8–9, 13, 24,
    52–3, 57–60, 73, 80, 81, 86, 87,
    111, 175, 323
  information services, 16–7, 19–20,
    157, 159, 175, 309, 323
  media collections, 6, 10, 72–5, 91,
    96, 100–5, 112–3, 114, 118,
    119–24, 128, 134–7, 150–3, 304,
    323, 331
  media integration, 4, 6, 8, 9, 13,
    15–7, 32, 41–51, 52–64, 73
  media programming, 111–8,
    119–26, 127–9, 134–7, 139–48,
    161–74, 175–80, 312
  media selection and evaluation,
    43–51, 70–1, 86–96, 101–2,
    113–4, 134–8, 140–2
  playback equipment, 176–7, 231–5
  public, 5, 13, 15–7, 19, 23, 28–30,
    52, 76–9, 80, 104, 111–8, 149–53,
    154–60, 161, 175–80, 265–72,
    307–11, 312–20, 323–5
  school, 15–6, 19, 23, 28–9, 52–64,
    80, 88, 104, 249–55, 273–5
  young adult services, 312–22
  zone services, 111–8
  See also Librarians; Library schools;
    Media centers; Schools
Library Bill of Rights, 330, 332
Library Journal, 18, 74, 312
Library of Babel, The (Jorge Luis Bor-
    ges), 11
Library of Congress (LC), 102, 126,
    256–8
  cataloging, 74, 104, 119, 267
Library schools, 28, 29, 44, 49, 56–7,
    279–84, 285–92, 293–7, 311, 330
Library Technology Reports, 62
Lieberman, Irving, 286, 293
LIFE Library of Photography, The, 106
Lipton, Lenny, 140, 141
Listening Post, 114
Little, Robert D., 273–5
Little White Crimes, 315, 318, 320
Liveliest Art, The (Arthur Knight), 289
LJ/SLJ Previews, 70, 71, 74, 219, 234
Lola Montes (Max Ophuls), 137
Long Island University, 294
Lottery, The, 78

MacDonald, Dwight, 132
McDowell, Curt, 140
McLuhan, Marshall, 3, 4, 12, 13–4,
   22–3, 31, 34, 161, 285
Makavejev, Dusan, 137
Maness, Dennis, 127–9
Manual on Film Evaluation (Emily
   Jones), 91
Marker, Chris, 137
Marshal, John, 141
Martin, Allie Beth, 4
Martin, Chet, 312
Massachusetts College of Arts, 102
Matsushita (Panasonic), 244
Media and Methods, 70, 71, 74, 83
Media centers, 25, 28, 29, 30, 52–64,
   73, 75, 100, 104, 204, 219, 237,
   238, 239, 288, 331
Media Equipment Testing Service
   (METS), 203, 204
Media Indexes and Review Sources
   (Chisholm), 70
Media producers, alternative, 325–9
Media Programs: District and School
   (AASL), 249–55
Media Quick Lists (Baker and Taylor),
   72
Media Review Digest, 70, 72
Media specialists, 3, 13, 15, 19, 25, 32,
   36, 42, 72–5, 95–7, 99–107,
   251–2, 281–2
Media symbols, 266
Media theory, 3, 33–9, 41–51
Mediagraphic tool, 10
Medium designators, 260
Mekas, Jonas, 140, 146
Meshes of the Afternoon (Maya Deren),
   145
Metropolitan Museum of Art, 102,
   103, 105
Michaelson, Annette, 140
Mitchell, Martin L., 285–94, 296
Moholy-Nagy, Laszlo, 107
Mokin, Arthur, 83, 84
Morning on the Lièvre, 78
Moynihan, Frank, 80
Mullin, John T., 220
Mumford, Lewis, 12–4, 34, 35
Munday, Karen S., 293–7
Museum of Fine Arts (Boston), 102
Museum of Modern Art (New York),
   127, 135, 167
Museums, 101–3, 134, 137
   See also individual museums

National Audio-Visual Association
   (NAVA), 83–4, 203, 231
National Commission on Library and
   Information Science (NCLIS),
   324
National Conference on Visual Lit-
   eracy (NCVL), 101
National Education Association
   (NEA), 23, 87, 288
National Educational Television
   (NET), 162
National Endowment for the Arts,
   309
National Opinion Research Center,
   254
National Project Center for Film and
   the Humanities, 137
National Union Catalog of Manu-
   script Collections (NUCMC),
   123, 126
Nelson, Gunvor, 140
Nelson, Robert, 140
New Media in Public Libraries (James
   Brown), 9
New York State Council on the Arts,
   134, 175
New York State Library, 13
New York Times Index, 197
New York University, 134, 138
New Yorker, The, 147
Newbery Award, 90–1
Newenhouse, Henk, 82
News Notes of California Libraries, 150
NICEM, 70, 72, 82, 88
Non-book Materials Cataloguing Rules,
   256
*Non-book Materials: The Organization
   of Integrated Collections* (Weihs,
   Lewis and Macdonald), 256,
   274–5
Nonfiction Film (Richard Barsam), 148
Nonprint Media Guidelines (Pearce S.
   Grove), 256–60
Noren, Andrew, 145
Norwood, Frank W., 154–60
Noyes, Jr., Eli, 131
Numbing the Audience (Pauline Kael),
   28

Occurrence at Owl Creek Bridge, 77
Offon (Scott Bartlett), 145
O'Neil, Pat, 140, 146
On My Mind, 30
Ophuls, Marcel, 137

Oral history, 119–24
Oral History Collections (Bowker), 123
Orgren, Carl F., 186–93
Ortega y Gasset, José, 43

Palmer, Joseph W., 149–53
Parable, 315, 317, 320
Partisan Review, 5
Passion of Joan of Arc, The (Carl Dreyer), 48
Pennebaker, D. A., 141
Perry, Ted, 134–7
Peyser, Jay R., 175–80
Philadelphia Museum of Art, 103, 105
Philips/MCA, 221, 241–3
Phonetic alphabet, 34–7
Photography, 99, 100, 102, 106, 127–9
    See also Slides
Piaget, Jean, 37
Pincus, Ed, 141
Pinto, Robert, 311
Poniatoff, Alexander M., 220
Porte, Masha R., 75–9
Pratt Institute, 286
Press, 14, 17, 19, 20
Previews. See LJ/SLJ Previews
Primer of Visual Literacy, A (Donis A. Dondis), 106
Prince George's Community College, Learning Resources Center, 104
Print, 4–5, 9–10, 13, 14, 20, 22–3, 31, 32, 34–9, 49, 56, 86, 146
    importance of content, 42–6
    literacy, 25–7, 33–8
    psychological effect of, 35–6, 47
    versus nonprint, 4, 15, 50–1, 56, 59, 69, 323, 331–2
    See also Books
Programmed Learning and Individually Paced Instruction (Hendershot), 70
Projectors, 204–10, 231–5, 237–40
    maintenance and operation, 232, 237–40
    screens, 232–3, 235
    zoom lenses, 205, 207, 208
Psycho (Alfred Hitchcock), 137
Publishers Weekly, 43

Radio, 4, 6, 8, 17, 42
Ramey, James W., 52–65

Ranganathan's First Law, 149–50
RCA, 113, 241–2
Reader's Advisor, The, 72
Reader's Guide to Periodical Literature, 197
Reading, 23–4, 25–7, 32, 33–9, 145
Reasoner, Harry, 312, 320
Record players, 212–9, 235, 238
Recordings, 13, 20, 23, 304
Red Balloon, The (Albert Lamorisse), 77, 130
Red Desert (Michelangelo Antonioni), 137
Reed, Paul, 96
Remedial Reading Comprehension, 145
Renoir, Jean, 137
Report (Bruce Conner), 8
Research Opportunities in Renaissance Drama, 71
Resnais, Alain, 137
Responsive Chord, The (Tony Schwartz), 5
Review journals, 71–2
Rice, Susan, 130–3
Riesman, David, 32, 36
Rimmer, David, 140
Robbe-Grillet, Alain, 137
Roberts, Don, 10, 323–32
Rock in the Road, 317, 319, 320
Rosary University, 294
Rosenberg, Kenyon C., 203–30
Run, 315
Rutgers University, 286, 296

San Jose University, 295
Sanyo, 244
Satyricon (Federico Fellini), 137
Schein, Harvey, 244
Schilling, Rick, 83
Schlueter, Jane, 273–5
Schofield, Edward T., 286, 293
School Library Journal (SLJ), 14, 71, 88, 89, 90
Schools, 15–6, 19–20, 23, 28, 52–64, 80, 87, 88, 100, 104, 178, 204, 249–55, 273–5, 302
    and cable TV, 155–6, 159
    See also Library schools; individual universities
Schwann Record and Tape Guide, 70, 113–4, 267
Schwartz, Tony, 5, 6

Science Teacher, 89
SEEK Program, 195–6
Senior Scholastic, 89
Sesame Street, 34, 176
Sharits, Paul, 140
Shoemaker, Dick, 312
Sightlines, 70, 71
Sigler, Ronald F., 312–20
Simon and Tansey slide classification system, 104
Sitney, P. Adams, 140, 145
Slide Buyers Guide, A (De Laurier), 70, 102
Slide Classification System for the Organization and Automatic Indexing of Interdisciplinary Collection of Slides and Pictures, A, 104
Slide Libraries: A Guide for Academic Libraries and Museums (Betty Jo Irvine), 100
Slide-tape programs, 186–94
  equipment, 192–3
Slides, 22–3, 74, 89, 99–108, 304
  cataloging, 103–5
  collections, 100–5
  equipment, 207–9
  sources, 70, 100–2
Sloan, Patricia, 105
Smoller, Merry Sue, 308
Snow, Michael, 140, 145
Social Education, 89
Social Responsibilities Roundtable (SRRT), 323
Soho Weekly News, 147
Some Sources of 2 × 2 Inch Color Slides, 70
Sonny and Cher, 176
Sony Corp. of America, 244
Sorrow and the Pity, The, (Marcel Ophuls), 137
Sources of Slides: The History of Art, 102
Special Libraries Association (SLA), 100
Speech Teacher, The, 70
Spoken Record (Roach), 70
Stafford, Jean, 28, 29, 31, 32
Standards, 15, 19, 23, 29, 249–55, 265, 288, 302
Standards for Cataloging Nonprint Materials, 256
Standards for College Libraries, 29
Standards for School Media Programs, 15, 19, 29, 249–55, 288

State University of New York (SUNY)
  Buffalo, 294, 295, 296
  Geneseo, 295
  Stony Brook, 243
Stevens, Frank, 15
Stoney, George C., 9, 307–11
Stratton, Jean, 314, 316, 319–22
String Bean, The, (Edmond Sechan), 77
Suburban Library System, Hinsdale, IL, 111–8

Tape recorders, 218–9, 220–30, 238
  cassette, 221–4, 235
  specifications, 226–8
Technology, 5, 8, 9, 10, 13, 14, 26, 30, 31, 42, 69, 159, 281
  computer, 53
  fear of, 6–7, 9, 54, 281
  instructional, 30–1, 42, 69
Teldec, 243
Telephones, 4, 9, 15, 19
Television, 4–6, 8, 12, 14–5, 16–20, 22, 30, 36, 42–3, 47–8, 50, 134, 154–5, 170, 175, 243, 301, 310
  cable, 154–60, 177, 307–11
  use in teaching, 54, 57–8, 60–1, 64
  See also Video; Videodisc
Television Information Office, 17
Texas Women's University, 294
Tickton, Sidney G., 29
To Improve Learning (Sidney G. Tickton), 12, 29
Toffler, Alvin, 7, 54
Totten, Herman L., 279–92, 293, 294, 296
Touch of Evil (Orson Welles), 137
Trans-American Video, Inc., 84
Trinkle, Robert, 309–10
Truffaut, Francois, 137
Tucker, B. R., 256–64

Ullman, Jeff, 309
Understanding Media (Marshall McLuhan), 3
Underwriters' Laboratory, 204
UNESCO, 127
Unheavenly City, The (Edward Banfield), 18
United States Office of Education, 282

Universal Studios, 243, 244
University Film Study Center, 147
University of California, 88, 104, 123
University of Illinois, 296
University of Kansas Medical Center, 54
University of Kentucky, 288, 296
University of Michigan, 81, 102, 294
University of Pittsburgh, 280
University of Washington, 288, 290
Uptight, 319

Vanderbeek, Stan, 145–6
Vertov, Dziga, 137
Video, 7–9, 71, 74, 83–4, 161–74, 177, 310–1, 323, 325
Betamax, 244–5
books and periodicals, 171–4
cassettes, 161–3, 211, 234, 244–5
cataloging, 161, 261, 263, 266
equipment, 161–4, 169–70, 176–7, 203–19, 231–5
portapak, 7–8, 176, 310
programming, 7, 162, 164–7, 169–70, 178–80
recording, 210–2, 236, 240
sources, 164–9, 325–9
tape, 157, 161–3, 175–80, 186, 195–9, 310–1, 325–9
See also Videodisc
Video Publisher, 84
Videodisc, 7–8, 163–4, 241–4
Disco-Vision, 241–3
Selecta-Vision, 241–2
TeD, 241–3
Thomson CFS, 241–2

Videoplay Program Guide, The, 71
Village Voice, The, 147, 167
Viridiana (Luis Buñuel), 136
Visionary Film: The American Avant-Garde (P. Adams Sitney), 148
Visual literacy, 25–7, 106–7, 177
Visual Literacy Newsletter, 101
Visual Thinking (Rudolf Arnheim), 106

Ward, Phyllis, 236–40
Warhol, Andy, 140, 141
Wayne State University, 294, 295
Weapons of Gordon Parks (Gordon Parks), 319
Weinstein, Miriam, 141
Welles, Orson, 137
What's Wrong With This Picture, 145
White House Record Library, The, 70
White Throat, 78
Whitney Museum of Art, 140
Wilcox, Lee, 243
Wild Bunch, The, 136
Wilson catalogs, 88
Window Water Baby Moving (Stan Brakhage), 145
Wisconsin Association of School Librarians, 275
Wiseman, Fred, 141
Woman Under the Influence (John Cassavetes), 135
Women and technology, 6–7, 54

Youngblood, Gene, 140

DATE DUE

GAYLORD			PRINTED IN U.S.A.